Study Guide

to accompany Bade and Parkin

FOUNDATIONS *of* MACROECONOMICS

Second Edition

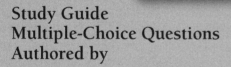

**Study Guide
Multiple-Choice Questions
Authored by**

Ali Ataiifar
Delaware County Community College

Diego Mendez-Carbajo
Illinois Wesleyan University

William Mosher
Assumption College

Terry Sutton
Southeast Missouri State University

Cindy Tori
Valdosta State University

Nora Underwood
University of California, Davis

Neil Garston
California State University, Los Angeles

Tom Larson
California State University, Los Angeles

Mark Rush
University of Florida

PEARSON

Addison
Wesley

Boston San Francisco New York
London Toronto Sydney Tokyo Singapore Madrid
Mexico City Munich Paris Cape Town Hong Kong Montreal

Table of Contents

Your Complete Learning Package

■ The Complete Package

Your *Foundations of Macroeconomics* package consists of:

- Textbook
- Study Guide
- Foundations Web site

The Foundations Web site is a powerful and tightly integrated online learning environment. For students, the site includes

- eText—the entire textbook in PDF format with animated figures accompanied by audio explanations prepared by us and with hyperlinks to all the other components of the Web site
- eStudy Guide—the entire Study Guide online with interactive quizzes
- Foundations Interactive—tutorials, quizzes, and graphing tools that make
- curves shift and graphs come to life with a click of the mouse
- Diagnostic quizzes for every Checkpoint with feedback that includes hyperlinks to the e-text, e-Study Guide, and Foundations Interactive
- Economics in the News updated daily during the school year
- Online "Office Hours"—ask a question via e-mail, and one of us will respond within 24 hours!
- Economic links—links to sites that keep students up to date with what's going on in the economy and that enable them to work end-of-chapter

Each new textbook arrives with a Student Access Kit that unlocks protected areas of the Web site.

■ Checklist and Checkpoints: The Glue That Holds Your Tools Together

Each chapter of your textbook opens with a Chapter Checklist that tells you what you'll be able to do when you've completed the chapter. The number of tasks varies from two to five and most often is three or four. Begin by reviewing this list thoughtfully and get a good sense of what you are about to learn.

Your Study Guide provides an Expanded Chapter Checklist that breaks down your tasks into detailed bite-size pieces. Use the Expanded Chapter Checklist to confirm that you have learned each one of the individual items.

Each part of a chapter in the textbook, Study Guide, and Foundations Web site is linked directly to a Checklist item to enable you to know exactly what you're studying and how it will enable you to accomplish your learning objective.

Each part of a chapter in the textbook ends with a Checkpoint—a page that offers you a Practice Problem to test your understanding of the key ideas of the part, a worked and illustrated solution to the Practice Problem, and a further (parallel) exercise. The Checkpoints enable you to review material when it's fresh in your mind—the most effective and productive time to do so. The Checkpoints guide you through the material in a step-by-step approach that takes the guesswork out of learning. The Study Guide reinforces each Checkpoint by providing a more detailed solution to the textbook Practice Problem and an Additional Practice Problem. Use these if you're still not sure you understand the material.

The self-test questions in the Study Guide, the Diagnostic quiz on the Foundations Web site, and the tutorials, quizzes, and practice exam in Foundations Interactive are organized by Checkpoint so that you can maintain your focus as you work through the material. So that you know exactly where to go in your Study Guide, the Study Guide page numbers are listed at every textbook Checkpoint.

■ Practice Makes Perfect

As you study, distinguish between *practice* and *self-test*. Practice is part of the learning process, learning by doing. Self-test is a check. It shows you where you need to go back and reinforce your understanding, and it helps you build confidence in your knowledge of the material.

The Checkpoint Practice Problems and Exercises, the end-of-chapter Exercises, and the quizzes in Foundations Interactive are designed for practice. The self-test questions in the Study Guide, the Diagnostic quiz on the Web site, and the practice exam in Foundations Interactive are designed to reveal your gaps in understanding and to target your final examination of the material.

The table that follows shows you how the different tools help you practice and learn the material. Take a look at it now and start thinking about which tools you think will be most useful to you.

■ Learn Your Learning Style

It is unlikely that you'll need to use all the tools that we've created all of the time. Try to discover how you learn best. Then exploit what you discover.

If you learn best by reading with a marker or pencil in your hand, you'll use the textbook and Study Guide more often than the other items. If you learn best by seeing the action, you'll often use the eText and Foundations Interactive Demos with their animated graphics. If you learn best by hearing, you'll use the eText audio explanations of the action in key figures. If you learn best by participating and acting, you'll often use the Action and Interactive Quiz in Foundations Interactive.

■ Tell Us What Works for *You*

Please tell us the tools that you find most helpful. And tell us what you think we can improve. You can email us at robin@econ100.com or michael.parkin@uwo.ca, or use the Office Hours in your Foundations Web site.

Robin Bade
Michael Parkin
Ontario, Canada
March, 2003

Your Learning Tools at a Glance

Activity	Print		Foundations Web Site	
	Textbook	**Study Guide**	**eText and eStudy Guide**	**Foundations Interactive**
Getting into a chapter	Chapter opener—previews and places chapter in context	Chapter in perspective—a short summary of the core material		
	Chapter checklist tells you what you'll be able to do when you've completed the chapter	Expanded chapter checklist breaks down your tasks into detailed bite-size pieces		
Learning the material	Explanations; matched tables and figures; figures with numbered captions		eText has exactly the same content as the print textbook plus: animated figures and audio explanations	Fast track summarizes each topic. Textbook figures are interactive in Action and animated in Demo
	Key terms defined in text and in margin	Key terms list for review	Key terms with hyperlinks to definitions, examples, and related terms in both tools	
	Chapter checkpoint • Key points • Key terms list			
Practice makes perfect	Checkpoints • Practice problem • Exercise • Solution to practice problem	Checkpoints • Practice problem • Additional practice problem • Expanded solution to practice problem	eText practice problems, exercises and solutions eStudy Guide additional practice problems and expanded solutions	Interactive Quiz with explanations. Five question types: • Fill in the blanks • True or False • Multiple Choice • Numeric • Complete the graph
	Chapter checkpoint exercises		Chapter checkpoint exercises with links to external sites	
Self Test		Self Test: • Fill in the blanks • True or False • Multiple Choice • Complete the graph • Short Answers and Numeric	eStudy Guide has the same content as the print Study Guide. Online quizzes with hyperlinks to eText for further review: • True or False • Multiple Choice	Self Test version of Interactive Quiz: • Fill in the blanks • True or False • Multiple Choice • Numeric • Complete the graph
Enrichment, Critical Thinking, and Applications	Eye On … • The U.S. economy • The global economy • The past Extensive end-of-chapter questions		Spreadsheets with data for most of the data graphs in the textbook	Economics in the News hyperlinks to news article and related sites Links for the Web Exercises in the textbook

Your Course and Your Study Guide

■ Introduction

My experience has taught me that what students want most from a study guide is help in mastering course material in order to do well on examinations. This Study Guide has been created to respond specifically to that demand. Using this Study Guide alone, however, is not enough to guarantee that you will earn an A or do well in your course. In order to help you overcome the problems and difficulties that most students encounter, I have some general advice on how to study, as well as some specific advice on how best to use this Study Guide.

Economics requires a different style of thinking than what you may encounter in other courses. Economists make extensive use of assumptions to break down complex problems into simple, analytically manageable parts. This analytical style, while ultimately not more demanding than the styles of thinking in other disciplines, feels unfamiliar to most students and requires practice. As a result, it is not as easy to do well in economics on the basis of your raw intelligence and high-school knowledge as it is in many other courses. Many students who come to my office are frustrated and puzzled by the fact that they are getting A's and B's in their other courses but only a C or worse in economics. They have not recognized that economics is different and requires practice. In order to avoid a frustrating visit to your instructor after your first test, I suggest you do the following.

■ Don't rely solely on your high-school economics.

If you took high-school economics, you have seen the material on supply and demand which your instructor will lecture on in the first few weeks. Don't be lulled into feeling that the course will be easy. Your high-school knowledge of economic concepts will be very useful, but it will not be enough to guarantee high scores on exams. Your college or university instructors will demand much more detailed knowledge of concepts and ask you to apply them in new circumstances.

■ Keep up with the course material on a weekly basis.

Skim the appropriate chapter in the textbook before your instructor lectures on it. In this initial reading, don't worry about details or arguments you can't quite follow — just try to get a general understanding of the basic concepts and issues. You may be amazed at how your instructor's ability to teach improves when you come to class prepared. As soon as your instructor has finished covering a chapter, complete the corresponding Study Guide chapter. Avoid cramming the day before or even just the week before an exam. Because economics requires practice, cramming is an almost certain recipe for failure.

■ Keep a good set of lecture notes.

Good lecture notes are vital for focusing your studying. Your instructor will only lecture on a subset of topics from the textbook. The topics your instructor covers in a lecture should usually be given priority when studying. Also give priority to studying the figures and graphs covered in the lecture.

Instructors differ in their emphasis on lecture notes and the textbook, so ask early on in the course which is more important in reviewing for exams — lecture notes or the textbook. If your instructor answers that both are important, then ask the following, typical economic question: which will be more beneficial — spending an extra hour re-reading your lecture notes or an extra hour re-reading the textbook? This question assumes that you have read each textbook chapter twice (once before lecture for a general understanding, and then later for a thorough understanding); that you have prepared a good set of lecture notes; and that you have worked through all of the problems in the appropriate Study Guide chapters. By applying this style of analysis to the problem of efficiently allocating your study time, you are already beginning to think like an economist!

■ Use your instructor and/or teaching assistants for help.

When you have questions or problems with course material, come to the office to ask questions. Remember, you are paying for your education and instructors are there to help you learn. I am often amazed at how few students come to see me during office hours. Don't be shy. The personal contact that comes from one-on-one tutoring is professionally gratifying for instructors as well as (hopefully) beneficial for you.

■ Form a study group.

A very useful way to motivate your studying and to learn economics is to discuss the course material and problems with other students. Explaining the answer to a question out loud is a very effective way of discovering how well you understand the question. When you answer a question only in your head, you often skip steps in the chain of reasoning without realizing it. When you are forced to explain your reasoning aloud, gaps and mistakes quickly appear, and you (with your fellow group members) can quickly correct your reasoning. The Exercises at the end of each textbook chapter are extremely good study group material. You might also get together after having worked the Study Guide problems, but before looking at the answers, and help each other solve unsolved problems.

■ Work old exams.

One of the most effective ways of studying is to work through exams your instructor has given in previous years. Old exams give you a feel for the style of question your instructor might ask, and give you the opportunity to get used to time pressure if you force yourself to do the exam in the allotted time. Studying from old exams is not cheating, as long as you have obtained a copy of the exam legally. Some institutions keep old exams in the library, others in the department. Students who have previously taken the course are usually a good source as well. Remember, though, that old exams are a useful study aid only if you use them to understand the reasoning behind each question. If you simply memorize answers in the hopes that your instructor will repeat the identical question, you are likely to fail. From year to year, instructors routinely change the questions or change the numerical values for similar questions.

■ Use *All Your Tools*

The authors of your book, Robin Bade and Michael Parkin, have created a rich array of learning tools that they describe in the preceding section, "Your Complete Learning Package." Make sure that you read this section because it makes sense to use *all* your tools!

USING THE STUDY GUIDE

You should only attempt to complete a chapter in the Study Guide after you have read the corresponding textbook chapter and listened to your instructor lecture on the material. Each Study Guide chapter contains the following sections.

Chapter in Perspective

This first section is a short summary of the key material. It is designed to focus you quickly and precisely on the core material that you must master. It is an excellent study aid for the night before an exam. Think of it as crib notes that will serve as a final check of the key concepts you have studied.

Expanded Chapter Checklist

A key point of the textbook is its use of Chapter Checkpoints. Each Checkpoint contains a complete exposition of a topic. At the beginning of each Checkpoint is a statement of what you will be able to accomplish after reading the Checkpoint. This Study Guide repeats the Checkpoint statement and then breaks down the material into smaller points. As you review, if you have mastered each of the detailed checkpoints, you can be confident that you understand the material.

Key Terms

One aspect many students find difficult about economics is its vocabulary. Similar to any science, to understand economics you must learn its vocabulary. The Study Guide lists the key terms found in the chapter and the page in the text upon which they are found. You can use this list to help you review for a test: Be certain that you can define and understand each term. When you review this way, be sure to note the links between some of the words and terms. If you understand connections between the terms, you will find it easier to understand the terms!

After the Key Terms, the Study Guide is divided into Checkpoints, exactly the same as your text. At the beginning of each checkpoint the basic learning objective is repeated. Always keep this objective in mind because it

helps place into perspective the material in the Checkpoint.

Practice Problem

At the end of each Checkpoint in the text is a Practice Problem with answers. These Practice Problems are repeated in the Study Guide and then answered. The answers in the Study Guide are more extended than the answers in the textbook, so they will add to your understanding of the question.

Additional Practice Problem

After the initial Practice Problem is presented and answered, the Study Guide presents another Practice Problem. The additional Practice Problems either extend the first Practice Problem or cover another important topic from the Checkpoint. Although the answer is given to the additional Practice Problem, try to solve it on your own before reading the answer.

Following the additional Practice Problem is the Self Test section of the Study Guide. This section has fill in the blank, true or false, multiple choice, complete the graph, and short answer and numeric questions. The questions are designed to give you practice and to test skills and techniques you must master to do well on exams. Before I describe the parts of the Self Test section, here are some general tips that apply to all parts.

First, use a pencil to write your answers in the Study Guide so you have neat, complete pages from which to study. Draw graphs wherever they are applicable. Some questions will ask explicitly for graphs; many others will not but will require a chain of reasoning that involves shifts of curves on a graph. Always draw the graph. Don't try to work through the reasoning in your head — you are much more likely to make mistakes that way. Whenever you draw a graph, even in the margins of the Study Guide, label the axes. You might think that you can keep the labels in your head, but you will be confronting many different graphs with many different variables on the axes. Avoid confusion and label. As an added incentive, remember that on exams where graphs are required, instructors often will deduct points for unlabelled axes.

Do the Self Test questions as if they were real exam questions, which means do them without looking at the answers. This is the single most important tip I can give you about effectively using the Study Guide to improve your exam performance. Struggling for the answers to questions that you find difficult is one of the most effective ways to learn. The adage — no pain, no gain — applies well to studying. You will learn the most from right answers you had to struggle for and from your wrong answers and mistakes. Only after you have attempted all the questions should you look at the answers. When you finally do check the answers, be sure to understand where you went wrong and why the right answer is correct.

Fill in the Blanks

This section covers the material in the checkpoint and has blanks for you to complete. Often suggested phrases are given but sometimes there are no hints—in that case you are on your own! Well, not really, because the answers are given at the end of each Study Guide chapter. This section also can help you review for a test because, once completed, they serve as a *very* brief statement of the important points within the important points within the checkpoint.

True or False

Next are true or false questions. Some instructors use true or false questions on exams or quizzes, so these questions might prove very valuable. The answers to the questions are given at the end of the chapter. The answer also has a page reference to the textbook. If you missed the question or did not completely understand the answer, definitely turn to the textbook and study the topic so that you will not miss similar questions on your exams.

Multiple Choice

Many instructors use multiple choice questions on exams, so pay particular attention to these questions. Similar to the true or false questions, the answers are given at the end of the Study Guide chapter and each answer references the relevant page in the text. If you had any difficulty with a question, use this page reference to look up the topic and then study it to remove this potential weakness.

Complete the Graph

The complete the graph questions allow you to practice using one of economists' major tools, graphs. If you will have essay questions on your exams, it is an extremely safe bet that you will be expected to use graphs on at least some of the questions. This section is designed to ensure that you are well prepared to handle these questions. Use the graph in the Study Guide to answer the questions. Although the answer is given at the end of the Study Guide chapter, do *not* look at the answer before you attempt to solve the problem. It is much too easy to deceive yourself into thinking you understand the answer when you simply look at the question and then read the answer. Involve yourself in the material by answering the question and then looking at the answer. If you cannot answer the question or if you got the answer wrong, the Study Guide again has a reference to the relevant page number in the text. Use the text and study the material!

Short Answer and Numeric Questions

The last set of questions are short answer and numeric questions. Short answer and numeric questions are classic exam questions, so pay attention to these questions. Approach them similarly to how you approach all the other questions: Answer them before you look at the answers in the back of the Study Guide. These questions are also excellent for use in a study group. If you and several friends are studying for an exam, you can use these questions to quiz your understanding. If you have disagreements about the correct answers, once again there are page references to the text so that you can settle these disagreements and be sure that everyone has a solid grasp of the point!

FINAL COMMENTS

This Study Guide combines the efforts of many talented individuals. The authors of the Chapter in Perspective, Expanded Chapter Checkpoint, answers to the Practice Problems, and the additional Practice Problem and answer are Neil Garston, from California State University, at Los Angeles, and Tom Larson, also from California State University, at Los Angeles. It was a pleasure to work with these fine gentlemen and scholars.

For the multiple choice questions, we assembled a team of truly outstanding teachers:
- Ali Ataiifar, Delaware County Community College
- Diego Mendez-Carbajo, Illinois Wesleyan University
- William Mosher, Assumption College
- Cynthia Tori, Valdosta State University
- Nora Underwood, University of California, Davis

I added a few multiple choice questions and wrote the fill in the blank, true or false, complete the graph, and short answer and numeric questions. I also served as an editor to assemble the material into the book before you.

The Study Guide and other supplements were checked for accuracy by a team of instructors, For a previous edition, the team included:
- David Bivin, Indiana University-Purdue University
- Geoffrey Black, Boise State University
- Jeffrey Davis, ITT Technical Institute
- Ken Long, New River Community College
- Barbara Wiens-Tuers, Penn State University, Altoona
- Joachim Zietz, Middle Tennessee State University

- Armand Zottola, Central CT State University

For this edition, checking the accuracy of material were
- Harry Ellis, University of North Texas
- Kate Krause, University of Mew Mexico

In this edition, Harry and Kate saved me from innumerable errors and without their help, this book would be a much inferior product.

Incredibly valuable was Cynthia Westermann-Clark, who proofread, copy-edited, and corrected my attempts to write in a language others could recognize. Aint' it the truth that without she efforts at improving my gramer and speling, this hear book wuld be much the pooorer! More seriously, thanks: I will use what I learned from you and your comments forever.

Jeannie Shearer-Gillmore, University of Western Ontario, checked every word, every sentence, every paragraph, and every page of the first edition of this book and many of the words, sentences, paragraphs, and pages of this edition. She made a huge number of corrections and comments. The easiest way to distinguish her work and mine is to determine if there is an error in a passage. If there is, it's my work; if there is not, it's her work.

Robin Bade and Michael Parkin, the authors of your book, also need thanks. Not only have they written such a superior book that it was easy to be enthusiastic about writing the Study Guide to accompany it, both Robin and Michael played a very hands-on role in creating this Study Guide. They corrected errors and made suggestions that vastly improved the Study Guide.

I want to thank my family: Susan, Tommy, Bobby, and Kathryn, who, respectively: allowed me to work all hours on this book; helped me master the intricacies of FTPing computer files; let me postpone working on our trains with him until after the book was concluded; and would run into my typing room to share her new discoveries. Thanks a lot!

Finally, I want to thank Butterscotch, Mik, Lucky, and Pearl, who sometimes sat on my lap and sometimes sat next to the computer in a box peering out the window (and occasionally meowed) while I typed.

We (all of us except the cats) have tried to make the Study Guide as helpful and useful as possible. Undoubtedly I have made some mistakes; mistakes that you may see. If you find any, I, and succeeding generations of students, would be grateful if you could point them out to me. At the end of my class at the University of Florida, when I ask my students for their advice, I point out to them that this advice won't help them at all because they have just completed the class. But comments they make will influence how future students are taught. Thus just as they owe a debt of gratitude for the comments and suggestions that I received from students before them, so too will students after them owe them an (unpaid and unpayable) debt. You are in the same situation. If you have questions, suggestions, or simply comments, let me know. My address follows, or you can reach me via e-mail at MARK.RUSH@CBA.UFL.EDU. Your input probably won't benefit you directly, but it will benefit following generations. And if you give me permission, I will note your name and school in following editions so that any younger siblings (or, years down the road, maybe even your children!) will see your name and offer up thanks.

Mark Rush
Economics Department
University of Florida
Gainesville, Florida 32611
March, 2003.

Getting Started

Chapter

1

Chapter 1 explains what economics is, what economists do and how they think, and why even those who do not plan on becoming economists should learn the essential elements of this discipline. Future chapters will rely on the ideas and definitions presented in this chapter.

■ **Define economics, distinguish between microeconomics and macroeconomics, and explain the questions of macroeconomics.**

Economic questions exist because of scarcity, the point that human wants exceed the resources available to satisfy them. Economics is the social science that studies the choices that individuals, businesses, government, and entire societies make as they cope with scarcity. Microeconomics studies choices made by individuals and businesses. Macroeconomics studies the national and global economies. Macroeconomic issues are the standard of living, the cost of living, and economic fluctuations. The standard of living is the number of goods and services people enjoy and is measured by average income per person. The cost of living is the number of dollars it takes to buy the goods and services to achieve a given standard of living. Economic fluctuations are reflected in the business cycle, the periodic but irregular up-and-down movement in production and jobs. Business cycles move from an expansion to a peak, then to a recession, then to a trough, and then back to an expansion.

■ **Describe what economists do and some of the problems they encounter.**

Statements about "what is" are positive statements; statements about "what should be" are normative statements. Economists use observation and measurement, model building, and testing to develop their theories. An economic model simplifies reality by including only those features needed for the purpose under study. *Ceteris paribus* is a Latin term that means "other things being equal" or "if all other relevant things remain the same." Correlation is the tendency for the values of two variables to move together in a predictable way. The *post hoc* fallacy is the error of reasoning that one event caused a second event because the first event occurred before the second.

■ **Explain four core ideas that define the way economists think about macroeconomic questions.**

The four core ideas are that people make rational choices by comparing marginal benefits and marginal costs so that they respond to incentives; the standard of living rises when productivity increases; the cost of living increases, that is, inflation occurs, when an increase in the quantity of money is not matched by an increase in the quantity of goods and services; and the sources of economic fluctuations are expenditure and productivity fluctuations.

■ **Explain why economics is worth studying.**

Studying economics provides understanding and expanded career opportunities. The costs of studying economics are the forgone knowledge of other subjects and the forgone leisure time.

EXPANDED CHAPTER CHECKLIST

When you have completed this chapter, you will be able to:

1 **Define economics, distinguish between microeconomics and macroeconomics, and explain the questions of macroeconomics.**

- Define economics and explain the meaning of scarcity.
- Distinguish between microeconomics and macroeconomics and discuss what subjects each studies.
- List and explain the three major macroeconomic issues.

2 **Describe what economists do and some of the problems they encounter.**

- Explain the difference between positive and normative statements.
- Describe the task of economic science.
- Discuss the correlation between two variables.
- Define and give examples of the *post hoc* fallacy.

3 **Explain four core ideas that define the way economists think about macroeconomic questions.**

- Define "rational choice" and explain why a rational decision is made on the margin.
- Explain the role productivity plays in increasing the standard of living.
- Discuss what leads to inflation.
- Discuss the factors that result in business cycles.

4 **Explain why economics is worth studying.**

- State the two benefits of studying economics.
- State the two costs of studying economics.

KEY TERMS

- Scarcity (page 2)
- Incentive (page 2)
- Economics (page 3)
- Microeconomics (page 3)
- Macroeconomics (page 3)
- Standard of living (page 4)
- Goods and services (page 4)
- Unemployment (page 4)
- Cost of living (page 5)
- Inflation (page 5)
- Business cycle (page 5)
- Great Depression (page 6)
- Economic model (page 9)
- Economic theory (page 9)
- *Ceteris paribus* (page 10)
- Correlation (page 11)
- *Post hoc* fallacy (page 11)
- Rational choice (page 13)
- Opportunity cost (page 13)
- Benefit (page 13)
- Margin (page 14)
- Marginal cost (page 14)
- Marginal benefit (page 14)
- Productivity (page 15)

CHECKPOINT 1.1

■ **Define economics, distinguish between microeconomics and macroeconomics, and explain the questions of macroeconomics.**

Practice Problems 1.1

1. Economics studies choices that arise from one fact. What is that fact?
2. Sort the following headlines into those that deal with (i) the standard of living, (ii) the cost of living, and (iii) unemployment and the business cycle:
   a. Production per person has grown for the tenth straight year.
   b. Another price hike for consumers?

c. Firms lay off more workers as orders decline.

d. States pay out more unemployment compensation.

e. New robots boost production across a wide range of industries.

f. Money doesn't buy what it used to.

Solution to Practice Problems 1.1

These Practice Problems involve definitions. The definitions are important because they focus on the key macroeconomic questions.

Quick Review

- *Standard of living* The level of consumption of goods and services that people enjoy, on the average; it is measured by average income per person.
- *Cost of living* The number of dollars it takes to buy the goods and services that achieve a given standard of living.
- *Economic fluctuations* The economy fluctuates in the business cycle, the periodic but irregular up-and-down movement in production and jobs.

1. **Economics studies choices that arise from one fact. What is that fact?**

The fact is scarcity, that is, our limited resources cannot meet people's unlimited wants. Scarcity influences all of economics.

2. **Sort the following headlines into those that deal with (i) the standard of living, (ii) the cost of living, and (iii) unemployment and the business cycle:**

   a. **Production per person has grown for the tenth straight year.**

Production per person affects the standard of living because with more goods and services per person being produced the consumption of goods and services per person can increase.

   b. **Another price hike for consumers?**

A price hike raises the cost of living because it increases the number of dollars it takes to buy the goods and services necessary to achieve a given standard of living.

c. **Firms lay off more workers as orders decline.**

Laying off workers increases the number of unemployed workers, so the headline deals with unemployment and the business cycle.

d. **States pay out more unemployment compensation.**

States pay out more unemployment compensation when there are more unemployed workers, so the headline deals with unemployment and the business cycle.

e. **New robots boost production across a wide range of industries.**

By boosting production, robots increase the number of goods people can consume, so the headline deals with the standard of living.

f. **Money doesn't buy what it used to.**

More dollars are needed to purchase the same quantity of goods and services as in the past. The headline deals with the cost of living.

Additional Practice Problem 1.1a

Which of the following headlines are microeconomic in nature and which are macroeconomic?

   a. Several manufacturers introduce gigabyte memory chips for personal computers.

   b. Bad weather destroys the wheat crop in several mid-western counties.

   c. The unemployment rate goes up.

   d. The federal government decides to regulate the production and price of electricity.

Solution to Additional Practice Problem 1.1a

   a. **Several manufacturers introduce gigabyte memory chips for personal computers.**

The new memory chips will have industry (and personal) effects, not nationwide effects. This change is microeconomic in nature.

   b. **Bad weather destroys the wheat crop in several mid-western counties.**

The bad weather has affected counties, not the nation, and so is a microeconomic topic.

c. The unemployment rate goes up.

An increase in the unemployment rate is macroeconomic in nature. Although it affects individuals and their choices, it involves the overall health of the national economy.

d. The federal government decides to regulate the production and price of electricity.

Even though the federal government is involved, this issue is a matter of how a particular product is produced and sold. As a result, it is microeconomic in nature.

■ Self Test 1.1

Fill in the blanks

Economic questions arise because ____ (human wants; resources) exceed the ____ (human wants; resources) available to satisfy them. Faced with ____, people must make choices. ____ (Macroeconomics; Microeconomics) is the study of the choices individuals make. The big issues macroeconomics studies are: ____, ____, ____.

True or false

1. Everyone faces scarcity.
2. The standard of living is measured by the inflation rate.
3. The cost of living is the number of dollars it takes to buy the goods and services to achieve a given standard of living.
4. The worst recession ever experienced is called the Great Depression.

Multiple choice

1. The characteristic from which all economic problems arise is
   a. political decisions.
   b. providing a minimal standard of living for every person.
   c. how to make a profit.
   d. scarcity.

2. Scarcity results from the fact that
   a. human wants exceed the resources available to satisfy them.
   b. not all goals are desirable.
   c. our standard of living keeps increasing.
   d. the population keeps growing.

3. ____ studies issues such as the standard of living, recessions, and interest rates.
   a. Macroeconomics
   b. Microeconomics
   c. International economics
   d. The history of economics

4. Last year, a country's average income per person increased. You can conclude that
   a. the country's standard of living decreased during the last year.
   b. scarcity is not a concern because labor resources increased.
   c. the country's standard of living increased during the last year.
   d. the country's cost of living decreased during the last year.

5. When inflation leads to a decrease in the value of the dollar, an economy experiences
   a. an increasing cost of living.
   b. an increasing standard of living.
   c. a decreasing cost of living.
   d. an expansionary period.

6. Business cycles are
   a. business law irregularities.
   b. the smooth, upward path of production and jobs.
   c. fluctuations in prices only.
   d. irregular fluctuations in production and jobs.

Complete the graph

■ FIGURE 1.1

Total production

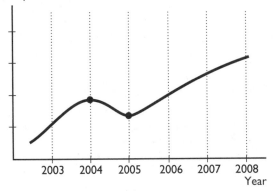

1. Figure 1.1 shows how total production changes over the years. In the figure, label the parts of the business cycle.

Short answer and numeric questions

1. Will there ever come a time without scarcity?
2. Explain the difference between microeconomics and macroeconomics.
3. What are the three big issues that macroeconomics studies?

CHECKPOINT 1.2

■ **Describe what economists do and some of the problems they encounter.**

Practice Problems 1.2

1. Classify each of the following statements as positive or normative:
   a. Unemployed workers have to wait too long before being rehired.
   b. Doctors earn, on the average, more than the governor of Florida.
2. Provide two examples of the *post hoc* fallacy.

Solution to Practice Problems 1.2

The key to whether a statement is positive or normative is whether the statement is testable. If the statement is testable, it is positive; if it is not testable, it is normative.

Quick Review

- *Positive statement* A positive statement tells what is currently understood about the way the world operates and is testable.
- *Normative statement* A normative statement tells what ought to be. It depends on values and is not testable.
- Post hoc *fallacy* The error of reasoning that a first event *causes* a second event because the first event occurred *before* the second.

1. Classify each of the following statements as positive or normative:
   a. **Unemployed workers have to wait too long before being rehired.**
   This statement is not testable. What one person thinks too long, another thinks too short. The statement is normative.

   b. **Doctors earn, on the average, more than the governor of Florida.**
   This statement can be tested to determine if it is correct, so it is a positive statement.

2. **Provide two examples of the *post hoc* fallacy.**
   Your examples will differ. The key is that the first event does not cause the second.
   i) JCPenney runs a sale on swim suits in April and it is warm in June.
   ii) I buy 100 shares of Pfizer stock today and its price falls tomorrow.

Additional Practice Problem 1.2a

Why is it harder to test theories in economics than in laboratory sciences, such as chemistry?

Solution to Additional Practice Problem 1.2a

In laboratory sciences it is possible to do controlled experiments. That means you can add all the same ingredients, in the same proportions, but just change the temperature of the mix and see what that does, or keep the temperature and everything else the same but change the amount of one ingredient. If you have a theory that predicts what the effect of each change should be, you can test the theory by matching the prediction with the results of the experiment.

In the area of macroeconomics, controlled experiments seem impossible. Even if a whole nation would consent to have an economist perform an experiment on the country to test a theory, there still would be no controlled experiment. That would require that the country (starting at the same date, with all the same conditions) go through the same period of time twice—for example once with a low money supply and again with a higher money supply. Clearly this isn't possible. Economists must use other methods to try to disentangle the effects of many things happening all at the same time.

■ Self Test 1.2

Fill in the blanks

A statement that tells "what is" is a ____ (positive; normative) statement. A statement that tells "what should be" is a ____ (positive; normative) statement. An economic ____ (model; theory) simplifies the reality it describes. The process of building and testing models creates ____. The Latin term meaning "other things remaining the same " is ____ (*ceteris paribus; post hoc*).

True or false

1. The statement, "If income per person grew more rapidly, crime rates would decrease" is a positive statement.

2. An economic model must include all the details about the real world.

3. Studying a situation that arises naturally in the ordinary course of life is called a natural experiment.

4. Assuming that one event causes another because the first occurs before the second is good economic reasoning.

Multiple choice

1. A positive statement
   a. must always be right.
   b. cannot be tested.
   c. might be right or wrong.
   d. cannot be negative.

2. Which of the following is an example of a normative statement?
   a. If cars become more expensive, fewer people will buy them.
   b. Car prices should be affordable.
   c. If wages increase, firms will fire some workers.
   d. Cars emit pollution.

3. If an economic theory conflicts with actual data,
   a. it is a good theory.
   b. the model needs adjustment.
   c. it becomes an economic law.
   d. the subject matter must be normative.

4. The Latin term *ceteris paribus* means
   a. after this, therefore because of this.
   b. other things remaining the same.
   c. what is correct for the part, is not correct for the whole.
   d. when one variable increases, the other variable decreases.

5. Economics is a nonexperimental science because controlled laboratory experiments are difficult to conduct. Consequently, economists must use which of the following to construct economic models?
   a. natural experiments
   b. econometric investigations
   c. economic experiments
   d. All of the above answers are correct

6. "The rooster crows every morning and then the sun comes out. Sunrise, therefore, is caused by the rooster's crowing." This statement is a
   a. true statement.
   b. *post hoc* fallacy.
   c. normative statement.
   d. negative statement.

Short answer and numeric questions

1. Becky is writing an essay about the law that requires all passengers in a car to use seat belts and its effectiveness. What might be a positive statement and a normative statement that she could include in her essay?.

2. What are the three steps used by economic science?

CHECKPOINT 1.3

■ **Explain four core ideas that define the way economists think about macroeconomic questions.**

Practice Problems 1.3

1. Kate usually plays tennis for two hours a week and her grade on math tests is usually 70 percent. Last week, after having played two hours of tennis, Kate thought long and hard about playing for another hour. She decided to play another hour of tennis and cut her study time by one additional hour. But the grade on last week's math test was 60 percent.
   a. What was Kate's opportunity cost of the third hour of tennis?
   b. Was Kate's decision to play the third hour of tennis rational?
   c. Did Kate make her decision on the margin?

2. Classify each of the following events as an influence on the standard of living or the cost of living, and as an expenditure or a productivity source of economic fluctuations.
   a. A new computer chip doubles the speed of a PC.
   b. A new process lowers the cost of producing fiber-optic cable.
   c. Telephone companies increase their spending on cellular networks.
   d. Expenditure is increasing, prices are rising, but production is stagnant.

Solution to Practice Problem 1.3

The first Practice Problem uses several ideas, including rational decision making. To understand rational decision making, you also need to understand marginal benefit and marginal cost because a rational choice compares the marginal benefit to the marginal cost. The second problem returns to the macroeconomic themes of this chapter, the standard of living, the cost of living, and business fluctuations.

Quick Review
- *Marginal cost* The cost that arises from a one-unit increase in an activity. The marginal cost of something is what you *must give up* to get one more unit of it.
- *Marginal benefit* The benefit that arises from a one-unit increase in an activity. The marginal benefit of something is *measured* by what you are *willing to give up* to get *one more* unit of it.
- *Rational choice* A choice that uses the available resources to most effectively satisfy the wants of the person making the choice.

a. What was Kate's opportunity cost of the third hour of tennis?

The opportunity cost of the third hour of tennis was the percentage drop in her math grade.

b. Was Kate's decision to play the third hour of tennis rational?

Kate's decision was rational if her marginal benefit exceeded her marginal cost.

c. Did Kate make her decision on the margin?

Kate's decision to play was made on the margin because she compared the cost and benefit of a one-unit change, in particular, a one-hour change, in the time she played tennis.

2. Classify each of the following events as an influence on the standard of living or the cost of living, and an expenditure or a productivity source of economic fluctuations.

a. A new computer chip doubles the speed of a PC.

The chip increases productivity and raises the standard of living. It is a productivity source of economic fluctuations.

b. A new process lowers the cost of producing fiber-optic cable.

The new process increases productivity and raises the standard of living. It is a productivity source of economic fluctuations.

c. Telephone companies increase their spending on cellular networks.

The new cellular networks will increase the standard of living. The spending is an expenditure source of economic fluctuations.

d. Expenditure is increasing, prices are rising, but production is stagnant.

When prices rise, the cost of living increases. The increase in expenditure is an expenditure source of economic fluctuations.

Additional Practice Problem 1.3a

Macroeconomics studies the standard of living, the cost of living, and economic fluctuations. Which of these three topics is the most important?

Solution to Additional Practice Problem 1.3a

It is impossible to state with certainty which topic is the most important because importance is a normative concept. However, from the vantage point of the public's opinion, the topic considered most important varies over time, depending on what is currently the weakest area of the nation's performance. For instance, during recessionary periods, the topic of economic fluctuations is reported as most important, while during inflationary periods, the cost of living is considered most important. Finally, in times during which there is neither a recession nor severe inflation, the standard of living is deemed key.

■ Self Test 1.3

Fill in the blanks

A rational choice compares the marginal benefit of an action to its ____. The standard of living increases only when ____ (prices rise; the number of people employed increases; productivity increases). A rising cost of living is called ____ and occurs when there is an increase in the quantity of ____ (money; wages) not matched by an increase in the quantity of ____ (money; goods and services). Economic fluctuations appear to be caused by fluctuations in ____ (ex-

penditure; wages; inflation) and ____ (marginal benefits; productivity). Most people think economic fluctuations are ____ (desirable; undesirable).

True or false

1. Instead of attending her macroeconomics class for two hours, Kim could have played tennis or watched a movie. Therefore, the opportunity cost of attending class is the tennis *and* the movie she had to give up.

2. An increase in the number of people employed increases the nation's production but does not increase its standard of living.

3. Inflation is caused by increases in productivity.

4. Macroeconomists know enough to eliminate the business cycle.

Multiple choice

1. Which of the following is NOT one of the four core macroeconomic ideas?
   a. The nation's macroeconomic performance has led people to make rational choices.
   b. The standard of living improves when production per person increases.
   c. The cost of living rises when the quantity of money increases faster than production.
   d. The sources of economic fluctuations are expenditure fluctuations and productivity fluctuations.

2. An increase in a country's standard of living *definitely* occurs if
   a. prices rise.
   b. the population grows.
   c. the dollar value of a nation's production increases.
   d. the production per person increases.

3. Which of the following increases the nation's standard of living?
   a. an increase in the quantity of money
   b. a decrease in the quantity of money
   c. an increase in productivity
   d. a decrease in productivity

4. When there is too much money chasing too few goods, the result is
   a. inflation.
   b. deflation.
   c. productivity.
   d. splurging.

5. Economic fluctuations appear to be the result of fluctuations
   a. in expenditures only.
   b. in productivity only.
   c. in expenditures and in productivity.
   d. in expenditures, in productivity, and in the seasons.

6. "Smoothing the business cycle" refers to
   a. predicting when a recession will occur.
   b. limiting the damage from a recession.
   c. eliminating expansions.
   d. decreasing productivity gains.

Short answer and numeric questions

1. Define opportunity cost. If you have a choice of buying dinner for $5 at Taco Bell or at KFC and you decide to eat at KFC, what is the opportunity cost of the decision?
2. Why will an increase in production per person boost the nation's standard of living?
3. What factors appear to cause business cycles?

CHECKPOINT 1.4

■ Explain why economics is worth studying.

Practice Problem 1.4

A student is choosing between an economics course and a popular music course. List two opportunity costs and two benefits from taking a course in economics.

Solution to Practice Problem 1.4

This Practice Problem helps you use the idea of making a rational decision discussed in the last section. To make a rational decision, the decision maker must compare the opportunity costs and benefits of the activity.

Quick Review

- *Opportunity cost* The opportunity cost of something is what you must give up to get it.

A student is choosing between an economics course and a popular music course. List two opportunity costs and two benefits from taking a course in economics.

The opportunity cost of taking the economics class is the fact that the student cannot take the popular music course. All the information from the popular music course is forgone and is an opportunity cost. Presumably the popular music course does not involve as much time studying, and so the forgone leisure is another opportunity cost. Benefits from taking the economics course are the knowledge gained from the class. These benefits include a better understanding of the world, better problem-solving skills, and expected career opportunities.

Additional Practice Problem 1.4a

What are the opportunity costs and benefits of using this *Study Guide*?

Solution to Additional Practice Problem 1.4a

The opportunity cost is mainly the time spent using the *Study Guide* because that time could be devoted to other endeavors. The highest-valued forgone endeavor, be it studying for another class, or sleeping, or some other activity, is the opportunity cost of using the *Study Guide*. The price you paid for the *Study Guide* is not an opportunity cost of using it because you have already paid for the *Study Guide*.

The benefits from the *Study Guide* are an enhanced understanding of the important topics in the book, which, likely will lead to a higher grade in the class. Over a longer time horizon, an increased understanding might influence the future courses you take and lead to career benefits.

■ Self Test 1.4

Fill in the blanks

A better understanding of important issues is a ____ (benefit; cost) from studying economics. The cost of buying textbooks ____ (is; is not) an opportunity cost of studying economics rather than another subject.

True or false

1. Economics requires thinking abstractly about concrete issues.

2. Economics graduates are among the highest-paid professionals.

3. Most students find that memorization is the way to get a good grade in an economics course.

4. The benefits to all students from majoring in economics exceed the costs.

Multiple choice

1. A benefit from studying economics is
   a. that the only jobs available to students studying economics are as economists.
   b. an understanding of many of today's events.
   c. the increased leisure time from the choice of economics as a major.
   d. that you will become as rich as Mick Jagger.

2. Economics is a good major for a ____ student.
   a. pre-med
   b. pre-law
   c. pre-MBA
   d. All of the above answers are correct.

3. On average, economics graduates earn less than ____ graduates and more than ____ graduates.
   a. engineering; business administration
   b. business administration; biology
   c. biology; accounting
   d. accounting; psychology

4. An opportunity cost of studying economics rather than another subject is the
   a. expense of the textbooks you buy and the tuition you pay.
   b. tuition you pay but not the expense of the textbooks you buy.
   c. the forgone leisure time from the choice of economics as a major.
   d. increased salary you might earn after you graduate.

5. Economics says that you should major in economics if
   a. your instructor tells you that the benefits from the major exceed the costs.
   b. you think the benefits from the major exceed the costs.
   c. you think you will make lots of money regardless of the costs.
   d. you are very good at memorization.

Short answer and numeric questions

1. What are the career benefits from taking economics courses?

2. Why do some students decide not to major in economics?

SELF TEST ANSWERS

■ CHECKPOINT 1.1

Fill in the blanks

Economic questions arise because <u>human wants</u> exceed the <u>resources</u> available to satisfy them. Faced with <u>scarcity</u>, people must make choices. <u>Microeconomics</u> is the study of the choices individuals make. The big issues macroeconomics studies are: <u>the standard of living</u>, <u>the cost of living</u>, and <u>economic fluctuations</u>.

True or false

1. True; page 2
2. False; page 4
3. True; page 5
4. True; page 6

Multiple choice

1. d; page 2
2. a; page 2
3. a; page 3
4. c; page 4
5. a; page 5
6. d; page 5

Complete the graph
■ FIGURE 1.2

Total production

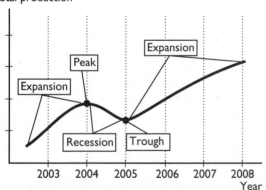

1. Figure 1.2 labels the parts of the business cycle; page 6.

Short answer and numeric questions

1. There will never be a time without scarcity because human wants are unlimited; page 2.
2. Microeconomics studies individual units within the economy, such as a consumer, a firm, a market, and so forth. Macroeconomics studies the overall, or aggregate, economy; page 3.
3. The three big issues macroeconomics studies are the standard of living, the cost of living, and economic fluctuations; page 4.

■ CHECKPOINT 1.2

Fill in the blanks

A statement that tells "what is" is a <u>positive</u> statement. A statement that tells "what should be" is a <u>normative</u> statement. An economic <u>model</u> simplifies the reality it describes. The process of building and testing models creates <u>theories</u>. The Latin term meaning "other things remaining the same " is <u>*ceteris paribus*</u>.

True or false

1. True; page 8
2. False; page 9
3. True; page 11
4. False; page 11

Multiple choice

1. c; page 8
2. b; page 8
3. b; page 9
4. b; page 10
5. d; pages 11-12
6. b; page 12

Short answer and numeric questions

1. A positive statement is "People who obey the law and wear seat belts are involved in fewer road deaths." This statement can be tested. A normative statement is "People should be free to choose whether to wear seat belts or

not." This statement cannot be tested; page 8.

2. The three steps are to observe and measure data; to build a model; and to test the model; page 8.

■ CHECKPOINT 1.3

Fill in the blanks

A rational choice compares the marginal benefit of an action to its <u>marginal cost</u>. The standard of living increases only when <u>productivity increases</u>. A rising cost of living is called <u>inflation</u> and occurs when there is an increase in the quantity of <u>money</u> not matched by an increase in the quantity of <u>goods and services</u>. Economic fluctuations appear to be caused by fluctuations in <u>expenditure</u> and <u>productivity</u>. Most people think economic fluctuations are <u>undesirable</u>.

True or false

1. False; page 13
2. True; page 15
3. False; page 15
4. False; page 16

Multiple choice

1. a; page 13
2. d; page 15
3. c; page 15
4. a; page 15
5. c; page 16
6. b; page 16

Short answer and numeric questions

1. The opportunity cost of a decision is the highest-valued alternative given up. The opportunity cost of eating at KFC is *not* $5. It is eating a meal at Taco Bell because that is the best forgone alternative; page 13.
2. The standard of living is the level of consumption of goods and services that people enjoy. An increase in production per person means that, on the average, the consumption of goods and service per person can increase,

which boosts the nation's standard of living; page 15.

3. Two factors are responsible for the business cycle: fluctuations in expenditure and fluctuations in productivity; page 16.

■ CHECKPOINT 1.4

Fill in the blanks

A better understanding of important issues is a <u>benefit</u> from studying economics. The cost of buying textbooks <u>is not</u> an opportunity cost of studying economics rather than another subject.

True or false

1. True; page 19
2. True; page 19
3. False; page 20
4. False; page 20

Multiple choice

1. b; page 18
2. d; page 19
3. a; page 19
4. c; page 20
5. b; page 20

Short answer and numeric questions

1. Economics courses stress thinking abstractly and logically about important subjects, which are valuable skills to possess. In addition, economics courses discuss many important economic concepts. A student's career benefits from the style of thought gained in economics classes and from the economic concepts covered in the classes; page 19.
2. There are students for whom the benefit of economics as a major is less than the cost. The costs might be high because the student does not enjoy economics or because the student finds the subject difficult. These students should not major in economics; page 20.

Appendix: Making and Using Graphs

Chapter 1

After you have completed the appendix, you will have thoroughly reviewed the graphs used in your economics course.

■ Making and using graphs.

Graphs represent quantities as distances. The vertical axis is the y-axis and the horizontal axis is the x-axis. A scatter diagram plots a graph of one variable against the value of another variable. A time-series graph measures time along the x-axis and the variable (or variables) of interest along the y-axis. A cross-section graph shows the values of an economic variable for different groups in the population at a point in time. Graphs can show the relationship between two variables in an economic model. Variables that move in the same direction have a positive, or direct relationship. Variables that move in the opposite direction have a negative, or inverse relationship. Some relationships have minimum or maximum points. The slope of a relationship is the change in the value of the variable measured on the y-axis divided by the change in the value of the variable measured on the x-axis. To graph a relationship among more than two variables, we use the *ceteris paribus* assumption and graph the relationship between two of the variables holding the other variables constant.

EXPANDED APPENDIX CHECKLIST

When you have completed this appendix, you will be able to:

1 Interpret a scatter diagram, time-series graph, and cross-section graph.

- Identify the x-axis, the y-axis, and the origin in a graph.
- Explain what is plotted in and the differences among a scatter diagram, a time-series diagram, and a cross-section graph.

2 Interpret the graphs used in economic models.

- Be able to draw a figure showing a positive (direct) relationship between two variables.

- Be able to draw a figure showing a negative (inverse) relationship between two variables.
- Be able to draw figures showing a maximum and a minimum.
- Be able to draw figures showing two variables that are unrelated.

3 Define and calculate slope.

- Present the formula used to calculate the slope of a relationship and use it to calculate slope.

4 Graph relationships among more than two variables.

- Describe how the *ceteris paribus* assumption is used to allow us to illustrate the relationship among more than two variables.

KEY TERMS

- Scatter diagram (page 26)
- Time-series graph (page 26)
- Trend (page 26)
- Cross-section graph (page 26)
- Positive relationship (page 28)
- Direct relationship (page 28)
- Linear relationship (page 28)
- Negative relationship (page 29)
- Inverse relationship (page 29)
- Slope (page 31)

CHECKPOINT 1

■ Making and using graphs.

Additional Practice Problems 1

1. You have data on the average monthly rainfall and the monthly expenditure on umbrellas in Seattle, Washington. What sort of graph would be the best to reveal if any relationship exists between these variables?

2. The table below has the annual average U.S. unemployment rate for the decade of the 1990s through 2001. In Figure A1.1, label the axes and then plot these data. What type of graph are you creating? What is the trend in the unemployment rate?

Year	Unemployment rate (percentage of labor force)
1990	5.6
1991	6.9
1992	7.5
1993	6.9
1994	6.1
1995	5.6
1996	5.4
1997	4.9
1998	4.5
1999	4.2
2000	4.0
2001	4.8

■ FIGURE A1.1

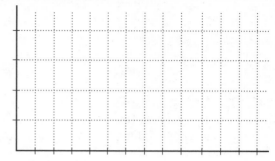

3. In Figure A1.2, draw a straight line showing a positive relationship and another straight line showing a negative relationship.

■ FIGURE A1.2

4. Figure A1.3 shows the relationship between the price of a paperback book and the quantity of paperback books a publisher is willing to sell. What is the slope of the line in Figure A1.3?

■ FIGURE A1.3

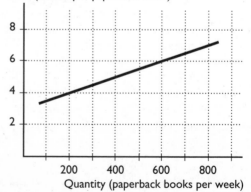

Price (dollars per paperback book)

Solution to Additional Practice Problems I

1. You have data on the average monthly rainfall and the monthly expenditure on umbrellas in Seattle, Washington. What sort of graph would be the best to reveal if any relationship exists between these variables?

A scatter diagram would be the best graph to use. A scatter diagram would plot the monthly value of, say, rainfall along the vertical axis (the y-axis) and the monthly value of umbrella expenditure along the horizontal axis (the x-axis).

2. The table has the annual average U.S. unemployment rate for the decade of the 1990s. In Figure A1.1, label the axis and then plot these data. What type of graph are you using?

Figure A1.4 labels the axes and plots the data in the table. The graph is a time-series graph. At least until 2001, the trend is negative because the unemployment rate has generally been decreasing.

■ FIGURE A1.4

Unemployment rate (percentage of labor force)

3. In Figure A1.2, draw a straight line showing a positive relationship and another straight line showing a negative relationship.

Figure A1.5 has two lines, one showing a positive relationship and the other showing a negative relationship. Your figure does not need to have identical lines. The key point your figure needs is that the line for the positive relationship slopes up as you move rightward along it and the line for the negative relationship slopes down as you move rightward along it.

■ FIGURE A1.5

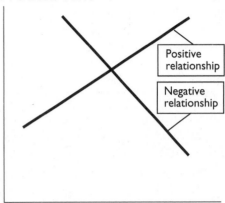

4. What is the slope of the line in Figure A1.3?

The slope of a line is the change in the variable measured on the y-axis divided by the change in the variable measured on the x-axis. To calculate the slope of the line in the figure, use points a and b in Figure A1.6. Between a and b, y rises by 2, from 4 to 6. And x increases by 400, from 200 to 600. The slope equals $2 \div 400 = 0.005$.

■ FIGURE A1.6

Price (dollars per paperback book)

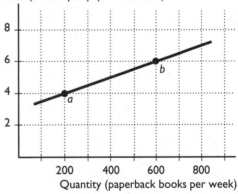

Quantity (paperback books per week)

■ Self Test I

Fill in the blanks

In a graph, the vertical line is called the ____ (x-axis; y-axis) and the horizontal line is called the ____ (x-axis; y-axis). A ____ (scatter diagram; time-series graph; cross-section graph) is a graph of the value of one variable against the value of another variable. A ____ (scatter diagram; time-series graph; cross-section graph) measures time along the x-axis and the variable along the y-axis. A ____ (scatter diagram; time-series graph; cross-section graph) shows the values of an economic variable for different groups in the population at a point in time. If the graph of a relationship between two variables slopes up to the right, the two variables have a ____ (positive; negative) relationship. If the graph between two variables is a vertical line, the two variables ____ (are; are not) related. The slope of a relationship is the change in the value of the variable measured along the ____ (x-axis; y-axis) divided by the change in the value of the variable measured along the ____ (x-axis; y-axis). By using the *ceteris paribus* assumption, it ____ (is; is not) possible to graph a relationship that involves more than two variables.

True or false

1. A point that is above and to the right of another point will have a larger value of the x-axis variable and a larger value of the y-axis variable.

2. A scatter diagram shows the values of an economic variable for different groups in a population at a point in time.

3. A time-series graph compares values of a variable for different groups at a single point in time.

4. A trend is a measure of the closeness of the points on a graph.

5. A positive relationship is always a linear relationship.

6. A relationship that starts out sloping upward and then slopes downward has a maximum.

7. A graph that shows a horizontal line indicates variables that are unrelated.

8. The slope of a relationship is calculated as the change in value of the variable measured on the x-axis divided by the change in the value of the variable measured on the y-axis.

9. The slope at a point on a curve can be found by calculating the slope of the line that

touches the point and no other point on the curve.

Multiple choice

1. Demonstrating how an economic variable changes from one year to the next is best illustrated by a
   a. scatter diagram.
   b. time-series graph.
   c. linear graph.
   d. cross-section graph.

2. To show the values of an economic variable for different groups in a population at a point in time, it is best to use a
   a. scatter diagram.
   b. time-series graph.
   c. linear graph.
   d. cross-section graph.

3. If whenever one variable increases, another variable also increases, then these two variables are ____ related.
   a. positively
   b. negatively
   c. inversely
   d. cross-sectionally

4. A graph of the relationship between two variables is a line that slopes down to the right. These two variables are ____ related.
   a. positively
   b. directly
   c. negatively
   d. not

5. Two variables are unrelated if their graph is
   a. a vertical line.
   b. a 45 degree line.
   c. a horizontal line.
   d. Both (a) and (c) are correct.

■ **FIGURE A1.7**

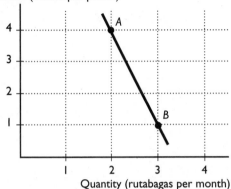

Price (dollars per pound)

6. Figure A1.7 shows the relationship between the price of rutabagas and the quantity purchased. Between points A and B, what is the slope of the line?
   a. 4
   b. 1
   c. 3
   d. –3

■ **FIGURE A1.8**

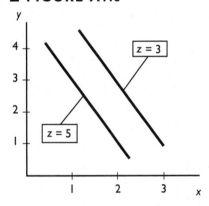

7. In Figure A1.8 an increase in z leads to a
   a. movement up along one of the lines showing the relationship between x and y.
   b. movement down along one of the lines showing the relationship between x and y.
   c. rightward shift of the line showing the relationship between x and y.
   d. leftward shift of the line showing the relationship between x and y.

8. In Figure A1.8, *ceteris paribus*, an increase in x is associated with
   a. an increase in y.
   b. a decrease in y.
   c. an increase in z.
   d. a decrease in z.

Complete the graph

1. The table below has the annual average U.S. inflation rate for the decade of the 1990s. In Figure A1.9, measure time on the horizontal axis and the inflation rate on the vertical axis, and then plot these data.

Year	Inflation rate (percent per year)
1990	6.3
1991	3.0
1992	3.0
1993	2.8
1994	2.6
1995	2.6
1996	3.2
1997	1.7
1998	1.6
1999	2.7

   a. What type of graph are you creating?
   b. In what year was the inflation rate the highest? The lowest?
   c. Using your figure, what was the trend in the inflation rate during the decade of the 1990s?

■ **FIGURE A1.9**

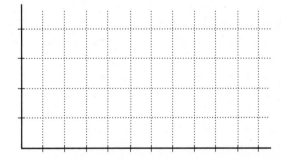

2. The table below has the annual average U.S. inflation rate and an annual interest rate for the decade of the 1990s. In Figure A1.10, measure the interest rate along the y-axis and

the inflation rate along the *x*-axis. Then plot these data.

Year	Interest rate (percent per year)	Inflation rate (percent per year)
1990	6.7	6.3
1991	4.1	3.0
1992	3.4	3.0
1993	3.3	2.8
1994	6.2	2.6
1995	5.1	2.6
1996	5.0	3.2
1997	5.2	1.7
1998	4.4	1.6
1999	5.4	2.7

a. What type of graph are you creating?

b. What is the relationship between the interest rate and the inflation rate that you see in your figure?

■ **FIGURE A1.10**

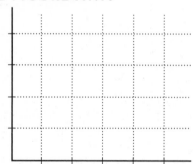

3. The number of sacks of premium cat food that cat lovers will buy depends on the price of a sack of cat food. The relationship is given in the table. In Figure A1.11, plot this relationship, putting the price on the vertical axis and the quantity on the horizontal axis.

Price (dollars per sack of cat food)	Quantity (sacks of cat food per month)
1	10,000
2	8,000
3	7,000
4	4,000

a. If the price of a sack of cat food is $2, how many sacks will be purchased?

b. If the price of a sack of cat food is $3, how many sacks will be purchased?

c. Is the relationship between the price and the quantity positive or negative?

■ **FIGURE A1.11**

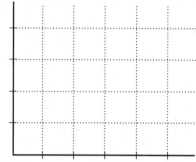

4. In Figure A1.12, label the maximum and minimum points.

■ **FIGURE A1.12**

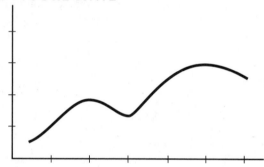

5. In Figure A1.13, draw a line through point *A* with a slope of 2. Label the line "1." Draw another line through point *A* with a slope of −2. Label this line "2."

■ **FIGURE A1.13**

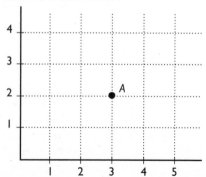

6. Bobby says that he buys fewer compact discs when the price of a compact disc is higher. Bobby also says that he will buy more com-

pact discs after he graduates and his income is higher. The table below shows the number of compact discs Bobby buys in a month at different prices when his income is low and when his income is high.

Price (dollars per compact disc)	Quantity of compact discs purchased, low income	Quantity of compact discs purchased, high income
11	4	5
12	3	4
13	1	3
14	0	2

a. In Figure A1.14, put the price on the vertical axis and the quantity purchased on the horizontal axis. Show the relationship between the number of discs purchased and the price when Bobby's income is low.

b. On the same figure, draw the relationship between the number of discs purchased and the price when his income is high.

c. Does an increase in Bobby's income cause the relationship between the price of a compact disc and the number purchased to shift rightward or leftward?

■ **FIGURE A1.14**

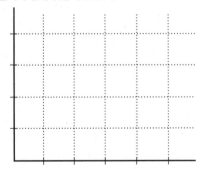

Short answer and numeric questions

1. What are the three types of graphs?

2. If two variables are positively related, will the slope of a graph of the two variables be positive or negative? If two variables are negatively related, will the slope of a graph of the two variables be positive or negative?

3. If a line slopes upward to the right, is its slope positive or negative? If a line slopes downward to the right, is its slope positive or negative?

4. In Figure A1.15, what is the slope of the curved line at point *A*? At point *B*?

■ **FIGURE A1.15**

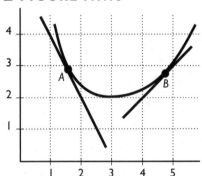

SELF TEST ANSWERS

■ CHECKPOINT I

Fill in the blanks

In a graph, the vertical line is called the _y-axis_ and the horizontal line is called the _x-axis_. A _scatter diagram_ is a graph of the value of one variable against the value of another variable. A _time-series graph_ measures time along the _x_-axis and the variable along the _y_-axis. _A cross-section graph_ shows the values of an economic variable for different groups in the population at a point in time. If the graph of a relationship between two variables slopes up to the right, the two variables have a _positive_ relationship. If the graph between two variables is a vertical line, the two variables _are not_ related. The slope of a relationship is the change in the value of the variable measured along the _y-axis_ divided by the change in the value of the variable measured along the _x-axis_. By using the _ceteris paribus_ assumption, it _is_ possible to graph a relationship that involves more than two variables.

True or false

1. True; page 25
2. False; page 26
3. False; page 26
4. False; page 26
5. False; page 28
6. True; page 30
7. True; page 30
8. False; page 31
9. True; page 31

Multiple choice

1. b; page 26
2. d; page 26
3. a; page 28
4. c; page 29
5. d; page 30
6. d; page 31
7. d; page 32
8. b; page 32

Complete the graph

■ FIGURE A1.16

Inflation rate (percent per year)

1. Figure A1.16 plots the data.
   a. This is a time-series graph; page 26.
   b. The inflation rate was highest in 1990 and lowest in 1998.
   c. The inflation rate generally fell during the decade so the trend is negative; page 26.

■ FIGURE A1.17

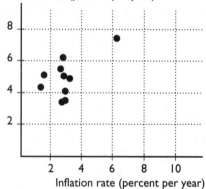

Interest rate (percent per year)

2. Figure A1.17 plots the data.
   a. The figure is a scatter diagram; page 26.
   b. The relationship between the interest rate and the inflation rate is positive; page 28.

■ **FIGURE A1.18**

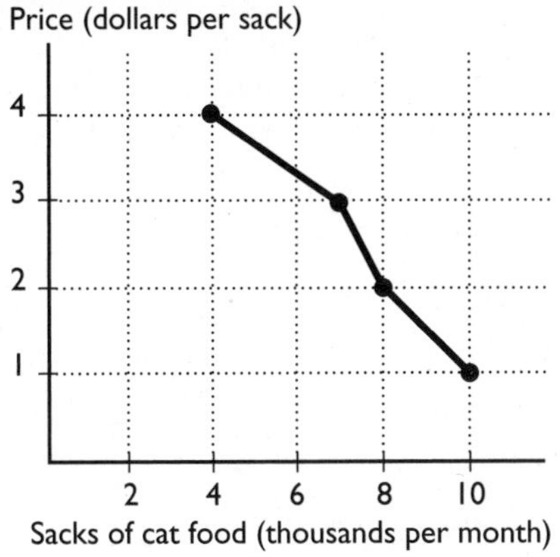

Price (dollars per sack)
4
3
2
1
2
4
6
8
10
Sacks of cat food (thousands per month)

3. Figure A1.18 plots the relationship.
   a. If the price is \$2 per sack, 8,000 sacks are purchased; page 25.
   b. If the price is \$3 per sack, 7,000 sacks are purchased; page 25.
   c. The relationship between the price and quantity of sacks is negative; page 29.

■ **FIGURE A1.19**

Maximum
Minimum

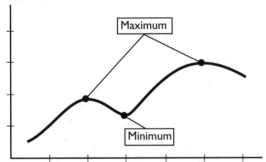

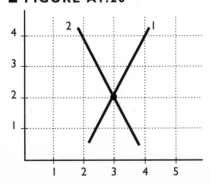

4. Figure A1.19 labels the two maximum points and one minimum point; page 30.

■ **FIGURE A1.20**

2
1
4
3
2
1
1
2
3
4
5

5. Figure A1.20 shows the two lines; page 31.

■ **FIGURE A1.21**

Price (dollars per compact disc)
14
13
12
11
High income
Low income
0
1
2
3
4
5
Compact discs

6. a. Figure A1.21 plots the relationship; page 32.
   b. Figure A1.21 plots the relationship; page 32.
   c. An increase in Bobby's income shifts the relationship rightward; page 32.

Short answer and numeric questions

1. The three types of graphs are scatter diagram, time-series graph, and cross-section graph; page 26.
2. If two variables are positively related, a graph of the relationship will have a positive slope. If two variables are negatively related, a graph of the relationship will have a negative slope; page 31.
3. If a line slopes upward to the right, its slope is positive. If a line slopes downward to the right, its slope is negative; page 31.
4. The slope of a curved line at a point equals the slope of a straight line that touches that point and no other point on the curve. The slope of the curved line at point *A* is –2 and the slope of the curved line at point *B* is 1; page 31.

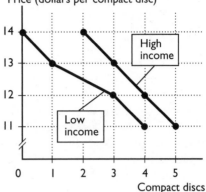

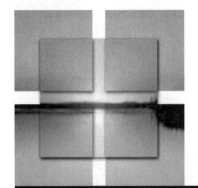

The U.S. and Global Economies

Chapter

2

Chapter 2 introduces fundamental concepts about how households, firms, markets, and government are linked together. A circular flow model is presented to show how goods and services and expenditures flow from and to households, firms, and the government. The measures of economic performance—the standard of living, cost of living, and economic fluctuations—are discussed.

■ **Describe what, how, and for whom goods and services are produced in the United States.**

The production of goods and services, the "what" question, is divided into four broad categories defined in terms of the ultimate buyer: individuals (consumption goods and services), businesses (investment goods), governments (government goods and services), and other countries (export goods and services). The "how" of production involves the factors of production: land, labor, capital, and entrepreneurship. Goods and services are sold to those who have income, so the personal distribution of income is one way of showing who ends up with our national output. The functional distribution of income shows how much is paid to the owners of each type of productive resource. The largest share of national income goes to labor, so workers get the largest share of our nation's goods and services.

■ **Use the circular flow model to provide a picture of how households, firms, and government interact.**

The circular flow model shows that households provide factors of production and firms hire factors of production in factor markets. The circular flow also shows that households purchase goods and services and firms sell goods and services in goods markets. The decisions made by households and firms (and the government) in these markets determine the answers to the "what," "how," and "for whom" questions. The federal government provides public goods and services and makes social security and other benefit payments. In the circular flow, the government purchases goods and services in goods markets. It makes transfers to firms and households and also taxes them. The federal government's largest expenditure is social security and its largest source of tax revenue is personal income taxes. State and local governments' largest expenditure is on education and its largest sources of revenue are sales taxes and transfers from the federal government.

■ **Describe the macroeconomic performance—standard of living, cost of living, and economic fluctuations—of the United States and other economies.**

Nations are divided into advanced, developing, and transition economies. The United States has the highest standard of living, measured in dollars per person per day, and one of the lowest unemployment rates. Along with most advanced countries, the United States has a low inflation rate. Developing nations have higher inflation rates. The United States had recessions in 1991 and 2001; the transition economies had severe recessions in the 1990s.

EXPANDED CHAPTER CHECKLIST

When you have completed this chapter, you will be able to:

1 Describe what, how, and for whom goods and services are produced in the United States.

- Define consumption goods and services, investment goods, government goods and services, and exports.
- Discuss the four factors of production.
- Distinguish between the functional and personal distributions of income.

2 Use the circular flow model to provide a picture of how households, firms, and government interact.

- Define households, firms, and markets.
- Tell what is bought and sold in goods markets and in factor markets.
- Draw the circular flow between households and firms showing factor markets and goods markets.
- Draw the circular flow model with the government added.
- State the main expenditures and sources of tax revenue for the federal government.
- State the main expenditures and sources of tax revenue for state and local governments.

3 Describe the macroeconomic performance—standard of living, cost of living, and economic fluctuations—of the United States and other economies.

- Distinguish between advanced, developing, and transition economies and give examples of each.
- Discuss how the United States compares to other countries in terms of its standard of living, its unemployment rate, its inflation rate, and its economic fluctuations.

KEY TERMS

- Consumption goods and services (page 36)
- Investment goods (page 36)
- Government goods and services (page 36)
- Export goods and services (page 36)
- Factors of production (page 37)
- Land (page 37)
- Labor (page 37)
- Human capital (page 38)
- Capital (page 38)
- Entrepreneurship (page 39)
- Rent (page 39)
- Wages (page 39)
- Interest (page 39)
- Profit (or loss) (page 39)
- Functional distribution of income (page 39)
- Personal distribution of income (page 40)
- Circular flow model (page 42)
- Households (page 42)
- Firms (page 42)
- Market (page 42)
- Goods markets (page 42)
- Factor markets (page 42)
- National debt (page 46)

CHECKPOINT 2.1

■ Describe what, how, and for whom goods and services are produced in the United States.

Practice Problems 2.1

1. Name the four broad categories of goods and services that we use in macroeconomics, provide an example of each (different from those in the chapter), and say what percentage of total production each accounted for in 2002.
2. Name the four factors of production and the incomes they earn.
3. Distinguish between the functional distribution of income and the personal distribution of income.
4. In the United States, which factor of production earns the largest share of income and what percentage does it earn?

Solution to Practice Problems 2.1

These Practice Problems involve definitions and facts. The definitions in the first problem are important because we will encounter them throughout our study of macroeconomics.

Quick Review

- *Consumption goods and services* Goods and services that are bought by individuals and used to provide personal enjoyment and contribute to a person's standard of living.
- *Investment goods* Goods that are bought by businesses to increase their productive resources.
- *Government goods and services* Goods and services that are bought by governments.
- *Exports* Goods and services produced in the United States and sold in other countries.

1. **Name the four broad categories of goods and services that we use in macroeconomics, provide an example of each (different from those in the chapter), and say what percentage of total production each accounted for in 2002.**

Purchases by households and individuals for themselves are consumption goods and services and comprise 61 percent of the value of all purchases. Consumption goods and services include everything from manicures to Playstation 2s, and from cheeseburgers to medical care. Firms purchase investment goods, which are used to produce other goods and services, and which comprise 13 percent of the value of all purchases. Investment goods include factories, desks, computer software, and machinery. Government goods and services are goods and services purchased by all levels of the government and comprise 17 percent of all goods and services. Government goods and services include military armaments and police protection. Exports of goods and services are goods and services produced in the United States and sold in other countries. Exports are 9 percent of all the goods and services. U.S. exports include movies, television shows, airplanes, and rice.

2. **Name the four factors of production and the incomes they earn.**

Land, labor, capital, and entrepreneurship are the four factors of production. Land earns rent; labor earns wages; capital earns interest; and, entrepreneurship earns profit or incurs loss.

3. **Distinguish between the functional distribution of income and the personal distribution of income.**

The functional distribution shows how income is divided among the factors of production: land, labor, capital, and entrepreneurship. The personal distribution shows the distribution of income among households.

4. **In the United States, which factor of production earns the largest share of income and what percentage does it earn?**

While many people think that business owners earn the largest share of income, in fact labor earns a larger share. The share of total income that goes to labor is 72 percent.

Additional Practice Problem 2.1a

How much labor is there in the United States? What determines the quantity of labor?

Solution to Additional Practice Problem 2.1a

In the United States, in 2002 about 144 million people had jobs or were available for work and they provided about 234 billion hours of labor a year. The quantity of labor depends on the size of the population, the percentage of the population that takes jobs, and on social relationships that influence things such as how many women take paid work. An increase in the proportion of women who have taken paid work has increased the quantity of labor in the United States over the past 50 years.

■ Self Test 2.1

Fill in the blanks

Goods and services that are bought by individuals and used to provide personal enjoyment and to contribute to a person's standard of living are _____ (consumption; investment; export) goods. Goods that are bought by businesses to increase their productive resources are ____ (consumption; investment; export) goods. Goods that are produced in the United States and sold in other countries are ____ (consumption; investment; export) goods. Of the four large groups of goods and services in the United States, ____ (consumption goods and services; investment goods; government goods and services; export goods and services) have the largest share of total production. Productive resources are called ____ and are grouped into four categories: ____, ____, ____, and ____. In 2002, ____ (labor; capital) received 72 percent of total income and ____ (labor; capital) received 17 percent. The distribution of income among households is called the ____ (functional; personal) distribution of income.

True or false
1. Consumption goods and services include a slice of pizza purchased to eat at home.
2. A gold mine is included in the "land" category of productive resources.
3. The income earned by people selling the services of their capital is profit or loss.
4. In the United States, the factor of production that earns the most income is labor.
5. In the United States, the richest 20 percent of individuals earn approximately 30 percent of total income.

Multiple choice
1. When the total U.S. production of goods and services is divided into consumption goods and services, investment goods, government goods and services, and export goods and services, the largest component is
   a. consumption goods and services.
   b. investment goods.
   c. government goods and services.
   d. export goods and services.
2. An example of an investment good is
   a. a fiber optic cable TV system.
   b. an insurance policy.
   c. a hair cut.
   d. a slice of pizza.

3. Goods and services produced in the United States and sold in other countries are called
   a. consumption goods and services.
   b. investment goods.
   c. government goods and services.
   d. export goods and services.
4. Which of the following correctly lists the categories of productive resources?
   a. machines, buildings, land, and money
   b. hardware, software, land, and money
   c. capital, money, and labor
   d. land, labor, capital, and entrepreneurship
5. Human capital is
   a. solely the innate ability we are born with.
   b. the money humans have saved.
   c. the knowledge humans accumulate through education and experience.
   d. machinery.
6. Wages are paid to ____ and interest is paid to ____.
   a. entrepreneurs; capital
   b. labor; capital
   c. labor; land
   d. None of the above answers are correct.
7. Dividing the nation's income among the factors of production, the largest percentage is paid to
   a. labor.
   b. land.
   c. capital.
   d. entrepreneurship.
8. The personal distribution of income shows
   a. that labor receives the largest percentage of total income.
   b. how profit accounts for the largest fraction of total income.
   c. that the richest 20 percent of households earn 23 percent of total income.
   d. that the poorest 20 percent of households earn 4 percent of total income.

Short answer and numeric questions
1. Is an automobile a consumption good or an investment good?
2. Compare the incomes earned by the poorest and richest 20 percent of households.

CHECKPOINT 2.2

■ **Use the circular flow model to provide a picture of how households, firms, and governments interact.**

Practice Problem 2.2

What are the real flows and money flows that run between households, firms, and governments in the circular flow model?

Solution to Practice Problem 2.2

The circular flow diagram shows the interactions between firms, households, and the government. It is used in later chapters to help explain some of the key macroeconomic relationships between income and expenditure, so you need to understand it.

Quick Review

- *Circular flow model* A model of the economy that shows the circular flow of expenditures and incomes that result from firms', households', and governments' choices.

What are the real flows and money flows that run between households, firms, and governments in the circular flow model?

Start with a circular flow diagram, illustrated in Figure 2.1. The circular flow diagram illustrates the flows between households, firms, and the government. The real flows are in gray. They are the flows of the factors of production through factor markets and the flows of goods and services through goods markets. In the goods markets, households and the government buy goods and services from firms. In the factor markets, households provide land, labor, capital, and entrepreneurship to firms. The money flows are in black. The money flows include payments to households for their factors of production (rent, wages, interest, and profit), expenditures made by households and the government on goods and services, and transfers and taxes from and to the government.

■ **FIGURE 2.1**

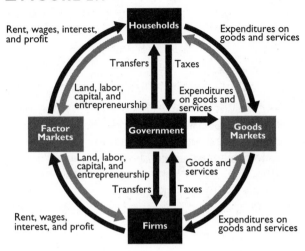

Additional Practice Problem 2.2a

In the circular flow, what is the relationship between the flow of expenditures into the goods markets (from households and the government) and the flow of revenues out of the goods markets to firms?

Solution to Additional Practice Problem 2.2a

The flow of expenditures into the goods markets–the funds that households and the government spend on the goods and services they purchase–equals the flow of revenue out of the goods markets.

■ **Self Test 2.2**

Fill in the blanks

The ____ model shows the flows of expenditure and incomes. An arrangement that brings buyers and sellers together is a ____ (firm; household; market). A market in which goods and services are bought and sold is a ____ (goods; factor) market and a market in which factors of production are bought and sold is a ____ (goods; factor) market. In 2002, as a percentage of the total value of the goods and services produced in the United States, the federal government spent about ____ (20; 13) percent while state and local governments spent about ____ (20; 13) percent. The largest part of what the federal government spends is ____ (social security payments; national defense spending).

Most of the federal government's tax revenue comes from ____. The largest part of the expenditures of state and local governments is spending on ____ (education; highways).

True or false

1. Firms own the factors of production.

2. A market is any arrangement where buyers and sellers meet face-to-face.

3. Factors of production flow from households to firms through goods markets.

4. Social security payments are made by state and local governments.

5. The largest part of the expenditures of state and local government is on education.

Multiple choice

1. Within the circular flow model, economists define households as
   a. families with at least 2 children.
   b. families living in their own houses.
   c. individuals or groups living together.
   d. individuals or groups within the same legally defined family.

2. A market is defined as
   a. the physical place where goods are sold.
   b. the physical place where goods and services are sold.
   c. any arrangement that brings buyers and sellers together.
   d. another name for a store such as a grocery store.

3. In the circular flow model,
   a. only firms sell in markets.
   b. only households buy from markets.
   c. some firms sell and some firms buy.
   d. both firms and households buy and sell in different markets.

4. ____ choose the quantities of goods and services to produce, while ____ choose the quantities of goods and services to buy.
   a. Households; firms
   b. Firms; households and the government
   c. The government; firms
   d. Households; the government

5. A circular flow model shows the interrelationship between the ____ market and the ____ markets.
   a. household; goods
   b. household; factor
   c. business; household
   d. goods; factor

6. In the circular flow model, the expenditures on goods and services flow in the
   a. same direction as goods and services.
   b. opposite direction as goods and services.
   c. same direction as factor markets.
   d. None of the above answers are correct.

7. The largest expenditure category of the federal government is
   a. the purchase of goods and services.
   b. interest on the national debt.
   c. grants to states and local governments.
   d. Social Security.

8. The largest source of revenue for the federal government is
   a. personal income taxes.
   b. Social Security taxes.
   c. corporate income taxes.
   d. lottery revenue.

Complete the graph

■ **FIGURE 2.2**

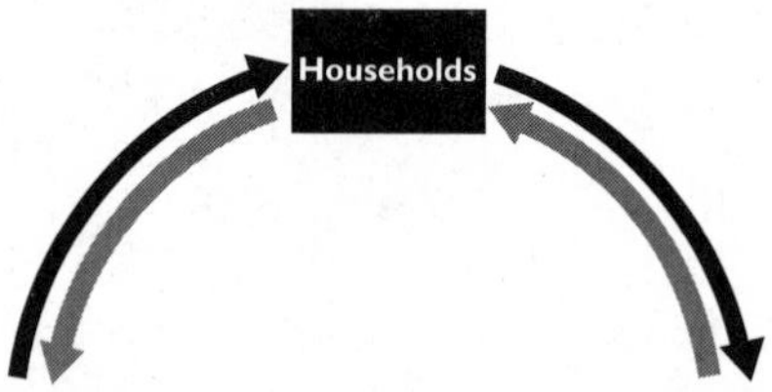

1. Figure 2.2 ignores the government and shows the flows into and out of households. Label the flows and identify who they come from and who they go to.

■ **FIGURE 2.3**

2. Figure 2.3 ignores the government and shows the flows into and out of firms. Label the flows and identify who they come from and who they go to.

■ **FIGURE 2.4**

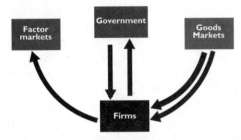

3. Figure 2.4 now includes the government and shows the money flows into and out of firms. Label the money flows.

Short answer and numeric questions

1. Ignoring taxes and transfer payments, what funds flow into firms and what funds flow out of them?

2. Is it possible for something to affect households and not firms? To affect firms and not households? Explain your answers.

3. In 2002, which spent more, the federal government or state and local governments?

4. In the circular flow model, what are the sources of expenditures on goods and services?

5. Compare the amount of the federal government's spending on social security and other transfers to persons to its spending on national defense and goods and services.

CHECKPOINT 2.3

■ **Describe the macroeconomic performance—standard of living,** cost of living, and economic fluctuations—of the United States and other economies.

Practice Problems 2.3

1. What percentage of the world's population live in developing economies, and what was the range of incomes that these people earned in 2002?

2. What percentage of the world's population live in advanced economies and what was the range of incomes that these people earned in 2002?

3. What percentage of the world's population live in the United States and what was the average income that Americans earned in 2002?

4. Which countries or regions experienced high inflation during the 1990s?

5. Which countries or regions experienced recession during the 1990s?

Solution to Practice Problems 2.3

These Practice Problems help you focus on the realities of the world, in particular, the vast differences in economic performance. Keep these facts in mind, both inside and outside of your course, because they should help shape your perceptions of the world.

Quick Review
- *Advanced economies* The 28 countries (or areas) that have the highest living standards.
- *Developing economies* The 128 countries in Africa, the Middle East, Europe, and Central and South America that have not yet achieved a high standard of living for their people.
- *Transition economies* The 28 countries in Europe and Asia that were until the early 1990s part of the Soviet Union or its satellites and are changing the way they organize their economies.

1. What percentage of the world's population live in developing economies, and what was

the range of incomes that these people earned in 2002?

The world's population is a bit over 6 billion. About 5 billion of the world's 6 billion people live in developing economies. So, approximately 80 percent of the world's population lives in developing economies. Average daily income in Africa is about $5, and because that is an average, many people live on less than that. Similarly, in South and Central America the average income per day is about $20.

2. What percentage of the world's population live in advanced economies and what was the range of incomes that these people earned in 2002?

About 1 billion people, or 16 percent of the world's population live in 28 advanced economies. The highest average income per person in 2002 was in the United States, at about $100 per day. The lowest average income per person was in the newly industrialized Asian economies, where it was about $54 per day.

3. What percentage of the world's population live in the United States and what was the average income that Americans earned in 2002?

The U.S. population in 2002 was 287 million, which is about 5 percent of the world's total population of 6.25 billion. The average income in the United States was $100 a day.

4. Which countries or regions experienced high inflation during the 1990s?

The group of nations with the highest inflation rates in the world has been the transition economies. The next highest inflation rates were in Central and South America.

5. Which countries or regions experienced recession during the 1990s?

Though most nations suffered from recession in the 1990s, of the advanced nations, Japan and the newly industrialized Asian nations have spent more time during this period in recession. However, the worst recessions have been in the transition economies.

Additional Practice Problem 2.3a

"For any economy, high unemployment rates mean lower living standards." To what extent is this statement true?

Solution to Additional Practice Problem 2.3a

If unemployment is high, society has resources that it is not using. These unused factors of production could be used to produce more goods and services, which means that a higher standard of living would exist. High unemployment lowers a nation's standard of living below what it could be otherwise.

However, keep in mind that a number of countries in Western Europe have high unemployment rates, but also have high living standards compared to most of the world. If an economy has high quality workers and lots of capital, it might be able to keep high living standards without using all its resources. It just won't have a standard of living as high as it could have had otherwise.

■ Self Test 2.3

Fill in the blanks

The lowest standard of living is in the ____ (advanced; developing; transition) economies and the highest standard of living is in the ____ (advanced; developing; transition) economies. In the United States, the average income is ____ a day and in India and the African continent it is ____ a day. The United States has one of the world's ____ (highest; lowest) unemployment rates. Inflation is ____ (high; low) in advanced economies. The deepest and longest recession in the 1990s occurred in ____ (Japan; the transition economies).

True or false

1. The standard of living depends on the amount of money it takes to buy the goods and services that a typical family consumes.

2. Mexico is a transition economy.

3. Most of the people in the world live in countries that have incomes below the world average of $20 a day.

4. During the 1980s and 1990s, the inflation rate in Central and South America was over 100 percent a year greater than in the United States.

5. The deepest and lengthiest recession in the 1990s occurred in the United States.

Multiple choice

1. The world population is approximately ____ people.
   a. 6.25 million
   b. 2 trillion
   c. 6.25 billion
   d. 550 million

2. The percentage of the world's population that lives in the advanced economies is
   a. 75 percent.
   b. 50 percent.
   c. 25 percent.
   d. less than 20 percent.

3. Which of following groups of countries are *all* advanced economies?
   a. Australia, Brazil, and the United States
   b. Canada, Japan, France, and the United Kingdom
   c. Italy, the United States, China, and Russia
   d. Mexico, Canada, Germany, and Egypt

4. The transition economies are
   a. the largest grouping including the nations of China and India.
   b. in transition from state-owned enterprises to free markets.
   c. most of the nations of Western Europe.
   d. nations with some of the highest standards of living.

5. Among the United States, Russia, Germany, and the United Kingdom, the country with the highest average income per person and the highest living standard is
   a. the United States.
   b. Russia.
   c. Germany.
   d. the United Kingdom.

6. Unemployment rates are lowest among ____ economies.
   a. developing
   b. transition
   c. advanced
   d. tropical

7. Inflation rates are lowest among ____ economies.
   a. developing
   b. transition
   c. advanced
   d. tropical

8. The mildest recession in the 1990s occurred in
   a. the United States.
   b. Asian countries, except Japan which had a deep recession.
   c. Japan.
   d. Russia.

Short answer and numeric questions

1. What are the three groups the International Monetary Fund uses to classify countries? Describe each group. Which group has the largest number of countries? The largest number of people?

2. How do inflation rates compare between advanced and developing economies?

3. Where were the deepest and most severe recessions in the 1990s?

SELF TEST ANSWERS

■ CHECKPOINT 2.1

Fill in the blanks

Goods and services that are bought by individuals and used to provide personal enjoyment and to contribute to a person's standard of living are <u>consumption</u> goods. Goods that are bought by businesses to increase their productive resources are <u>investment</u> goods. Goods that are produced in the United States and sold in other countries are <u>export</u> goods. Of the four large groups of goods and services in the United States, <u>consumption goods and services</u> have the largest share of total production. Productive resources are called <u>factors of production</u> and are grouped into four categories: <u>labor</u>, <u>land</u>, <u>capital</u>, and <u>entrepreneurship</u>. In 2002, <u>labor</u> received 72 percent of total income and <u>capital</u> received 17 percent. The distribution of income among households is called the <u>personal</u> distribution of income.

True or false

1. True; page 36
2. True; page 37
3. False; page 39
4. True; page 39
5. False; page 40

Multiple choice

1. a; page 36
2. a; page 36
3. d; page 36
4. d; page 37
5. c; page 38
6. b; page 39
7. a; page 39
8. d; page 40

Short answer and numeric questions

1. An automobile might be either a consumption or an investment good. It is a consumption good if it is purchased by a household. It is an investment good if it is purchased by a business for use within the business; page 36.

2. The richest 20 percent of households earn about 50 percent of the total U.S. income. The poorest 20 percent of households have an average income of about $10,000 and earn about 4 percent of the total U.S. income; page 40.

■ CHECKPOINT 2.2

Fill in the blanks

The <u>circular flow</u> model shows the flows of expenditures and incomes. An arrangement that brings buyers and sellers together is a <u>market</u>. A market in which goods and services are bought and sold is a <u>goods</u> market and a market in which factors of production are bought and sold is a <u>factor</u> market. In 2002, as a percentage of the total value of the goods and services produced in the United States, the federal government spent about <u>20</u> percent while state and local governments spent about <u>13</u> percent. The largest part of what the federal government spends is <u>social security payments</u>. Most of the federal government's tax revenue comes from <u>personal income taxes</u>. The largest part of the expenditures of state and local governments is spending on <u>education</u>.

True or false

1. False; page 42
2. False; page 42
3. False; pages 42-43
4. False; page 44
5. True; page 47

Multiple choice

1. c; page 42
2. c; page 42
3. d; page 42
4. b; page 42
5. d; pages 42-43
6. b; page 43
7. d; page 46
8. a; page 46

Complete the graph

1. Figure 2.5 labels the flows. Rent, wages, interest, and profits (or losses) flow from the labor market while land, labor, capital, and entrepreneurship flow to the factor market. In addition, expenditures on goods and services flow to the goods market, and goods and services flow from the goods market; page 43.

■ FIGURE 2.5

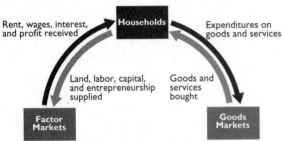

2. Figure 2.6 labels the flows. Revenues from the sale of goods and services flow into firms from the goods market and payments of rent, wages, interest, and profit (or loss) flow from firms into the factor market. Land, labor, capital, and entrepreneurship flow into firms from the factors markets, and goods and services flow from firms to the goods markets; page 43.

■ FIGURE 2.6

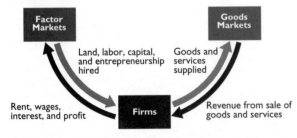

3. Figure 2.7 labels the money flows into and out of firms. The difference between this figure and Figure 2.6 is the addition of transfers and taxes; page 45.

■ FIGURE 2.7

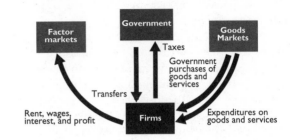

Short answer and numeric questions

1. Funds that flow into firms are households' expenditures and government purchases of goods and services. Funds that flow out of firms are payments for rent, wages, interest, and profit (or loss) to households in exchange for the factors of production; pages 43, 45.

2. The circular flow shows that at the macroeconomic level it is impossible for something to influence only firms or only households. An influence that changes households' buying behavior in goods markets affects firms because they sell to households in goods markets; page 43.

3. In 2002, the federal government spent more than $2 trillion and state and local governments spent more than $1.3 trillion. The federal government spent significantly more than state and local governments; page 44.

4. The circular flow identifies two sources of expenditures on goods and services, expenditures by households and expenditures by the government; page 45.

5. The federal government spends more on social security and other transfers to persons than on national defense and other goods and services combined. In 2002, 43 percent of government expenditure was on social security and other transfers to persons, while a total of 27 percent was spent on national defense plus other goods and services; page 46.

■ CHECKPOINT 2.3

Fill in the blanks

The lowest standard of living is in the <u>developing</u> economies and the highest standard of living is in the <u>advanced</u> economies. In the United States, the average income is <u>$100</u> a day and in India and the African continent it is <u>$5</u> a day. The United States has one of the world's <u>lowest</u> unemployment rates. Inflation is <u>low</u> in advanced economies. The deepest and longest recession in the 1990s occurred in <u>the transition economies</u>.

True or false

1. False; page 49
2. False; page 49
3. True; page 50
4. True; page 52
5. False; page 52

Multiple choice

1. c; page 49
2. d; page 49
3. b; page 49
4. b; page 50
5. a; page 50
6. c; page 51
7. c; page 52
8. a; page 52

Short answer and numeric questions

1. The three groups are advanced economies, developing economies, and transition economies. Advanced economies have the highest standard of living. Developing economies have yet to achieve a high standard of living. Transition economies are changing their economies from government management and state-ownership of capital to market-based economies similar to that in the United States. There are more nations, 128, and more people, almost 5 billion, in developing economies; page 49.

2. Inflation rates are lowest in advanced economies and significantly higher in many developing economies; page 52.

3. The deepest and most severe recessions in the 1990s occurred in the transition economies, in particular, in Russia and Russia's neighbors. In some of these nations, production decreased by almost 30 percent; page 52.

The Economic Problem

CHAPTER IN PERSPECTIVE

Chapter 3 develops a second economic model, the production possibilities frontier or *PPF* model, that further highlights limits and scarcity. The production possibilities frontier shows how the opportunity cost of a good or service increases as more of the good or service is produced. The *PPF* also shows how societies and individuals gain by specializing according to comparative advantage. Finally, the production possibilities frontier sheds light on economic growth and the opportunity cost of growth.

■ Use the production possibilities frontier to illustrate the economic problem.

The production possibilities frontier, *PPF*, is the boundary between the combinations of goods and services that can be produced and those that cannot be produced, given the available factors of production and technology. Production points outside the *PPF* are unattainable. Points on and inside the *PPF* are attainable. With full employment of resources the economy produces at a point on the *PPF*. With unemployed resources, the economy produces at a point inside the *PPF*. As we move along the *PPF* producing more of one good, less of another good is produced. We face a tradeoff as we move along the *PPF*. When we move from inside the *PPF* to a point on the *PPF*, more of some goods and services can be produced without producing less of others—a free lunch.

■ Calculate opportunity cost.

Along the *PPF* all choices involve a tradeoff. The *PPF* allows us to calculate opportunity cost—how much of one good we have to give up to get an additional unit of another good. Along the *PPF*, the opportunity cost of the good on the *x*-axis is equal to the decrease in the good on the *y*-axis divided by the increase in the good on the *x*-axis. As more of a good is produced, its opportunity cost increases, so the *PPF* is bowed outward. The opportunity cost increases because resources are not equally productive in all activities. In the real world, most activities have increasing opportunity cost.

■ Explain how people gain from specialization and trade.

A person has a comparative advantage in an activity if he or she can perform the activity at lower opportunity cost than someone else. People can gain from specializing in production according to comparative advantage and then trading with others. An absolute advantage occurs when one person is more productive than another person in several or even all activities. A person can have an absolute advantage in all activities but cannot have a comparative advantage in all activities.

■ Explain how technological change and increases in capital and human capital expand production possibilities.

The available resources as well as technology set limits on production possibilities. If technology improves, or more capital is accumulated, or more or better (human capital) labor is developed, production possibilities increase, and the *PPF* shifts outward. The (opportunity) cost of economic growth is that resources used to improve technology, increase capital, or develop human capital cannot be used to produce current consumption goods and services.

EXPANDED CHAPTER CHECKLIST

When you have completed this chapter, you will be able to:

1 Use the production possibilities frontier to illustrate the economic problem.

- Define the production possibilities frontier, *PPF*, and explain the relationship between the *PPF* and the available factors of production and technology.
- State which production points are attainable and which are unattainable.
- Discuss production when resources are fully employed and when resources are unemployed.
- Discuss the difference between tradeoff and free lunch.

2 Calculate opportunity cost.

- Measure opportunity cost along the *PPF*.
- Explain why opportunity costs increase and tell how this affects the shape of the *PPF*.

3 Explain how specialization and trade expand production possibilities.

- Define comparative advantage and tell its relationship to the gains from trade.
- Determine which of two people has a comparative advantage in the production of a good.
- Define absolute advantage and tell why it is different from comparative advantage.

4 Explain how technological change and increases in capital and human capital expand production possibilities.

- State the three factors that influence economic growth and illustrate economic growth using a *PPF*.
- Explain the opportunity cost of economic growth.

KEY TERMS

- Production possibilities frontier (page 60)
- Tradeoff (page 63)
- Comparative advantage (page 70)
- Absolute advantage (page 72)

CHECKPOINT 3.1

■ Use the production possibilities frontier to illustrate the economic problem.

Practice Problems 3.1

1. Robinson Crusoe, the forerunner of the televsion program *Survivor*, lived alone on a deserted island. He spent his day fishing and picking fruit. He varied the time spent on these two activities and kept a record of his production. The table shows the numbers that Crusoe wrote in the sand. Use these numbers to make Crusoe's *PPF* if he can work only 8 hours a day.

Hours	Fish (pounds)		Fruit (pounds)
0	0	or	0
1	4.0	or	8
2	7.5	or	15
3	10.5	or	21
4	13.0	or	26
5	15.0	or	30
6	16.5	or	33
7	17.5	or	35
8	18.0	or	36

2. Which combinations (pounds of each) are attainable and which are unattainable: (i) 10 fish and 30 fruit, (ii) 13 fish and 26 fruit, (iii) 20 fish and 21 fruit?

3. Which combinations (pounds of each) use all of Crusoe's available 8 hours a day: (i) 15 fish and 21 fruit, (ii) 7 fish and 30 fruit, (iii) 18 fish and 0 fruit?

4. Which combinations (pounds of each) provide Crusoe with a free lunch and which confront him with a tradeoff when he increases fruit by 1 pound: (i) 0 fish and 36 fruit, (ii) 15 fish and 15 fruit, (iii) 13 fish and 26 fruit?

Solution to Practice Problems 3.1

These Practice Problems involve construction of a production possibilities frontier and then interpreting it.

Quick Review

- *Production possibilities frontier* The boundary between combinations of goods and services that can be produced and combinations that cannot be produced given the available factors of production and the state of technology.
- *Unattainable points* Production points outside the *PPF* are unattainable.
- *Full employment* With full employment, the economy produces at a point on the *PPF*.
- *Unemployment* At production points inside the *PPF* some resources are unemployed.

1. Make Crusoe's *PPF* if he can work only 8 hours a day.

Possibility	Fish (pounds)		Fruit (pounds)
A	0.0	and	36.0
B	4.0	and	35.0
C	7.5	and	33.0
D	10.5	and	30.0
E	13.0	and	26.0
F	15.0	and	21.0
G	16.5	and	15.0
H	17.5	and	8.0
I	18.0	and	0.0

The table above shows Crusoe's *PPF*. To calculate the *PPF*, suppose that Crusoe puts all 8 hours into gathering fruit, so that he gets 36 pounds. But there is no time left for fishing, so he gets 0 pounds of fish. If he takes an hour off from gathering fruit, he gets 35 pounds of fruit and has an hour in which to fish—so he gets 4 pounds of fish. The rest of the *PPF* is constructed similarly.

2. Which combinations (pounds of each) are attainable and which are unattainable: (i) 10 fish and 30 fruit, (ii) 13 fish and 26 fruit, (iii) 20 fish and 21 fruit?

i) Row *D* shows that Crusoe can produce 10.5 fish and 30 fruit, so he can produce 10 fish and 30 fruit. Hence (i) is attainable.

ii) 13 fish and 26 fruit is on the production possibilities frontier, row *E*. So (ii) is attainable.

iii) 20 fish and 21 fruit is unattainable because if Crusoe spends the entire 8 hours fishing he can catch only 18 pounds of fish.

3. Which combinations (pounds of each) use all of Crusoe's available 8 hours a day: (i) 15 fish and 21 fruit, (ii) 7 fish and 30 fruit, (iii) 18 fish and 0 fruit?

i) If Crusoe spends enough time to pick 21 fruit, he has just enough time left to catch 15 fish. This combination uses all his time and is on the *PPF*, row *F*.

ii) Row *C* shows that he can get 7.5 fish and 33 fruit if he works the full 8 hours, so combination (ii) does not require the full 8 hours

iii) Catching 18 fish takes the full 8 hours, leaving no time for picking fruit, so 0 fruit is as much as he can get. So this combination uses all 8 hours and is row *I* on the *PPF*.

4. Which combinations (pounds of each) provide Crusoe with a free lunch and which confront him with a tradeoff when he increases fruit by 1 pound: (i) 0 fish and 36 fruit, (ii) 15 fish and 15 fruit, (iii) 13 fish and 26 fruit?

i) Picking 36 fruit is on the *PPF*, row *A*, so there is a tradeoff but no free lunch.

ii) Row *F* shows that this combination is inside the *PPF* and so there is a free lunch.

iii) This combination is Row *E* in the *PPF*, so there is a tradeoff but no free lunch.

Additional Practice Problem 3.1a

Can Crusoe gather 21 pounds of fruit and catch 30 pounds of fish? Explain your answer. Suppose that Crusoe discovers another fishing pond with more fish, so that he can catch twice as many fish as before. Now can Crusoe gather 21 pounds of fruit and catch 30 pounds of fish? Explain your answer.

Solution to Additional Practice Problem 3.1a

Initially, Crusoe cannot gather 21 pounds of fruit and catch 30 pounds of fish. This production point lies outside his *PPF* and so is unattainable. Once Crusoe discovers the new pond, however, he can gather 21 pounds of fruit and catch 30 pounds of fish. (In Row *F*, double the amount of Crusoe's fish.) The *PPF* depends on the available factors of production and when the factors of production increase, Crusoe's production possibilities change.

■ Self Test 3.1

Fill in the blanks

The _____ is the boundary between the combinations of goods and services that can and that cannot be produced given the available _____ (goods; factors of production) and _____ (number of services; state of technology). Production points outside the *PPF* _____ (are unattainable; are attainable; represent a free lunch). Society has the possibility of a free lunch if production occurs _____ (inside; on; outside) the *PPF*. When resources are fully employed, we face a _____ (free lunch; tradeoff).

True or false

1. Our production capacity is limited by our available resources and technology.

2. A point outside the production possibilities frontier is unattainable.

3. If all the factors of production are fully employed, the economy will produce at a point on the production possibilities frontier.

4. Moving from one point on the *PPF* to another point on the *PPF* illustrates a free lunch.

Multiple choice

1. A reason the production possibilities frontier exists is
   a. unlimited resources and technology.
   b. scarcity of resources.
   c. scarcity of resources and unlimited technology.
   d. unemployment.

2. The production possibilities frontier is a graph showing the
   a. exact point of greatest efficiency for producing goods and services.
   b. tradeoff between free lunches.
   c. maximum combinations of goods and services that can be produced.
   d. minimum combinations of goods and services that can be produced.

3. The production possibilities frontier is a boundary that separates
   a. the combinations of goods that can be produced from the combinations of services.
   b. attainable combinations of goods and services that can be produced from unattainable combinations.
   c. equitable combinations of goods that can be produced from inequitable combinations.
   d. reasonable combinations of goods that can be consumed from unreasonable combinations.

4. Points inside the *PPF* are all
   a. unattainable and use fully employed resources.
   b. attainable and use fully employed resources.
   c. unattainable and have some unemployed resources.
   d. attainable and have some unemployed resources.

5. During a period of time with high unemployment, a country can increase the production of one good or service
   a. without decreasing the production of something else.
   b. but must decrease the production of something else.
   c. and must increase the production of something else.
   d. by using resources in the production process twice.

6. Moving along the production possibilities frontier itself illustrates
   a. the existence of tradeoffs.
   b. the existence of unemployment of productive resources.
   c. the benefits of free lunches.
   d. how free lunches can be exploited through trade.

Complete the graph

■ **FIGURE 3.1**
Computers (millions per year)

Food (tons per year)

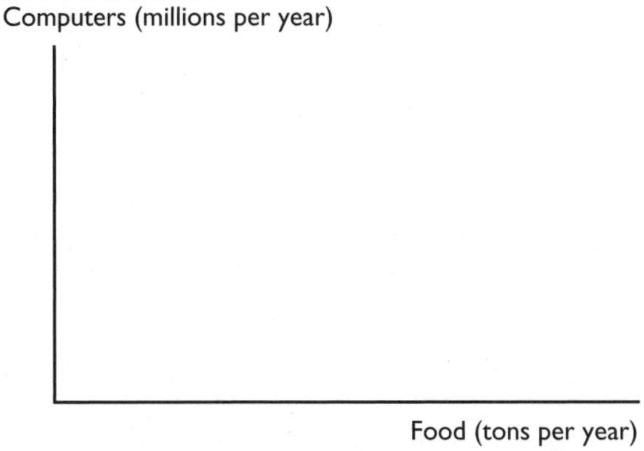

1. In Figure 3.1, draw a production possibilities frontier showing combinations of computers and food. Label the points that are attainable and unattainable. Label the points that have full employment and the points that have unemployment.

Short answer and numeric questions

1. What factors limit the amount of our production?
2. What is the relationship between unemployment and a free lunch? Between full employment and a tradeoff?

CHECKPOINT 3.2

■ **Calculate opportunity cost.**

Practice Problems 3.2

1. Use Robinson Crusoe's production possibilities shown in the table to calculate his opportunity cost of a pound of fish. Make a table that shows Crusoe's opportunity cost of a pound of fish as he increases the time he spends fishing and decreases the time he spends picking fruit.

Possibility	Fish (pounds)		Fruit (pounds)
A	0.0	and	36.0
B	4.0	and	35.0
C	7.5	and	33.0
D	10.5	and	30.0
E	13.0	and	26.0
F	15.0	and	21.0
G	16.5	and	15.0
H	17.5	and	8.0
I	18.0	and	0.0

2. If Crusoe increases his production of fruit from 21 pounds to 26 pounds and decreases his production of fish from 15 pounds to 13 pounds, what is his opportunity cost of a pound of fruit? Explain your answer.

3. If Crusoe is producing 10 pounds of fish and 20 pounds of fruit, what is his opportunity cost of a pound of a fruit and a pound of fish? Explain your answer.

Solution to Practice Problems 3.2

Keep in mind that cost is the highest-valued alternative forgone and questions dealing with opportunity cost will be more straightforward.

Quick Review

- *Opportunity cost is a ratio* Along a *PPF*, the opportunity cost of one good equals the quantity of the other good forgone divided by the increase in the good.

1. Make a table that shows Crusoe's opportunity cost of a pound of fish as he increases the time he spends fishing and decreases the time he spends picking fruit.

Move from	Increase in fish (pounds)	Decrease in fruit (pounds)	Opportunity cost of fish (pounds of fruit)
A to B	4.0	1.0	0.25
B to C	3.5	2.0	0.57
C to D	3.0	3.0	1.00
D to E	2.5	4.0	1.60
E to F	2.0	5.0	2.50
F to G	1.5	6.0	4.00
G to H	1.0	7.0	7.00
H to I	0.5	8.0	16.00

The opportunity cost of a pound of fish is the decrease in fruit divided by the increase in fish as Crusoe moves along his *PPF*. If he increases the time fishing from 0 hours to 1 hour he gets 4 more fish (from 0 fish to 4 fish). At the same time, he loses 1 fruit (he gets 35 pounds of fruit instead of 36). In this case the cost of 4 more fish is 1 less fruit. The cost per fish is 1 fruit/4 fish or 0.25. The rest of the answers in the table are calculated similarly.

2. **If Crusoe increases his production of fruit from 21 pounds to 26 pounds and decreases his production of fish from 15 pounds to 13 pounds, what is his opportunity cost of a pound of fruit? Explain your answer**

If he raises fruit production from 21 to 26, he gains 5 pounds of fruit. Production of fish decreases from 15 to 13 pounds, a decrease of 2 pounds. The 5 more pounds of fruit cost 2 pounds of fish. The cost of 1 pound of fruit equals 2 pounds of fish forgone divided by the gain of 5 pounds of fruit, which is 2/5 of a pound of fish per pound of fruit.

3. **If Crusoe is producing 10 pounds of fish and 20 pounds of fruit, what is his opportunity cost of a pound of a fruit and a pound of fish? Explain your answer.**

This combination of fish and fruit lies inside his *PPF*, so Crusoe enjoys a free lunch. He can gather more fruit without giving up fish and catch more fish without giving up fruit, so the opportunity cost of either is zero.

Additional Practice Problem 3.2a

How does Crusoe's opportunity cost of a pound of fish change as he catches more fish?

Solution to Additional Practice Problem 3.2a

The table answering Practice Problem 1 shows that Crusoe's opportunity cost of a pound of fish increases as he catches more fish. As Crusoe moves from point *A* to point *B* and catches his first fish, the opportunity cost is only 0.25 pounds of fruit per pound of fish. But, as he catches more fish, the opportunity cost increases. As he moves from point *H* to point *I* and catches only fish, the opportunity cost has increased to 16.0 pounds of fruit per pound of fish.

■ Self Test 3.2

Fill in the blanks

Along a production possibilities frontier, the opportunity cost of obtaining one more unit of a good is the amount of another good that is ____ (gained; forgone). The opportunity cost is equal to the quantity of the good forgone ____ (plus; divided by) the increase in the quantity of the other good. As more of a good is produced, its opportunity cost ____.

True or false

1. Moving from one point on the *PPF* to another point on the *PPF* has no opportunity cost.

2. When we move along the *PPF*, the quantity of CDs increases by 2 and the quantity of DVDs decreases by 1, so the opportunity cost is 2 CDs minus 1 DVD.

3. The opportunity cost of a good increases as more of the good is produced.

4. Increasing opportunity costs are common.

Multiple choice

1. The opportunity cost of one more slice of pizza in terms of sodas is the
   a. number of pizza slices we have to give up to get one extra soda.
   b. number of sodas we have to give up to get one extra slice of pizza.
   c. total number of sodas that we have divided by the total number of pizza slices that we have.
   d. total number of pizza slices that we have divided by the total number of sodas that we have.

2. Moving between two points on a *PPF*, a country gains 6 automobiles and forgoes 3 trucks. The opportunity cost of 1 automobile is
   a. 3 trucks.
   b. 6 automobiles – 3 trucks.
   c. 2 trucks.
   d. 1/2 of a truck.

3. A country produces only cans of soup and pens. If the country produces on its *PPF* and increases the production of cans of soup, the opportunity cost of the
   a. cans of soup is increasing.
   b. cans of soup is decreasing.
   c. cans of soup remain unchanged.
   d. pens is increasing.

4. The bowed-out shape of the *PPF* reflects
   a. different rates of unemployment.
   b. increasing availability of resources and improved technology.
   c. decreasing opportunity costs.
   d. increasing opportunity costs.

5. Moving along a country's *PPF*, a reason opportunity costs increase is that
   a. unemployment decreases as a country produces more and more of one good.
   b. unemployment increases as a country produces more and more of one good.
   c. technology declines as a country produces more and more of one good.
   d. some resources are better suited for producing one good rather than the other.

6. Increasing opportunity costs exist
   a. in the real world.
   b. as long as there is high unemployment.
   c. only in theory but not in real life.
   d. for a country but not for an individual.

Complete the graph

Production point	MP3 players (millions per year)		DVD players (millions per year)
A	4.0	and	0.0
B	3.0	and	3.0
C	2.0	and	4.0
D	1.0	and	4.7
E	0.0	and	5.0

1. The table shows the production possibilities for a nation.
   a. Placing MP3 players on the vertical axis, label the axes in Figure 3.2 and graph the production possibilities frontier.
   b. What is the opportunity cost per DVD player of moving from point *A* to point *B*?

B to *C*? *C* to *D*? *D* to *E*? How does the opportunity cost change as more DVD players are produced?

■ FIGURE 3.2

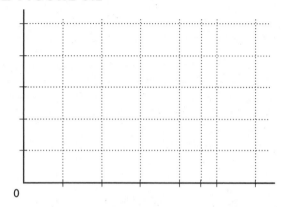

Short answer and numeric questions

1. What is the opportunity cost of increasing the production of a good while moving along a *PPF*? Why does this opportunity cost increase?

2. What does it mean for the opportunity cost to be a ratio?

CHECKPOINT 3.3

■ Explain how people gain from specialization and trade.

Practice Problem 3.3

Tony and Patty produce scooters and snowboards. The figure shows their production possibilities per day.

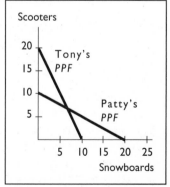

a. Calculate Tony's opportunity cost of a snowboard.

b. Calculate Patty's opportunity cost of a snowboard.

c. Who has a comparative advantage in producing snowboards?

d. Who has a comparative advantage in producing scooters?

e. If they specialize and trade, how many snowboards and scooters will they produce?

Solution to Practice Problem 3.3

This problem uses what you learned in the last checkpoint about how to measure opportunity cost along a *PPF* along with the definition of comparative advantage. Keep the definition in mind and once you have calculated the opportunity costs the problem is straightforward.

Quick Review

*   *Comparative advantage* The ability of a person to perform an activity or produce a good or service at a lower opportunity cost than someone else.

a. Calculate Tony's opportunity cost of a snowboard.

In the figure Tony has a constant opportunity cost because the *PPF* is a straight line. If he uses all his resources producing scooters he can make 20, and if he uses all his resources to producing snowboards he can make 10. Each snowboard produced decreases his scooter production by 2. So the opportunity cost of a snowboard is 2 scooters.

b. Calculate Patty's opportunity cost of a snowboard.

Patty's *PPF* shows she can make 20 snowboards and no scooters, or 10 scooters and no snowboards. For each snowboard she produces, she forgoes the production of 1/2 of a scooter.

c. Who has the comparative advantage in producing snowboards?

The opportunity cost of a snowboard for Patty is 1/2 a scooter and for Tony is 2 scooters. Patty has a lower opportunity cost and therefore she has the comparative advantage in snowboards.

d. Who has the comparative advantage in producing scooters?

The opportunity cost of a scooter for Patty is 2 snowboards and for Tony is 1/2 of a snow-

board. Tony has a lower opportunity cost and so he has the comparative advantage in scooters.

e. If they specialize and trade, how many snowboards and scooters will they produce?

If they specialize, Patty will produce (only) snowboards and Tony will produce (only) scooters. Patty can produce 20 snowboards and Tony 20 scooters, so a total of 20 snowboards and 20 scooters will be produced.

Additional Practice Problem 3.3a

If Patty acquires new equipment for scooter production that lets her produce a maximum of 60 rather than 10 scooters a day, should Patty and Tony specialize and trade?

Solution to Additional Practice Problem 3.3a

Once Patty can produce 60 scooters a day, her opportunity costs change. Her opportunity cost of a scooter falls to 1/3 snowboard per scooter and her opportunity cost of a snowboard rises to 3 scooters per snowboard. With these opportunity costs, the comparative advantages have switched: Patty now has the comparative advantage in scooters and Tony in snowboards. Patty and Tony should still specialize and trade, only now Patty will specialize in scooters and Tony will specialize in snowboards.

■ Self Test 3.3

Fill in the blanks

A person has ____ (a comparative; an absolute) advantage in an activity if that person can perform the activity at a lower opportunity cost than someone else. If people specialize according to ____ (comparative; absolute) advantage and then trade, they can get ____ (outside; inside) their production possibilities frontiers. A person has ____ (a comparative; an absolute) advantage if they are more productive than someone else in all activities. It ____ (is; is not) possible for someone to have a comparative advantage in all activities. It ____ (is; is not) possible for someone to have an absolute advantage in all activities.

True or false

1. A person has an absolute advantage in an activity if the person can perform the activity at lower opportunity cost than someone else.

2. If Kevin can produce ice cream at a lower opportunity cost than Pat can, Kevin has a comparative advantage in ice cream only if he can produce more ice cream than Pat in an hour.

3. To achieve the gains from trade, a producer specializes in the product in which he or she has a comparative advantage and then trades with others.

4. Specialization and trade can make both producers better off even if one of them has an absolute advantage in producing all goods.

Multiple choice

1. The term "comparative advantage" is defined as a situation in which one person can produce
   a. more of all goods than another person.
   b. more of only one good than another person.
   c. one good for a lower dollar cost than another person.
   d. one good for a lower opportunity cost than another person.

2. Bob produces baseballs and softballs. In one hour he can produce 10 baseballs or he can produce 2 softballs. Bob's opportunity cost of producing 1 softball is
   a. 2 softballs.
   b. 10 baseballs.
   c. 5 baseballs.
   d. 1 baseball.

For the next three questions, use the following information: Scott and Cindy both produce only pizza and tacos. In one hour, Scott can produce 20 pizzas or 40 tacos. In one hour, Cindy can produce 30 pizzas or 40 tacos.

3. Scott's opportunity cost of producing 1 taco is
   a. 1/2 of a pizza.
   b. 1 pizza.
   c. 2 pizzas.
   d. 20 pizzas.

4. Cindy's opportunity cost of producing 1 taco is
   a. 3/4 of a pizza.
   b. 1 pizza.
   c. 30 pizzas.
   d. 40 pizzas.

5. Based on the data given,
   a. Cindy has a comparative advantage in producing tacos.
   b. Scott has a comparative advantage in producing tacos.
   c. Cindy and Scott have the same comparative advantage when producing tacos.
   d. neither Cindy nor Scott has a comparative advantage when producing tacos.

6. In one hour John can produce 20 loaves of bread or 8 cakes. In one hour Phyllis can produce 30 loaves of bread or 15 cakes. Which of the following statements is true?
   a. Phyllis has a comparative advantage when producing bread.
   b. John has a comparative advantage when producing cakes.
   c. Phyllis has an absolute advantage in both goods.
   d. John has an absolute advantage in both goods.

Complete the graph

■ **FIGURE 3.3**

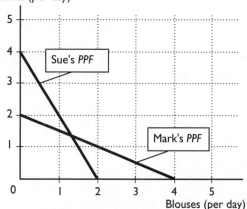

Shirts (per day)

Sue's PPF

Mark's PPF

Blouses (per day)

1. Figure 3.3 shows Mark and Sue's *PPF*s.
   a. Who has the comparative advantage in producing shirts?

b. Who has the comparative advantage in producing blouses?

c. Who should specialize in producing blouses and who should specialize in producing shirts?

d. If Mark and Sue specialize according to their comparative advantage, indicate the total production of shirts and blouses by putting a point in Figure 3.3 showing the total production. Label the point *A*.

e. How does point *A* show the gains from trade?

Short answer and numeric questions

1. Why should people specialize according to their comparative advantage?

2. To achieve gains from trade, the opportunity costs of the trading partners must diverge. Why?

3. When it comes to trading one good for another, why is comparative advantage crucial and absolute advantage unimportant?

CHECKPOINT 3.4

■ **Explain how technological change and increases in capital and human capital expand production possibilities.**

Practice Problem 3.4

1. The table shows a nation that produces education services and consumption goods. If the nation currently produces 500 graduates a year and 2,000 units of consumption goods, what is the opportunity cost of growth?

Possibility	Education services (graduates)	Consumption goods (units)
A	1,000	0
B	750	1,000
C	500	2,000
D	0	3,000

Solution to Practice Problem 3.4

Economic growth has an opportunity cost because we must consume fewer goods and services today. This opportunity cost of growth must be paid regardless of whether growth is through the development of better technology or the accumulation of more capital.

Quick Review

- *Opportunity cost of growth* The opportunity cost of economic growth is the current consumption goods and services forgone.

1. The table shows a nation that produces education services and consumption goods. If the nation currently produces 500 graduates a year and 2,000 units of consumption goods, what is the opportunity cost of growth?

The opportunity cost of the economic growth is the consumption goods forgone. If the nation produced no graduates, it would have 3,000 units of consumption goods. Because it produces 500 graduates, it has only 2,000 units of consumption goods. The difference—1,000 units of consumption goods—is the opportunity cost of economic growth.

Additional Practice Problem 3.4a

Does economic growth eliminate scarcity?

Solution to Additional Practice Problem 3.4a

Economic growth does not eliminate scarcity. Scarcity exists as long as people's wants exceed what can be produced. Economic growth increases the goods and services that can be produced, but people's wants will continue to outstrip the ability to produce. While economic growth means that additional wants can be satisfied, people's wants are infinite and so scarcity will continue to be present even with economic growth.

■ **Self Test 3.4**

Fill in the blanks

A sustained expansion of production possibilities is called ____. Three factors influence economic growth: ____, ____, and ____. Economic growth shifts the *PPF* ____ (inward; outward). The *PPF* shows that economic growth requires ____ (a decrease; an increase) in the current production of consumption goods.

True or false

1. The three key factors that influence economic growth are technological change, income, and capital accumulation.
2. Economic growth abolishes scarcity.
3. The opportunity cost of economic growth is less consumption goods in the future.
4. Production possibilities per person in the United States have remained constant during the last 30 years.

Multiple choice

1. To increase its economic growth, a nation should
   a. limit the number of people in college because they produce nothing.
   b. encourage spending on goods and services.
   c. encourage education because that leads to increased human capital.
   d. increase current consumption.
2. Other things being equal, if Mexico devotes more resources to train its population than Spain,
   a. Mexico will be able to eliminate opportunity cost faster than Spain.
   b. Mexico will be able to eliminate scarcity faster than Spain.
   c. Spain will grow faster than Mexico.
   d. Mexico will grow faster than Spain.
3. If we decide to increase the current production of consumption goods, then
   a. economic growth will slow down.
   b. the *PPF* will shift outward.
   c. the *PPF* will shift inward.
   d. some productive factors will become unemployed.
4. Which of the following statements is correct?
   a. As the economy grows, the opportunity costs of economic growth necessarily decrease.
   b. Economic growth has no opportunity cost.
   c. The greater the opportunity costs of economic growth, the more rapid the economic growth.
   d. The opportunity cost of economic growth is current consumption forgone.

5. When a country's production possibilities frontier shifts outward over time, the country is experiencing
   a. no opportunity cost.
   b. economic growth.
   c. higher unemployment of resources.
   d. a decrease in unemployment of resources.

6. The *PPF* shows economic growth when the *PPF*
   a. shifts outward, away from the origin.
   b. shifts inward, towards the origin showing lower costs.
   c. changes from a bowed out *PPF* to a flatter *PPF*.
   d. changes from a flatter *PPF* to a more bowed out curve.

Complete the graph

■ FIGURE 3.4

Automobiles (millions per year)

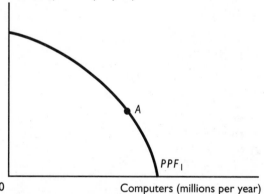

0   Computers (millions per year)

1. In the above figure, illustrate what happens if there is a technological breakthrough in the production of computers but not in the production of automobiles.
   a. Suppose the economy was initially producing at point *A*. After the breakthrough, is it possible for the economy to produce more computers *and* more automobiles?

Short answer and numeric questions

1. What are the three factors that influence economic growth?
2. What is the opportunity cost of economic growth?

SELF TEST ANSWERS

■ CHECKPOINT 3.1

Fill in the blanks

The <u>production possibilities frontier or *PPF*</u> is the boundary between the combinations of goods and services that can and that cannot be produced given the available <u>factors of production</u> and <u>state of technology</u>. Production points outside the *PPF* <u>are unattainable</u>. Society has the possibility of a free lunch if production occurs <u>inside</u> the *PPF*. When resources are fully employed, we face a <u>tradeoff</u>.

True or false

1. True; page 60
2. True; page 62
3. True; page 62
4. False; page 63

Multiple choice

1. b; page 60
2. c; page 60
3. b; page 62
4. d; page 63
5. a; page 64
6. a; page 64

Complete the graph

■ FIGURE 3.5

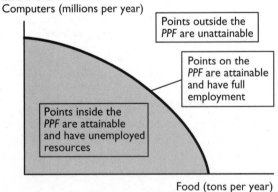

Computers (millions per year)

Points outside the *PPF* are unattainable

Points on the *PPF* are attainable and have full employment

Points inside the *PPF* are attainable and have unemployed resources

Food (tons per year)

1. Figure 3.5 shows a production possibilities frontier between computers and food; pages 62-63.

Short answer and numeric questions

1. The factors that limit the amount of our production are the available resources and the state of technology; page 60.
2. When the nation is producing at a point with unemployment, there are free lunches available because the production of some goods and services can be increased without decreasing the production of anything else. When the nation is producing at full employment, it is on the *PPF* and so only tradeoffs are available: If the production of one good or service is increased, the production of something else must be decreased; page 63.

■ CHECKPOINT 3.2

Fill in the blanks

Along a production possibilities frontier, the opportunity cost of obtaining one more unit of a good is the amount of another good that is <u>forgone</u>. The opportunity cost is equal to the quantity of the good forgone <u>divided by</u> the increase in the quantity of the other good. As more of a good is produced, its opportunity cost <u>increases</u>.

True or false

1. False; page 66
2. False; page 67
3. True; page 68
4. True; page 68

Multiple choice

1. b; page 66
2. d; page 66
3. a; page 68
4. d; page 68
5. d; page 68
6. a; page 68

Complete the graph

■ FIGURE 3.6

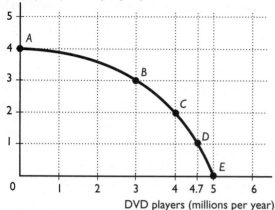

MP3 players (millions per year)

DVD players (millions per year)

1. a. Figure 3.6 illustrates the production possibilities frontier; page 66.

   b. The opportunity cost of moving from point *A* to point *B* to is 0.33 MP3 players per DVD player; from *B* to *C* is 1.00 MP3 player per DVD player; from *C* to *D* is 1.43 MP3 players per DVD player; and, from *D* to *E* is 3.33 MP3 players per DVD player. The opportunity cost increases; page 68.

Short answer and numeric questions

1. The opportunity cost of increasing production of one good is the production of some other good forgone. The opportunity cost increases, so that increasingly large amounts of the other good are forgone, because resources are not equally productive in all activities. When initially increasing the production of one good, resources that are well suited for its production are used. When still more of the good is produced, resources that are less well suited must be used. Because the resources are ill suited, more are necessary to increase the production of the first good, and the forgone amount of the other good increases; page 68.

2. The opportunity cost is the amount of a good forgone to gain an additional unit of another good. We divide the quantity of the good forgone by the increase in the other good. So opportunity cost is a ratio—the change in the quantity of one good divided by the change in the quantity of another good; pages 67-68.

■ CHECKPOINT 3.3

Fill in the blanks

A person has <u>a comparative</u> advantage in an activity if that person can perform the activity at a lower opportunity cost than someone else. If people specialize according to <u>comparative</u> advantage and then trade, they can get <u>outside</u> their production possibilities frontiers. A person has <u>an absolute</u> advantage if they are more productive than someone else in all activities. It <u>is not</u> possible for someone to have a comparative advantage in all activities. It <u>is</u> possible for someone to have an absolute advantage in all activities.

True or false

1. False; page 70
2. False; page 70
3. True; page 72
4. True; page 72

Multiple choice

1. d; page 70
2. c; page 70
3. a; page 70
4. a; page 70
5. b; page 72
6. c; page 72

Complete the graph

1. a. Sue has the comparative advantage in producing shirts. Her opportunity cost of a shirt is 1/2 of a blouse and Mark's opportunity cost of a shirt is 2 blouses; page 70.

   b. Mark has the comparative advantage in producing blouses. His opportunity cost of a blouse is 1/2 of a shirt and Sue's opportunity cost of a blouse is 2 shirts; page 70.

   c. Mark should specialize in producing blouses and Sue should specialize in producing shirts; page 71.

   d. Mark produces 4 blouses and Sue produces 4 shirts, so a total of 4 shirts and 4 blouses

■ FIGURE 3.7

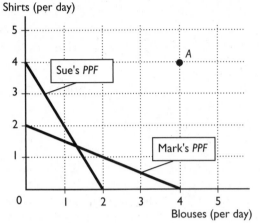

Shirts (per day)

are produced. Figure 3.7 shows this production as point A; page 71.

e. If the total production at point A is divided evenly, both Mark and Sue will receive 2 shirts and 2 blouses. When both were producing only for themselves, they could not produce 2 shirts and 2 blouses because this point is beyond both their *PPFs*. By specializing and trading, Mark and Sue get outside their *PPFs*; page 72.

Short answer and numeric questions

1. A person's comparative advantage is the good that the person can produce at a lower opportunity cost than other people. When this person specializes in the production of the good, it is produced at the lowest cost; page 70.

2. If the trading partners' opportunity costs are the same, there is no incentive for them to trade. For instance, if two people produce either gum or soda and both have the same opportunity cost of 5 gums for 1 soda, neither is willing to buy or sell to the other. Only when opportunity costs diverge will one person be willing to buy (the person with the higher opportunity cost) and the other willing to sell (the person with the lower opportunity cost); page 72.

3. People are willing to trade if they can obtain a good at lower opportunity cost than what it costs them to produce the good. Comparative advantage tells which person has a lower opportunity cost. Even if a person has

an absolute advantage in all goods, he or she does not have a comparative advantage in all goods. So comparative advantage determines who produces a product and who buys it; page 72.

■ CHECKPOINT 3.4

Fill in the blanks

A sustained expansion of production possibilities is called <u>economic growth</u>. Three factors influence economic growth: <u>technological change</u>, <u>expansion of human capital</u>, and <u>capital accumulation</u>. Economic growth shifts the *PPF* <u>outward</u>. The *PPF* shows that economic growth requires <u>a decrease</u> in the current production of consumption goods.

True or false

1. False; page 74
2. False; page 74
3. False; page 74
4. False; page 74

Multiple choice

1. c; page 74
2. d; page 74
3. a; page 74
4. d; page 74
5. b; page 74
6. a; page 74

Complete the graph

■ FIGURE 3.8

Automobiles (millions per year)

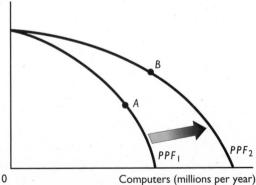

1. Figure 3.8 illustrates the new production possibilities frontier. Because the technologi-

cal breakthrough did not affect automobile production, the maximum amount of automobiles that can be produced on the vertical axis does not change; pages 74-75.

1. a. Figure 3.8 shows that it is possible for the production of *both* automobiles and computers to increase, as a movement from the initial point *A* to a possible new point *B* illustrates; page 75.

Short answer and numeric questions

1. The three factors that influence economic growth are technological change, the expan-

sion of human capital, and capital accumulation; page 74.

2. Economic growth requires either developing new technologies, accumulating more human capital, or accumulating more capital. All of these avenues require resources, so the opportunity cost of economic growth is the decrease in the current production of goods and services; page 74.

Demand and Supply

Chapter

4

The tools of demand and supply explain how competitive markets work. We use the demand and supply tools to determine the quantities and prices of the goods and services produced and consumed.

■ **Distinguish between quantity demanded and demand and explain what determines demand.**

The quantity demanded is the amount that buyers are willing and able to buy during a specified period at a specified price. The law of demand states that other things remaining the same, if the price of a good falls (rises), the quantity demanded of that good increases (decreases). A demand curve graphs the relationship between the quantity demanded of a good and its price. A change in price leads to a *change in the quantity demanded*, a movement along the demand curve. Influences on buying plans that *change demand* are: prices of related goods (substitutes and complements); income; expectations; number of buyers; and preferences. If demand increases (decreases), the demand curve shifts rightward (leftward).

■ **Distinguish between quantity supplied and supply and explain what determines supply.**

The quantity supplied is the amount that sellers will sell during a specified period at a specified price. The law of supply states that other things remaining the same, if the price of a good falls (rises), the quantity supplied decreases (increases). A supply curve graphs the relationship between the price and the quantity supplied. A change in price creates a *change in the quantity supplied*, a movement along the supply curve. Influences on selling plans that *change supply* are: prices of related goods; prices of inputs; expectations; number of sellers; and productivity. If supply increases (decreases), the supply curve shifts rightward (leftward).

■ **Explain how demand and supply determine price and quantity in a market and explain the effects of changes in demand and supply.**

The equilibrium price is the price at which the quantity demanded equals the quantity supplied, and the quantity at this price is the equilibrium quantity. An increase (decrease) in demand raises (lowers) the price and increases (decreases) the quantity. An increase (decrease) in supply lowers (raises) the price and increases (decreases) the quantity. An increase (decrease) in both demand and supply increases (decreases) the quantity but the effect on the price is ambiguous. An increase in demand and a decrease in supply raises the price but the effect on the quantity is ambiguous. A decrease in demand and an increase in supply lowers the price but the effect on the quantity is ambiguous.

■ **Explain how price ceilings, price floors, and sticky prices cause shortages, surpluses, and unemployment.**

A price ceiling set below the equilibrium price creates a shortage. A price floor set above the equilibrium price creates a surplus. Sticky prices can create temporary shortages or surpluses.

EXPANDED CHAPTER CHECKLIST

When you have completed this chapter, you will be able to:

1 Distinguish between quantity demanded and demand and explain what determines demand.

- Define quantity demanded.
- State and explain the law of demand.
- Define demand, demand schedule, and demand curve.
- Illustrate the law of demand using a demand schedule and a demand curve.
- List the influences on buying plans that change demand.
- Distinguish between a change in the quantity demanded and a change in demand.

2 Distinguish between quantity supplied and supply and explain what determines supply.

- Define quantity supplied.
- State and explain the law of supply.
- Define supply, supply schedule, and supply curve.
- Illustrate the law of supply using a supply schedule and a supply curve.
- List the influences on selling plans that change supply.
- Distinguish between a change in the quantity supplied and a change in supply.

3 Explain how demand and supply determine the price and quantity in a market and explain the effects of changes in demand and supply.

- Determine the equilibrium price and quantity in a supply and demand diagram.
- Indicate the amount of a surplus or shortage if the price is not the equilibrium price.
- Illustrate the effects of a change in demand and a change in supply.

4 Explain how price ceilings, price floors, and sticky prices cause shortages, surpluses, and unemployment.

- Explain the effect of a price ceiling.
- Explain the effect of a price floor.
- Discuss why some prices might be sticky and illustrate how sticky prices create shortages or surpluses.

KEY TERMS

- Quantity demanded (page 83)
- Law of demand (page 83)
- Demand (page 83)
- Demand schedule (page 84)
- Demand curve (page 84)
- Change in the quantity demanded (page 85)
- Change in demand (page 85)
- Substitute (page 85)
- Complement (page 85)
- Normal good (page 85)
- Inferior good (page 85)
- Quantity supplied (page 88)
- Law of supply (page 88)
- Supply (page 88)
- Supply schedule (page 89)
- Supply curve (page 89)
- Change in the quantity supplied (page 90)
- Change in supply (page 90)
- Substitute in production (page 90)
- Complement in production (page 90)
- Market equilibrium (page 93)
- Equilibrium price (page 93)
- Equilibrium quantity (page 93)
- Surplus or excess supply (page 94)
- Shortage or excess demand (page 94)
- Price ceiling (page 101)
- Rent ceiling (page 101)
- Price floor (page 103)
- Minimum wage law (page 103)

CHECKPOINT 4.1

■ **Distinguish between quantity demanded and demand and explain what determines demand.**

Practice Problem 4.1

In the market for scooters, several events occur, one at a time. Explain the influence of each event on the quantity demanded of scooters and on the demand for scooters. Illustrate the effects of each event by either a movement along the demand curve or a shift in the demand curve for scooters and say which event (or events) illustrates the law of demand in action. These events are:

a. The price of a scooter falls.

b. The price of a bicycle falls.

c. Citing rising injury rates, cities and towns ban scooters from sidewalks.

d. Income increases.

e. Rumor has it that the price of a scooter will rise next month.

f. Scooters become unfashionable and the number of buyers decreases.

Solution to Practice Problem 4.1

This problem emphasizes the distinction between a change in the quantity demanded and a change in demand.

Quick Review

- *Change in the quantity demanded* A change in the quantity of a good that people plan to buy that results from a change in the price of the good.

- *Law of demand* A rise in the price of a good brings a decrease in the quantity demanded of that good; a fall in the price of a good brings an increase in the quantity demanded of that good.

- *Change in demand* A change in the quantity that people plan to buy when any influence on buying plans, other than the price of the good, changes. These other influences include: prices of related goods, income, expectations, number of buyers, and preferences.

a. The price of a scooter falls.

A fall in the price of a scooter brings an increase in the quantity demanded of scooters, which is illustrated by a movement down along the demand curve for scooters. This event illustrates the law of demand in action.

b. The price of a bicycle falls.

A bicycle is a substitute for a scooter. With the lower price of a bicycle, some people who would previously have bought a scooter will now buy a bicycle instead. So a fall in the price of a bicycle decreases the demand for scooters. The demand curve for scooters shifts leftward.

c. Citing rising injury rates, cities and towns ban scooters from sidewalks.

Rising injury rates and banning scooters from sidewalks changes preferences. The demand for scooters decreases and the demand curve for the scooters shifts leftward.

d. Income increases.

A scooter is probably a normal good. So, people will buy more scooters when their income increases. The demand for scooters increases and the demand curve shifts rightward as illustrated in the figure.

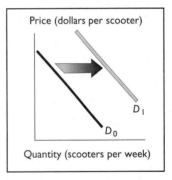

e. Rumor has it that the price of a scooter will increase next month.

A rise in the expected future price of a scooter increases the demand for scooters now. The demand curve shifts rightward.

f. Scooters become unfashionable and the number of buyers decreases.

A decrease in the number of buyers decreases the demand for scooters. The demand curve shifts leftward.

Additional Practice Problem 4.1a

Price (dollars per scooter)	Quantity (scooters per week)
100	0
75	10
50	40
25	60

The information in the table shows the demand schedule for scooters in a town. Using this information, label the axes in Figure 4.1 and then graph the demand curve.

■ **FIGURE 4.1**

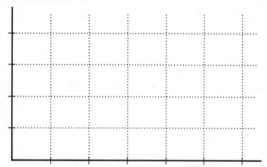

Solution to Additional Practice Problem 4.1a

The axes are labeled and the demand curve is graphed in Figure 4.2.

■ **FIGURE 4.2**

Price (dollars per scooter)

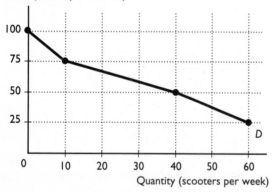

Quantity (scooters per week)

■ Self Test 4.1

Fill in the blanks

The _____ (demand schedule; law of demand) states that other things remaining the same, if the price of a good rises, the _____ (quantity demanded of; demand for) that good decreases. A _____ is a graph of the relationship between the quantity demanded of a good and its price. Demand curves are _____ (downward; upward) sloping. An increase in demand shifts the demand curve _____. Factors that change demand lead to a _____ (shift of; movement along) the demand curve. Factors that change demand are _____, _____, _____, _____, and _____.

True or false

1. The law of demand states that other things remaining the same, if the price of a good rises, the quantity demanded of that good increases.

2. If the quantity of ice cream demanded at each price increases and other influences on buying plans do not change, there is a movement along the demand curve for ice cream.

3. When Sue's income increases, her demand for movies increases. For Sue, movies are a normal good.

4. If average income falls and all other influences on buying plans remain the same, the demand for computers will decrease and there will be a movement along the demand curve.

Multiple choice

1. Other things remaining the same, the quantity of a good or service demanded will increase if the price of the good or service
   a. rises.
   b. falls.
   c. does not change.
   d. rises or falls.

2. Hot dogs and hot dog buns are complements. If the price of a hot dog falls, then
   a. the demand for hot dogs will increase.
   b. the demand for hot dog buns will decrease.
   c. the quantity demanded of hotdogs will decrease.
   d. the demand for hot dog buns will increase.

3. Over the next few years the number of buyers in the market for sport utility vehicles decreases sharply. As a result,
   a. the demand curve for sport utility vehicles shifts leftward.
   b. the demand curve for sport utility vehicles shifts rightward.
   c. there is neither a shift nor a movement along the demand curve for sport utility vehicles.
   d. there is a movement downward along the demand curve for sport utility vehicles.

4. When moving along a demand curve, which of the following changes?
   a. the consumers' incomes
   b. the prices of other goods
   c. the number of buyers
   d. the price of the good

5. If the price of a CD falls,
   a. the demand for CDs will increase and the demand curve for CDs will shift rightward.
   b. the demand for CDs will be unaffected, so the demand curve for CDs will not shift.
   c. the quantity of CDs demanded will increase and there will be a movement along the demand curve for CDs.
   d. Both answers (b) and (c) are correct.

6. Pizza and tacos are substitutes and the price of a pizza rises. Which of the following correctly indicates what happens?
   a. The demand for pizzas decreases and the demand for tacos increases.
   b. The demand for both goods decreases.
   c. The quantity of tacos demanded increases and the quantity of pizza demanded decreases.
   d. The quantity of pizza demanded decreases and the demand for tacos increases.

Complete the graph

1. The demand schedule for cotton candy is given in the following table. In Figure 4.3, draw the demand curve. Label the axes.

Price (dollars per bundle of cotton candy)	Quantity (bundles of cotton candy per month)
1	10,000
2	8,000
3	7,000
4	4,000

a. If the price of cotton candy is $2 a bundle, what is the quantity demanded?
b. If the price of cotton candy is $3 a bundle, what is the quantity demanded?
c. Does the demand curve you drew slope upward or downward?

■ **FIGURE 4.3**

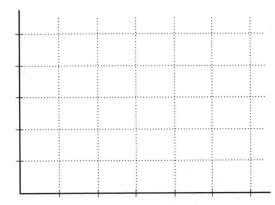

Short answer and numeric questions

1. Explain the difference between a change in the quantity demanded and a change in demand.

2. What is the difference between a movement along a demand curve and a shift of a demand curve?

CHECKPOINT 4.2

■ **Distinguish between quantity supplied and supply and explain what determines supply.**

Practice Problem 4.2

In the market for timber beams, several events occur one at a time. Explain the influence of each event on the quantity supplied of timber beams and the supply of timber beams. Illustrate the effects of each event by either a movement along the supply curve or a shift in the supply curve of timber beams and say which event (or events) illustrates the law of supply in action. These events are

    a. The wage rate of sawmill workers rises.

    b. The price of sawdust rises.

    c. The price of a timber beam rises.

    d. The price of a timber beam is expected to rise next year.

    e. Environmentalists convince Congress to introduce a new law that reduces the amount of forest that can be cut for timber products.

    f. A new technology lowers the cost of producing timber beams.

Solution to Practice Problem 4.2

Practice Problem 4.2 stresses a key point, the distinction between a change in the quantity supplied and a change in supply.

Quick Review

- *Change in the quantity supplied* A change in the quantity of a good that suppliers plan to sell that results from a change in the price of the good.

- *Change in supply* A change in the quantity that suppliers plan to sell when any influence on selling plans, other than the price of the good, changes. These other influences include: prices of related goods, prices of inputs, expectations, number of sellers, and productivity.

a. The wage rate of sawmill workers rises.

Sawmill workers are resources used to produce timber beams. So a rise in their wage rate decreases the supply of timber beams and shifts the supply curve leftward, as illustrated.

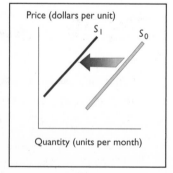

b. The price of sawdust rises.

Sawdust is produced when timber beams are produced, so sawdust and timber beams are complements in production. A rise in the price of a complement in production increases the supply of timber beams and the supply curve of timber beams shifts rightward.

c. The price of a timber beam rises.

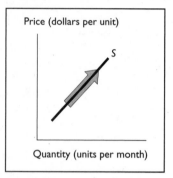

The law of supply states that a rise in the price of a good increases the quantity supplied. So a rise in the price of a timber beam increases the quantity of timber beams supplied and there is a movement up along the supply curve as shown in the figure.

d. The price of a timber beam is expected to rise next year.

The higher price expected next year decreases the current supply of beams as producers store their beams in order to sell them at the (expected) higher price next year. The supply curve of timber beams shifts leftward.

e. Environmentalists convince Congress to introduce a new law that reduces the amount of forest that can be cut for timber products.

The new law decreases the supply of timber beams. The supply of trees decreases and so the price of a tree, a resource for timber beams, rises. The supply curve of beams shifts leftward.

f. A new technology lowers the cost of producing timber beams.

With the lower cost from the new technology, the supply of timber beams increases. The supply curve shifts rightward.

Additional Practice Problem 4.2a

The information in the table shows the supply schedule for scooters in a town. Using this information, label the axes in Figure 4.4 and then graph the supply curve.

Price (dollars per scooter)	Quantity (scooters per week)
100	60
75	50
50	30
25	10

■ **FIGURE 4.4**

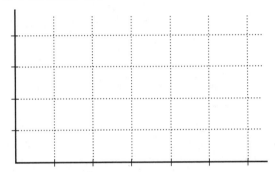

Solution to Additional Practice Problem 4.2a
The axes are labeled and the supply curve is graphed in Figure 4.5.

■ **FIGURE 4.5**

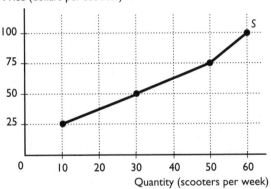

■ **Self Test 4.2**

Fill in the blanks
The ____ (quantity supplied; supply) of a good is the amount people are willing and able to sell during a specified period at a specified price. The law of supply states that other things remaining the same, if the price of a good rises, the quantity supplied ____. A supply curve is ____ (upward; downward) sloping. A change in the price of a good changes ____ (supply; the quantity supplied) and is illustrated by a ____ the supply curve. Factors that change supply are ____, ____, ____, ____, and ____.

True or false
1. The law of supply states that other things remaining the same, if the price of a good rises, the quantity supplied increases.

2. If the wage rate paid to chefs rises and all other influences on selling plans remain the same, the supply of restaurant meals will increase.

3. If the price of coffee is expected to rise next month, the supply of coffee this month will decrease.

4. When new technology for producing computers is used by manufacturers, the supply of computers increases.

Multiple choice
1. The quantity supplied is ____ during a specified period and at a specified price.
   a. the amount that people are able to sell
   b. the amount that people are willing to sell
   c. the amount that people are able and willing to sell
   d. the amount that people are willing and able to buy

2. An increase in supply is shown by a
   a. rightward shift of the supply curve.
   b. leftward shift of the supply curve.
   c. movement up along the supply curve but no shift in the supply curve.
   d. movement down along the supply curve but no shift in the supply curve.

3. If the costs to produce pizza increase, which will occur?
   a. The supply of pizza will decrease.
   b. The quantity of pizzas supplied will increase as sellers try to cover their costs.
   c. Pizza will cease to be produced and sold.
   d. The demand curve for pizza will shift leftward when the price of a pizza increases.

4. A rise in the price of a substitute in production for a good will lead to
   a. an increase in the supply of that good.
   b. a decrease in the supply of that good.
   c. no change in the supply of that good.
   d. a decrease in the quantity of that good supplied.

5. A technological advancement in the production of jeans will bring about which of the following?
   a. The quantity of jeans supplied will increase.
   b. The supply of jeans will increase.
   c. Buyers will demand more jeans because they are now more efficiently produced.
   d. The impact on the supply of jeans is impossible to predict.

6. Suppose the price of leather used to produce shoes increases. As a result, there is ____ in the supply of shoes and the supply curve of shoes shifts ____.
   a. an increase; rightward
   b. an increase; leftward
   c. a decrease; rightward
   d. a decrease; leftward

Complete the graph

1. Suppose that the supply schedule for cotton candy is given in the table below. In Figure 4.3, you previously drew a demand curve for cotton candy. Now use the supply schedule to draw the supply curve in Figure 4.3.

Price (dollars per bundle of cotton candy)	Quantity (bundles of cotton candy per month)
1	4,000
2	8,000
3	10,000
4	12,000

   a. If the price of cotton candy is $2 a bundle, what is the quantity supplied?
   b. If the price of cotton candy is $3 a bundle, what is the quantity supplied?
   c. Does the supply curve you drew slope upward or downward?

■ **FIGURE 4.6**
Price (dollars per box of rubber bands)

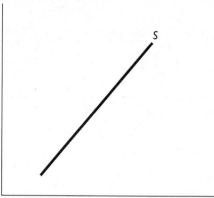

Quantity (boxes of rubber bands per year)

2. Figure 4.6 shows a supply curve for rubber bands. Suppose the technology used to produce rubber bands advances. In Figure 4.6, illustrate the effect of this event.

■ **FIGURE 4.7**
Price (dollars per ton of copper)

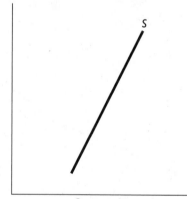

Quantity (tons of copper per year)

3. Figure 4.7 shows a supply curve for copper. The cost of the natural gas used to refine copper ore into copper rises. In Figure 4.7, show the effect of this event.

Short answer and numeric questions
1. What is the law of supply?

2. What influence(s) lead to a change in the quantity supplied?

3. What influences(s) cause a change in supply?

CHECKPOINT 4.3

■ **Explain how demand and supply determine price and quantity in a market and explain the effects of changes in demand and supply.**

Practice Problem 4.3

Price (dollars per carton)	Quantity demanded	Quantity supplied
	(cartons per day)	
1.00	200	110
1.25	175	130
1.50	150	150
1.75	125	170
2.00	100	190

The table shows the demand and supply schedules for milk:

a. What is the market equilibrium in the milk market?

b. Describe the situation in the milk market if the price is $1.75 a carton.

c. If the price is $1.75 a carton, explain how the market reaches equilibrium.

d. A drought decreases the quantity supplied by 45 cartons a day at each price. What is the new equilibrium and how does the market adjust to it?

e. Milk becomes more popular and the quantity demanded increases by 5 cartons a day at each price. Improved feeds for dairy cows increase the quantity of milk supplied by 50 cartons a day at each price. If there is no drought, what is the new equilibrium and how does the market adjust to it?

Solution to Practice Problem 4.3

This Practice Problem uses the idea of market equilibrium and puts to work all you learned in the previous checkpoints about changes in demand and supply.

Quick Review

• *Market equilibrium* When the quantity demanded equals the quantity supplied.

a. What is the market equilibrium in the milk market?

Scan the table to find the row in which the quantity supplied and the quantity demanded

are equal. The price that equates quantity demanded and quantity supplied is the equilibrium price and, in the table, is $1.50 per carton. The equilibrium quantity is 150 cartons per day.

b. Describe the situation in the milk market if the price is $1.75 a carton.

At prices that are higher than the equilibrium price, the quantity supplied will exceed the quantity demanded, so there is a surplus. At a price of $1.75 per carton, the surplus is 45 cartons (170 cartons minus 125 cartons).

c. If the price is $1.75 a carton, explain how the market reaches equilibrium.

The surplus means that sellers cannot sell all the milk they have for sale, 170 cartons. The price falls, which increases the quantity demanded and decreases the quantity supplied. The price falls to its equilibrium level.

d. A drought decreases the quantity supplied by 45 cartons per day at each price. What is the new equilibrium and how does the market adjust to it?

The new supply curve shifts leftward by 45 cartons a day at each price. At the old equilibrium price of $1.50 a carton, there now is a shortage of milk. The law of markets tells us that the price rises. The (new) equilibrium price is $1.75 a carton and the (new) equilibrium quantity is 125 cartons a day.

e. Milk becomes more popular and the quantity demanded increases by 5 cartons a day at each price. Improved feeds for dairy cows increase the quantity of milk supplied by 50 cartons a day at each price. If there is no drought, what is the new equilibrium and how does the market adjust to it?

The change in preferences shifts the demand curve rightward by 5 cartons a day at all prices and the advanced technology shifts the supply curve rightward by 50 cartons. Because the increase in supply exceeds the increase in demand, at the initial equilibrium price there is a surplus. The price falls until it reaches its new equilibrium of $1.25 a carton. At $1.25 a carton, the (new) quantity demanded equals the (new) quantity supplied at the equilibrium quantity of 180 cartons a day.

Additional Practice Problem 4.3a

The price of a hot dog bun falls and, simultaneously, the number of hot dog producers increases. The effect of the fall in the price of a hot dog bun is less than the effect of the increase in the number of producers. What happens to the equilibrium price and quantity of hot dogs?

Solution to Additional Practice Problem 4.3a

The fall in the price of a complement, hot dog buns, increases the demand for hot dogs and the demand curve for hot dogs shifts rightward. The increase in the

number of producers increases the supply of hot dogs and the supply curve shifts rightward. Because the increase in supply exceeds the increase in demand, the price of a hot dog falls and the quantity increases, as shown in the figure.

■ Self Test 4.3

Fill in the blanks

The price at which the quantity demanded equals the quantity supplied is the ____. In a diagram, the ____ is determined where the supply and demand curves intersect. If the price exceeds the equilibrium price, the price ____ (rises; falls). An increase in demand ____ (raises; lowers) the equilibrium price and ____ (increases; decreases) the equilibrium quantity. An increase in supply ____ (raises; lowers) the equilibrium price and ____ (increases; decreases) the equilibrium quantity. If both the demand and supply increase, definitely the equilibrium ____ increases but the effect on the equilibrium ____ is ambiguous.

True or false

1. If the price of asparagus is below the equilibrium price, there is a shortage of asparagus and the price of asparagus will rise until the shortage disappears.

2. When the demand for skateboards decreases and the supply of skateboards remains unchanged, the quantity supplied of skateboards decreases as the price rises.

3. As summer comes to an end and winter sets in, the demand for and supply of hamburger buns decrease. The price of a hamburger bun will definitely remain the same.

4. The number of buyers of grapefruit juice increases and at the same time severe frost decreases the supply of grapefruit juice. The price of grapefruit juice will rise.

Multiple choice

1. The equilibrium price of a good occurs when the
   a. quantity of the good demanded equals the quantity of the good supplied.
   b. quantity of the good demanded is greater than the quantity of the good supplied.
   c. quantity of the good demanded is less than the quantity of the good supplied.
   d. demand for the good is equal to the supply of the good.

2. Which of the following is correct?
   a. A surplus puts downward pressure on the price of a good.
   b. A shortage puts upward pressure on the price of a good.
   c. There is no surplus or shortage at equilibrium.
   d. All of the above answers are correct.

3. Which of the following is the best explanation for why the price of gasoline rises and the quantity increases during the summer months?
   a. Oil producers have higher costs of production in the summer.
   b. Sellers have to earn profits during the summer to cover losses in the winter.
   c. There is increased driving by families going on vacation.
   d. There is less competition among oil refineries in the summer.

4. Suppose that the price of lettuce used to produce tacos increases. As a result, the equilibrium price of a taco ____ and the equilibrium quantity ____.
   a. rises; increases
   b. rises; decreases
   c. falls; increases
   d. falls; decreases

5. The technology associated with manufacturing computers has advanced enormously. This change has led to the equilibrium price of a computer ____ and the equilibrium quantity ____.
   a. rising; increasing
   b. rising; decreasing
   c. falling; increasing
   d. falling; decreasing

6. During 2003 the supply of petroleum decreased while at the same time the demand for petroleum increased. If the magnitude of the increase in demand was greater than the magnitude of the decrease in supply, which of the following occurred?
   a. The equilibrium price of gasoline increased and the equilibrium quantity increased.
   b. The equilibrium price of gasoline increased and the equilibrium quantity decreased.
   c. The equilibrium price of gasoline increased and the equilibrium quantity did not change.
   d. The equilibrium price of gasoline decreased and the equilibrium quantity did not change.

Complete the graph

1. In Checkpoint 4.1 you drew a demand curve in Figure 4.3; in Checkpoint 4.2, you drew a supply curve in that figure. Return to Figure 4.3 and answer the following questions.
   a. If the price of cotton candy is $1 a bundle, what is the situation in the market?
   b. If the price of cotton candy is $3 a bundle, what is the situation in the market?
   c. What is the equilibrium price and equilibrium quantity of cotton candy?

Short answer and numeric questions

1. How is a shortage different from a surplus?

Price (dollars per sweatshirt)	Quantity demanded (sweatshirts per season)	Quantity supplied (sweatshirts per season)
35	13	32
30	15	25
25	19	19
20	27	12
15	37	8

2. The table gives the demand and supply schedules for sweatshirts. At what price will the quantity demanded be equal to the quantity supplied? What is the equilibrium quantity?

3. People read that drinking orange juice helps prevent heart disease. What is the effect on the equilibrium price and quantity of orange juice?

4. The cost of memory chips used in computers falls. What is the effect on the equilibrium price and quantity of computers?

5. The demand for Japanese yen (the currency of Japan) increases while simultaneously the Japanese government decreases the supply of yen. What is the effect on the price of yen?

CHECKPOINT 4.4

■ **Explain how price ceilings, price floors, and sticky prices cause shortages, surpluses, and unemployment.**

Practice Problems 4.4

1. The figure shows the rental market for apartments in Corsicana, Texas.

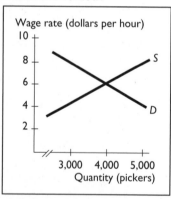

   a. What is the rent and how many apartments are rented?

   b. If the city government imposes a rent ceiling of $900 a month, what is the rent and how many apartments are rented?

   c. If the city government imposes a rent ceiling of $600 a month, what is the rent and how many apartments are rented?

2. The figure shows the market for tomato pickers in southern California:

   a. What is the equilibrium wage rate of tomato pickers and what is the equilibrium quantity of tomato pickers employed?

   b. If California introduces a minimum wage for tomato pickers of $4 an hour, how many tomato pickers are employed and how many are unemployed?

   c. If California introduces a minimum wage for tomato pickers of $8 an hour, how many tomato pickers are employed and how many are unemployed?

Solution to Practice Problems 4.4

These problems study cases in which markets cannot adjust to their equilibrium. In later chapters we use these ideas to help explain unemployment and the overall level of production in the economy.

Quick Review

- *Price ceiling* The highest price at which it is legal to trade a good, service, or factor of production. An interest rate ceiling is a price ceiling.
- *Price floor* The lowest price at which it is legal to trade a good, service, or factor of production. The minimum wage is a price floor.

1a. What is the rent and how many apartments are rented?

At equilibrium, the quantity supplied equals the quantity demanded. The equilibrium rent is $800 a month and the equilibrium quantity of apartments rented is 3,000.

1b. If the city government imposes a rent ceiling of $900 a month, what is the rent and how many apartments are rented?

With a rent ceiling of $900 a month, apartments cannot be rented for more than $900. Because the equilibrium rent is below $900, this requirement has no effect. The rent remains at $800 a month and 3,000 apartment are rented.

1c. If the city government imposes a rent ceiling of $600 a month, what is the rent and how many apartments are rented?

The rent ceiling is below the equilibrium rent. The rent cannot adjust to the equilibrium amount, $800. The rent will be $600 a month, equal to the ceiling rate, and the quantity of apartments rented is 1,000, determined from the supply curve.

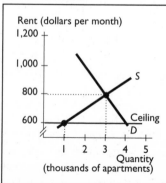

2a. What is the equilibrium wage rate of tomato pickers and what is the equilibrium quantity of tomato pickers employed?

The quantity supplied equals the quantity demanded at a wage rate of $6 an hour. $6 an hour is the equilibrium wage rate. The equilibrium quantity of tomato pickers employed is 4,000.

2b. If California introduces a minimum wage for tomato pickers of $4 an hour, how many tomato pickers are employed and how many are unemployed?

The minimum wage of $4 an hour is less than the equilibrium wage, so the minimum wage has no effect. The wage rate remains equal to $6 an hour. Zero pickers are unemployed and 4,000 pickers are employed.

2c. If California introduces a minimum wage for tomato pickers of $8 an hour, how many tomato pickers are employed and how many are unemployed?

The minimum wage is above the equilibrium wage of $6 an hour, so the wage cannot adjust to its equilibrium. The figure shows that at the minimum wage, the quantity demanded is 3,000 pickers, so 3,000 pickers will be employed. But 5,000 people would like to work, so 2,000 pickers (5,000 – 3,000) are unemployed.

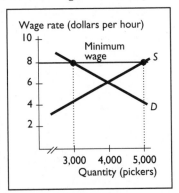

Additional Practice Problem 4.4a

What is a sticky price and how can a sticky price in the labor market create unemployment?

Solution to Additional Practice Problem 4.4a

A sticky price occurs when buyers and sellers agree on a price for a fixed period of time or a seller sets a price that changes infrequently. Many workers have contracts with their employers in which the wage rate to be paid for several years is specified. This wage rate can create unemployment when the demand for labor decreases. The wage rate cannot fall to its new equilibrium value. At the relatively high sticky wage, the quantity of labor demanded is less than the quantity of labor supplied. The surplus of workers are unemployed.

■ Self Test 4.4

Fill in the blanks

A price _____ (ceiling; floor) is the highest price at which it is legal to trade a particular good, service, or factor of production. In order to affect the market price and quantity, a price floor must be set _____ (above; below) the equilibrium price. A minimum wage is an example of a price _____ (ceiling; floor). A minimum wage creates unemployment when it is set _____ (above; below) the equilibrium wage rate. Sticky prices _____ (can; cannot) create unemployment.

True or false

1. A rent ceiling always lowers the rent paid.

2. A minimum wage is an example of a price ceiling.

3. Firms hire labor, so they determine how much labor to supply in a market.

4. When firms enter into long-term contracts with labor unions that fix wage rates for several years, the wage rate is sticky.

Multiple choice

1. Price ceilings
   a. prevent the market price from going above a certain value.
   b. prevent the market price from going below a certain value.
   c. keep the market prices higher than would otherwise be the case.
   d. match the quantity demanded with the quantity supplied of any given good or service.

2. When the government imposes a price ceiling on a product below the equilibrium price, the government creates
   a. a shortage.
   b. a surplus.
   c. equilibrium in the market.
   d. None of the above answers is correct.

3. To affect the market's price and quantity, a price floor must be set
   a. above the equilibrium price.
   b. below the equilibrium price.
   c. at the equilibrium price.
   d. None of the above answers are correct.

4. The minimum wage is an example of
   a. an equilibrium price.
   b. a price floor.
   c. a price ceiling.
   d. None of the above answers is correct.

5. A two-year labor contract is an example of a
   a. price ceiling.
   b. price floor.
   c. sticky price.
   d. shortage.

6. The result of sticky prices in a market is
   a. quicker adjustment of prices.
   b. no adjustment of prices.
   c. a slower adjustment of prices.
   d. to change the price but not the quantity bought and sold.

Complete the graph

1. In Checkpoint 4.1 you drew a demand curve in Figure 4.3; in Checkpoint 4.2, you drew a supply curve in that figure. Return to Figure 4.3 and answer the following questions.
   a. Suppose the government imposes a price ceiling for cotton candy of $1. What is the situation in the market?
   b. Suppose the government imposes a price floor for cotton candy of $3. What is the situation in the market?
   c. How do your answers to parts (a) and (b) compare with your answers to Checkpoint 4.3 complete the graph question parts (a) and (b)?

Short answer and numeric questions

Price (cents per kilowatt-hour)	Quantity demanded (kilowatt-hours)	Quantity supplied (kilowatt-hours)
17	2,700	2,700
15	2,900	2,600
13	3,100	2,500
11	3,300	2,400
9	3,500	2,300
7	3,700	2,100

1. The table gives the demand and supply schedules for electricity. At what price will the quantity demanded be equal to the quantity supplied? Suppose the government tries to keep the price of electricity low by setting a price ceiling of 7¢ per kilowatt. What is the impact of this price ceiling?

2. What is the effect of a minimum wage set below the equilibrium wage rate? Set above the equilibrium wage rate? Explain why your answers to the two questions differ.

SELF TEST ANSWERS

■ CHECKPOINT 4.1

Fill in the blanks

The <u>law of demand</u> states that other things remaining the same, if the price of a good rises, the <u>quantity demanded of</u> that good decreases. A <u>demand curve</u> is a graph of the relationship between the quantity demanded of a good and its price. Demand curves are <u>downward</u> sloping. An increase in demand shifts the demand curve <u>rightward</u>. Factors that change demand lead to a <u>shift of</u> the demand curve. Factors that change demand are <u>prices of related goods</u>, <u>income</u>, <u>expectations</u>, <u>number of buyers</u>, and <u>preferences</u>.

True or false

1. False; page 83
2. False; page 85
3. True; page 85
4. False; page 85

Multiple choice

1. b; page 83
2. d; page 85
3. a; page 86
4. d; page 86
5. d; page 86
6. d; page 86

Complete the graph

1. Figure 4.8 (above) illustrates the demand curve, labeled *D* in the diagram.
   a. 8,000 bundles per month
   b. 7,000 bundles per month
   c. The demand curve slopes downward.

Short answer and numeric questions

1. A change in the quantity demanded occurs when the price of the good changes. A change in demand occurs when any other influence on buying plans other than the price of the good changes; page 85.
2. A movement along a demand curve reflects a change in the quantity demanded and is the result of a change in the price of the good.

■ FIGURE 4.8

Price (dollars per bundle of cotton candy)

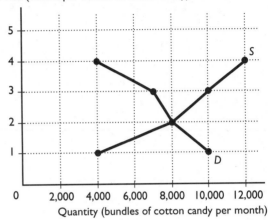

Quantity (bundles of cotton candy per month)

A shift of a demand curve reflects a change in demand and is the result of a change in any influence on buying plans other than the price of the good; page 83.

■ CHECKPOINT 4.2

Fill in the blanks

The <u>quantity supplied</u> of a good is the amount people are willing and able to sell during a specified period at a specified price. The law of supply states that other things remaining the same, if the price of a good rises, the quantity supplied <u>increases</u>. A supply curve is <u>upward</u> sloping. A change in the price of a good changes <u>the quantity supplied</u> and is illustrated by a <u>movement along</u> the supply curve. Factors that change supply are <u>prices of related goods</u>, <u>prices of resources and other inputs</u>, <u>expectations</u>, <u>number of sellers</u>, and <u>productivity</u>.

True or false

1. True; page 88
2. False; page 90
3. True; page 90
4. True; page 91

Multiple choice

1. c; page 88
2. a; page 91
3. a; page 90
4. b; page 90

5. b; page 91

6. d; page 91

Complete the graph

1. The supply curve is illustrated in Figure 4.8, labeled *S* in the diagram.
   a. 8,000 bundles per month
   b. 10,000 bundles per month
   c. The supply curve slopes upward.

■ FIGURE 4.9

Price (dollars per box of rubber bands)

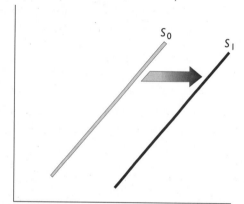

Quantity (boxes of rubber bands per year)

2. An advance in technology increases the supply. Figure 4.9 illustrates the shift of the supply curve; page 90.

■ FIGURE 4.10

Price (dollars per ton of copper)

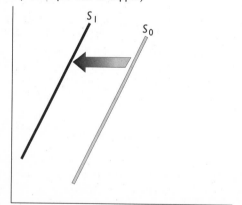

Quantity (tons of copper per year)

3. A rise in the price of a resource decreases the supply. Figure 4.10 illustrates the leftward shift of the supply curve; page 90.

Short answer and numeric questions

1. If other things remain the same, when the price of a good falls (rises), the quantity supplied of that good decreases (increases); page 88.

2. Change in the price of the good; page 88.

3. Changes in: prices of related goods; prices of resources and other inputs; expectations; number of sellers; and productivity; page 90.

■ CHECKPOINT 4.3

Fill in the blanks

The price at which the quantity demanded equals the quantity supplied is the <u>equilibrium price</u>. In a diagram, the <u>equilibrium</u> <u>price</u> is determined where the supply and demand curves intersect. If the price exceeds the equilibrium price, the price <u>falls</u>. An increase in demand <u>raises</u> the equilibrium price and <u>increases</u> the equilibrium quantity. An increase in supply <u>lowers</u> the equilibrium price and <u>increases</u> the equilibrium quantity. If both the demand and supply increase, definitely the equilibrium <u>quantity</u> increases but the effect on the equilibrium <u>price</u> is ambiguous.

True or false

1. True; page 94
2. False; page 95
3. False; page 98
4. True; page 99

Multiple choice

1. a; page 93
2. d; page 94
3. c; page 95
4. b; page 96
5. c; page 96
6. a; page 99

Complete the graph

1. a. A shortage of 6,000 bundles a day; page 94.
   b. A surplus of 3,000 bundles a day; page 94.
   c. The equilibrium price is $2 a bundle of cotton candy and the equilibrium quantity is 8,000 bundles a day; page 94.

Short answer and numeric questions

1. When a shortage exists, the price of the good is below the equilibrium price. The quantity demanded is greater than the quantity supplied. When a surplus exists, the price of the good is above the equilibrium price. The quantity demanded is less than the quantity supplied; page 94.

2. The quantity demanded equals the quantity supplied when the price is $25. The equilibrium quantity is 19 sweatshirts; page 93.

3. The increase in preferences increases the demand for orange juice and the demand curve shifts rightward. The price of orange juice rises and the quantity increases; page 95.

4. The fall in cost increases the supply of computers. The supply curve of computers shifts rightward. The price falls and the quantity increases; page 96.

5. The increase in demand shifts the demand curve for yen rightward. The decrease in supply shifts the supply curve of yen leftward. The price of a yen rises; page 98.

■ CHECKPOINT 4.4

Fill in the blanks

A price <u>ceiling</u> is the highest price at which it is legal to trade a particular good, service, or factor of production. In order to affect the market price and quantity, a price floor must be set <u>above</u> the equilibrium price. A minimum wage is an example of a price <u>floor</u>. A minimum wage creates unemployment when it is set <u>above</u> the equilibrium wage rate. Sticky prices <u>can</u> create unemployment.

True or false

1. False; page 102
2. False; page 103
3. False; page 103
4. True; pages 104-105

Multiple choice

1. a; page 101
2. a; page 102

3. a; pages 103-104
4. b; page 103
5. c; pages 104-105
6. c; page 105

Complete the graph

1. a. With a price ceiling of $1, there is a shortage of 6,000 bundles; page 102.

   b. With a price floor of $3, there is a surplus of 3,000 bundles; page 104.

   c. The shortages and surpluses in the answers above are the same as the shortages and surpluses in the answers to questions in Checkpoint 4.3. Government-imposed price ceilings and floors create shortages and surpluses *exactly* the same way that non-equilibrium prices create shortages and surpluses, though government created shortages and surpluses persist as long as the policies persist; pages 102, 104.

Short answer and numeric questions

1. The quantity demanded equals quantity supplied at the equilibrium price of 17¢ per kilowatt-hour. A price ceiling of 7¢ per kilowatt is below the equilibrium price. At the price ceiling, the quantity demanded is 3,700 kilowatt-hours and the quantity supplied is 2,100 kilowatt-hours, so a shortage of 1,600 kilowatt-hours exists; page 102.

2. A minimum wage set below the equilibrium wage rate has no effect. The minimum wage is the lowest legal wage. When set below the equilibrium wage rate, the equilibrium wage remains legal. Nothing is changed because the market wage remains equal to the equilibrium wage. When the minimum wage is set above the equilibrium wage, the equilibrium wage becomes illegal. The wage becomes the minimum wage. At the higher minimum wage, the quantity of labor demanded is less than the quantity of labor supplied and unemployment results; page 104.

GDP and the Standard of Living

Chapter

5

CHAPTER IN PERSPECTIVE

Chapter 5 explains GDP and how it is measured. It shows why GDP is the same whether measured as income, as expenditure, or as the value of production. It explains the difference between real and nominal GDP, and the limitations of GDP as a measure of the standard of living.

■ **Define GDP and explain why the value of production, income, and expenditure are the same for an economy.**

Gross Domestic Product, GDP, is the market value of all the final goods and services produced within a country in a given time period. Only final goods and services are included in GDP; intermediate goods and services are not included. Expenditures are consumption expenditure (*C*), investment (*I*), government purchases of goods and services (*G*), and net exports (*NX*). Total expenditure equals *C* + *I* + *G* + *NX*. Firms pay out everything they receive as incomes to the factors of production. We call total income *Y*. The circular flow shows that total expenditure equals total income so that *Y* = *C* + *I* + *G* + *NX*.

■ **Describe how economic statisticians measure GDP in the United States.**

GDP is measured using the expenditure approach and the income approach. The expenditure approach adds the four sources of expenditure: consumption expenditure, investment, government purchases of goods and services, and net exports. The income approach adds the National Income and Products Accounts five categories of income (compensation of employees, net interest, rental income of persons, corporate profits, and proprietors' income). This sum is net domestic product at factor cost. To get GDP, indirect taxes are added, subsidies are subtracted, and depreciation is added to net domestic product at factor cost. Value added is the value of a firm's production minus the value of the intermediate goods it uses.

■ **Distinguish between nominal GDP and real GDP and define the GDP deflator.**

GDP changes when prices or production change. Real GDP is the value of final goods and services produced in a given year valued at constant prices; nominal GDP is the value of final goods and services produced in a given year using prices that prevailed in that year. The GDP deflator is an average of current prices expressed as a percentage of base-year prices and equals (nominal GDP ÷ real GDP) × 100.

■ **Explain and describe the limitations of real GDP as a measure of the standard of living.**

GDP measures the value of goods and services that are bought in markets. It does not measure household production, underground production, the value of leisure time, the environmental quality, health and life expectancy, and political freedom and justice.

EXPANDED CHAPTER CHECKLIST

When you have completed this chapter, you will be able to:

1 **Define GDP and explain why the value of production, income, and expenditure are the same for an economy.**

- Define GDP.
- Explain the difference between a final good or service and an intermediate good or service, and tell why only final goods and services are included in GDP.
- Discuss the four types of expenditure.
- State why the value of production equals income, which equals expenditure.

2 **Describe how economic statisticians measure GDP in the United States.**

- Explain the expenditure approach to measuring GDP.
- Discuss why used goods and financial assets are not included in GDP.
- Explain the income approach to measuring GDP and discuss each of the components.
- State what adjustments must be made to net domestic product at factor cost to convert it to GDP.
- Define value added and calculate it.

3 **Distinguish between nominal GDP and real GDP and define the GDP deflator.**

- Define nominal GDP and real GDP, and explain the difference between them.
- Calculate real GDP.
- Define the GDP deflator and calculate it.

4 **Explain and describe the limitations of real GDP as a measure of the standard of living.**

- List the goods and services omitted from GDP and explain why each of these goods and services are not measured in GDP.

- Discuss how these omitted factors affect the standard of living.

KEY TERMS

- Gross domestic product (GDP) (page 112)
- Final good or service (page 112)
- Intermediate good or service (page 112)
- Consumption expenditure (page 113)
- Investment (page 113)
- Government purchases of goods and services (page 114)
- Net exports of goods and services (page 114)
- Exports of goods and services (page 114)
- Imports of goods and services (page 114)
- Net domestic product at factor cost (page 120)
- Depreciation (page 120)
- Value added (page 121)
- Real GDP (page 123)
- Nominal GDP (page 123)
- GDP deflator (page 125)

CHECKPOINT 5.1

■ Define GDP and explain why the value of production, income, and expenditure are the same for an economy.

Practice Problems 5.1

1. Classify each of the following items as a final good or service or an intermediate good or service:
   a. Banking services bought by a student.
   b. New cars bought by Hertz, the car rental firm.
   c. Newsprint bought by *USA Today* from International Paper.
   d. Ice cream bought by a diner and used to produce sundaes.

2. During 2001 on Lotus Island, net taxes were $10 billion; consumption expenditure was $30 billion; government purchases of goods and

services were $12 billion; investment was $15 billion; and net exports were $3 billion. Calculate:

  a. Total expenditure.

  b. Total income.

  c. GDP.

Solution to Practice Problems 5.1

For the first question, ask if the good is used to produce another good or service. If so, it is an intermediate good. For the second question, keep in mind the equality between total expenditure, total income, and GDP.

Quick Review

- *Total expenditure* Total expenditure is the total amount received by producers of final goods and services and equals $C + I + G + NX$.

- *Total income* Total income is the income paid to all factors of production and equals total expenditure.

1a. Banking services bought by a student.

Because the student uses the services and does not use them to produce or sell anything else, the banking services are a final service

1b. New cars bought by Hertz, the car rental firm.

Hertz is the final buyer of the cars so they are a final good. The cars are additions to capital and are part of investment when they are bought.

1c. Newsprint bought by *USA Today* from International Paper.

Because the newsprint was bought to be processed into newspapers that will be sold to others, this is an intermediate good. The newspapers are the final goods, not the newsprint itself.

1d. Ice cream bought by a diner and used to produce sundaes.

The sundaes are the final goods. The ice cream that was bought by the diner to make the sundaes is an intermediate good.

During 2001 on Lotus Island, net taxes were $10 billion; consumption expenditure was $30 billion; government purchases of goods and services were $12 billion; investment was $15 billion; and net exports were $3 billion. Calculate:

2a. Total expenditure.

Total expenditure is the sum of consumption expenditure, investment, government purchases of goods and services and net exports. Total expenditure $= C + I + G + NX$, or $30 billion + $15 billion + $12 billion + $3 billion = $60 billion.

2b. Total income.

Total income is always equal to total expenditure, so it also is $60 billion. You don't have the information about wages, rents, interest, and profits that would allow a separate calculation of total income, but you don't need to make that calculation.

2c. GDP.

GDP can be measured either as total income or as total expenditure. So GDP is $60 billion.

Additional Practice Problem 5.1a

Last year consumption expenditure was $70 billion, investment was $16 billion, government purchases of goods and services were $12 billion, exports were $4 billion, and imports were $3 billion. This year imports increased to $5 billion. If all the other types of expenditure stay the same, what was GDP last year, GDP this year, and how did GDP change from last year?

Solution to Additional Practice Problem 5.1a

To solve this problem use the equality between GDP and expenditure, GDP $= C + I + G + NX$. Last year's GDP $= $70 billion + $16 billion + $12 billion + ($4 billion − $3 billion) = $99 billion. This year, imports increased from $3 billion to $5 billion, so replace the $3 billion in the calculation with $5 billion and GDP for this year is $97 billion. The $2 billion increase in imports results in a $2 billion decrease in GDP.

■ Self Test 5.1

Fill in the blanks

The market value of all the final goods and services produced within a country in a given time period is ____ (GDP; investment). ____ (Two; Three; Four) groups buy the final goods and services produced. Net exports equals the value of ____ (imports; exports) minus the value of ____ (imports; exports). $C + I + G + NX$ equals ____ and ____.

True or false

1. The computer chip that Dell Corp. buys from Intel Corp. is a final good.

2. Expenditure on a bulldozer is consumption expenditure.

3. The value of net exports of goods and services can be negative.

4. The value of production equals income, which equals expenditure.

Multiple choice

1. The abbreviation "GDP" stands for
   a. Gross Domestic Product.
   b. Gross Domestic Prices.
   c. General Domestic Prices.
   d. Great Domestic Prices.

2. GDP is equal to the ____ value of all the final goods and services produced within a country in a given period of time.
   a. production
   b. market
   c. wholesale
   d. retail

3. The following are all *final* goods except
   a. flour used by the baker to make cup cakes.
   b. bread eaten by a family for lunch.
   c. pencils used by a 6th grader in class.
   d. Nike shoes used by a basketball player.

4. Investment is defined as
   a. the purchase of a stock or bond.
   b. financial capital.
   c. what consumers do with their savings.
   d. the purchase of new capital goods by firms.

5. In one year, a firm increases its production by $9 million worth of computers and increases sales by $8 million. All other things in the economy remaining the same, which of the following is true?
   a. GDP increases by $8 million and inventory investment decreases by $1 million.
   b. GDP increases by $9 million and inventory investment increases by $1 million.
   c. Inventory investment decreases by $1 million.
   d. GDP increases by $8 million and investment increases by $1 million.

6. Total expenditure equals
   a. $C + I + G + NX$.
   b. $C + I + G - NX$.
   c. $C + I - G + NX$.
   d. $C - I + G + NX$.

Short answer and numeric questions

1. Why aren't intermediate goods or services counted in GDP?

2. Classify each of the following into the components of U.S. GDP: consumption expenditure, investment, government purchases of goods and services, exports, or imports.
   a. The purchase of a Sony DVD player made in Japan.
   b. A family's purchase of a birthday cake at the local Safeway grocery store.
   c. Microsoft's purchase of 1,000 Dell computers.
   d. The purchase of a new pizza oven by Pizza Hut.
   e. The government's purchase of 15 stealth fighters.

3. Why does total expenditure equal total income?

CHECKPOINT 5.2

■ **Describe how economic statisticians measure GDP in the United States.**

Practice Problem 5.2

1. The table below gives some of the items in the U.S. National Income and Product Accounts in 2001.

Item	Amount (billions of dollars)
Compensation of employees	5,875
Consumption expenditure	6,987
Indirect taxes less subsidies	630
Net interest	650
Corporate profits	732
Capital consumption	1,329
Rental income of persons	138
Investment	1,586
Net exports	−349
Proprietors' income	728

a. Calculate U.S. GDP in 2001.
b. Did you use the expenditure approach or the income approach to make this calculation?
c. How much did the U.S. government spend on goods and services in 2001?
d. By how much did capital in the United States depreciate in 2001?

Solution to Practice Problem 5.2

This question focuses on calculating GDP. To solve problems such as this, you need to know how to use the expenditure approach and the income approach. The expenditure approach adds four categories of expenditure while the income approach adds five income categories and then makes a few additional adjustments.

Quick Review

- *Expenditure approach* GDP equals the sum of consumption expenditure, investment, government purchases, and net exports.
- *Income approach* GDP equals the sum of compensation of employees, net interest, rental income of persons, corporate profits and proprietors' income, plus indirect taxes minus subsidies, and depreciation.

The sum of the first five income categories is net domestic product at factor cost.

a. Calculate U.S. GDP in 2001.

To calculate GDP using the expenditure approach you need to know the values of consumption, investment, government purchases, and net exports. The table does not give the value of government purchases, so you cannot find GDP using the expenditure approach. To calculate GDP using the income approach you need to know the values of compensation of employees, net interest, rental income of persons, corporate profits, proprietors' incomes, indirect taxes less subsidies, and depreciation, called capital consumption. All these items are listed in the table, so GDP can be calculated using the income approach. In this case,

GDP = $5,875 billion + $650 billion + $138 billion + $732 billion + $728 billion + $630 billion + $1,329 billion, which is $10,082 billion.

b. Did you use the expenditure approach or the income approach to make this calculation?

The only way you could get GDP in (a) is by the income approach, which is the approach used.

c. How much did the U.S. government spend on goods and services in 2001?

You calculated GDP in (a) using the income approach. The expenditure approach notes that GDP = C + I + G + NX. Subtract C, I, and NX from both sides of the equation to show that G = GDP − C − I − NX. Using the values of GDP, C, I, and NX yields G = $10,082 billion − $6,987 billion − $1,586 billion + $349 billion = $1,858 billion. (The net exports were negative, so −(−$349 billion) equals + $349 billion).

d. By how much did capital in the United States depreciate in 2001?

Depreciation is the loss of value of capital that results from use and obsolescence. Depreciation also is called "capital consumption," so the amount of depreciation is the amount of capital consumption, listed in the table as $1,329 billion.

Additional Practice Problem 5.2a

What are the ways value added can be calculated? Suppose that the local Taco Bell sells $700,000 of food and it pays $300,000 for wages, $180,000 for ingredients, $20,000 for paper products, $150,000 for rent, and has a profit of $50,000. What is Taco Bell's value added?

Solution to Additional Practice Problem 5.2a

Value added equals the value of a firm's production minus the value of the intermediate goods it buys. Value added also equals the sum of the incomes, including profits, it paid for the factors of production it used.

The value of Taco Bell's production is $700,000. The intermediate goods Taco Bell uses are the ingredients and paper products. Taco Bell's value added equals $700,000 − $180,000 − $20,000 = $500,000. Alternatively, Taco Bell paid people incomes in the form of wages, rent, and profit. From this approach, value added equals the sum of the incomes or $300,000 + $150,000 + $50,000 = $500,000.

■ Self Test 5.2

Fill in the blanks

The ____ approach and the ____ approach are two methods used to calculate GDP. Expenditure on used goods ____ (is; is not) included in GDP. Compensation of employees is part of the ____ (expenditure; income) approach to calculating GDP. To calculate GDP, depreciation is ____ (added to; subtracted from) net domestic product at factor cost. The value of a firm's production minus the value of the intermediate goods it buys is called the firm's ____ (profit; valued added).

True or false

1. The expenditure approach measures GDP by using data on consumption expenditure, investment, government purchases of goods and services and net exports of goods and services.

2. In the United States, expenditure on used goods is becoming an increasingly large fraction of GDP.

3. The income approach uses data on consumption expenditure, investment, government purchases of goods and services, and net exports of goods and services to calculate GDP.

4. A firm's value added equals the value of its production minus the incomes it pays to the factors of production it uses.

Multiple choice

1. In calculating GDP, economists
   a. measure total expenditure as the only true measure.
   b. can measure either total expenditure or total income.
   c. measure total income as the only true measure.
   d. measure total income minus total expenditure.

2. The expenditure approach to measuring GDP is based on summing
   a. compensation of employees, net interest, rental income of persons, corporate profits, and proprietors' income.
   b. the value added by each industry.
   c. the total values of final goods, intermediate goods, used goods, and financial assets.
   d. consumption expenditure, investment, government purchases of goods and services, and net exports of goods and services.

3. Suppose GDP is $10 billion, consumption expenditure is $7 billion, investment is $2 billion, and government purchases of goods and services is $2 billion. Net exports of goods and services must be
   a. $1 billion.
   b. −$1 billion.
   c. $2 billion.
   d. −$2 billion.

4. According to the expenditure approach to measuring GDP, in the United States in 2002, the largest component of GDP is
   a. consumption expenditure.
   b. investment.
   c. government purchases of goods and services.
   d. net exports of goods and services.

5. Which of the following is <u>NOT</u> one of the income categories used in the income approach to measuring GDP?
   a. compensation of employees
   b. rental income of persons
   c. net interest
   d. tax revenues paid by persons

6. Once income is totaled across the five income categories of the income approach, to calculate GDP we must
   a. add the amount of income saved and spent.
   b. add indirect taxes and depreciation and subtract subsidies.
   c. subtract indirect taxes and subsidies and add depreciation.
   d. do nothing because the income sum equals GDP.

Short answer and numeric questions
1. The table below gives data for a small nation:

Item	Amount (dollars)
Compensation of employees	3,900
Consumption expenditure	4,000
Indirect taxes minus subsidies	400
Net interest	300
Corporate profits	500
Government purchases	1,000
Rental income	300
Investment	1,100
Net exports	300
Proprietors' income	300

   a. What is the nation's GDP?
   b. What is the net domestic product at factor cost?
   c. What does depreciation equal?

2. What adjustments must be made to net domestic product at factor cost to convert it to GDP? Why must these adjustments be made?

3. Suppose a gallon of oil is sold by a driller to a refinery for $0.80. The refinery converts the oil to gasoline and sells it to a consumer for $2.00. What is the increase in GDP? The driller uses no intermediate goods. What is the driller's value added? The refiner's? What is the sum of the driller's value added and the refiner's value added?

CHECKPOINT 5.3

■ **Distinguish between nominal GDP and real GDP and define the GDP deflator.**

Practice Problem 5.3
An island economy produces only bananas and coconuts. The table gives the quantities produced and prices in 2001 and 2002. The base year is 2001.

Item	Data for 2001		Data for 2002	
	Quantity	Price	Quantity	Price
Bananas	100	$10.00	110	$15.00
Coconuts	50	$12.00	60	$10.00

Calculate
   a. Nominal GDP in 2001.
   b. Nominal GDP in 2002.
   c. The value of 2002 production in 2001 prices.
   d. The percentage increase in production when valued at 2001 prices.
   e. The value of 2001 production in 2002 prices.
   f. The percentage increase in production when valued at 2002 prices.
   g. Real GDP in 2001 and 2002 by using the chain-linking method.
   h. The GDP deflator in 2002.

Solution to Practice Problem 5.3
This question gives you practice in how real GDP is calculated. Take each part step-by-step.

Quick Review

- *Nominal GDP* The value of the final goods and services produced in a given year valued at the prices that prevailed in that year.

a. Nominal GDP in 2001.

Nominal GDP in 2001 equals the 2001 expenditure on bananas, (100 × $10), plus the expenditure on coconuts, (50 × $12), which is $1,000 + $600 = $1,600.

b. Nominal GDP in 2002.

Similar to part (a), nominal GDP in 2002 = (110 × $15) + (60 × $10) = $1,650 + $600 = $2,250.

c. The value of 2002 production in 2001 prices.

The value of 2002 production in 2001 prices equals the expenditure on bananas, (110 × $10), plus the expenditure on coconuts, (60 × $12), which is $1,100 + $720 = $1,820.

d. The percentage increase in production when valued at 2001 prices.

In 2001 prices, the value of production increases from $1,600, in part (a), to $1,820, in part (c). The increase is $220, so the percentage increase is equal to ($220 ÷ $1,600) × 100, or 13.75 percent.

e. The value of 2001 production in 2002 prices.

The value of 2001 production in 2002 prices equals the expenditure on bananas, (100 × $15), plus the expenditure on coconuts, (50 × $10), which is $1,500 + $500 = $2,000.

f. The percentage increase in production when valued at 2002 prices.

In 2002 prices, the value of production increases from $2,000, in part (e), to $2,250, in part (b). The increase is $250, so the percentage increase is equal to ($250 ÷ $2,000) × 100, which is 12.50 percent.

g. Real GDP in 2001 and 2002 using the chain-linking method.

Because 2001 is the base year, real GDP in 2001 equals nominal GDP in 2001, which is $1,600. To calculate real GDP in 2002 it is necessary to compute the growth rate of real GDP between 2001 and 2002. That growth rate is the average of the growth rates between 2001 and 2002 using prices from 2001 and from 2002. Using the answers to parts (d) and (f), the average percentage increase is 13.125 percent. Real GDP in 2002 is 13.125 percent greater than real GDP in 2001. Real GDP in 2001 is $1,600, so real GDP in 2002 equals ($1,600) × (1.13125), which is $1,810.

h. The GDP deflator in 2002.

GDP deflator = (Nominal GDP ÷ Real GDP) × 100 = ($2,250 ÷ $1,810) × 100 = 124.3.

Additional Practice Problem 5.3a

Answer the following questions.

a. Nominal GDP = $10 trillion, real GDP = $9 trillion. What is the GDP deflator?

b. Real GDP = $8 trillion, GDP deflator = 120. What is nominal GDP?

c. Nominal GDP = $12 trillion, GDP deflator = 120. What is real GDP?

Solution to Additional Practice Problem 5.3a

a. Nominal GDP = $10 trillion, real GDP = $9 trillion. What is the GDP deflator?

GDP deflator = (Nominal GDP ÷ Real GDP) × 100 = ($10 trillion ÷ $9 trillion) × 100 = 111.1.

b. Real GDP = $8 trillion, GDP deflator = 120. What is nominal GDP?

Rearranging the formula used in part (a) gives (GDP deflator × Real GDP) ÷ 100 = Nominal GDP, so (120 × $8 trillion) ÷ 100 = $9.6 trillion.

c. Nominal GDP = $12 trillion, GDP deflator = 120. What is real GDP?

Once again rearranging the formula used in part (a) gives (Nominal GDP ÷ GDP deflator) × 100 = Real GDP, so ($12 trillion ÷ 120) × 100 = $10 trillion.

■ Self Test 5.3

Fill in the blanks

_____ (Real; Nominal) GDP values production during the year using constant prices; _____ (real; nominal) GDP values production using prices that prevailed during the year. If the

GDP deflator rises, nominal GDP rises more ____ (rapidly; slowly) than real GDP. The GDP deflator equals 100 times ____ (real nominal) GDP divided by ____ (real; nominal) GDP.

True or false

1. Nominal GDP increases only if the production of final goods and services increases.
2. Real GDP is just a more precise name for GDP.
3. Real GDP equals nominal GDP in the base year.
4. If real GDP is $600 billion and nominal GDP is $750 billion, then the GDP deflator is 125.

Multiple choice

1. Nominal GDP can change
   a. only if prices change.
   b. only if the quantities of goods and services change.
   c. only if prices increase.
   d. if either prices or the quantities of goods and services change.

2. The difference between nominal GDP and real GDP is
   a. the indirect taxes used in their calculations.
   b. the prices used in their calculations.
   c. that nominal GDP includes the depreciation of capital and real GDP does not.
   d. that nominal GDP includes net exports and real GDP includes net imports.

3. Real GDP measures the value of goods and services produced in a given year valued using
   a. constant prices.
   b. prices that prevail the same year.
   c. no prices.
   d. future prices.

4. If nominal GDP increases, then real GDP
   a. must decrease.
   b. must increase.
   c. must not change.
   d. could increase, decrease, or not change.

5. The GDP deflator is a measure of
   a. taxes and subsidies.
   b. changes in quantities.
   c. prices.
   d. depreciation.

6. The GDP deflator is calculated as
   a. (nominal GDP ÷ real GDP) × 100.
   b. (real GDP ÷ nominal GDP) × 100.
   c. (nominal GDP + real GDP) ÷ 100.
   d. (nominal GDP − real GDP) ÷ 100.

Short answer and numeric questions

1. An economy produces only pizza and soda. The table gives the quantities produced and prices in 2003 and 2004. The base year is 2003.

Item	Data for 2003 Quantity	Price	Data for 2004 Quantity	Price
Pizza	100	$10.00	150	$20.00
Soda	50	$2.00	75	$4.00

   a. What is nominal GDP in 2003?
   b. What is real GDP in 2003?
   c. What is nominal GDP in 2004?
   d. What is real GDP in 2004?

2. If you want to measure the change in production, is it better to use nominal GDP or real GDP? Why?

3. How does the term "chain linking" apply to real GDP?

CHECKPOINT 5.4

■ **Explain and describe the limitations of real GDP as a measure of the standard of living.**

Practice Problem 5.4

The United Nations Human Development Report gives the following data for real GDP per person in 2000: China $3,976; Russia, $8,377; Canada, $27,840; United States, $34,142. Other information suggests that household production is similar in Canada and the United States and smaller in these two countries than in the other two. The underground economy is largest in Russia and China and a similar proportion of the economy in these two cases. Canadians and Americans enjoy more leisure hours than do the Chinese and Russians. Canada and the United States spend significantly more to protect the environment, so that air, water, and land pollution is less in those countries than in China and Russia. Given this information and ignoring any other influences on the standard of living

a. In which pair (or pairs) of these four countries is it easiest to compare the standard of living? Why?

b. In which pair (or pairs) of these four countries is it most difficult to compare the standard of living? Why?

c. What more detailed information would we need to be able to make an accurate assessment of the relative standard of living in these four countries?

d. Do you think that real-GDP-per-person differences correctly rank the standard of living in these four countries?

Solution to Practice Problem 5.4
Comparing GDP per person is perhaps the most common method of comparing the standard of living among different countries. This question reminds us that other factors also matter when it comes to determining the standard of living.

Quick Review
- *Goods and services omitted from GDP* Household production, underground production, leisure time, and environmental quality are omitted from GDP.

a. In which pair (or pairs) of these four countries is it easiest to compare the standard of living? Why?
The factors that affect the standard of living, but which are not measured by real GDP per person, are similar in Canada and the United States. Comparing these two countries' living standards based on real GDP per person likely would give a proper ranking. Similarly, Russia and China are stated to be similar in the areas not measured by real GDP per person, so a comparison between these two countries based

on measurement of real GDP per person is likely to rank their standard of living correctly.

b. In which pair (or pairs) of these countries is it most difficult to compare the standard of living? Why?
Comparing either the United States or Canada to Russia or China would be the most difficult. Take the comparison between the United States and Russia for an example. The fact that household production in Russia is a larger proportion of the economy than in the United States means that a comparison based on real GDP per person looks less favorable to Russia than the actual differences in living standards warrant. On the other hand, Russia does less to protect the environment than does the United States, so Russians would suffer more of the consequences of pollution. That would make the comparison based on real GDP per person more favorable to Russia than it really should be. Similarly, less leisure in Russia makes the comparison too favorable to Russia. Because some of the problems make Russia look better and some make it look worse, it is hard to tell what a proper comparison would be. A similar conclusion is true for the United States to China, Canada to Russia, and Canada to China comparisons.

c. What more detailed information would we need to be able to make an accurate assessment of the relative standard of living in these four countries?
If we knew the actual value of the underground economy in each country (the value of household production, the value of leisure, and the value of environmental quality), we could adjust real GDP per person in each country to make a more accurate assessment of the relative standard of living.

d. Do you think that real-GDP-per-person differences correctly rank the standard of living in these four countries?
The areas where real GDP per person fails to measure living standards are similar in the United States and Canada, so the comparison between the United States and Canada based

on real GDP per person is probably correct. Similarly, it is likely that an accurate measure of living standards would put Russia ahead of China, just as real GDP per person does. Finally, the difference between real GDP per person in Canada and in Russia is so large that the ranking based on real GDP per person is correct.

Additional Practice Problem 5.4a

How do you think the standard of living in the United States today compares with the standard of living 150 years ago?

Solution to Additional Practice Problem 5.4a

The standard of living now is dramatically higher than it was 150 years ago. First, even though no totally accurate data on real GDP per person is available from 150 years ago, it is certain that real GDP per person is much higher today even after taking account of the fact that household production was more common 150 years ago. The underground economy is larger today, which boosts today's standard of living, and people today enjoy significantly more leisure time, which also boosts today's standard of living. Perhaps the edge on environment quality goes to the past. Considering health and life expectancy, and political freedom and social justice, people today are much better off than people 150 years ago. It is likely true that no country in history has ever enjoyed a standard of living as high as that in the United States today.

■ Self Test 5.4

Fill in the blanks

The value of household production ____ (is; is not) included in GDP. The value of people's leisure time ____ (is; is not) included in GDP. As it is calculated, GDP ____ (does; does not) subtract the value of environmental degradation resulting from production. Real GDP ____ (takes; does not take) into account the extent of a country's political freedom.

True or false

1. As currently measured, real GDP does not include the value of home production.
2. Production in the underground economy is part of the "investment" component of GDP.
3. The production of anti-pollution devices installed by electric utilities is not counted in GDP because the devices are designed only to eliminate pollution.
4. The measure of a country's real GDP does not take into account the extent of political freedom in the country.

Multiple choice

1. The measurement of GDP handles household production by
   a. estimating a dollar value of the goods purchased to do housework.
   b. estimating a dollar value of the services provided.
   c. ignoring it.
   d. including it in exactly the same way that all other production is included.

2. You hire some of your friends to help you move to a new house and pay them a total of $200 and buy them dinner at Pizza Hut. Which of the following is true?
   a. The $200 should be counted as part of GDP but not the dinner at Pizza Hut.
   b. If your friends do not report the $200 on their tax forms, it becomes part of the underground economy.
   c. The dinner at Pizza Hut should be counted as part of GDP but not the $200.
   d. Hiring your friends is an illegal activity and should not be counted in GDP.

3. The value of leisure time is
   a. directly included in GDP.
   b. excluded from GDP.
   c. zero.
   d. None of the above answers is correct.

4. A new technology is discovered that results in all new cars producing 50 percent less pollution. The technology costs nothing to produce. As a result of the technology, there is a reduction in the number of visits people

make to the doctor to complain of breathing difficulties. Which of the following is true?

a. GDP will decrease as a result of fewer doctor services being provided.

b. GDP is not affected.

c. GDP will increase to reflect the improvement in the health of the population.

d. GDP will increase to reflect the improvement in the health of the population, and the likely increase in the cost of the car.

5. The calculation of GDP using the income approach excludes

a. rental income.

b. proprietors' income.

c. environmental quality.

d. compensation of employees.

6. Good health and life expectancy are

a. included in GDP but not in our standard of living.

b. included in both GDP and in our standard of living.

c. included in our standard of living but not in GDP.

d. not included in either our standard of living or in GDP.

Short answer and numeric questions

1. What general categories of goods and services are omitted from GDP? Why is each omitted?

2. If you cook a hamburger at home, what happens to GDP? If you go to Burger King and purchase a hamburger, what happens to GDP?

SELF TEST ANSWERS

■ CHECKPOINT 5.1

Fill in the blanks

The market value of all the final goods and services produced within a country in a given time period is <u>GDP</u>. <u>Four</u> groups buy the final goods and services produced. Net exports equals the value of <u>exports</u> minus the value of <u>imports</u>. *C* + *I* + *G* + *NX* equals <u>total expenditure</u> and <u>total income</u>.

True or false

1. False; page 112
2. False; page 113
3. True; page 114
4. True; page 115

Multiple choice

1. a; page 112
2. b; page 112
3. a; page 112
4. d; page 113
5. b; page 113
6. a; page 114

Short answer and numeric questions

1. Intermediate goods or services are not counted in GDP because if they were, they would be double counted. A computer produced by Dell Corp. is included in GDP. But if the Intel chip that is part of the computer is also included in GDP, then that production is counted twice: once when it is produced by Intel, and again when it is included in the computer produced by Dell; page 112.

2. a. Import; page 114.
   b. Consumption expenditure; page 113.
   c. Investment; page 113.
   d. Investment; page 113.
   e. Government purchases of goods and services; 114.

3. Total expenditure is the amount received by producers of final goods and services. Because firms pay out everything they re-

ceive as incomes to the factors of production, total expenditure equals total income. From the viewpoint of firms, the value of production is the cost of production, which equals income. From the viewpoint of consumers of goods and services, the value of production is the cost of buying it, which equals expenditure; page 115.

■ CHECKPOINT 5.2

Fill in the blanks

The <u>expenditure</u> approach and the <u>income</u> approach are two methods used to calculate GDP. Expenditure on used goods <u>is not</u> included in GDP. Compensation of employees is part of the <u>income</u> approach to calculating GDP. To calculate GDP, depreciation is <u>added to</u> net domestic product at factor cost. The value of a firm's production minus the value of the intermediate goods it buys is called the firm's <u>valued added</u>.

True or false

1. True; page 117
2. False; page 118
3. False; page 119
4. False; page 121

Multiple choice

1. b; page 117
2. d; page 117
3. b; page 117
4. a; page 117
5. d; page 119
6. b; page 120

Short answer and numeric questions

1. a. GDP = $6,400, the sum of consumption expenditure, investment, government purchases of goods and services, and net exports; page 117.
   b. Net domestic product at factor cost equals $5,300, the sum of compensation of employees, net interest, corporate

profits, rental income and proprietors' income; page 119.

  c. The difference between GDP and net domestic product at factor cost ($1,100) is indirect taxes minus subsidies plus depreciation. Indirect taxes minus subsidies equals $400, so depreciation equals $700; page 120.

2. To change net domestic product at factor cost to GDP, two sets of adjustments must be made. First, net domestic product at factor cost is measured at firms' costs; to convert costs to equal the market prices paid, taxes must be added and subsidies subtracted. Second, net domestic product does not include depreciation but GDP does. So, depreciation must be added; page 120.

3. GDP increases by $2.00, the market value of the final product, the gallon of gasoline. Because the driller uses no intermediate goods, the driller's value added is $0.80. The refiner's value added is the value of the gasoline, $2.00, minus the value of the intermediate good, the oil at $0.80. The refiner's value added is $1.20. The sum of the driller's value added and the refiner's value added is $2.00, the same as the increase in GDP; page 121.

■ CHECKPOINT 5.3

Fill in the blanks

<u>Real</u> GDP values production during the year using constant prices; <u>nominal</u> GDP values production using prices that prevailed during the year. If the GDP deflator rises, nominal GDP rises more <u>rapidly</u> than real GDP. The GDP deflator equals 100 times <u>nominal</u> GDP divided by <u>real</u> GDP.

True or false

1. False; page 123
2. False; page 123
3. True; page 123
4. True; page 125

Multiple choice

1. d; page 123
2. b; page 123
3. a; page 123
4. d; page 123
5. c; page 125
6. a; page 125

Short answer and numeric questions

1. a. Nominal GDP = $(100 \times \$10) + (50 \times \$2)$ = $1,100, the sum of expenditure on pizza and expenditure on soda; page 123.

  b. Because 2003 is the base year, real GDP = nominal GDP, so real GDP = $1,100; page 123.

  c. Nominal GDP = $(150 \times \$20) + (75 \times \$4)$ = $3,300, the sum of expenditure on pizza and expenditure on soda; page 123.

  d. Using 2003 prices, GDP grew from $1,100 in 2003 to $1,650 in 2004, a percentage increase of 50 percent. Using 2004 prices, GDP grew 50 percent between 2003 and 2004. The average growth is 50 percent, so real GDP in 2004 is 50 percent higher than in 2003, so that real GDP in 2004 is $1,650; page 124.

2. To measure the change in production, it is necessary to use real GDP. Nominal GDP changes whenever production *or* prices change. Real GDP uses constant prices and changes only when production changes; page 123.

3. From one year to the next, real GDP is scaled by the percentage change from the first year to the next. Real GDP in 2002 is linked to real GDP in 2001 by the percentage change from 2001, and real GDP in 2001 in turn is linked to real GDP in 2000 by the percentage change from 2000, and so on. These links are like the links in a chain that link real GDP back to the base year and the base year prices; page 124.

■ CHECKPOINT 5.4

Fill in the blanks

The value of household production <u>is not</u> included in GDP. The value of people's leisure time <u>is not</u> included in GDP. As it is calculated, GDP <u>does not</u> subtract the value of environmental degradation resulting from production. Real GDP <u>does not take</u> into account the extent of a country's political freedom.

True or false

1. True; page 127
2. False; page 127
3. False; page 128
4. True; page 129

Multiple choice

1. c; page 127
2. b; page 127
3. b; page 128
4. a; page 128
5. c; page 128
6. c; page 128

Short answer and numeric questions

1. Goods and services omitted from GDP are household production, underground production, leisure time, and environmental quality. GDP measures the value of goods and services that are bought in markets. Because household production, leisure time, and environmental quality are not purchased in markets, they are excluded from GDP. Even though underground production frequently is bought in markets, the activity is unreported and is not included in GDP; pages 127-128.

2. If you cook a hamburger at home, the meat you purchased is included in GDP but the production of the hamburger is not included in GDP because it is household production. If you buy a hamburger at Burger King, the production of the hamburger is included in GDP; page 127.

Jobs and Unemployment

CHAPTER IN PERSPECTIVE

Chapter 6 explores one of the economy's important markets, the labor market, by defining indicators of its performance and explaining how these indicators have changed over time. Chapter 6 also discusses unemployment and its relationship to real GDP.

■ Define the unemployment rate and other labor market indicators.

The Current Population Survey is a monthly survey of 50,000 households across the country that is the basis for the nation's labor market statistics. The working-age population is non-institutionalized people aged 16 and over. The labor force is the sum of the employed and unemployed. To be unemployed, a person must have no employment, be available for work, and either have made an effort to find a job during the previous four weeks or be waiting to be recalled to a job from which he or she was laid off. The unemployment rate is the percentage of people in the labor force who are unemployed. The labor force participation rate is the percentage of the working-age population who are members of the labor force. A discouraged worker is a person who is available and willing to work but has not made specific efforts to find a job within the previous four weeks. Part-time workers are those who usually work less than 35 hours per week. Involuntary part-time workers part-time workers who are looking for full-time work. Aggregate hours are the total number of hours worked by all the people employed.

■ Describe the trends and fluctuations in the indicators of labor market performance in the United States.

From 1962 to 2002, the average unemployment rate was 6 percent. The lowest unemployment rates were achieved in the late 1960s and in the late 1990s through 2000. Over the last decade, the U.S. unemployment rate has been below those of Europe and Canada. From 1962 to 2002, the labor force participation rate had an upward trend and is about 67 percent. The labor force participation rate for men decreased and for women increased. About 17 percent of workers have part-time jobs. The involuntary part-time rate rises during recessions and falls during expansions. Aggregate hours have an upward trend. The average workweek has fallen from about 39 hours in 1960 to 34 hours in the 1990s.

■ Describe the sources and types of unemployment, define full employment, and explain the link between unemployment and real GDP.

People who become unemployed are job losers, job leavers, entrants, or reentrants. People who leave unemployment are hires, recalls, or withdrawals. Unemployment is either frictional (normal labor turnover), structural (changes in necessary job skills or job locations), seasonal (changes in the seasons), or cyclical (changes in the business cycle). The duration of unemployment increases in recessions. Full employment occurs when there is no cyclical unemployment. At full employment, the unemployment rate is the natural unemployment rate and the GDP produced is potential GDP.

EXPANDED CHAPTER CHECKLIST

When you have completed this chapter, you will be able to:

1 Define the unemployment rate and other labor market indicators.

- Define working-age population and labor force.
- Tell the criteria the Current Population Survey uses to classify a person as employed or unemployed.
- Define and calculate the unemployment rate.
- Define and calculate the labor force participation rate.
- Define discouraged workers.
- Tell the criteria used to classify a worker as full time or part time.
- Define involuntary part-time workers.
- Define and calculate aggregate hours.

2 Describe the trends and fluctuations in the indicators of labor market performance in the United States.

- Describe how the unemployment rate changed between 1962 and 2002.
- Tell what happens to the unemployment rate in recessions and in expansions.
- Compare the unemployment rate in the United States with that in other nations.
- Describe how the labor force participation rate changed between 1962 and 2002.
- Describe how the male and female labor force participation rates have changed and explain these changes.
- Describe the changes in the percentage of part-time workers between 1972 and 2002.
- Tell how the involuntary part-time rate changes in recessions.
- Tell how aggregate labor hours and average weekly work hours have changed between 1962 and 2002.

3 Describe the sources and types of unemployment, define full employment, and explain the link between unemployment and real GDP.

- List the sources of unemployment.
- Describe how unemployment ends.
- List and explain four types of unemployment.
- Discuss the duration of unemployment and explain what happens to the duration of unemployment in a recession.
- Discuss the uneven demographic impacts of unemployment.
- Identify the relationships between full employment, the natural unemployment rate, and potential GDP.

KEY TERMS

- Working-age population (page 136)
- Labor force (page 136)
- Unemployment rate (page 137)
- Labor force participation rate (page 138)
- Discouraged workers (page 138)
- Full-time workers (page 138)
- Part-time workers (page 138)
- Involuntary part-time workers (page 138)
- Aggregate hours (page 139)
- Frictional unemployment (page 149)
- Structural unemployment (page 150)
- Seasonal unemployment (page 150)
- Cyclical unemployment (page 150)
- Full employment (page 152)
- Natural unemployment rate (page 152)
- Potential GDP (page 152)

CHECKPOINT 6.1

■ **Define the unemployment rate and other labor market indicators.**

Practice Problem 6.1

The Bureau of Labor Statistics reported that in January 2000, the labor force was 140.9 million, employment was 135.2 million, and the working-age population was 208.6 million. Average weekly hours were 34.5.

Calculate for that month the:

  a. Unemployment rate.
  b. Labor force participation rate.
  c. Aggregate hours worked in a week.

Solution to Practice Problem 6.1

This question focuses on the calculations required to determine the three labor market indicators: the unemployment rate, the labor force participation rate, and aggregate hours.

Quick Review

  • *Unemployment rate* The unemployment rate is the percentage of the people in the labor force who are unemployed. That is,

$$\text{Unemployment rate} = \frac{(\text{Unemployed people})}{(\text{Labor force})} \times 100$$

  • *Labor force participation rate* The labor force participation rate is the percentage of the working-age population who are members of the labor force. It equals

$$\text{Participation rate} = \frac{(\text{Labor force})}{(\text{Working - age people})} \times 100$$

  • *Aggregate hours* The aggregate hours are the total number of hours worked by all the people employed, both full time and part time, during a year.

a. Unemployment rate

The labor force equals the sum of the number of people employed and the number of people unemployed. Subtracting the number employed from the labor force gives the number of unemployed. The labor force is 140.9 million and the number of employed is 135.2 million, so

the number unemployed is 140.9 million – 135.2 million, which is 5.7 million. To calculate the unemployment rate, divide the number of unemployed by the labor force and multiply by 100. The unemployment rate equals (5.7 million ÷ 140.9 million) × 100, which is 4.0 percent.

b. Labor force participation rate

The labor force participation rate is the percentage of the working-age population who are members of the labor force. The labor force participation rate equals the labor force divided by the working-age population all multiplied by 100, which is (140.9 million ÷ 208.6 million) × 100 = 67.5 percent.

c. Aggregate hours worked in a week

In January, 2000, 135.2 million people worked an average of 34.5 hours a week, so the aggregate hours worked in a week is 135.2 million × 34.5 hours, which is 4,664.4 million hours.

Additional Practice Problem 6.1a

Determine the labor market status of each of the following people:

  a. Don is 21 and a full-time college student.
  b. Shirley works for 20 hours a week as an administrative assistant and is looking for a full-time job.
  c. Clarence was laid off from his job selling keyboards to computer manufacturers and is actively seeking a new job.
  d. Pat quit her job as an account executive 6 months ago but, unable to find a new position, has stopped actively searching.

Solution to Additional Practice Problem 6.1a

a. Don is 21 and a full-time college student.
Don is neither working nor looking for work, so he is not in the labor force.

b. Shirley works for 20 hours a week as an administrative assistant and is looking for a full-time job.
Shirley is working for pay for more than 1 hour a week, so she is employed and part of the labor force. She is working less than 35 hours a week, so she is a part-time worker. Because she is looking for a full-time job, Shirley is an involuntary part-time worker.

c. Clarence was laid off from his job selling keyboards to computer manufacturers and is actively seeking a new job.

Clarence is actively seeking a new job, so he is unemployed. Clarence is part of the labor force.

d. Pat quit her job as an account executive 6 months ago but, unable to find a new position, has stopped actively searching.

Pat is neither working nor actively looking for work, so she is not in the labor force. Pat is a discouraged worker.

■ Self Test 6.1

Fill in the blanks

The ____ (working-age population; labor force) is the total number of people aged 16 years and over and who are not in jail, hospital, or some other form of institutional care. The unemployment rate equals the ____ divided by the ____, all multiplied by 100. The labor force participation rate equals the ____ divided by the ____, all multiplied by 100. Involuntary part-time workers ____ (are; are not) counted as employed. The total number of hours worked in a year by all the people employed are ____.

True or false

1. When contacted by the Bureau of Labor Statistics, Bob states that he has been laid off by Ford Motor Corporation, but expects to be recalled within the next three weeks. Bob is considered part of the labor force.

2. People are counted as unemployed as long as they are working less than 40 hours per week.

3. The unemployment rate decreases when unemployed workers find jobs.

4. The labor force participation rate measures the percentage of the labor force that is employed.

5. If the number of discouraged workers increases, the unemployment rate will increase.

Multiple choice

1. Assume the U.S. population is 300 million. If the working age population is 240 million, 150 million are employed, and 6 million are unemployed, what is the size of the labor force?
   a. 300 million
   b. 240 million
   c. 156 million
   d. 150 million

2. Which of the following statements about the United States is <u>FALSE</u>?
   a. The size of the labor force is greater than the number of employed people.
   b. The size of the labor force is greater than the number of unemployed people.
   c. The number of unemployed people is greater than the number of employed people.
   d. None of the above because they are all true statements.

3. To be counted as employed by the BLS, you must have worked for pay _____ in the week before the survey.
   a. at least 1 hour
   b. at least 5 hours
   c. more than 20 hours
   d. 40 hours

4. If you are available and willing to work but have not actively looked for work in the past month, then
   a. you are part of the labor force because you are willing to work.
   b. you are counted as unemployed because you are willing to work and do not have a job.
   c. you are not part of the labor force because you are not looking for a job.
   d. you are part of the labor force but are not counted as unemployed.

5. The unemployment rate is calculated as 100 times
   a. (number of people without a job) ÷ (population)
   b. (number of people unemployed) ÷ (labor force)
   c. (number of people without a job) ÷ (working-age population)
   d. (number of people unemployed) ÷ (population)

6. A discouraged worker is
   a. counted as employed by the BLS but is not part of the labor force.
   b. counted as employed by the BLS and is part of the labor force.
   c. counted as unemployed by the BLS and is part of the labor force.
   d. not part of the labor force.

7. While in school, Kiki spends 20 hours a week as a computer programmer for Microsoft and studies 30 hours a week.
   a. Kiki is classified as a full-time worker, working 50 hours a week.
   b. Kiki is classified as a part-time worker, working 30 hours a week.
   c. Kiki is classified as a part-time worker, working 20 hours a week.
   d. Because Kiki is a student, she is not classified as working.

8. Part-time workers for noneconomic reasons are people who
   a. work less than 35 hours a week but would like to work more than 35 hours a week.
   b. work more than 35 hours a week but would like to work less than 35 hours a week.
   c. have lost their jobs within the last four weeks and are seeking another job.
   d. do not want to work full time.

Short answer and numeric questions

Category	Number of people
Total population	2,600
Working-age population	2,000
Not in the labor force	500
Employed	1,300

1. The table above gives the status of the population of a (small!) nation.
   a. What is the size of the labor force?
   b. What is the number of unemployed workers?
   c. What is the unemployment rate?
   d. What is the labor force participation rate?

Category	Number of people
Working-age population	3,000
Unemployed	100
Employed	1,900

2. The table above gives the status of the population of another (small!) nation.
   a. What is the size of the labor force?
   b. What is the unemployment rate?
   c. What is the labor force participation rate?

3. What criteria must a person meet to be counted as unemployed?

4. What is a discouraged worker? Explain why a discouraged worker is not counted as part of the labor force.

5. Are involuntarily part-time workers counted as employed or unemployed?

CHECKPOINT 6.2

■ **Describe the trends and fluctuations in the indicators of labor market performance in the United States.**

Practice Problem 6.2

Use the link on your Foundations Web site and view the data for Figures 6.2, 6.3, 6.4, and 6.5. Then answer the following questions:
   a. In which decade—the 1960s, 1970s, 1980s, or 1990s—was the unemployment rate the

lowest? What brought low unemployment in that decade?

b. In which decade was the unemployment rate the highest? What brought high unemployment in that decade?

c. Describe the trends in the participation rates of men and women and all workers. Why did these trends occur?

d. Describe the trends and fluctuations in part-time work. Why is part-time work on the increase?

e. Do aggregate hours increase at the same rate as the increase in employment? Explain why or why not.

Solution to Practice Problem 6.2

This question focuses on labor market trends. These facts should help shape your future perceptions about how well the economy is performing.

Quick Review

- *Labor force participation rate* The percentage of the working-age population who are members of the labor force.

- *Aggregate hours* The total number of hours worked by all the people employed, both full time and part time, during a year.

a. **In which decade—the 1960s, 1970s, 1980s, or 1990s—was the unemployment rate the lowest? What brought low unemployment in that decade?**

The average unemployment rate was lowest in the 1960s, at 4.8 percent with low rates of 3.6 percent and 3.5 percent in 1968 and 1969, respectively. The 1960s saw a rapid rate of job creation due in part to defense spending on the Vietnam War and an expansion of social programs.

b. **In which decade was the unemployment rate the highest? What brought high unemployment in that decade?**

The unemployment rate was the highest during the 1980s. The unemployment rate peaked during the sharp recession of 1981-1982. But even after 1982 the unemployment rate in the United States remained relatively high and did not decrease below its average of 5.9 percent until the end of the 1980s.

c. **Describe the trends in the participation rates of men and women and all workers. Why did these trends occur?**

The labor force participation rate of women is generally increasing and the labor force participation rate of men is generally decreasing. The overall labor force participation rate of all workers is generally increasing. There are several reasons why women have entered the paid labor force. First, more women attend college and earn degrees, which results in higher pay. Technological change has decreased the time necessary to work in the home and has increased the number of white collar jobs with flexible hours. Also, more families want both spouses to work to earn more income. Men have withdrawn from the labor force because more men remain in college longer and because increases in wealth allow more men to retire at earlier ages. Also, some men lose their jobs at more advanced ages and are unable to find new employment.

d. **Describe the trends and fluctuations in part-time work. Why is part-time work on the increase?**

As a percent of workers, part-time work increased slightly from 1972 to 2002. It tends to rise during recessions and fall during expansions. Part-time jobs can be attractive to employers because they don't have to pay benefits to part-time workers and are less constrained by government regulations. Hiring part-time workers can decrease the firm's costs. And, many people desire part-time work because it provides flexible hours.

e. **Do aggregate hours increase at the same rate as the increase in employment? Explain why or why not.**

Aggregate hours have increased more slowly than employment because of a reduction in length of the average weekly hours from about 39 hours in 1962 to about 34 hours in 2002.

Additional Practice Problem 6.2a

Are involuntary part-time workers counted as unemployed when calculating the unemployment rate? If they are, how do they affect the unemployment rate; if they are not, how would their inclusion affect the unemployment rate?

Solution to Additional Practice Problem 6.2a

Involuntary part-time workers are *not* counted as unemployed. Indeed, they are counted as employed when computing the unemployment rate. If they were counted as, say, "partially" unemployed, the unemployment rate would increase. And, as Figure 6.4 in the textbook shows, the increase would be larger during recessions when the number of involuntary part-time workers increases.

■ Self Test 6.2

Fill in the blanks

The unemployment rate in 2002 was slightly _____ (higher; lower) than the average between 1962 and 2002. Since 1962, the male labor force participation rate _____ and the female participation rate _____. Since 1972, the percentage of workers who have part-time jobs _____ (rose; fell) slightly. Since 1962, the total number of labor hours _____ and the length of the average workweek _____.

True or false

1. The average unemployment rate in the United States during the 1970s and 1980s was above the average unemployment rate during the 1960s and 1990s.

2. In recent years the U.S. unemployment rate rose above its 40-year average because of layoffs brought about by the technology that has created the "new economy."

3. Although the female labor force participation rate increased over the last 40 years, it is still below the male labor force participation rate.

4. The percentage of involuntary part-time workers rises during a recession.

5. The aggregate hours worked in the United States have not grown as quickly as the number of people employed.

Multiple choice

1. From 1962 to 2002, the average unemployment rate in the United States was approximately
   a. 3 percent.
   b. 6 percent.
   c. 12 percent.
   d. 24 percent.

2. During the 1990s, the unemployment rate in the United States
   a. was always lower than the unemployment rate in Japan.
   b. almost always equaled the unemployment rate in Canada.
   c. rose while the unemployment rate in France, Germany, and Italy fell.
   d. fell while the unemployment rate in France, Germany, and Italy rose.

3. Which of the following statements about the United States is correct?
   a. Between 1962 and 2002, both the male and female labor force participation rates increased.
   b. Between 1962 and 2002, the male labor force participation rate decreased rapidly, the female labor force participation rate decreased slowly, and the two rates are now equal.
   c. Between 1962 and 2002, the male labor force participation rate decreased and the female labor force participation rate increased.
   d. Between 1962 and 2002, both the male and female labor force participation rates decreased slowly.

4. The total U.S. labor force participation rate increased since 1962 because
   a. the female labor force participation rate increased.
   b. more men are retiring early.
   c. fewer women are attending college.
   d. many blue-collar jobs with rigid work hours have been created in the last decade.

5. The female labor force participation rate is
   a. larger in Japan than in the United States.
   b. larger in the United States than in France.
   c. the largest in Spain.
   d. None of the above answers is correct.

6. Part-time workers increased from ____ of the labor force in 1972 to ____ in 2002.
   a. 16 percent; 50 percent
   b. 16 percent; 17 percent
   c. 2 percent; 4 percent
   d. 10 percent; 40 percent

7. In the United States, involuntary part-time workers
   a. account for more than 66 percent of all part-time workers.
   b. account for about 50 percent of all part-time workers.
   c. account for about 5 percent of all part-time workers.
   d. None of the above answers are correct.

8. In the United States since 1962, aggregate hours have ____ and average weekly hours per worker have ____.
   a. increased; increased
   b. increased; decreased
   c. decreased; increased
   d. decreased; decreased

Short answer and numeric questions

1. During a recession, what happens to:
   a. the unemployment rate?
   b. aggregate hours?
   c. average weekly hours?

2. Compare the U.S. unemployment rate between 1990 to 2002 to the unemployment rate in
   a. Japan.
   b. Canada.

3. How does the unemployment rate during the Great Depression compare with more recent unemployment rates?

CHECKPOINT 6.3

■ **Describe the sources and types of unemployment, define full employment, and explain the link between unemployment and real GDP.**

Practice Problem 6.3

A labor force survey in a Polynesian island records the following data for December 31, 2002: employed, 13,500; unemployed, 1,500; not in the labor force; 7,500. The survey also recorded during 2003: hires and recalls, 1,000; job losers, 750; job leavers 300; entrants, 150; reentrants, 450; withdrawals, 500. The working-age population increased during 2003 by 100. (All the job losers, entrants, and reentrants became unemployed.) Calculate for the end of 2003,
   a. The unemployment rate
   b. The labor force participation rate

Solution to Practice Problem 6.3

This question focuses on labor market flows. Some of the data given are sources that flow into unemployment; others are flows out of unemployment.

Quick Review

- *Sources of unemployment* People who become unemployed are job losers, job leavers, entrants, or reentrants.
- *How unemployment ends* People who end a period of unemployment are either hires and recalls, or withdrawals.

Calculating the unemployment rate and labor force participation rate for 2003 requires finding the number unemployed and the number employed in 2003. To find the number unemployed in 2003, start with the number unemployed in 2002, then add those who enter unemployment in 2003 and subtract those who leave unemployment in 2003. So to the number unemployed at the end of 2002, add the number of job losers, job leavers, entrants and reentrants and then subtract the number of hires, recalls, and withdrawals. Unemployment at the end of 2003 is 1,500 + 750 + 300 + 150 + 450 − 1,000 − 500, which is 1,650.

Next we need to find the number employed at the end of 2003. To the number employed at the end of 2002 add the number of hires and recalls and subtract the number of job losers and job leavers. So employment at the end of 2003 is 13,500 + 1,000 − 750 − 300, which is 13,450.

We also can calculate the labor force, which is the sum of the number unemployed and the number employed. The labor force equals 1,650 + 13,450 = 15,100.

a. The unemployment rate

The unemployment rate is the percentage of the people in the labor force who are unemployed. The unemployment rate in 2003 equals $(1,650 \div 15,100) \times 100$, which is 10.9 percent.

b. The labor force participation rate

The labor force participation rate is the percentage of the working-age population who are members of the labor force. The working-age population is the total number of people aged 15 years and over. In 2002, the working-age population is the sum of the number employed (13,500), the number unemployed (1,500), and the number not in the labor force (7,500), which is 22,500. The working-age population increased by 100 during 2003, so the working-age population in 2003 is 22,600. The labor force participation rate at the end of 2003 is $(15,100 \div 22,600) \times 100$, which is 66.8 percent.

Additional Practice Problem 6.3a

Each of the following people is actively seeking work. Classify each as either frictionally, structurally, seasonally, or cyclically unemployed:

a. Perry lost his job because his company went bankrupt when faced with increased foreign competition.
b. Sam did not like his boss and so he quit his job.
c. Sherry just graduated from college.
d. Hanna lost her job selling cotton candy on the boardwalk when winter arrived and the tourists left.
e. Jose was fired when his company downsized in response to a recession.
f. Pat was laid off from her job at the Gap because customers decided they liked the fashions at JCPenney better.

Solution to Additional Practice Problem 6.3a

a. Perry lost his job because his company went bankrupt when faced with increased foreign competition.

Perry is structurally unemployed.

b. Sam did not like his boss and so he quit his job.

Sam is frictionally unemployed.

c. Sherry just graduated from college.

Sherry is frictionally unemployed.

d. Hanna lost her job selling cotton candy on the boardwalk when winter arrived and the tourists left.

Hanna is seasonally unemployed.

e. Jose was fired when his company downsized in response to a recession.

Jose is cyclically unemployed.

f. Pat was laid off from her job at the Gap because customers decided they liked the fashions at JCPenney better.

Pat is frictionally unemployed.

■ Self Test 6.3

Fill in the blanks

People who become unemployed are ____, ____, or ____. Unemployed people who stop looking for jobs are ____ (recalls; job losers; withdrawals). The normal unemployment from labor market turnover is called ____ unemployment, and the unemployment that fluctuates over the business cycle is called ____ unemployment. When ____ (frictional; structural; cyclical) unemployment equals zero, the economy is experiencing ____ employment. When potential GDP exceeds real GDP, the unemployment rate ____ (is higher than; is lower than) the natural unemployment rate.

True or false

1. If Amazon.Com Inc. must lay off 20 percent of its workers, the laid-off workers would be considered job leavers.

2. The only way to end a spell of unemployment is by finding a job.

3. The unemployment that arises when technology changes is termed technological unemployment.

4. When the U.S. economy is at full employment, the unemployment rate is zero.

5. Potential GDP is the level of real GDP produced when the economy is at full employment.

Multiple choice

1. Generally, most unemployed workers are ____; the fewest number of unemployed workers are ____.
   a. job losers; job leavers
   b. job leavers; reentrants and entrants
   c. job losers; reentrants and entrants
   d. reentrants and entrants; job leavers

2. Reentrants are people who
   a. are laid off.
   b. leave the labor force voluntarily.
   c. recently left school.
   d. have returned to the labor force.

3. Tommy graduates from college and starts to look for a job. Tommy is ____ unemployed.
   a. frictionally
   b. structurally
   c. cyclically
   d. seasonally

4. If an entire industry relocates to a foreign country, the relocation leads to a higher rate of ____ unemployment.
   a. frictional
   b. structural
   c. seasonal
   d. cyclical

5. Of the following, who is cyclically unemployed?
   a. Casey, who lost his job because the technology changed so that he was no longer needed.
   b. Katrina, an assistant manager who quit her job to search for a better job closer to home.
   c. Kathy, a steelworker who was laid off but has stopped looking for a new job because she can't find a new job.
   d. David, a new car salesman who lost his job because of a recession.

6. In the United States, the highest unemployment rates occur among
   a. white female teenagers.
   b. black male teenagers.
   c. white females aged 20 and over.
   d. black males aged 20 and over.

7. When the economy is at full employment,
   a. the natural unemployment rate equals zero.
   b. the amount of cyclical unemployment equals zero.
   c. the amount of structural unemployment equals zero.
   d. there is no unemployment.

8. When the unemployment rate is less than the natural unemployment rate, real GDP is _____ potential GDP.
    a. greater than
    b. less than
    c. unrelated to
    d. equal to

Short answer and numeric questions

1. What are sources of unemployment? How does unemployment end?
2. What are the four types of unemployment?
3. How does the average duration of unemployment change during a recession?
4. What is the relationship between full employment, the natural unemployment rate, and potential GDP?
5. If the unemployment rate exceeds the natural unemployment rate, what is the relationship between real GDP and potential GDP?

SELF TEST ANSWERS

■ CHECKPOINT 6.1

Fill in the blanks

The <u>working-age population</u> is the total number of people aged 16 years and over and who are not in jail, hospital, or some other form of institutional care. The unemployment rate equals the <u>number of people unemployed</u> divided by the <u>labor force</u>, all multiplied by 100. The labor force participation rate equals the <u>labor force</u> divided by the <u>working-age population</u>, all multiplied by 100. Involuntary part-time workers <u>are</u> counted as employed. The total number of hours worked in a year by all the people employed are <u>aggregate hours</u>.

True or false

1. True; page 136
2. False; page 136
3. True; page 137
4. False; page 138
5. False; page 138

Multiple choice

1. c; page 136
2. c; page 136
3. a; page 136
4. c; page 136
5. b; page 137
6. d; page 138
7. c; page 138
8. d; page 138

Short answer and numeric questions

1. a. 1,500; page 136.
   b. 200; page 136.
   c. 13.3 percent; page 137.
   d. 75.0 percent; page 138.

2. a. 2,000; page 136.
   b. 5.0 percent; page 137.
   c. 66.7 percent; page 138.

3. The person must be without employment, available for work, and actively searching or waiting to be recalled to a job from which he or she was laid off; page 136.

4. A discouraged worker is an unemployed worker who is not actively looking for a job. A discouraged worker is not unemployed because the worker is not actively seeking a job; page 138.

5. Employed; page 138.

■ CHECKPOINT 6.2

Fill in the blanks

The unemployment rate in 2002 was slightly <u>lower</u> than the average between 1962 and 2002. Since 1962, the male labor force participation rate <u>fell</u> and the female participation rate <u>rose</u>. Since 1972, the percentage of workers who have part-time jobs <u>rose</u> slightly. Since 1962, the total number of labor hours <u>rose</u> and the length of the average workweek <u>fell</u>.

True or false

1. True; page 141
2. False; page 141
3. True; pages 142-143
4. True; page 144
5. True; page 144

Multiple choice

1. b; page 141
2. d; page 143
3. c; pages 142-143
4. a; page 143
5. b; page 145
6. b; page 144
7. d; page 144
8. b; pages 144-145

Short answer and numeric questions

1. a. The unemployment rate rises; page 141.

b. Aggregate hours fall; page 144.

c. Average weekly hours falls; page 144.

2. a. The Japanese unemployment rate in 1990 was below the U.S. unemployment rate but by 2002 the unemployment rates were about the same; page 143.

b. The Canadian unemployment rate has mirrored changes in the U.S. unemployment rate but has been about 4 percentage points higher; page 143.

3. The unemployment rate during the Great Depression was *much* higher (reaching almost 25 percent) than the recent unemployment rate (which reached a maximum of approximately 10 percent in 1982); pages 141-142.

■ CHECKPOINT 6.3

Fill in the blanks

People who become unemployed are <u>job losers</u>, <u>job leavers</u>, or <u>entrants and reentrants</u>. Unemployed people who stop looking for jobs are <u>withdrawals</u>. The normal unemployment from labor market turnover is called <u>frictional</u> unemployment, and the unemployment that fluctuates over the business cycle is called <u>cyclical</u> unemployment. When <u>cyclical</u> unemployment equals zero, the economy is experiencing <u>full</u> employment. When potential GDP exceeds real GDP, the unemployment rate <u>is higher than</u> the natural unemployment rate.

True or false

1. False; page 147

2. False; page 148

3. False; page 150

4. False; page 152

5. True; page 153

Multiple choice

1. a; pages 147-148

2. d; page 147

3. a; page 149

4. b; page 150

5. d; page 150

6. b; page 151

7. b; page 152

8. a; page 153

Short answer and numeric questions

1. Sources of unemployment are job losers, job leavers, entrants, and reentrants. People who end a period of unemployment rate are hires, recalls, or withdrawals; pages 147-148.

2. Unemployment is either frictional, structural, seasonal, or cyclical; pages 149-150.

3. The average duration of unemployment (the length of time a person is unemployed) rises in a recession; page 151.

4. When the economy is at full employment, the unemployment rate is the natural unemployment rate. When the economy is at full employment, the amount of GDP produced is potential GDP; page 152.

5. If the unemployment rate exceeds the natural unemployment rate, real GDP is less than potential GDP; page 153.

The CPI and the Cost of Living

CHAPTER IN PERSPECTIVE

Chapter 7 explores how the cost of living is measured. It discusses the Consumer Price Index, CPI, explains how it is constructed, and examines its biases. Chapter 7 demonstrates how to adjust money values for changes in the price level. In addition, Chapter 7 discusses the real wage rate and the real interest rate, and also shows how both are calculated.

■ Explain what the Consumer Price Index (CPI) is and how it is calculated.

The Consumer Price Index (CPI) measures the average of the prices paid by urban consumers for a fixed market basket of consumer goods and services. The CPI compares the cost of the fixed basket of goods and services at one time with the cost of the fixed basket in the reference base period, currently 1982–1984. The CPI in the base period is 100. If the CPI is now 150, it costs 50 percent more to buy the same goods and services than it cost in the base period. To construct the CPI basket, households are surveyed on what they buy. Then, each month the Bureau of Labor Statistics checks the prices of the 80,000 goods and services in the basket. To calculate the CPI, the cost of the basket using current prices is divided by the cost of the basket using base period prices and the result is multiplied by 100. The inflation rate is the percentage change in the price level from one year to the next and is equal to [(CPI in current year – CPI in previous year) ÷ (CPI in previous year)] × 100.

■ Explain the limitations of the CPI as a measure of the cost of living.

The CPI has four sources of bias that lead to an inaccurate measure of the cost of living. These biases are the new goods bias (new goods replace old goods), the quality change bias (goods and services increase in quality), the commodity substitution bias (changes in relative prices lead consumers to change the items they buy), and the outlet substitution bias (consumers switch to shopping more often in discount stores). The overall CPI bias has been estimated to overstate inflation by 1.1 percentage points per year. The CPI bias distorts private contracts and increases government outlays. The GDP deflator is constructed using, in part, the CPI, and so the GDP deflator inherits the same biases as the CPI. The GDP deflator is not a good measure of the cost of living because it includes prices of goods and services households never buy.

■ Adjust money values for inflation and calculate real wage rates and real interest rates.

Comparing values measured in dollars in different years is misleading if the value of money changes. To make the comparison, the nominal values must be converted to real values. The real wage rate measures the quantity of goods and services that an hour's work can buy and equals the nominal wage rate divided by the CPI and multiplied by 100. The real interest rate equals the nominal interest rate minus the inflation rate.

EXPANDED CHAPTER CHECKLIST

When you have completed this chapter, you will be able to:

1 **Explain what the Consumer Price Index (CPI) is and how it is calculated.**

- Define the CPI and discuss the meaning of the CPI numbers.
- Explain the construction of the CPI, including the role played by the fixed CPI basket and the reference base period.
- Discuss how the cost of the CPI basket is calculated and show how the CPI is calculated.
- Define and calculate the inflation rate.

2 **Explain the limitations of the CPI as a measure of the cost of living.**

- Explain the new goods bias.
- Explain the quality change bias.
- Explain the commodity substitution bias.
- Explain the outlet substitution bias.
- State the estimated size of the CPI bias.
- Explain the consequences of the CPI bias for private contracts and government outlays.
- Compare the GDP deflator and the CPI as measures of the cost of living.

3 **Adjust money values for inflation and calculate real wage rates and real interest rates.**

- Explain how changes in the price level can be used when comparing the price of a good at different dates.
- Discuss the difference between the nominal wage rate and the real wage rate.
- Explain how the real wage rate is calculated.
- Define nominal interest rate and real interest rate.
- Explain the relationship between the nominal interest rate, the real interest rate, and the inflation rate.

- Explain how the real interest rate is calculated.

KEY TERMS

- Consumer Price Index CPI (page 160)
- Reference base period (page 160)
- Inflation rate (page 163)
- Cost of living index (page 166)
- Nominal wage rate (page 172)
- Real wage rate (page 172)
- Nominal interest rate (page 175)
- Real interest rate (page 175)

CHECKPOINT 7.1

■ **Explain what the Consumer Price Index (CPI) is and how it is calculated.**

Practice Problems 7.1

1. A Consumer Expenditure Survey in Sparta shows that people consume only juice and cloth. In 2003, the year of the Consumer Expenditure Survey and also the reference base year, the average household spent $40 on juice and $25 on cloth. The price of juice in 2003 was $4 a bottle and the price of cloth was $5 a yard. In the current year, 2004, the price of juice is $4 a bottle and the price of cloth is $6 a yard. Calculate
   a. The CPI basket.
   b. The percentage of the average household's budget spent on juice in the base year.
   c. The CPI in 2004.

2. The table shows the CPI in Russia. Calculate Russia's inflation rate in 2001 and 2002. Did the price level rise or fall in 2002? Did the inflation rate increase or decrease in 2002?

Year	CPI
2000	225
2001	274
2002	310

Solution to Practice Problems 7.1

The two problems concentrate on different aspects of the CPI. The first question examines how the CPI is calculated; the second looks at a major use of the CPI. To solve the first question, recall that to compute the CPI, you need the cost of the CPI basket in the period being examined and the cost of the CPI basket in the base period. The second question requires that you use the formula for the inflation rate.

Quick Review

- *CPI basket* The goods and services in the CPI and the relative importance attached to each of them.
- *CPI formula* The CPI equals:

$$\frac{\text{Cost of CPI basket at current period prices}}{\text{Cost of CPI basket at base period prices}} \times 100.$$

- *Inflation rate* The inflation rate equals:

$$\frac{(\text{CPI in current year} - \text{CPI in previous year})}{\text{CPI in previous year}} \times 100.$$

1a. The CPI basket.

In the reference base year, the price of juice is $4 a bottle and the average household spent $40 on juice. The household bought $40 ÷ $4 = 10 bottles of juice. The household spent $25 on cloth that was $5 a yard, so the household purchased $25 ÷ $5 = 5 yards of cloth. The CPI basket is the quantities of goods and services purchased during the Consumer Expenditure Survey year, so the basket is 10 bottles of juice and 5 yards of cloth.

1b. The percentage of the average household's budget spent on juice in the base year.

The household's budget in the base year was $40 (juice) plus $25 (cloth), which is $65. The percentage of the budget spent on juice is the amount spent on juice divided by the budget, multiplied by 100, or ($40 ÷ $65) × 100, which is 61.5 percent.

1c. The CPI in 2004.

In 2004, the 10 bottles of juice in the market basket cost $4 each and the 5 yards of cloth cost $6 each. So the total cost of the market basket in 2004 is $70. The CPI basket in the base period, 2003, cost $65. The CPI is equal to the cost of the basket in 2004 divided by the cost of the basket in 2003, all multiplied by 100, or ($70/$65) × 100, which is 107.7.

2. Calculate Russia's inflation rate in 2001 and 2002. Did the price level rise or fall in 2002? Did the inflation rate increase or decrease in 2002?

The inflation rate is the percentage change in the price level from one year to the next. In 2000, the CPI was 225 and in 2001, it was 274. The inflation rate in 2001 is [(274 − 225) ÷ 225] × 100, which is 21.8 percent. The inflation rate in 2002 is [(310 − 274) ÷ 274] × 100, which is 13.1 percent. The price level rose in 2002 because the CPI is higher in 2002 than in 2001. The inflation rate in 2001 was 21.8 percent and in 2002 was 13.1 percent, so the inflation rate decreased from 2001 to 2002.

Additional Practice Problem 7.1a

Suppose the price level in Russia remained equal to 310 in 2003, the same level as in 2002. What then would be the inflation rate in Russia in 2003?

Solution to Additional Practice Problem 7.1a

The inflation rate can be calculated two ways. First, because the price level did not change, immediately the inflation rate is 0 percent. Alternatively, the inflation rate formula can be used, which yields [(310 − 310) ÷ 310] × 100 = 0 percent.

■ Self Test 7.1

Fill in the blanks

The ____, also called the CPI, is a measure of the average of the prices paid by urban consumers for a fixed market basket of consumer goods and services. In the base reference period, the CPI equals ____. Each ____ (month; year) the Bureau of Labor Statistics checks the prices of the goods and services in the CPI basket. The CPI equals the cost of the CPI basket at current prices ____ (plus; minus; divided by) the cost of the CPI basket at base period prices, all multiplied by 100. To measure changes in the cost of living, the ____ (inflation rate; CPI in the base reference period) is used.

True or false

1. In the reference base period, the CPI equals 1.0.

2. The CPI market basket is changed from one month to the next.

3. If the cost of the CPI basket at current period prices equals $320, then the CPI equals 320.

4. If the cost of the CPI basket at current period prices exceeds the cost of the CPI basket at base period prices, the inflation rate between these two periods is positive.

5. If the CPI increases from 110 to 121, the inflation rate is 11 percent.

Multiple choice

1. The Consumer Price Index (CPI) is a measure of
   a. the prices of a few consumer goods and services.
   b. the prices of those consumer goods and services that increased in price.
   c. the average of the prices paid by urban consumers for a fixed market basket of goods and services.
   d. consumer confidence in the economy.

2. The CPI is reported once every
   a. year.
   b. quarter.
   c. month.
   d. week.

3. If a country has a CPI of 105.0 in 2002 and a CPI of 102.0 in 2003, then
   a. the average prices of goods and services increased between 2002 and 2003.
   b. the average prices of goods and services decreased between 2002 and 2003.
   c. the average quantity of goods and services decreased between 2002 and 2003.
   d. there was an error when calculating the CPI in 2003.

4. The period for which the Consumer Price Index is defined to equal 100 is called
   a. the reference base period.
   b. the base year.
   c. the starting point.
   d. the zero period.

5. The good or service given the most weight in the CPI basket when calculating the CPI is
   a. food and beverages.
   b. taxes.
   c. housing.
   d. medical care.

6. Suppose a basket of consumer goods and services costs $180 using the base period prices, and the same basket of goods and services costs $300 using the current period prices. The CPI for the current year period equals
   a. 166.7.
   b. 66.7.
   c. 160.0.
   d. 60.0.

7. Suppose the CPI for 1980 was 82.3 and for 1981 was 90.9. Based on this information, we can calculate that the inflation rate in 1981 was
   a. 10.4 percent.
   b. 8.6 percent.
   c. 90.9 percent.
   d. 82.3 percent.

8. If we look at the annual inflation rate in the United States since 1970, we see that inflation on average in the last ten years was
   a. higher than in the 1970s.
   b. higher than in the 1980s.
   c. lower than in the 1970s.
   d. non-existent.

Short answer and numeric questions

Item	Quantity (2002)	Price (2002)	Quantity (2003)	Price (2003)
Pizza	10	$10.00	15	$10.00
Burritos	20	$1.00	25	$0.75
Rice	30	$0.50	20	$1.00

1. The table above gives the expenditures of households in the small nation of Studenvia.

In Studenvia, 2002 is the reference base period.

a. What is the cost of the CPI basket in 2002?

b. What is the cost of the CPI basket in 2003?

c. What is the CPI in 2002?

d. What is the CPI in 2003?

e. What is the inflation rate in 2003?

2. Suppose the CPI was 100.0 in 2002, 110.0 in 2003, 121.0 in 2004, and 133.1 in 2005. What is the inflation rate in 2003, 2004, and 2005?

3. If the price level rises slowly, is the inflation rate positive or negative? Why?

CHECKPOINT 7.2

■ **Explain the limitations of the CPI as a measure of the cost of living.**

Practice Problem 7.2

Item	2001 Quantity	2001 Price	2002 Quantity	2002 Price
Broccoli	10	$3.00	15	$3.00
Carrots	15	$2.00	10	$4.00

1. Economists in the Statistics Bureau decide to check the substitution bias in the CPI. To do so they conduct a Consumer Expenditure Survey in both 2001 and 2002. The above table shows the results of the survey. It shows the items that consumers buy and their prices. The Statistics Bureau fixes the reference base year as 2001 and asks you to:

a. Calculate the CPI in 2002 using the 2001 CPI basket.

b. Calculate the CPI in 2002 using the 2002 CPI basket.

c. Explain whether there is any substitution bias in the CPI that uses the 2001 basket.

Solution to Practice Problem 7.2

The commodity substitution bias is one of the four sources that makes the CPI a biased measure of changes in the cost of living. The commodity substitution bias occurs because consumers change their buying patterns when relative prices change, but the CPI uses a fixed basket. Because the CPI basket is fixed, it cannot take account of the changes in buying patterns.

Quick Review

- *Commodity substitution bias* People cut back on their purchases of items that become relatively more costly and increase their consumption of items that become relatively less costly.

a. Calculate the CPI in 2002 using the 2001 CPI basket.

The CPI basket in 2001 consists of 10 broccoli and 15 carrots. The cost of the basket in 2001 is $60 ($3 × 10 + $2 × 15, where the prices and quantities are both from 2001), and its cost in 2002 is $90 ($3 × 10 + $4 × 15, where the prices are from 2002 and the quantities are from the 2001 CPI basket). The CPI in 2002, using the 2001 basket, equals the cost of the basket in 2002 divided by the cost of the basket in 2001 all multiplied by 100, which is ($90 ÷ $60) × 100 = 150.

b. Calculate the CPI in 2002 using the 2002 CPI basket.

The CPI basket in 2002 consists of 15 broccoli and 10 carrots. The cost of the basket in 2001 is $65 and its cost in 2002 is $85. The CPI in 2002, using the 2002 basket, equals ($85 ÷ $65) × 100, which is 131.

c. Explain whether there is any substitution bias in the CPI that uses the 2001 basket.

There is substitution bias because the price of broccoli was the same in both years, but the price of carrots rose between 2001 and 2002. In response, households substituted the now relatively cheaper broccoli for the now relatively more expensive carrots. Thus in 2002 people bought more broccoli and fewer carrots than in 2001. Consumers spent $60 on vegetables in 2001 and $85 in 2002, an increase of 42 percent. By using a fixed CPI basket, the CPI ignores the substitution. The CPI, using the 2001 CPI basket, concludes that the cost of vegetables rose 50 percent, which overstates the actual impact of the price rise because it ignores the ability of households to partially escape the increased price of carrots by substituting broccoli. Because consumers make substitutions, the cost of vegetables increases by only 42 percent. (The second CPI measure, using the 2002 CPI basket, concluded that the price of vegetables increased 31 percent. This amount understates the impact of the price change, because it assumes people don't mind switching from carrots to broccoli.)

Additional Practice Problem 7.2a

Nowadays when households buy broccoli, they discard some of it because it is bruised. Suppose 20 percent is discarded. Now new, genetically engineered broccoli is developed that does not bruise so that all the broccoli that is purchased can be used. People prefer the new broccoli, so they switch to buying the new broccoli. If the price of the new broccoli is 10 percent higher than the old, what actually happens to the CPI and what should happen to the CPI?

Solution to Additional Practice Problem 7.2a

With the introduction of the new broccoli, the CPI will rise because the new broccoli's price is higher (10 percent) than the old broccoli. But, the CPI should actually decrease because people pay only 10 percent more for 20 percent more (useable) broccoli. This problem illustrates how the quality change bias can bias the CPI upwards.

■ Self Test 7.2

Fill in the blanks

The sources of bias in the CPI as a measure of the cost of living are the ____, ____, ____, and ____. The Boskin Commission concluded that the CPI ____ (overstates; understates) inflation by ____ (1.1; 2.2; 3.3) percentage points a year. The CPI bias leads to ____ (an increase; a decrease) in government outlays.

True or false

1. The CPI is a biased measure of the cost of living.
2. Commodity substitution bias refers to the ongoing replacement of old goods by new goods.
3. The bias in the CPI is estimated to overstate inflation by approximately 1.1 percentage points a year.

4. The CPI bias can distort private contracts.
5. The GDP deflator gives a better measure of the cost of living than does the CPI.

Multiple choice

1. All of the following create bias in the CPI except the
   a. new goods bias.
   b. outlet substitution bias.
   c. commodity substitution bias.
   d. GDP deflator bias.

2. An example of the new goods bias in the calculation of the CPI is a price increase in
   a. butter relative to margarine.
   b. an MP3 player relative to a Walkman.
   c. a 2003 Honda Civic LX relative to a 1998 Honda Civic LX.
   d. textbooks bought through the campus bookstore relative to textbooks bought through Amazon.com.

3. Over the last decade, the price of a dishwasher has remained relatively constant while the quality of dishwashers has improved. The CPI
   a. is adjusted monthly to reflect the improvement in quality.
   b. is increased monthly to reflect the increased quality of dishwashers.
   c. has an upward bias if it is not adjusted to take account of the higher quality.
   d. has an upward bias because it does not reflect the increased production of dishwashers.

4. Joe buys chicken and beef. If the price of beef rises and the price of chicken does not change, Joe will
   a. buy more beef and help create a new goods bias for the CPI.
   b. buy more chicken and help create a commodity substitution bias for the CPI.
   c. buy the same quantity of beef and chicken and help create a commodity substitution bias for the CPI.
   d. buy less chicken and beef and thus help create a quality change bias for the CPI.

5. The CPI bias was estimated by the Congressional Advisory Commission on the Consumer Price Index as
   a. understating the actual inflation rate by about 5 percentage points a year.
   b. understating the actual inflation rate by more than 5 percentage points a year.
   c. overstating the actual inflation rate by about 1 percentage point a year.
   d. overstating the actual inflation rate by more than 5 percentage points a year.

6. A consequence of the CPI bias is that it
   a. decreases government outlays.
   b. increases international trade.
   c. reduces outlet substitution bias.
   d. distorts private contracts.

7. The fact that the CPI is a biased measure of the inflation rate means government outlays will
   a. increase at a faster rate than the actual inflation rate.
   b. increase at the same rate as the actual inflation rate.
   c. increase at a slower rate than the actual inflation rate.
   d. None of the above, because the bias in inflation measured using the CPI has nothing to do with government outlays.

8. If we compare the recent measurements of inflation as recorded by the CPI and the GDP deflator we find that the
   a. two measures fluctuate together.
   b. CPI has consistently been at least 5 percentage points above the GDP deflator.
   c. GDP deflator has consistently been at least 5 percentage points above the CPI.
   d. two measures give very different inflation rates for most years.

Short answer and numeric questions

1. What are the sources of bias in the CPI? Briefly explain each.

2. Once you graduate, you move to a new town and sign a long-term lease on a townhouse. You agree to pay $1,000 a month rent and to change the monthly rent annually by the percentage change in the CPI. For the next 4 years, the CPI increases 5 percent each year. What will you pay in monthly rent for the second, third, and fourth years of your lease? Suppose the CPI overstates the inflation rate by 1 percentage point a year. If the CPI bias was eliminated, what would you pay in rent for the second, third, and fourth years?

CHECKPOINT 7.3

■ **Adjust money values for inflation and calculate real wage rates and real interest rates.**

Practice Problems 7.3

1. The table shows some gas prices and the CPI for three years. The reference base period is 1982–1984.

Year	Price of gasoline (cents)	CPI
1971	36	40.5
1981	138	90.9
1991	112	136.2

   a. Calculate the real price of gasoline in each year in 1982–1984 dollars.
   b. In which year was gasoline the most costly in real terms?
   c. In which year was gasoline the least costly in real terms?

2. Amazon.com agreed to pay its workers $20 an hour in 1999 and $22 an hour in 2001. The CPI for these years was 166 in 1999 and 180 in 2001.
   a. Calculate the real wage rate in each year.
   b. Did these workers get a pay raise between 1999 and 2001?

3. Sally worked hard all year so she could go to school full time the following year. She put her savings into a mutual fund that paid a nominal interest rate of 7 percent a year. The CPI was 165 at the beginning of the year and 177 at the end of the year. What was the real interest rate that Sally earned?

Solution to Practice Problems 7.3

Using the CPI to adjust nominal values to real values is a key use of the CPI. Keep in mind that to convert a nominal price (such as the nominal wage rate) into a real price (such as the real wage rate), you divide by the CPI and multiply by 100, but to convert the nominal interest rate into the real interest rate, you subtract the inflation rate.

Quick Review

- *Real wage rate* The real wage rate equals the nominal wage rate divided by the CPI and multiplied by 100.
- *Real interest rate* The real interest rate equals the nominal interest rate minus the inflation rate.

1a. Calculate the real price of gasoline in each year in 1982–1984 dollars.

To convert the current prices in the table to real prices, divide the price by the CPI in that year and then multiply by 100. In 1971, the nominal price of gas was $0.36 a gallon and the CPI was 40.4, so the real price of gasoline is ($0.36 ÷ 40.5) × 100 = $0.89. In 1981 the nominal price was $1.38 a gallon, the CPI was 90.9, and so the real price is ($1.38 ÷ 90.9) × 100 = $1.52. In 1991 the nominal price was $1.12 a gallon, the CPI was 136.2, and so the real price was $0.82.

1b. In which year was gasoline the most costly in real terms?

The highest real price for gasoline was 1981, when the real price was $1.52. In 1981 you gave up more in terms of other goods and services to get a gallon of gas than in 1971 or 1991.

1c. In which year was gasoline the least costly in real terms?

The lowest real price for gasoline was 1991, when the real price was $0.82. In 1991 you gave up less in terms of other goods and services to get a gallon of gas than in 1971 or 1981.

2. Amazon.com agreed to pay its workers $20 an hour in 1999 and $22 an hour in 2001. The CPI for these years was 166 in 1999 and 180 in 2001.

2a. Calculate the real wage rate in each year.

The real wage rate equals the nominal wage rate divided by the CPI and multiplied by 100. The nominal wage rate in 1999 was $20 an hour, and the CPI was 166, so the real wage rate was ($20 ÷ 166) × 100 = $12.05. Similarly, the real wage in 2001 was ($22 ÷ 180) × 100 = $12.22.

2b. Did these workers get a pay raise between 1999 and 2001?

The workers got a real pay raise from $12.05 an hour in 1999 to $12.22 an hour in 2001. Although they didn't get a 10 percent increase in the real wage (they received a 10 percent increase in the nominal wage) they did get a 1.4 percent increase in the real wage.

3. Sally worked hard all year so she could go to school full time the following year. She put her savings into a mutual fund that paid a nominal interest rate of 7 percent a year. The CPI was 165 at the beginning of the year and 177 at the end of the year. What was the real interest rate that Sally earned?

The real interest rate equals the nominal interest rate minus the inflation rate. Sally earned a nominal interest rate of 7 percent a year. The inflation rate is the percentage change in the price level from one year to the next, which equals [(177 − 165) ÷ 165] × 100 = 7.3 percent a year. The real interest rate is 7 percent − 7.3 percent = −0.3 percent. Sally had less purchasing power (0.3 percent less) at the end of the year than she had at the beginning of the year!

Additional Practice Problem 7.3a

Suppose Sally (from Practice Problem 3) had wanted a 3 percent real interest rate on her savings. What nominal interest rate would she have needed to receive with an inflation rate of 7 percent?

Solution to Additional Practice Problem 7.3a

The real interest rate equals the nominal rate minus the inflation rate. Rearranging this formula shows that the nominal interest rate equals the real interest rate plus the inflation rate. To get a 3 percent real interest rate with a 7 percent inflation rate, Sally needs the nominal interest rate to equal 3 percent plus 7 percent, or 10 percent.

■ Self Test 7.3

Fill in the blanks

The nominal wage rate is the average hourly wage rate measured in ____ (current; reference base year) dollars. The real wage rate is the average hourly wage rate measured in dollars of the ____ (current; given base) year. The real wage rate equals the nominal wage rate (plus; times; divided by) the CPI multiplied by 100. The real interest rate equals the nominal interest rate ____ (plus; minus; divided by) the ____ (CPI; inflation rate).

True or false

1. The CPI was 171 in 2000 and 24.4 in 1950, so the price level in 2000 was 7 times higher than what it was in 1950.

2. Real GDP equals nominal GDP divided by the CPI, multiplied by 100.

3. A change in the real wage rate measures the change in the goods and services that an hour's work can buy.

4. The nominal interest rate is the percentage return on a loan expressed in dollars; the real interest rate is the percentage return on a loan expressed in purchasing power.

5. If the nominal interest rate is 8 percent a year and the inflation rate is 4 percent a year, then the real interest rate is 4 percent a year.

Multiple choice

1. In 2002, in New York, apples cost $1.49 a pound. Suppose the CPI was 120 in 2002 and 140 in 2003. If there is no change in the real price of an apple in the year 2003, how much would a pound of apples sell for in 2003?
   a. $2.74
   b. $1.69
   c. $1.66
   d. $1.74

2. In 1970, the CPI was 39 and in 2000 it was 172. A local phone call cost $0.10 in 1970. What is the price of this phone call in 2000 dollars?
   a. $1.42
   b. $0.39
   c. $1.72
   d. $0.44

3. The nominal wage rate is the
   a. minimum hourly wage that a company can legally pay a worker.
   b. average hourly wage rate measured in the dollars of a given reference base year.
   c. minimum hourly wage rate measured in the dollars of a given reference base year.
   d. average hourly wage rate measured in current dollars.

4. In 2001, the average starting salary for an economics major was $29,500. If the CPI was 147.5, the real salary was
   a. $200.00 an hour.
   b. $20,000.
   c. $35,000.
   d. $43,513.

5. If we compare the nominal wage versus the real wage in the United States since 1972, we see that
   a. real wages increased steadily.
   b. nominal wages increased more than real wages.
   c. real wages increased more than nominal wages.
   d. nominal wages increased at an uneven pace whereas the increase in real wages was steady and constant.

6. The real interest rate is equal to the
   a. nominal interest rate plus the inflation rate.
   b. nominal interest rate minus the inflation rate.
   c. nominal interest rate times the inflation rate.
   d. nominal interest rate divided by the inflation rate.

7. You borrow at a nominal interest rate of 10 percent. If the inflation rate is 4 percent, then the real interest rate is
   a. the $10 in interest you have to pay.
   b. 16 percent.
   c. 2.5 percent.
   d. 6 percent.

8. In the United States between 1972 and 2002, the
   a. nominal and real interest rates both generally decreased.
   b. nominal and real interest rates were both constant.
   c. real interest rate was constant and the nominal interest rate fluctuated.
   d. nominal interest rate was greater than the real interest rate.

Short answer and numeric questions

Job	Salary (dollars per year)	CPI
Job A	20,000	105
Job B	25,000	120
Job C	34,000	170

1. Often the cost of living varies from state to state or from large city to small city. After you graduate, suppose you have job offers in 3 locales. The nominal salary and the CPI for each job is given in the table above.
   a. Which job offers the highest real salary?
   b. Which job offers the lowest real salary?
   c. In determining which job to accept, what is more important: the real salary or the nominal salary? Why?

Year	Real interest rate (percent per year)	Nominal interest rate (percent per year)	Inflation rate (percent per year)
1999	____	10	5
2000	____	6	1
2001	4	6	____
2002	5	____	3

2. The table above gives the real interest rate, nominal interest rate, and inflation rate for various years in a foreign country. Complete the table.

3. In 1980, the nominal interest rate was 12 percent. In 2002, the nominal interest rate was 8 percent. From this information, can you determine if you would rather have saved $1,000 in 1980 or 2002? Explain your answer.

SELF TEST ANSWERS

■ CHECKPOINT 7.1

Fill in the blanks

The <u>Consumer Price Index</u>, also called the CPI, is a measure of the average of the prices paid by urban consumers for a fixed market basket of consumer goods and services. In the base reference period, the CPI equals <u>100</u>. Each <u>month</u> the Bureau of Labor Statistics checks the prices of the goods and services in the CPI basket. The CPI equals the cost of the CPI basket at current prices <u>divided by</u> the cost of the CPI basket at base period prices, all multiplied by 100. To measure changes in the cost of living, the <u>inflation rate</u> is used.

True or false

1. False; page 160
2. False; page 160
3. False; page 163
4. True; page 163
5. False; page 163

Multiple choice

1. c; page 160
2. c; page 160
3. b; page 160
4. a; page 160
5. c; page 161
6. a; page 163
7. a; page 163
8. c; pages 163-164

Short answer and numeric questions

1. a. The cost is $135; page 162.
   b. The cost is $145. The quantities used to calculate this cost are the base period, 2002, quantities; page 162.
   c. The CPI is 100; page 163.
   d. The CPI is 107.4; page 163.
   e. The inflation rate is 7.4 percent; page 163.
2. The inflation rate for each year is 10 percent; page 163.

3. Whenever the price level rises, the inflation rate is positive. If the price level rises slowly, the inflation rate is small; if the price level rises rapidly, the inflation rate is large; page 163.

■ CHECKPOINT 7.2

Fill in the blanks

The sources of bias in the CPI as a measure of the cost of living are the <u>new goods bias</u>, <u>quality change bias</u>, <u>commodity substitution bias</u>, and <u>outlet substitution bias</u>. The Boskin Commission concluded that the CPI <u>overstates</u> inflation by <u>1.1</u> percentage points a year. The CPI bias leads to <u>an increase</u> in government outlays.

True or false

1. True; page 164
2. False; page 165
3. True; page 165
4. True; page 166
5. False; pages 166-167

Multiple choice

1. d; page 164
2. b; page 164
3. c; page 164
4. b; page 165
5. c; page 165
6. d; pages 165-166
7. a; page 166
8. a; page 167

Short answer and numeric questions

1. There are four sources of bias in the CPI: the new goods bias, the quality change bias, the commodity substitution bias, and the outlet substitution bias. The new goods bias refers to the fact that new goods replace old goods. The quality change bias occurs because at times price increases in existing goods are the result of increased quality. The commodity substitution bias occurs because consumers buy fewer goods and services when their

prices rise compared to other, comparable products. The fixed basket approach taken in the CPI's calculation cannot take account of this method by which households offset higher prices. Finally, the outlet substitution bias refers to the fact that when prices rise, people shop more frequently at discount stores to take advantage of the lower prices in these stores; pages 164-165.

2. The monthly rent increases by 5 percent each year. For the second year the monthly rent equals $1,000 × 1.05, which is $1,050. For the third year the monthly rent equals $1,050 × 1.05, which is $1,102.50. And for the third year the monthly rent equals $1,102.50 × 1.05, which is $1,157.63. If the CPI bias was eliminated, the monthly rent would increase by 4 percent each year. The monthly rent would be $1,040 for the second year, $1,081.60 for the third year, and $1,124.86 for the third year; page 166.

■ CHECKPOINT 7.3

Fill in the blanks

The nominal wage rate is the average hourly wage rate measured in <u>current</u> dollars. The real wage rate is the average wage rate measured in dollars of the <u>given base</u> year. The real wage rate equals the nominal wage rate <u>divided by</u> the CPI multiplied by 100. The real interest rate equals the nominal interest rate <u>minus</u> the <u>inflation rate</u>.

True or false

1. True; page 169
2. False; page 169
3. True; page 171
4. True; page 173
5. True; page 173

Multiple choice

1. d; page 169
2. d; page 169
3. d; page 170
4. b; page 170
5. b; page 171
6. b; page 173
7. d; page 173
8. d; page 173

Short answer and numeric questions

1. a. The real salary equals (nominal salary ÷ CPI) times 100. The real salary is $19,048 for Job A, $20,833 for Job B, and $20,000 for Job C. The real salary is highest for Job B; page 170.
   b. The real salary is lowest for Job A; page 170.
   c. The real salary is more important than the nominal salary because the real salary measures the quantity of goods and services you will be able to buy; pages 171-172.

Year	Real interest rate (percent per year)	Nominal interest rate (percent per year)	Inflation rate (percent per year)
1999	<u>5</u>	10	5
2000	<u>5</u>	6	1
2001	4	6	<u>2</u>
2002	5	<u>8</u>	3

2. The completed table is above; page 173.
3. You cannot determine when you would rather have been a saver. Savers are interested in the real interest rate because the real interest rate is the percentage return expressed in purchasing power. Without knowing the inflation rate, there is not enough data given to compute the real interest rate; page 173.

Chapter

8

AS-AD and Potential GDP

CHAPTER IN PERSPECTIVE

In Chapter 8 we study the forces that determine potential GDP and the natural unemployment rate.

■ **Preview the aggregate supply–aggregate demand (*AS-AD*) model and explain why real GDP and unemployment fluctuate in a business cycle.**

The classical dichotomy states that if the economy is at full employment, the forces that determine the real variables are independent of those that determine the nominal variables. Potential GDP is the level of real GDP produced at full employment. Aggregate supply is the relationship between the quantity of real GDP supplied and the price level when all other influences on production plans remain the same. Other things remaining the same, a rise in the price level increases the quantity of real GDP supplied. Aggregate demand is the relationship between the quantity of real GDP demanded and the price level when all other influences on expenditure plans remain the same. Other things remaining the same, a rise in the price level decreases the quantity of real GDP demanded. Macroeconomic equilibrium occurs at the intersection of the aggregate supply and aggregate demand curves. The macroeconomic equilibrium can be a full-employment equilibrium (real GDP equals potential GDP), an above full-employment equilibrium (real GDP exceeds potential GDP), or a below full-employment equilibrium (real GDP is less than potential GDP).

■ **Explain the forces that determine potential GDP and the distribution of income between labor and other factors of production.**

The production function shows the maximum quantity of real GDP that can be produced as the quantity of labor employed changes and all other influences on production remain the same. The quantity of labor employed is determined in the labor market. The quantity of labor demanded increases (decreases) as the real wage rate falls (rises). The quantity of labor supplied increases (decreases) as the real wage rate rises (falls). Labor market equilibrium occurs at the intersection of the labor supply curve and the labor demand curve. When the labor market is in equilibrium, the economy is at full employment and real GDP equals potential GDP.

■ **Explain what creates unemployment when the economy is at full employment and describe the influences on the natural unemployment rate.**

The natural unemployment rate is the unemployment rate at full employment and consists of frictional, structural, and seasonal unemployment. Two fundamental causes of unemployment are job search, which is the activity of looking for an acceptable vacant job, and job rationing, which occurs when the real wage rate is above the full-employment equilibrium level. The amount of job search depends on demographic change, unemployment benefits, and structural change. Job rationing occurs when there is an efficiency wage, a minimum wage, or a union wage.

EXPANDED CHAPTER CHECKLIST

When you have completed this chapter, you will be able to:

1 Preview the aggregate supply–aggregate demand (*AS-AD*) model and explain why real GDP and unemployment fluctuate in a business cycle.

- Distinguish between real and nominal variables and explain the importance of the classical dichotomy.
- Define potential GDP.
- Discuss aggregate supply and explain the relationship between the quantity of real GDP supplied and the price level.
- List factors that change aggregate supply and shift the aggregate supply curve.
- Discuss aggregate demand and explain the relationship between the quantity of real GDP demanded and the price level.
- List factors that change aggregate demand and shift the aggregate demand curve.
- Explain and illustrate macroeconomic equilibrium.
- Illustrate the three types of macroeconomic equilibrium: full-employment equilibrium, above full-employment equilibrium, and below full-employment equilibrium.

2 Explain the forces that determine potential GDP and the distribution of income between labor and other factors of production.

- Describe the production function and explain how it displays diminishing returns.
- Discuss the relationship between the real wage rate and the quantity of labor demanded.
- Discuss the relationship between the real wage rate and the quantity of labor supplied.

- Discuss how equilibrium in the labor market is achieved and the relationship between the labor market equilibrium and potential GDP.
- Use the full-employment model to explain the functional distribution of income.

3 Explain what creates unemployment when the economy is at full employment and describe the influences on the natural unemployment rate.

- Define the natural unemployment rate.
- Define job search and describe the factors that influence it.
- Define job rationing and explain why it occurs.
- Explain how job rationing affects the natural unemployment rate.

KEY TERMS

- Classical dichotomy (page 182)
- Potential GDP (page 183)
- Aggregate supply (page 183)
- Aggregate demand (page (185)
- Macroeconomic equilibrium (page 186)
- Full-employment equilibrium (page 187)
- Above full-employment equilibrium (page 187)
- Below full-employment equilibrium (page 187)
- Production function (page 190)
- Diminishing returns (page 190)
- Quantity of labor demanded (page 191)
- Demand for labor (page 191)
- Quantity of labor supplied (page 193)
- Supply of labor (page 193)
- Job search (page 199)
- Job rationing (page 200)
- Efficiency wage (page 201)
- Union wage (page 201)

CHECKPOINT 8.1

■ **Preview the aggregate supply-aggregate demand (*AS-AD*) model and explain why real GDP and unemployment fluctuate in a business cycle.**

Practice Problems 8.1

1. The table shows aggregate demand and aggregate supply schedules for the United Kingdom.

Price level (GDP deflator)	Real GDP demanded (billions of	Real GDP supplied 1995 pounds)
90	800	650
100	775	700
110	750	750
120	725	800
130	700	850

   a. Plot the aggregate demand curve.
   b. Plot the aggregate supply curve.
   c. What is the macroeconomic equilibrium?
   d. If potential GDP in the United Kingdom is £800 billion, what is the type of macroeconomic equilibrium?

2. The U.S. economy is at full employment when the following events occur:
   - A deep recession hits the world economy, and real GDP in the rest of the world decreases.
   - The world oil price tumbles.
   a. Explain the effect of each event separately on aggregate demand and aggregate supply in the United States.
   b. Explain the combined effect of the two events on the U.S. price level and real GDP.

Solution to Practice Problems 8.1

The aggregate supply–aggregate demand model will be explored in greater detail in future chapters. These problems give you some initial practice in using it. Keep in mind the difference between a movement along a curve and a shift of a curve. When the price level changes, there is a movement along the aggregate supply curve and the aggregate demand curve. When other factors change, the curve shifts.

Quick Review

- *Aggregate demand* The relationship between the quantity of real GDP demanded and the price level when all other influences on expenditure plans remain the same.
- *Aggregate supply* The relationship between the quantity of real GDP supplied and the price level when all other influences on production plans remain the same.

1a. Plot the aggregate demand curve.

The aggregate demand curve is plotted in the figure to the right. The aggregate demand curve has a negative slope, so as the price level falls, the quantity of real GDP demanded increases.

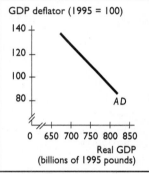

1b. Plot the aggregate supply curve.

The aggregate supply curve is plotted in the figure. The aggregate supply curve has a positive slope, so as the price level rises, the quantity of real GDP supplied increases.

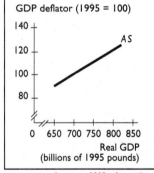

1c. What is the macroeconomic equilibrium?

The macroeconomic equilibrium is at a price level of 110 and real GDP of £750 billion. The macroeconomic equilibrium is at the intersection of the aggregate supply curve and the aggregate demand curve.

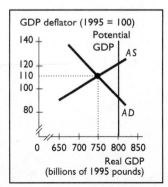

1d. If potential GDP in the United Kingdom is £800 billion, what is the type of macroeconomic equilibrium?

Because potential GDP is £800 billion and the macroeconomic equilibrium is £750 billion, the economy is in a below full-employment equilibrium. Real GDP is less than potential GDP.

2. The U.S. economy is at full employment when the following events occur:

- **A deep recession hits the world economy and real GDP in the rest of the world decreases.**
- **The world oil price tumbles.**

2a. Explain the effect of each event separately on aggregate demand and aggregate supply in the United States.

If real GDP in the rest of the world decreases, people in the rest of the world buy less from the United States. U.S. aggregate demand decreases and the U.S. aggregate demand curve shifts leftward. A fall in the price of oil reduces the cost of production for U.S. firms. When costs fall, U.S. aggregate supply increases and the aggregate supply curve shifts rightward.

2b. Explain the combined effect of the two events on the U.S. price level and real GDP.

The effect on the price level is unambiguous: It falls because both the decrease in aggregate demand and increase in aggregate supply reduce the price level. The effect on real GDP is ambiguous. The decrease in aggregate demand decreases real GDP while the increase in aggregate supply increases real GDP. The net change in real GDP depends on which effect is larger.

Additional Practice Problem 8.1a

What factors increase aggregate demand? What effect does an increase in aggregate demand have on the price level and real GDP?

Solution to Additional Practice Problem 8.1a

Factors that increase aggregate demand include a fall in the interest rate, an increase in the quantity of money in the economy, an increase in government purchases, a tax cut, and an increase in real GDP in the rest of the world. An increase in aggregate demand raises the price level and increases real GDP.

■ Self Test 8.1

Fill in the blanks

The discovery that at full employment, the forces that determine real variables are independent of the forces that determine nominal variables is the ____. The inflation rate is a ____ (real; nominal) variable; employment is a ____ (real; nominal) variable. Other things remaining the same, the higher the price level, the ____ (greater; smaller) the quantity of real GDP supplied. Potential GDP ____ (changes; does not change) when the price level increases. Other things remaining the same, the higher the price level, the ____ (greater; smaller) the quantity of real GDP demanded. The aggregate demand curve ____ (does not shift; shifts) when government purchases change. Macroeconomic equilibrium occurs at the point of intersection of the *AD* curve and ____ (potential GDP; the *AS* curve). When equilibrium real GDP exceeds potential GDP, there is ____ equilibrium.

True or false

1. The aggregate supply–aggregate demand model applies to the economy as a whole.

2. Other things remaining the same, the higher the price level, the greater the quantity of real GDP supplied.

3. Potential GDP increases as the price level increases because firms plan to produce a larger quantity of goods and services.

4. Other things remaining the same, the higher the price level, the greater the quantity of real GDP demanded.

5. Macroeconomic equilibrium occurs at the point where aggregate demand equals potential GDP.

Multiple choice

1. The classical dichotomy states that
   a. the forces that determine the real variables are the same as those that determine the nominal variables.
   b. at full employment, the forces that determine the real variables are independent of

those that determine the nominal variables.

c. at zero unemployment, the forces that determine the real variables are independent of those that determine the nominal variables.

d. None of the above answers is correct.

2. The level of real GDP that the economy produces at full employment is called

a. real GDP.

b. nominal GDP.

c. potential GDP.

d. sustainable GDP.

3. The aggregate supply curve shows that, all other influences on production plans remaining the same, as the

a. price level rises, the quantity of real GDP supplied decreases.

b. price level rises, the quantity of real GDP supplied increases.

c. quantity of labor employed increases, potential GDP increases.

d. natural unemployment rate falls, potential GDP increases.

4. If the price level rises, then potential GDP

a. increases.

b. decreases.

c. does not change.

d. causes the natural unemployment rate to decrease.

5. Because there is a _____ relationship between the price level and the quantity of real GDP demanded, the aggregate demand curve is _____ curve.

a. negative; an upward-sloping

b. positive; a downward-sloping

c. positive; an upward-sloping

d. negative; a downward-sloping

6. A rise in the interest rate _____ aggregate demand and a tax cut _____ aggregate demand.

a. decreases; increases

b. increases; decreases

c. increases; increases

d. decreases; decreases

7. If the quantity of real GDP supplied equals the quantity of real GDP demanded, then

a. nominal GDP equals zero.

b. real GDP must equal potential GDP.

c. real GDP must be below potential GDP.

d. real GDP might be below, equal to, or above potential GDP.

8. If the equilibrium real GDP is less than potential GDP, the economy is in _____ full-employment equilibrium; if equilibrium real GDP is greater than potential GDP, the economy is in _____ full-employment equilibrium.

a. an above; an above

b. an above; a below

c. a below; an above

d. a below; a below

Complete the graph

■ **FIGURE 8.1**

Price level (GDP deflator, 1996 = 100)

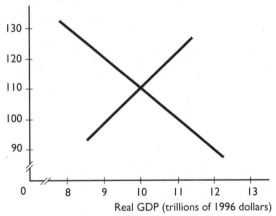

1. In Figure 8.1, label the curves. What is the equilibrium price level and real GDP? Suppose the money wage rate falls so that real GDP becomes $11 trillion. Show which curve shifts. What is the new price level?

Short answer and numeric questions

1. What is the classical dichotomy and why is it important?

Price level (GDP deflator)	Quantity of real GDP demanded (trillions of 1996 dollars)	Quantity of real GDP supplied (trillions of 1996 dollars)
110	14	11
120	13	13
130	12	15
140	11	17

2. The table gives the aggregate demand and aggregate supply schedules. What is the equilibrium price level and real GDP?

3. When the price level rises, what happens to aggregate supply and the quantity of real GDP supplied? Aggregate demand and the quantity of real GDP demanded? Potential GDP?

4. When the price level falls, what happens to aggregate supply and the quantity of real GDP supplied? Aggregate demand and the quantity of real GDP demanded? Potential GDP?

5. What is a below full-employment equilibrium?

CHECKPOINT 8.2

■ **Explain the forces that determine potential GDP and the distribution of income between labor and other factors of production.**

Practice Problem 8.2

Quantity of labor demanded (billions of hours per year)	Real GDP (billions of 2001 dollars)	Real wage rate (2001 dollars per hour)
0	0	50
1	40	40
2	70	30
3	90	20
4	100	10

1. The table above describes an economy's production function and its demand for labor. The table below describes the supply of labor in this economy.

   a. Make graphs of the production function and the labor market.

Quantity of labor supplied (billions of hours per year)	Real wage rate (2001 dollars per hour)
0	10
1	20
2	30
3	40
4	50

   b. Find the equilibrium employment, real wage rate, and potential GDP.

   c. What percentage of real GDP does labor earn?

Solution to Practice Problem 8.2

To solve this Practice Problem, first find the equilibrium in the labor market. Then use the production function to determine how much GDP is produced, which is the potential GDP.

Quick Review

• *Full employment and potential GDP* When the economy is at full employment, real GDP equals potential GDP.

a. **Make graphs of the production function and the labor market.**

The production function is a graph of the first two columns of the first table. The figure to the right shows the production function.

The second figure to the right shows the labor market. The labor demand curve is the first and third columns in the first table. It shows the relationship between the real wage rate and the quantity of labor demanded. The la-

bor supply curve is from the second table and shows the relationship between the real wage rate and the quantity of labor supplied.

b. **Find the equilibrium employment, real wage rate, and potential GDP.**

Equilibrium employment occurs at the point where the labor demand curve and the labor supply curve intersect. The second figure in part (a) shows that the equilibrium real wage rate is $30 an hour and the equilibrium employment is 2 billion hours a year. The production function, in the first figure in part (a), shows that when 2 billion hours of labor are employed, GDP is $70 billion, so potential GDP equals $70 billion.

c. **What percentage of GDP does labor earn?**

Workers earn $30 an hour and work for 2 billion hours a year, so workers earn $60 billion. GDP is $70 billion, so the percentage of GDP earned by labor is ($60 billion ÷ $70 billion) × 100 = 85.7 percent of GDP.

Additional Practice Problem 8.2a

The population in Practice Problem 8.1 grows so that the quantity of labor supplied increases by 2 billion hours at every real wage rate. What is the effect on potential GDP?

Solution to Additional Practice Problem 8.2a

Quantity of labor (billions of hours per year)	Real wage rate (2001 dollars per hour)
2	10
3	20
4	30
5	40
6	50

The new labor supply schedule is given in the table above and shown in the figure. In the figure, the labor supply curve shifts rightward from LS_1 to LS_2. The equilibrium quantity of labor increases to 3

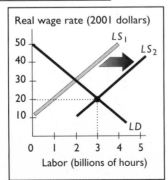

billion hours and the equilibrium real wage rate falls to $20. The production function in the first table in the practice problem shows that when labor is 3 billion hours, real GDP is $90 billion. The increase in the population increases potential GDP to $90 billion.

■ Self Test 8.2

Fill in the blanks

The relationship that shows the maximum quantity of real GDP that can be produced as the quantity of labor employed changes is ____ (the production function; potential GDP). The quantity of labor demanded ____ (increases; decreases) as the real wage rate falls, and the quantity of labor supplied ____ (increases; decreases) as the real wage rate falls. If the real wage rate exceeds the equilibrium real wage rate, there is a ____ (shortage; surplus) of labor. When the labor market is in equilibrium, there is ____ and real GDP equals ____.

True or false

1. Real GDP can exceed potential GDP permanently.

2. The production function shows how the quantity of labor hired depends on the real wage rate.

3. The nominal wage rate influences the quantity of labor demanded because what matters to firms is the number of dollars they pay for an hour of labor.

4. A rise in the real wage rate has two opposing effects on the quantity of labor supplied.

5. When the labor market is in equilibrium, the economy is at full employment and real GDP equals potential GDP.

Multiple choice

1. Potential GDP
   a. is the quantity of GDP produced when the economy is at full employment.
   b. can never be exceeded.
   c. can never be attained.
   d. None of the above answers is correct.

2. With fixed quantities of capital, land, and entrepreneurship and fixed technology, real GDP depends on
   a. the quantity of labor employed.
   b. the inflation rate.
   c. the price level.
   d. all of the above.

3. The production function graphs the relationship between
   a. nominal GDP and real GDP.
   b. real GDP and the quantity of labor employed.
   c. real GDP and capital.
   d. nominal GDP and the quantity of labor employed.

4. The quantity of labor demanded definitely increases if the
   a. real wage rate rises.
   b. real wage rate falls.
   c. nominal wage rate rises.
   d. nominal wage rate falls.

5. The supply of labor curve has a
   a. negative slope because as the real wage rate rises, firms hire fewer workers.
   b. positive slope because as the real wage rate rises, the opportunity cost of leisure rises.
   c. positive slope because as the real wage rate rises, the opportunity cost of leisure falls.
   d. negative slope because as the real wage rate rises, households work more hours.

6. The real wage rate is $35 an hour. At this wage rate there are 100 billion labor hours supplied and 200 billion labor hours demanded. There is a
   a. shortage of 300 billion hours of labor.
   b. shortage of 100 billion hours of labor.
   c. surplus of 100 billion hours of labor.
   d. surplus of 300 billion hours of labor.

7. When the labor market is in equilibrium, real GDP ____ potential GDP.
   a. is greater than
   b. is equal to
   c. is less than
   d. might be greater than, less than, or equal to

8. Compared to the 1960s, U.S. potential GDP in the 1990s is
   a. smaller.
   b. approximately the same amount.
   c. larger.
   d. not comparable because the U.S. production function shifted.

Complete the graph

Quantity of labor (billions of hours per year)	Real GDP (billions of 2000 dollars)
0	0
10	400
20	725
30	900
40	960
50	1,000

1. The above table gives data for a nation's production function. In Figure 8.2, draw the production function. Label the axes. How are diminishing returns reflected in the table and in the figure?

■ **FIGURE 8.2**

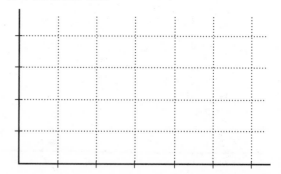

■ **FIGURE 8.3**

Real wage rate (2000 dollars per hour)

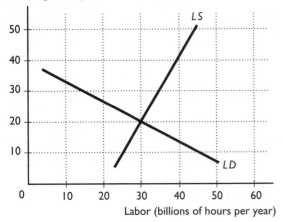

Labor (billions of hours per year)

2. Figure 8.3 illustrates the labor market for the nation with the production function given in the previous problem. In the figure, identify the equilibrium real wage rate and employment. Using the production function in Figure 8.2, what is the nation's potential GDP?

Short answer and numeric questions

1. What is the relationship between equilibrium in the labor market and potential GDP? Be sure to explain the role played by the production function.

2. Suppose a nation's production function shifts upward. If the equilibrium quantity of labor does not change, what is the effect on the nation's potential GDP?

CHECKPOINT 8.3

■ **Explain what creates unemployment when the economy is at full employment and describe the influences on the natural unemployment rate.**

Practice Problem 8.3

1. The economy of Singapore has seen huge changes during the past 50 years. It has experienced rapid population growth and has re-

structured its economy several times to remain at the forefront of latest technology. Singapore has modest unemployment benefits, no minimum wage, and weak labor unions.

   a. Does the unemployment that Singapore experiences arise primarily from job search or job rationing?
   b. Which factors mentioned above suggest that Singapore has a higher natural unemployment rate than the United States?
   c. Which factors mentioned above suggest that Singapore has a lower natural unemployment rate than the United States?

Solution to Practice Problem 8.3

The natural unemployment rate exists because of job search and job rationing. This Practice Problem gives you the opportunity to apply your knowledge of job search and job rationing to the real-world Singapore economy.

Quick Review

- *Job search* Job search is the activity of looking for an acceptable vacant job. Job search is influenced by demographic changes, unemployment benefits, and structural change.
- *Job rationing* Job rationing is a situation that arises when the real wage rate is above the full-employment equilibrium level. An efficiency wage, a minimum wage, or a union wage can lead to job rationing.

   a. **Does the unemployment that Singapore experiences arise primarily from job search or job rationing?**

Singapore does not have a minimum wage, so there is no minimum wage impact on job rationing. Similarly, with weak unions, union wage setting is not likely to cause much job rationing. Of the sources of job rationing, only efficiency wages applies. The most likely source of unemployment is from job search, because rapid population growth means lots of young workers who spend time job searching. And restructuring means workers losing old (vanishing) jobs and searching for new jobs, another source of job search.

b. Which factors mentioned above suggest that Singapore has a higher natural unemployment rate than the United States?

Rapid population growth and restructuring to remain at the forefront of the latest technology suggest that Singapore has a higher natural unemployment rate than the United States.

c. Which factors mentioned above suggest that Singapore has a lower natural unemployment rate than the United States?

The United States has a minimum wage, more generous unemployment benefits, and stronger unions than Singapore. These factors suggest that the United States has a higher natural unemployment rate than Singapore.

Additional Practice Problem 8.3a

Since the 1960s, how has the minimum wage as a percentage of the average wage rate changed in the United States ? What effect would you expect this trend to have on the natural unemployment rate?

Solution to Additional Practice Problem 8.3a

Since 1960 there has been a general downward trend in the minimum wage as a percentage of the average wage rate. The drop was most pronounced between 1967 and 1988, after which the minimum wage has hovered near 40 percent of the average wage rate. We would expect the general downward trend in the minimum wage to reduce the amount of job rationing, decreasing the natural unemployment rate.

■ Self Test 8.3

Fill in the blanks

The unemployment rate at full employment is the ____. The activity of looking for an acceptable vacant job is called ____ (job search; job rationing). An increase in unemployment benefits ____ (decreases; increases) job search. Job rationing occurs when the real wage rate is ____ (above; below) the full-employment equilibrium level. A minimum wage set above the equilibrium wage rate ____ (creates; does not create) unemployment. If the real wage rate is above the full-employment equilibrium level,

the natural unemployment rate ____ (increases; decreases).

True or false

1. The amount of job search depends on a number of factors including demographic change.

2. An increase in unemployment benefits, other things remaining the same, will increase the amount of time spent on job search.

3. Job rationing has no effect on the natural unemployment rate.

4. Job rationing results in a shortage of labor

5. Teenage labor is not affected by the minimum wage.

Multiple choice

1. The two fundamental causes of unemployment are
   a. seasonal jobs and technological change.
   b. foreign competition and financial bankruptcies.
   c. job search and job rationing.
   d. decreases in labor productivity and retirement benefits.

2. In the United States since 1950, the average unemployment rate was highest during the decade of the
   a. 1950s.
   b. 1960s.
   c. 1970s.
   d. 1980s.

3. Job search is defined as
   a. the activity of looking for an acceptable, vacant job.
   b. saying you are looking when you are actually not looking.
   c. attending school to increase your employability.
   d. equivalent to job rationing.

4. The higher unemployment benefits are, the
   a. higher the opportunity cost of job search.
   b. lower the opportunity cost of job search.
   c. shorter the time spent searching and ac-
      cepting a suitable job.
   d. shorter the time spent searching for a suit-
      able job and the higher the opportunity
      cost of being unemployed.

5. The existence of union wages, efficiency
   wages, and the minimum wage
   a. raises the real wage rate above the full-
      employment equilibrium wage rate and
      creates a shortage of labor.
   b. lowers the real wage rate below the full-
      employment equilibrium wage rate and cre-
      ates a shortage of labor.
   c. raises the real wage rate above the full-
      employment equilibrium wage rate and
      raises the natural unemployment rate.
   d. does not have an impact on the full-
      employment equilibrium wage rate or on
      the amount of unemployment.

6. Job rationing occurs if
   a. the minimum wage is set below the equi-
      librium wage rate.
   b. an efficiency wage is set below the equi-
      librium wage rate.
   c. a union wage is set below the equilibrium
      wage rate.
   d. the real wage rate is pushed above the
      equilibrium wage rate.

7. IBM wants to attract the most productive
   and knowledgeable workers. To achieve this
   goal it should pay ____ wage.
   a. an efficiency
   b. a minimum
   c. a nominal
   d. an equilibrium

8. Collective bargaining by unions can result in
   a union wage rate that is ____ the equilibrium real wage rate and creates a ____ of labor.
   a. above; surplus
   b. above; shortage
   c. below; surplus
   d. below; shortage

Complete the graph

■ FIGURE 8.4

Real wage rate (2000 dollars per hour)

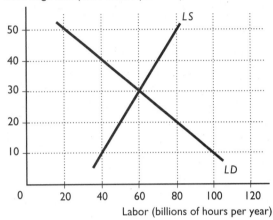

Labor (billions of hours per year)

1. Figure 8.4 illustrates a nation's labor market.
   a. What is the equilibrium wage rate?
   b. What must a firm do to set an efficiency
      wage?
   c. Suppose the government imposes a mini-
      mum wage that creates a surplus of 60 bil-
      lion hours of labor a year. What is the
      minimum wage?
   d. If a union negotiates on behalf of its mem-
      bers, what can you say about the range of
      wage rates the union will try to obtain?
   e. How do your answers to parts (b), (c), and
      (d) compare?

Short answer and numeric questions

Real wage rate (2001 dollars per hour)	Quantity of labor demanded (billions of hours per year)	Quantity of labor supplied (billions of hours per year)
10	180	150
20	160	160
30	140	170
40	120	180

1. The above table gives the labor demand and
   labor supply schedules for a nation.
   a. What is the equilibrium wage rate?
   b. Suppose firms set an efficiency wage of
      $30 an hour. What is the effect of this
      wage rate?

c. Suppose the government sets a minimum wage of $30 an hour. What is the effect of the minimum wage?

d. Suppose unions negotiate a wage rate of $30 an hour. What is the effect of the union wage?

e. How do your answers to parts (b), (c), and (d) compare?

2. The demographics of the United States are such that there will be an increase of young people entering the labor force between 2004 and 2012. What do you predict will be the effect on the U.S. unemployment rate?

3. Why do unemployment benefits affect the natural unemployment rate?

4. An efficiency wage is a real wage rate that is set above the full-employment equilibrium wage rate. Why would a firm pay an efficiency wage?

SELF TEST ANSWERS

■ CHECKPOINT 8.1

Fill in the blanks

The discovery that at full employment, the forces that determine real variables are independent of the forces that determine nominal variables is the <u>classical dichotomy</u>. The inflation rate is a <u>nominal</u> variable; employment is a <u>real</u> variable. Other things remaining the same, the higher the price level, the <u>greater</u> the quantity of real GDP supplied. Potential GDP <u>does not change</u> when the price level increases. Other things remaining the same, the higher the price level, the <u>smaller</u> the quantity of real GDP demanded. The aggregate demand curve <u>shifts</u> when government purchases change. Macroeconomic equilibrium occurs at the point of intersection of the *AD* curve and <u>the *AS* curve</u>. When equilibrium real GDP exceeds potential GDP, there is <u>an above full-employment</u> equilibrium.

True or false

1. True; page 183
2. True; page 183
3. False; page 184
4. False; page 185
5. False; page 186

Multiple choice

1. b; page 182
2. c; page 183
3. b; page 184
4. c; page 184
5. d; page 185
6. d; page 185
7. d; page 186
8. c; page 186

Complete the graph

1. Figure 8.5 labels the two curves. The equilibrium price level is 110 and equilibrium real GDP is $10 trillion. A fall in the money wage rate increases aggregate supply and shifts the aggregate supply curve rightward, from

■ FIGURE 8.5

Price level (GDP deflator, 1996 = 100)

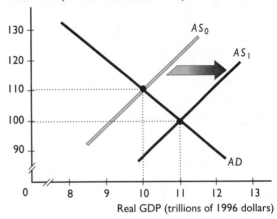

Real GDP (trillions of 1996 dollars)

AS_0 to AS_1. At the new equilibrium real GDP equals $11 trillion and the new equilibrium price level is 100; pages 184-186.

Short answer and numeric questions

1. The classical dichotomy states that when the economy is operating at full employment, the forces that determine the real variables are independent of those that determine the nominal variables. The importance is that we can divide the economy into two sets of variables (the dichotomy), real variables and nominal variables. Then, if we want to study the factors that determine real variables at full employment we can ignore the nominal variables; page 182.

2. The equilibrium price level is 120 and equilibrium real GDP is $13 billion; page 186.

3. When the price level rises, aggregate supply does not change but the quantity of real GDP supplied increases. When the price level rises, aggregate demand does not change but the quantity of real GDP demanded decreases. Potential GDP does not change; pages 183-185.

4. When the price level falls, aggregate supply does not change but the quantity of real GDP supplied decreases. When the price level falls, aggregate demand does not change but the quantity of real GDP demanded in-

creases. Potential GDP does not change; pages 183-185.

5. A below full-employment equilibrium occurs when real GDP is less than potential GDP; page 186.

■ CHECKPOINT 8.2

Fill in the blanks

The relationship that shows the maximum quantity of real GDP that can be produced as the quantity of labor employed changes is the production function. The quantity of labor demanded increases as the real wage rate falls, and the quantity of labor supplied decreases as the real wage rate falls. If the real wage rate exceeds the equilibrium real wage rate, there is a surplus of labor. When the labor market is in equilibrium, there is full employment and real GDP equals potential GDP.

True or false

1. False; page 189
2. False; page 190
3. False; page 191
4. True; page 194
5. True; page 195

Multiple choice

1. a; page 189
2. a; page 189
3. b; page 190
4. b; page 191
5. b; pages 193-194
6. b; pages 194-195
7. b; page 195
8. c; page 196

Complete the graph

1. Figure 8.6 illustrates the production function. In the table, diminishing returns are demonstrated by the fact that each additional 10 billion hours of labor increases real GDP by a smaller amount. In the figure, diminishing returns are illustrated by the slope of the production function, which becomes less steep as the quantity of labor increases; page 190.

■ FIGURE 8.6

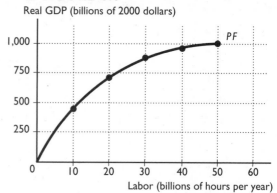

Real GDP (billions of 2000 dollars)

2. The equilibrium real wage rate is $20 an hour and equilibrium employment is 30 billion hours. Potential GDP is $900 billion; page 195.

Short answer and numeric questions

1. The equilibrium quantity of labor is the amount of labor at full employment. The production function shows how much GDP this full-employment quantity of labor produces, and this quantity of GDP is potential GDP; page 195.

2. If the production function shifts upward, the amount of real GDP produced by every quantity of labor increases. The nation's potential GDP increases; pages 195-196.

■ CHECKPOINT 8.3

Fill in the blanks

The unemployment rate at full employment is the natural unemployment rate. The activity of looking for an acceptable, vacant job is called job search. An increase in unemployment benefits increases job search. Job rationing occurs when the real wage rate is above the full-employment equilibrium level. A minimum wage set above the equilibrium wage rate creates unemployment. If the real wage rate is above the full-employment equilibrium level, the natural unemployment rate increases.

True or false

1. True; page 199
2. True; page 199

3. False; page 202
4. False; pages 200-201
5. False; page 201

Multiple choice

1. c; page 199
2. d; page 198
3. a; page 199
4. b; page 199
5. c; page 202
6. d; pages 200-201
7. a; page 201
8. a; page 201

Complete the graph

1. a. The equilibrium wage is $30; page 202.
   b. An efficiency wage is set higher than the equilibrium wage, so the firm must set the wage above $30; pages 201-202.
   c. A minimum wage of $50 an hour creates a labor surplus of 60 billion hours a year; pages 201-202.
   d. The union will strive to set a wage rate that is higher than the competitive wage, so the union will try to set a wage that is higher than $30; pages 201-202.
   e. In each of the answers to parts (b), (c), and (d) there is a labor surplus. So, all three of the events raise the wage rate above its equilibrium and create unemployment; pages 201-202.

Short answer and numeric questions

1. a. The equilibrium wage rate is $20 an hour because that is the wage rate at which the quantity of labor demanded equals the quantity supplied; page 202.

   b. If firms set an efficiency wage of $30 an hour, there is a labor surplus of 30 billion hours a year (170 billion hours supplied minus 140 billion hours demanded); pages 201-202.
   c. If the government sets a minimum wage of $30 an hour, there is a labor surplus of 30 billion hour a year; page 202.
   d. If unions negotiate a wage of $30 an hour, there is a labor surplus of 30 billion hours a year; pages 201-202.
   e. In each of the answers to parts (b), (c), and (d) there is a labor surplus of 30 billion hours a year. All three of the events raise the wage rate above its equilibrium and create unemployment; pages 201-202.

2. The natural unemployment rate increases as more young people enter the labor force and search for jobs. The natural unemployment rate in the United States likely will increase between 2004 and 2012; page 199.

3. If unemployment benefits increase, the opportunity cost of job search decreases. Workers spend more time searching for jobs, so they are unemployed longer and the natural unemployment rate increases; page 199.

4. A firm pays an efficiency wage rate as an incentive to its employees to work hard. The employees will work hard to avoid being fired because they know that if they have to take another job, they are likely to be paid the lower equilibrium wage rate; page 201.

Investment and Saving

Chapter 9

Chapter 9 shows how the nation's capital is replaced and increased through investment. Saving is the amount of income that is not paid in taxes or spent on consumption goods and services. At the financial market equilibrium, the quantity of saving supplied equals the quantity of investment demanded.

■ **Define and explain the relationships among capital, investment, wealth, and saving.**

Physical capital, also called capital, is the tools, machines, buildings, and other constructions that have been produced in the past and are used to produce additional goods and services. Financial capital is the funds firms use to buy and operate physical capital. Gross investment is the total amount spent on new capital goods. Net investment equals gross investment minus depreciation. Net investment is the change in the quantity of capital. Wealth is the value of all the things a person owns. Saving is the amount of income that is not paid in taxes or spent on consumption goods or services. Saving adds to wealth. Financial markets are the collection of households, firms, governments, banks, and other financial markets that lend and borrow. Financial markets determine the price of financial capital, which is expressed as an interest rate.

■ **Explain how investment and saving decisions are made and how these decisions interact in financial markets to determine the real interest rate.**

Firms demand investment goods. Other things remaining the same, the higher the real interest rate, the smaller is the quantity of investment demanded, and the lower the real interest rate, the larger is the quantity of investment demanded. Investment demand is the relationship between the quantity of investment demanded and the real interest rate, other things remaining the same. Investment demand changes when the expected rate of profit changes. Households supply savings. Other things remaining the same, the higher the real interest rate, the greater is the quantity of saving supplied, and the lower the real interest rate, the smaller is the quantity of saving supplied. Saving supply is the relationship between saving and the real interest rate, other things remaining the same. The three main factors that influence saving supply are disposable income, the buying power of net assets, and expected future disposable income. The financial market equilibrium occurs at the real interest rate where the quantity of investment demanded equals the quantity of saving supplied.

■ **Explain how government influences the real interest rate, investment, and saving.**

In the global economy, $I = S + (NT - G)$ where I is investment, S is private saving, and $NT - G$ is government saving. A government budget surplus adds to private saving, lowering the real interest rate and increasing investment. A government budget deficit decreases saving, raising the real interest rate and decreasing (crowding out) investment. The Ricardo-Barro effect says that private saving increases to offset a government budget deficit so that no crowding out occurs.

EXPANDED CHAPTER CHECKLIST

When you have completed this chapter, you will be able to:

1 Define and explain the relationships among capital, investment, wealth, and saving.

- Define physical capital and financial capital, and state how the two are related.
- Define gross investment and net investment and explain the relationship between net investment and capital.
- Define wealth and saving and explain how the two are related.
- Describe financial markets, including stock markets, bond markets, short-term securities markets, and loan markets.

2 Explain how investment and saving decisions are made and how these decisions interact in financial markets to determine the real interest rate.

- Discuss the relationship between the quantity of investment demanded and the real interest rate.
- Draw an investment demand curve and discuss what factors influence investment demand.
- Discuss the relationship between the quantity of saving supplied and the real interest rate.
- Draw a saving supply curve and discuss what factors influence saving supply.
- Draw a figure showing equilibrium in the financial market and use the figure to show how changes in investment demand and saving supply change the real interest rate.

3 Explain how government influences the real interest rate, investment, and saving.

- Explain the formula $I = S + (NT - G)$.

- Describe and illustrate the effect a government budget surplus has on the real interest rate and quantity of investment.
- Describe and illustrate the effect a government budget deficit has on the real interest rate and quantity of investment.
- Define crowding out and describe why it occurs.
- Explain how the Ricardo-Barro effect modifies the conclusions from the crowding-out effect.

KEY TERMS

- Physical capital (page 210)
- Financial capital (page 210)
- Gross investment (page 210)
- Net investment (page 210)
- Wealth (page 212)
- Saving (page 212)
- Financial markets (page 212)
- Stock (page 212)
- Stock market (page 213)
- Bond (page 213)
- Bond market (page 213)
- Investment demand (page 215)
- Saving supply (page 218)
- Disposable income (page 218)
- Crowding-out effect (page 227)

CHECKPOINT 9.1

■ Define and explain the relationships among capital, investment, wealth, and saving.

Practice Problems 9.1

1. Michael is an Internet service provider. On December 31, 2000, he bought an existing business with servers and a building worth $400,000. During his first year of operation, his business grew and he bought new servers for $500,000. The market value of some of his older servers fell by $100,000.

   a. What was Michael's gross investment during 2001?

b. What was Michael's depreciation during 2001?

c. What was Michael's net investment during 2001?

d. What was Michael's capital at the end of 2001?

2. Lori is a student who teaches golf on the weekend and in a year earns $20,000 in fees after paying her taxes. At the beginning of 2000, Lori owned $1,000 worth of books, CDs, and golf clubs and she had $5,000 in a savings account at the bank. During 2000, the interest on her savings account was $300 and she spent a total of $15,300 on consumption goods and services. There was no change in the market values of her books, CDs, and golf clubs.

a. How much did Lori save in 2000?

b. What was Lori's wealth at the end of 2000?

Solution to Practice Problems 9.1

The first problem concentrates on the relationships between investment, net investment, and depreciation. The second problem studies the relationship between saving and wealth.

Quick Review

- *Net investment* Net investment is the change in the quantity of capital and equals gross investment minus depreciation.
- *Wealth* Wealth is the value of all things that a person owns. Wealth at the end of the year equals wealth at the beginning of the year plus saving over the year.

1a. What was Michael's gross investment during 2001?

Gross investment is the total amount spent on new capital goods. Michael's gross investment is what he spent on servers during 2001, so his gross investment was $500,000.

1b. What was Michael's depreciation during 2001?

Depreciation is the decrease in the value of capital that results from its use and obsolescence. Michael's depreciation was $100,000, the

decrease in the market value of some of his servers.

1c. What was Michael's net investment during 2001?

Net investment equals gross investment minus depreciation. Michael's net investment during 2001 is $500,000 – $100,000 = $400,000.

1d. What was Michael's capital at the end of 2001?

Michael's capital at the end of 2001 equals his capital at the beginning of 2000, $400,000, plus his net investment, during 2001, also $400,000, which equals $800,000.

2. **Lori is a student who teaches golf on the weekend and in a year earns $20,000 in fees after paying her taxes. At the beginning of 2000, Lori owned $1,000 worth of books, CDs, and golf clubs and she had $5,000 in a savings account at the bank. During 2000, the interest on her savings account was $300 and she spent a total of $15,300 on consumption goods and services.**

2a. How much did Lori save in 2000?

Lori's saving is her after-tax income minus the amount she spent on consumption. Lori's income was the $20,000 from teaching plus $300 in interest, which is $20,300. Her spending was $15,300, so she saved the difference, $20,300 – $15,300, which is $5,000.

2b. What was Lori's wealth at the end of 2000?

Lori's wealth at the end of 2000 is the wealth she had at the beginning of 2000 plus her saving during 2000. At the start of 2000, she had $1,000 worth of books, CDs, and golf clubs, as well as a savings account balance of $5,000, so her wealth was $6,000. She saved another $5,000 during the year, so her wealth at the end of 2000 is $6,000 + $5,000 = $11,000.

Additional Practice Problem 9.1a

In 2000, the 3-D graphics accelerator company Nvidia wanted to raise $200 million to build a new headquarters building and buy other physical capital. What methods could Nvidia have used to obtain the funds to purchase the capital it needed?

Solution to Additional Practice Problem 9.1a

Nvidia had a number of choices. It could have sold new shares of stock, so the current stockholders would share future profits with new stockholders. Nvidia could have sold bonds, which means it would be borrowing the funds from the buyers of the bonds. The company could have sold short-term securities. Nvida could have arranged a bank loan. If Nvidia sold bonds, short-term securities, or borrowed from a bank, Nvidia would have increased its debt and would be required at some time to repay whoever loaned it the funds. As it happens, Nvidia actually financed its new capital by selling bonds.

■ Self Test 9.1

Fill in the blanks

_____ (Physical; Financial) capital consists of tools, instruments, machines, buildings, and other constructions that have been produced in the past and that are used to produce goods and services. Net investment equals _____ (gross investment; depreciation) minus _____ (gross investment; depreciation). _____ (Saving; Wealth) is the value of all the things people own. A _____ (bond; stock) is a certificate of ownership and claim to the profit that a firm makes and a _____ (bond; stock) is a debt for the issuer.

True or false

1. Financial capital and physical capital are two different names for the same thing.
2. Net investment equals gross investment minus depreciation.
3. The nation's capital stock at the end of 2004 equals the capital stock at the beginning of 2004 plus gross investment during 2004.
4. Wealth and income are the same thing.
5. A bond issued by a firm is a certificate of ownership and claim to the profits that the firm makes.

Multiple choice

1. Which of the following is <u>NOT</u> an example of physical capital?
   a. a building
   b. a bond
   c. a dump truck
   d. a lawn mower

2. The decrease in the value of capital that results from its use and obsolescence is
   a. appreciation.
   b. deconstruction.
   c. depreciation.
   d. None of the above answers are correct.

3. Which of the following formulas is correct?
   a. Net investment = gross investment + depreciation
   b. Net investment = gross investment + capital
   c. Net investment = gross investment – depreciation
   d. Gross investment = net investment – depreciation

4. Intel's capital at the end of the year equals Intel's capital at the beginning of the year
   a. minus its stock dividends.
   b. plus net investment.
   c. minus depreciation.
   d. plus gross investment.

5. U.S. capital at the end of 2003 equals U.S. capital at the beginning of 2003 plus
   a. nothing, because capital can't change in just one year.
   b. gross investment during 2003.
   c. gross investment during 2002 minus net investment in 2003.
   d. net investment during 2003.

6. The Ng's family's wealth at the end of the year equals their wealth at the beginning of the year
   a. minus personal income taxes.
   b. plus saving.
   c. minus consumption.
   d. plus income.

7. Economists use the term "financial markets" to mean the markets in which
   a. firms purchase their physical capital.
   b. firms supply their goods and services.
   c. households supply their labor services.
   d. firms get the funds that they use to buy physical capital.

8. A stockholder ____ an owner of the firm and a bondholder ____ an owner of the firm.
   a. is; is
   b. is; is not
   c. is not; is
   d. is not; is not

Short answer and numeric questions

1. What is the relationship between physical capital and financial capital?

2. What is the difference between gross investment and capital?

3. In 2003, Regis Hair Salon purchased 10 hair dryers for $3,300 each. During the year, depreciation was $13,000. What was the amount of Regis' gross investment and net investment?

Year	Gross investment (trillions of 1996 dollars)	Depreciation (trillions of 1996 dollars)	Net investment (trillions of 1996 dollars)
2003	2.3	0.2	____
2004	2.5	0.3	____
2005	2.8	0.4	____

4. The table above gives gross investment and depreciation for three years.
   a. Complete the net investment column.
   b. If the capital was $22.3 trillion at the beginning of 2003, what was it at the beginning of 2004? 2005? 2006?

CHECKPOINT 9.2

■ **Explain how investment and saving decisions are made and how these decisions interact in financial markets to determine the real interest rate.**

Practice Problems 9.2

1. First Call, Inc. is a cellular phone company. It plans to build an assembly plant that costs $10 million if the real interest rate is 6 percent a year. If the real interest rate is 5 percent a year, First Call will build a larger plant that costs $12 million. And if the real interest rate is 7 percent a year, First Call will build a smaller plant that costs $8 million.
   a. Draw a graph of First Call's investment demand curve.
   b. First Call expects its profit from the sale of cellular phones to double next year. If everything else remains the same, explain how this increase in expected profit influences First Call's investment demand.
   c. In 2005, First Call plans to incorporate a new technology into its cellular phones. If the demand for its phones increases and other things remain the same, explain the influence of the new technology on First Call's investment demand.

2. In 2002, the King family had a disposable income of $50,000, net assets of $100,000, and an expected future disposable income of $50,000 a year. At a real interest rate of 4 percent a year, the King family would save $10,000 a year; at a real interest rate of 6 percent a year, they would save $12,500 a year; and at a real interest rate of 8 percent a year, they would save $15,000 a year.
   a. Draw a graph of the King family's saving supply curve.
   b. In 2003, the King family expects its future disposable income to increase to $60,000 a year. If other things remain the same, explain how this change influences the King family's saving supply.

c. In 2004, the stock market booms and the King family's net assets increase in value. If the King family expects its future disposable income to be $50,000 and other things remain the same, explain how this change influences the King family's saving supply.

3. Draw graphs that illustrate how an increase in saving supply and:

   a. A decrease in investment demand can lower the real interest rate and leave the equilibrium quantity of saving and investment unchanged.

   b. An even larger increase in investment demand increases the equilibrium quantity of saving and investment and raises the real interest rate.

Solution to Practice Problems 9.2

The figure that shows the investment demand curve and the saving supply curve illustrates how the real interest rate is determined. Use this diagram the same way you use the supply and demand figures you studied in Chapter 4. Equilibrium occurs where the investment demand curve intersects the saving supply curve and a shift in either curve changes the equilibrium real interest rate and the equilibrium quantity of investment and saving.

Quick Review

- *Investment demand* The relationship between the quantity of investment demanded and the real interest rate, other things remaining the same.

- *Saving supply* The relationship between the quantity of saving supplied and the real interest rate, other things remaining the same.

1. First Call, Inc. is a cellular phone company. It plans to build an assembly plant that costs $10 million if the real interest rate is 6 percent a year. If the real interest rate is 5 percent a year, First Call will build a larger plant that costs $12 million. And if the real interest rate is 7 percent a year, First Call will build a smaller plant that costs $8 million.

1a. Draw a graph of First Call's investment demand curve.

The investment demand curve shows the relationship between the quantity of investment demanded and the real interest rate. The real interest rate is the opportunity cost of investment, so the quantity of investment First Call demands decreases as the real interest rate rises (because First Call builds a smaller assembly plant). First Call's investment demand curve is the downward sloping curve labeled ID_0 in the figure.

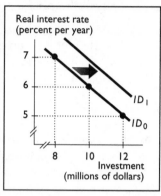

1b. First Call expects its profit from the sale of cellular phones to double next year. If everything else remains the same, explain how this increase in expected profit influences First Call's investment demand.

An increase in expected profit increases investment demand and shifts the investment demand curve rightward. In the above figure, First Call's investment demand curve shifts rightward from ID_0 to ID_1.

1c. In 2005, First Call plans to incorporate a new technology into its cellular phones. If the demand for its phones increases and other things remain the same, explain the influence of the new technology on First Call's investment demand.

To use the new technology, the firm must replace existing equipment and buy new equipment. Investment demand increases and the investment demand curve shifts rightward. In the above figure, First Call's investment demand curve shifts rightward from ID_0 to ID_1.

2. In 2002, the King family had a disposable income of $50,000, net assets of $100,000, and an expected future disposable income of $50,000 a year. At a real interest rate of 4 percent a

year, the King family would save $10,000 a year; at a real interest rate of 6 percent a year, they would save $12,500 a year; and at a real interest rate of 8 percent a year, they would save $15,000 a year.

2a. Draw a graph of the King family's saving supply curve.

The figure illustrates the King family's saving supply curve. The saving supply curve, SS_0, slopes upward because an increase in the real interest rate increases the quantity the King family will save.

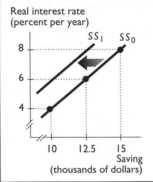

2b. In 2003, the King family expects its future disposable income to increase to $60,000 a year. If other things remain the same, explain how this change influences the King family's saving supply.

An increase in expected future income decreases the amount of saving at each real interest rate. The King family's saving supply decreases and the saving supply curve shifts leftward. In the above figure, the saving supply curve shifts leftward from SS_0 to SS_1.

2c. In 2004, the stock market booms and the buying power of the King family's net assets increase in value. If the King family expects its future disposable income to be $50,000 and other things remain the same, explain how this change influences the King family's saving supply.

An increase in the buying power of net assets decreases the amount people save at each real interest rate. The King family's saving supply decreases and the saving supply curve shifts leftward, In the above figure, the saving supply curve shifts leftward from SS_0 to SS_1.

3. Draw graphs that illustrate how an increase in saving supply and:

3a. A decrease in investment demand can lower the real interest rate and leave the equilibrium quantity of saving and investment unchanged.

An increase in saving supply shifts the saving supply curve rightward. A decrease in investment demand shifts the investment demand curve leftward. If the two shifts are same magnitude, the equilibrium quantity does not change. In the figure, the real interest rate falls from 6 percent a year to 5 percent a year and the equilibrium of saving and investment remains at $10 trillion.

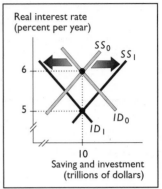

3b. An even larger increase in investment demand increases the equilibrium quantity of saving and investment and raises the real interest rate.

The increase in saving supply shifts the saving supply curve rightward. The increase in investment demand shifts the investment demand curve rightward. The shift in the investment demand curve exceeds the shift in the saving supply curve, so, as illustrated in the figure, the real interest rate rises and the quantity of investment and saving increases.

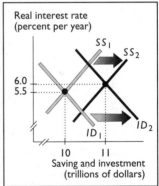

Additional Practice Problem 9.2a

Suppose you buy a lottery ticket and the top prize is $10 million. Your current income is $30,000 a year and you save $1,500 a year. Glory be, you win the lottery and your income this year is $10,030,000! Do you think you will save more or less than $1,500 this year? In your answer, focus on the amount of your income this year and what you expect it to be in the future.

Solution to Additional Practice Problem 9.2a

You will save more than $1,500 this year. First, your disposable income is much higher this year, and saving increases when disposable income increases. Second, your expected future income is much lower than your income this year because you cannot expect to win the lottery two years running! When expected future income is lower, saving increases. For both reasons you will save a *lot* more than $1,500.

■ Self Test 9.2

Fill in the blanks

Other things remaining the same, the higher the real interest rate, the ____ (greater; smaller) the quantity of investment demanded. Population growth ____ (increases; decreases) investment demand. Other things remaining the same, the higher the real interest rate, the ____ (greater; smaller) the quantity of saving supplied. An increase in disposable income ____ (increases; decreases) saving. When saving supply increases, the saving supply curve shifts ____ (rightward; leftward). The financial market is in equilibrium when the quantity of saving supplied ____ the quantity of investment demanded.

True or false

1. Other things remaining the same, the higher the real interest rate, the smaller the quantity of investment demanded.

2. When the expected rate of profit changes, there is a movement along the investment demand curve.

3. The real interest rate is the opportunity cost of consumption expenditure.

4. An increase in the buying power of net assets leads to a decrease in saving.

5. If the real interest rate is greater than the equilibrium real interest rate, there is a shortage of saving in the financial market.

Multiple choice

1. If the real interest rate decreases, other things being the same, the quantity of investment
   a. demanded increases.
   b. demanded decreases.
   c. supplied increases.
   d. demanded and supplied does not change.

2. Investment demand
   a. increases in a recession.
   b. decreases in an expansion.
   c. increases when firms are optimistic about their future prospects.
   d. None of the above is correct.

3. As the real interest rate rises, the quantity of saving supplied ____ and the quantity of investment demanded ____.
   a. increases; increases
   b. increases; decreases
   c. decreases; increases
   d. decreases; decreases

4. An increase in the buying power of a household's net assets leads to
   a. an increase in savings.
   b. an increase in investment.
   c. a decrease in savings.
   d. a decrease in investment.

5. If the real interest rate falls, there is
   a. an upward movement along the saving supply curve.
   b. a downward movement along the saving supply curve.
   c. a rightward shift of the saving supply curve.
   d. a leftward shift of the saving supply curve.

6. If, at the current interest rate, the quantity of saving supplied is less than the quantity of investment demanded, then the
   a. saving supply curve will shift rightward and the interest rate will rise.
   b. saving supply curve will shift leftward and the interest rate will fall.
   c. interest rate will fall.
   d. interest rate will rise.

7. In the financial market, the real interest rate changes until
   a. saving supply is greater than investment demand.
   b. saving supply is smaller than investment demand.
   c. saving supply and investment demand are equal.
   d. the quantity of saving supplied equals the quantity of investment demanded.

8. If the economy enters a recession, the investment demand curve shifts _____ and the real interest rate _____.
   a. rightward; rises
   b. rightward; falls
   c. leftward; rises
   d. leftward; falls

Complete the graph

■ FIGURE 9.1

Real interest rate (percent per year)

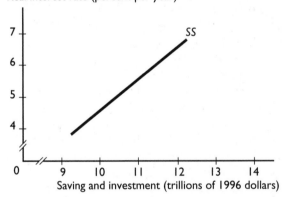

Saving and investment (trillions of 1996 dollars)

1. Figure 9.1 shows a saving supply curve.
   a. Suppose disposable income increases. Show the effect of this change on saving supply in Figure 9.1.
   b. Suppose the buying power of net assets increases. Show the effect of this change on saving supply in Figure 9.1.

2. The table in the right column gives a saving supply schedule and an investment demand schedule.
   a. Label the axes and then draw the saving supply curve and investment demand curve in Figure 9.2.

Real interest rate (percent per year)	Investment (trillions of 1996 dollars)	Saving (trillions of 1996 dollars)
4	12	10
5	11	11
6	10	12
7	9	13

■ FIGURE 9.2

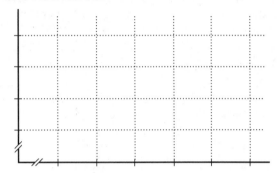

   b. What is the equilibrium real interest rate? What is the equilibrium quantity of investment and saving?
   c. Suppose that firms become more optimistic about the expected rate of profit. In Figure 9.2, show this change. What is the effect on the real interest rate and quantity of investment and saving?

Short answer and numeric questions

1. Why does an increase in the real interest rate decrease the quantity of investment demanded?
2. What factors shift the investment demand curve? The saving supply curve?
3. Why is the real interest rate the opportunity cost of consumption expenditure?
4. Suppose the real interest rate is less than its equilibrium value. What forces drive the real interest rate to its equilibrium?

CHECKPOINT 9.3

■ **Explain how government influences the real interest rate, investment, and saving.**

Practice Problem 9.3

1. The table shows the investment demand schedule and the supply schedule of private saving.

Real interest rate (percent per year)	Investment	Private saving
	(trillions of 1996 dollars per year)	
4	8.5	5.5
5	8.0	6.0
6	7.5	6.5
7	7.0	7.0
8	6.5	7.5
9	6.0	8.0
10	5.5	8.5

   a. If the government budget surplus is $1 trillion, what are the real interest rate, the quantity of investment, and the quantity of private saving? Is there any crowding out in this situation?

   b. If the government budget deficit is $1 trillion, what are the real interest rate, the quantity of investment, and the quantity of private saving? Is there any crowding out in this situation?

   c. If the Ricardo-Barro effect occurs, how do your answers to part (a) and part (b) change?

Solution to Practice Problem 9.3

The effect of the government budget on the real interest rate is almost always newsworthy. Financial commentators frequently discuss the effect of changing the budget surplus on interest rates. This problem gives you valuable practice in understanding this key macroeconomic issue.

Quick Review

- *Government saving* Government saving equals net taxes minus government purchases, or $NT - G$.

- *Crowding-out effect* The tendency for a government budget deficit to decrease investment.

- *Ricardo-Barro effect* A government deficit has no effect on the real interest rate or investment.

a. **If the government budget surplus is $1 trillion, what are the real interest rate, the quantity of investment, and the quantity of private saving? Is there any crowding out in this situation?**

With no budget deficit or surplus, private saving is total saving. The real interest rate is 7 percent a year and the quantity of investment and saving is $7.0 trillion. When the government has a $1 trillion surplus, it is adding that amount to saving, so at an interest rate of 7 percent, there is a surplus of saving. The real interest rate falls. When the real interest rate falls to 6 percent, the quantity of private saving is $6.5 trillion and the total quantity of saving is $7.5 trillion. The quantity of investment demand is also $7.5 trillion. The total quantity of saving supplied equals the quantity of investment demanded. So the real interest rate is 6 percent, the quantity of private saving is $6.5 trillion, and the quantity of investment is $7.5 trillion. There is no crowding out.

b. **If the government budget deficit is $1 trillion, what are the real interest rate, the quantity of investment, and the quantity of private saving? Is there any crowding out in this situation?**

If the government runs a $1 trillion deficit, total saving at every real interest rate is $1 trillion less than the private saving shown in the table. When the real interest rate is 8 percent, the quantity of total saving supplied is $6.5 trillion (the $7.5 private saving "plus" the negative $1 trillion government saving). The quantity of investment demanded is $6.5 trillion, so the real interest rate of 8 percent is the equilibrium rate. Private saving is $7.5 trillion and investment is $6.5 trillion. In comparison to the situation with no government deficit, $0.5 trillion of investment has been crowded out.

c. **If the Ricardo-Barro effect occurs, how do your answers to part (a) and part (b) change?**

If the Ricardo-Barro effect occurs, then when the government has a $1 trillion surplus in part (a), private saving decreases by $1 trillion and there is no change in the equilibrium real interest rate. And when the government has a deficit of $1 trillion in part (b), private saving increases by $1 trillion and again there is no change in the equilibrium real interest rate. There is no crowding out because the real interest rate does not change.

Additional Practice Problem 9.3a

If the Ricardo-Barro effect occurs, what is the impact of a government budget deficit or surplus? Does the size of the deficit or surplus matter?

Solution to Additional Practice Problem 9.3a

The Ricardo-Barro effect says that government deficits and surpluses do not matter. They have no effect on the real interest rate or on investment. Whether a deficit or surplus is large or small is inconsequential; it still does not change the real interest rate. According to the Ricardo-Barro effect, concern about the government's budget is misplaced!

■ Self Test 9.3

Fill in the blanks

Total saving equals private saving _____ (plus; minus) government saving. A government budget surplus _____ (increases; decreases) government saving. The crowding-out effect is the tendency for a government budget deficit to _____ (increase; decrease) private investment. The Ricardo-Barro effect says that an increase in the government deficit will lead to _____ (an increase; a decrease) in private saving supply.

True or false

1. Investment, I, is financed by private saving, S, and government saving, $G - NT$.

2. An increase in government saving leads to a fall in the real interest rate.

3. An increase in government saving leads to an increase in investment.

4. The crowding-out effect is the tendency of a government budget surplus to crowd out private saving.

5. The Ricardo-Barro effect holds that the government budget deficit has no effect on the real interest rate or investment.

Multiple choice

1. A government budget surplus
   a. increases total saving supply in the global economy.
   b. increases investment demand in the global economy.
   c. decreases total saving supply in the global economy.
   d. decreases investment demand in the global economy.

2. For the world as a whole, suppose net taxes are greater than government purchases. Then
   a. private saving is equal to investment.
   b. private saving is greater than investment.
   c. private saving is less than investment.
   d. there is a budget deficit.

3. $(NT - G)$ is
   a. always positive.
   b. always negative.
   c. positive if the government runs a budget surplus.
   d. negative if the government runs a budget surplus.

4. During 2004, the world has net taxes of $5 trillion, government purchases of $4 trillion, and private savings of $6 trillion. Investment equals
   a. $5 trillion.
   b. $7 trillion.
   c. $10 trillion.
   d. $15 trillion.

5. If there is no Ricardo-Barro effect, a government surplus means that the real interest rate
   a. increases because the investment demand curve shifts rightward.
   b. falls because the investment demand curve shifts leftward.
   c. increases because the saving supply curve shifts leftward.
   d. falls because the saving supply curve shifts rightward.

6. The "crowding-out effect" refers to how a government budget deficit
   a. shifts the saving supply curve leftward.
   b. shifts the investment demand curve leftward.
   c. increases the equilibrium quantity of investment.
   d. decreases the equilibrium quantity of investment.

7. If there is no Ricardo-Barro effect, a government budget deficit will ____ the equilibrium real interest rate and ____ the equilibrium quantity of investment.
   a. raise; increase
   b. raise; decrease
   c. lower; increase
   d. lower; decrease

8. The Ricardo-Barro effect says that government budget deficits lead to
   a. a higher real interest rate.
   b. a lower real interest rate.
   c. no change in the real interest rate.
   d. an increase in investment demand.

Complete the graph

Real interest rate (percent per year)	Investment (trillions of 1996 dollars)	Private saving (trillions of 1996 dollars)
4	12	10
5	11	11
6	10	12
7	9	13

1. The above table has a private saving supply schedule and an investment demand schedule.
   a. Label the axes and then draw the private saving supply and investment demand curves in Figure 9.3.
   b. If the government has no budget deficit or surplus, what is the equilibrium real interest rate and quantity of investment?
   c. If the government has a $2 trillion deficit, and there is no Ricardo-Barro effect, draw the saving supply curve in Figure 9.3. What is the equilibrium real interest rate and quantity of investment?

■ **FIGURE 9.3**

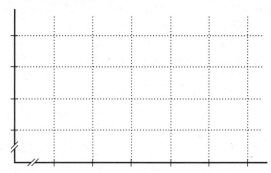

   d. If the government has a $2 trillion deficit, and there is a Ricardo-Barro effect, draw the saving supply curve in Figure 9.3. What is the equilibrium real interest rate and quantity of investment?

Short answer and numeric questions

Row	Investment	Private saving	Net taxes	Government purchases
		(trillions of 1996 dollars)		
A	12	13	5	___
B	12	11	5	___
C	___	10	6	4
D	11	___	7	6

1. The above table gives global data for investment, private saving, net taxes, and government purchases.
   a. Complete the table.
   b. What was government saving in Row A? Row B? Row C? Row D?
   c. In which rows did the government have a budget deficit? A budget surplus?
   d. What is the relationship between your answers to parts (b) and (c)?

2. What is the crowding-out effect?

3. How does the Ricardo-Barro effect modify the conclusion of the crowding-out effect?

SELF TEST ANSWERS

■ CHECKPOINT 9.1

Fill in the blanks

<u>Physical</u> capital consists of tools, instruments, machines, buildings, and other constructions that have been produced in the past and that are used to produce goods and services. Net investment equals <u>gross investment</u> minus <u>depreciation</u>. <u>Wealth</u> is the value of all the things people own. A <u>stock</u> is a certificate of ownership and claim to the profits that a firm makes and a <u>bond</u> is a debt for issuer.

True or false

1. False; page 210
2. True; page 210
3. False; page 211
4. False; page 212
5. False; page 213

Multiple choice

1. b; page 210
2. c; page 210
3. c; page 210
4. b; page 210
5. d; page 211
6. b; page 212
7. d; page 212
8. b; pages 212-213

Short answer and numeric questions

1. Physical capital is the tools, machines, buildings, and other constructions that have been produced in the past and are used to produce additional goods and services. Financial capital is the funds firms use to buy and operate physical capital. Hence a firm needs financial capital in order to buy a piece of physical capital; page 210.
2. Capital is the tools, machines, buildings, and other constructions that have been produced in the past and are used to produce additional goods and services. Investment is the purchase of new capital, so investment adds to the total amount of the nation's capital; page 210.

3. Regis' gross investment was $33,000, and net investment, which equals gross investment minus depreciation, was $20,000; page 210.
4. a. Net investment is gross investment minus depreciation, and is $2.1 trillion in 2003, $2.2 trillion in 2004, and $2.4 trillion in 2005; page 210.
   b. The capital changes by the amount of net investment. The capital stock at the beginning of 2004 is $24.4 trillion, at the beginning of 2005 is $26.6 trillion, and at the beginning of 2006 is $29.0 trillion; page 211.

■ CHECKPOINT 9.2

Fill in the blanks

Other things remaining the same, the higher the real interest rate, the <u>smaller</u> the quantity of investment demanded. Population growth <u>increases</u> investment demand. Other things remaining the same, the higher the real interest rate, the <u>greater</u> the quantity of saving supplied. An increase in disposable income <u>increases</u> saving. When saving supply increases, the saving supply curve shifts <u>rightward</u>. The financial market is in equilibrium when the quantity of saving supplied <u>equals</u> the quantity of investment demanded.

True or false

1. True; page 215
2. False; pages 216-217
3. True; page 218
4. True; page 219
5. False; page 221

Multiple choice

1. a; page 215
2. c; page 217
3. b; pages 215, 218
4. c; page 219
5. b; page 218
6. d; page 221
7. d; page 221
8. d; pages 216, 221

Complete the graph

■ FIGURE 9.4

Real interest rate (percent per year)

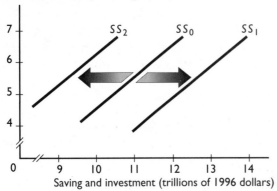

Saving and investment (trillions of 1996 dollars)

1. a. An increase in disposable income increases saving and the saving supply curve shifts rightward, from SS_0 to SS_1 in Figure 9.4; pages 218-219.

   b. An increase in the buying power of net assets decreases saving and the saving supply curve shifts leftward, from SS_0 to SS_2; page 219.

■ FIGURE 9.5

Real interest rate (percent per year)

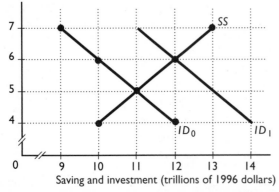

Saving and investment (trillions of 1996 dollars)

2. a. The axes are labeled and the curves are drawn in Figure 9.5. The saving supply curve is SS and the investment demand curve is ID_0; page 221.

   b. The equilibrium real interest rate is 5 percent a year. The equilibrium quantity of investment and saving is $11 trillion; page 221.

c. The increase in optimism increases investment demand and shifts the investment demand curve rightward from ID_0 to ID_1. The real interest rate rises and the quantity of investment and saving increases; page 217.

Short answer and numeric questions

1. The real interest rate is the opportunity cost of the funds used to finance the purchase of capital. The funds used to finance investment might be borrowed, or they might be the financial resources of the firm's owners. The opportunity cost of both sources of funds is the real interest rate. In the case of borrowed funds, the real interest rate is the opportunity cost because it is what is really paid to the lender. In the case of the owners' funds, the real interest rate is the opportunity cost because the funds could be loaned and earn the real interest rate. An increase in the real interest rate increases the opportunity cost of financing investment and so the quantity of investment demanded decreases; page 215.

2. The investment demand curve shifts when the expected rate of profit changes. Technological change, changes in the phase of the business cycle, population growth, subjective influences, and contagion effects all change the expected rate of profit and shift the investment demand curve. The saving supply curve shifts when disposable income, the buying power of net assets, and expected future disposable income change; pages 216, 219, 220.

3. If a dollar is spent on current consumption, it cannot be saved. If the dollar is saved, it would earn the real interest rate. Hence the real interest rate is what is forgone by spending a dollar on consumption and so the real interest rate is the opportunity cost of consumption; page 217.

4. If the real interest rate is less than the equilibrium real interest rate, the quantity of investment demanded exceeds the quantity of saving supplied. Borrowers can't find all the loans they want, but lenders are able to lend

all the funds they have available. So the real interest rate rises and the quantity of investment demanded decreases, while the quantity of saving supplied increases. The equilibrium occurs when the quantity of investment demanded equals the quantity of saving supplied; page 221.

■ CHECKPOINT 9.3

Fill in the blanks

Total saving equals private saving <u>plus</u> government saving. A government budget surplus <u>increases</u> government saving. The crowding-out effect is the tendency for a government budget deficit to <u>decrease</u> private investment. The Ricardo-Barro effect says that an increase in the government deficit will lead to <u>an increase</u> in private saving supply.

True or false

1. False; page 225
2. True; pages 225-226
3. True; page 226
4. False; page 227
5. True; page 227

Multiple choice

1. a; page 225
2. c; page 225
3. c; page 225
4. b; page 225
5. d; pages 225-226
6. d; page 227
7. b; page 227
8. c; page 227

Complete the graph

■ FIGURE 9.6

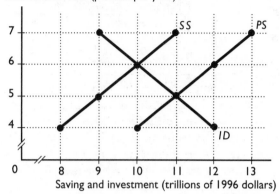
Real interest rate (percent per year)

Saving and investment (trillions of 1996 dollars)

1. a. Figure 9.6 labels the axes and plots the curves. The private saving supply curve is *PS* and the investment demand curve is *ID*; page 226.

   b. If the government has no budget deficit or surplus, the private saving supply curve is the same as the total saving supply curve. The equilibrium real interest rate is 5 percent a year and the equilibrium quantity of investment is $11 trillion; page 226.

   c. The total saving supply is labeled *SS* in Figure 9.6. At any interest rate, the quantity of total saving equals the quantity of private saving minus the government budget deficit of $2 trillion. The equilibrium real interest rate is 6 percent and the equilibrium quantity of investment is $10 trillion; page 227

   d. With a Ricardo-Barro effect and a $2 trillion government deficit, private saving increases. At every interest rate, the quantity of private saving is $2 trillion more than the amount given in the table. Total saving, the sum of private saving plus the government deficit, is the same as the initial total saving curve, *PS*. The equilibrium real interest rate is 5 percent and the equilibrium quantity of investment is $11 trillion, the same as in part (a); page 227.

Short answer and numeric questions

Row	Investment	Private saving	Net taxes	Government purchases
		(trillions of 1996 dollars)		
A	12	13	5	<u>6</u>
B	12	11	5	<u>4</u>
C	<u>12</u>	10	6	4
D	11	<u>10</u>	7	6

1. a. The completed table is above; page 225.

   b. Government saving is –$1 trillion in Row A; $1 trillion in Row B; $2 trillion in Row C; and $1 trillion in Row D; page 225.

   c. The government has a budget deficit in Row A and budget surpluses in Rows B, C, and D; page 225.

   d. When government saving is negative, as in Row A, the government has a budget deficit. When government saving is positive, as in Rows B, C, and D, the government has a budget surplus; page 225.

2. The crowding-out effect is the tendency for a government budget deficit to decrease private investment; page 227.

3. The Ricardo-Barro effect says that private savers increase their saving in response to a government budget deficit. The private saving supply curve shifts to offset any change in government saving. In this case, a government budget deficit has no effect on investment or the real interest rate; page 227.

Economic Growth

CHAPTER IN PERSPECTIVE

Chapter 10 discusses the factors that determine economic growth, studies different theories that explain economic growth, and examines possible government polices to speed economic growth.

■ **Define and calculate the economic growth rate, and explain the implications of sustained growth.**

Economic growth is a sustained expansion of production possibilities measured as the increase in real GDP over a given time period. The economic growth rate is the annual percentage change of real GDP. The standard of living depends on real GDP per person, which equals real GDP divided by the population. The Rule of 70 is that the number of years it takes a variable to double approximately equals 70 divided by the annual growth rate of the variable.

■ **Identify the main sources of economic growth.**

Real GDP grows when the quantities of the factors of production grow or when technology advances. Labor productivity is the quantity of real GDP produced by one hour of labor. When labor productivity grows, real GDP per person grows. Growth of labor productivity depends on saving and investment in more physical capital, acquisition of more human capital, and discovery of better technologies. The productivity curve is a relationship that shows how labor productivity changes as the amount of physical capital per hour of labor changes with a given state of technology. The one third rule is that on the average with no change in human capital or technology, a one percent increase in capital per hour of labor brings about a one third percent increase in labor productivity. The productivity curve shifts upward when technology advances or human capital increases.

■ **Review the theories of economic growth that explain why growth rates vary over time and across countries.**

The classical theory predicts that labor productivity growth is temporary. If real GDP rises above the subsistence level, a population explosion occurs so that labor productivity falls and real GDP per person returns to the subsistence level. The neoclassical theory asserts that real GDP per person will increase as long as technology keeps advancing. But technological change is assumed to be random. The new growth theory emphasizes that technological change results from our choices, and predicts that our unlimited wants will lead us to ever greater productivity and perpetual economic growth.

■ **Describe policies that might speed economic growth.**

The preconditions for economic growth are economic freedom, property rights, and markets. Governments can increase economic growth by creating incentives to save, invest, and innovate; by encouraging saving; by encouraging research and development; by encouraging international trade; and by improving the quality of education.

EXPANDED CHAPTER CHECKLIST

When you have completed this chapter, you will be able to:

1 Define and calculate the economic growth rate, and explain the implications of sustained growth.

- Define the economic growth rate.
- Calculate the growth rate of real GDP.
- Explain the relationship between the standard of living and real GDP per person.
- Calculate the growth rate of real GDP per person.
- Explain and be able to use the Rule of 70.

2 Identify the main sources of economic growth.

- Explain why growth in real GDP can be divided into growth in aggregate hours and growth in labor productivity.
- Tell how labor productivity is calculated, and discuss the importance of growth in labor productivity.
- List and explain the three sources of growth in labor productivity.
- Illustrate a productivity curve and distinguish the factors that shift the curve from those that create a movement along the curve.
- Explain the law of diminishing returns.
- Use the one third rule to identify the contribution of capital growth to labor productivity growth.

3 Review the theories of economic growth that explain why growth rates vary over time and across countries.

- Describe the classical growth theory and explain why it predicts a return to the subsistence level.
- Describe the neoclassical growth theory and explain why it predicts that the na-

tional level of real GDP per person and national growth rates will converge.
- Describe the new growth theory and explain why it predicts national growth rates will not necessarily converge.
- Compare the predictions of each growth theory with the facts in the global economy.

4 Describe policies that might speed economic growth.

- List and explain the preconditions for economic growth.
- Describe the five policies the government can take to achieve faster economic growth.
- Discuss the extent to which government policy can affect economic growth.

KEY TERMS

- Economic growth rate (page 234)
- Real GDP per person (page 234)
- Rule of 70 (page 235)
- Labor productivity (page 238)
- Productivity curve (page 241)
- One third rule (page 243)
- Classical growth theory (page 245)
- Malthusian theory (page 245)
- Neoclassical growth theory (page 247)
- New growth theory (page 249)
- Economic freedom (page 255)
- Property rights (page 255)

CHECKPOINT 10.1

■ **Define and calculate the economic growth rate, and explain the implications of sustained growth.**

Practice Problem 10.1

Mexico's real GDP was 1,448 billion pesos in 1998 and 1,501 billion pesos in 1999. Mexico's population growth rate in 1999 was 1.8 percent. Calculate

a. Mexico's economic growth rate in 1999.

b. The growth rate of real GDP per person in Mexico in 1999.

c. The approximate number of years it takes for real GDP per person in Mexico to double if the 1999 economic growth rate and population growth rate are maintained.

d. The approximate number of years it takes for real GDP per person in Mexico to double if the 1999 economic growth rate is maintained but the population growth rate slows to 1 percent per year.

Solution to Practice Problem 10.1

This question uses three growth rate formulas. The first is the formula that calculates the economic growth rate; the second is the formula that calculates the growth rate of real GDP per person; the third is the Rule of 70.

Quick Review

- *Growth rate* The growth rate of real GDP equals

$$\frac{\left(\begin{array}{c}\text{Real GDP in}\\\text{current year}\end{array}\right) - \left(\begin{array}{c}\text{Real GDP in}\\\text{previous year}\end{array}\right)}{\left(\text{Real GDP in previous year}\right)} \times 100$$

- *Growth rate of real GDP per person* The growth rate of real GDP per person is

(growth rate of real GDP)–(growth rate of population).

- *Rule of 70* The number of years it takes for the level of any variable to double is approximately 70 divided by the annual percentage growth rate of the variable.

a. Mexico's economic growth rate in 1999.

The economic growth rate is the growth rate of real GDP. Mexico's economic growth rate in 1999 equals [(Real GDP in 1999 – Real GDP in 1998) ÷ Real GDP in 1998] × 100. Real GDP in 1998 is 1,448 billion pesos and real GDP in 1999 is 1,501 billion pesos. So the economic growth rate is [(1,501 billion – 1,448 billion) ÷ 1,448 billion] × 100, which is 3.7 percent.

b. The growth rate of real GDP per person in Mexico in 1999.

The growth rate of real GDP per person equals the growth rate of real GDP minus the growth rate of the population. The rate of growth of

real GDP is 3.7 percent from part (a) and the population growth rate is 1.8 percent. The growth rate of real GDP per person is 3.7 percent – 1.8 percent, which equals 1.9 percent.

c. The approximate number of years it takes for real GDP per person in Mexico to double if the 1999 economic growth rate and population growth rate are maintained.

The number of years it takes for real GDP per person to double is given by the Rule of 70, which tells us that the level of a variable that grows at 1.9 percent per year will double in 70 ÷ 1.9 or approximately 37 years.

d. The approximate number of years it takes for real GDP per person in Mexico to double if the 1999 economic growth rate is maintained, but the population growth rate slows to 1 percent per year.

A change in the population growth rate, with all other things remaining the same, changes the growth rate of real GDP per person. The new growth rate of real GDP per person equals the growth rate of real GDP, 3.7 percent, minus the growth rate of the population, 1 percent, so the growth rate of real GDP person is 2.7 percent. Next, use the Rule of 70 to determine how long it will take for real GDP per person to double: real GDP per person doubles in 70 ÷ 2.7 or approximately 26 years.

Additional Practice Problem 10.1a

In the nation of Transylvania in 2001, real GDP was $3.0 million and the population was 1,000. In 2002, real GDP was $3.3 million and the population was 1,050.

a. What is Transylvania's economic growth in 2002?

b. What is the population growth rate?

c. What is Transylvania's growth rate of real GDP per person?

d. Did Transylvania's standard of living rise?

e. Approximately how long will it take for real GDP per person to double?

Solution to Additional Practice Problem 10.1a

a. What is Transylvania's economic growth in 2002?

Transylvania's economic growth rate equals [($3.3 million − $3.0 million) ÷ $3.0 million] × 100 = 10 percent.

b. What is the population growth rate?

Transylvania's population growth rate equals [(1,050 − 1,000) ÷ 1,000] × 100 = 5 percent.

c. What is Transylvania's real GDP per person growth rate?

Transylvania's real GDP per person growth rate equals the growth rate of real GDP minus the growth rate of the population, or 10 percent − 5 percent = 5 percent.

d. Did Transylvania's standard of living rise?

Transylvania's real GDP per person rose, so Transylvania's standard of living increased.

e. Approximately how long will it take for real GDP per person to double?

Transylvania's real GDP per person is growing at 5 percent per year, so it will take approximately 70 ÷ 5 or 14 years for Transylvania's real GDP per person to double.

■ Self Test 10.1

Fill in the blanks

The growth rate of real GDP equals real GDP in the current year minus real GDP in the previous year divided by real GDP ____ in the (current; previous) year, all multiplied by 100. The growth rate of real GDP per person equals the growth rate of real GDP ____ (minus; plus) the growth rate of the population. The number of years it takes for the level of any variable to double is approximately ____ divided by the annual percentage growth rate of the variable.

True or false

1. If real GDP last year was $1.00 trillion and real GDP this year is $1.05 trillion, the growth rate of real GDP this year is 5 percent.

2. Real GDP per person equals real GDP divided by the population.

3. If a nation's population grows at 2 percent and its real GDP grows at 4 percent, then the growth rate of real GDP per person is 2 percent.

4. If real GDP is growing at 2 percent a year, it will take 70 years for real GDP to double.

Multiple choice

1. The economic growth rate is measured as the
   a. annual percentage change of real GDP.
   b. annual percentage change of employment.
   c. level of real GDP.
   d. annual percentage change of the population.

2. Real GDP is $9 trillion in the current year and $8.6 trillion in the previous year. The economic growth rate in the current year is
   a. 10.31 percent.
   b. 4.65 percent.
   c. 5.67 percent.
   d. 7.67 percent.

3. The standard of living is measured by
   a. real GDP.
   b. employment.
   c. employment per person.
   d. real GDP per person.

4. If the growth rate of population is greater than a nation's growth rate of real GDP, then its real GDP per person
   a. falls.
   b. rises.
   c. does not change.
   d. might rise or fall.

5. If real GDP increases by 3 percent a year and at the same time the population increases by 1 percent a year, then real GDP per person grows by
   a. 4 percent.
   b. 2 percent.
   c. 3 percent.
   d. by some amount that cannot be determined without more information.

6. If a country experiences a real GDP growth rate of 4 percent a year, real GDP will double in
   a. 14 years.
   b. 17.5 years.
   c. 23.3 years.
   d. 35 years.

Short answer and numeric questions

Year	Real GDP (billions of 1996 dollars)
2000	100.0
2001	110.0
2002	121.0
2003	133.1

1. The above table gives the real GDP of a nation. What is the growth rate of real GDP in 2001? In 2002? In 2003?

2. The table below gives the growth rate of real GDP and the growth rate of population for a nation.

Year	Real GDP growth rate (percent)	Population growth rate (percent)
2000	3	2
2001	4	2
2002	1	2
2003	4	4

   a. What is the growth rate of real GDP per person for each year?
   b. In what years did the standard of living improve?

3. If a nation's real GDP grows at 4 percent a year, how long does it take for real GDP to double? If the growth rate is 5 percent, how long does it take for real GDP to double?

CHECKPOINT 10.2

■ **Identify the main sources of economic growth.**

Practice Problem 10.2

The table below provides some data on the Canadian economy in 1998 and 1999.

Item	1998	1999
Aggregate hours (billions)	25.0	25.2
Real GDP (billions of 1992 dollars)	840	880
Capital per hour of labor (1992 dollars)	127	130

   a. Calculate the growth rate of real GDP in 1999.
   b. Calculate labor productivity in 1998 and 1999.
   c. Calculate the growth rate of labor productivity in 1999.
   d. If the one third rule applies in Canada, what were the sources of labor productivity growth in 1999? Explain your answer.

Solution to Practice Problem 10.2

This question focuses on growth rates, labor productivity, and the one third rule.

Quick Review

- *Labor productivity* Labor productivity equals real GDP divided by aggregate hours. When labor productivity grows, real GDP per person grows.
- *One third rule* On the average, with no change in human capital or technology, a *one percent* increase in capital per hour of labor brings a *one third percent* increase in labor productivity.

   a. Calculate the growth rate of real GDP in 1999.

The growth rate of real GDP in 1999 is [($880 billion − $840 billion) ÷ $840 billion] × 100, which is 4.8 percent.

   b. Calculate labor productivity in 1998 and 1999.

Labor productivity is real GDP divided by aggregate hours. So labor productivity in 1998 is $840 billion ÷ 25.0 billion hours, which is $33.60 per hour of labor. In 1999 labor productivity is $880 billion ÷ 25.2 billion hours, which is $34.92 per hour of labor.

   c. Calculate the growth rate of labor productivity in 1999.

The growth rate of labor productivity is labor productivity in 1999 minus the labor productivity in 1998, divided by labor productivity in

1998, all multiplied by 100. The growth rate of labor productivity equals [($34.92 per hour − $33.60 per hour) ÷ $33.60 per hour] × 100, which is 3.93 percent.

d. If the one third rule applies in Canada, what were the sources of labor productivity growth in 1999? Explain your answer.

To use the one third rule, we need the growth rate of capital per hour. The growth rate of capital per hour equals [($130 − $127) ÷ $127] × 100, which is 2.36 percent. The one third rule tells us that (1/3) × 2.36 percent, or 0.79 percent, of labor productivity growth came from capital. The remaining labor productivity growth, 3.93 percent minus 0.79 percent or 3.14 percent, came from technological change and human capital growth.

Additional Practice Problem 10.2a

The table above gives data on capital per hour of labor and real GDP per hour of labor for a small nation.

a. Label the axes in Figure 10.1 and plot this nation's productivity curve.

Capital per hour of labor (1996 dollars)	Real GDP per hour of labor (1996 dollars)
0	0
30	20.0
45	23.3
60	25.9

■ FIGURE 10.1

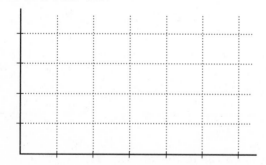

b. When capital per hour of labor equals $30 or more, does this nation's productivity curve agree with the one third rule?

Solution to Additional Practice Problem 10.2a

a. The productivity curve is in Figure 10.2.

■ FIGURE 10.2

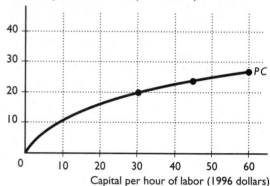

b. Yes, the productivity curve agrees with the one third rule. Between $30 and $45 of capital per hour of labor, capital per hour of labor grows 50 percent and GDP per hour of labor grows one third of 50 percent, or 16.67 percent. Between $45 and $60 of capital per hour of labor, capital per hour of labor grows 33 percent and GDP per hour of labor grows one third of 33 percent, or 11 percent.

■ Self Test 10.2

Fill in the blanks

All influences on real GDP growth can be divided into those that increase aggregate hours and ____ (labor productivity; population). Education, training, and job experience increase ____ (investment in physical capital; human capital). The ____ is the relationship that shows how labor productivity changes when the amount of physical capital per hour of labor changes with a given state of technology. A change in capital per hour of labor creates a ____ (movement along; shift of) the productivity curve and a technological change creates a ____ (movement along; shift of) the productivity curve. The one third rule tells us that a ____ (one; one third) percent increase in capital per hour of labor brings a ____ (one; one third) percent increase in labor productivity.

True or false

1. Real GDP increases if aggregate hours increase or labor productivity increases.
2. If labor productivity increases and aggregate hours do not change, then real GDP per person increases.
3. Higher wages are a source of growth in labor productivity.
4. A technological advance shifts the productivity curve upward.

Multiple choice

1. The only source of growth in aggregate labor hours that is sustainable over long periods of time is
   a. an increase in the labor force participation rate.
   b. population growth.
   c. a decrease in labor productivity.
   d. a decrease in the unemployment rate.

2. Real GDP equals aggregate hours
   a. divided by labor productivity.
   b. minus labor productivity.
   c. plus labor productivity.
   d. multiplied by labor productivity.

3. If real GDP is $1,200 billion, the population is 60 million, and aggregate hours are 80 billion, labor productivity is
   a. $5.00 an hour.
   b. $6.67 an hour.
   c. $15.00 an hour.
   d. $20,000.

4. Which of the following lists gives factors that increase labor productivity?
   a. saving and investment in physical capital, and wage increases
   b. expansion of human capital, labor force increases, and discovery of new technologies
   c. expansion of human capital, population growth, and discovery of new technologies
   d. saving and investment in physical capital, expansion of human capital, and discovery of new technologies

5. An increase in the amount of capital per hour of labor leads to ____ the productivity curve.
   a. a downward movement along
   b. an upward movement along
   c. an upward shift of
   d. a downward shift of

6. If the capital per hour of labor grows by 6 percent, then, with no growth in technology, labor productivity increases by
   a. 6 percent.
   b. 3 percent.
   c. 2 percent.
   d. 4 percent.

Complete the graph

■ **FIGURE 10.3**

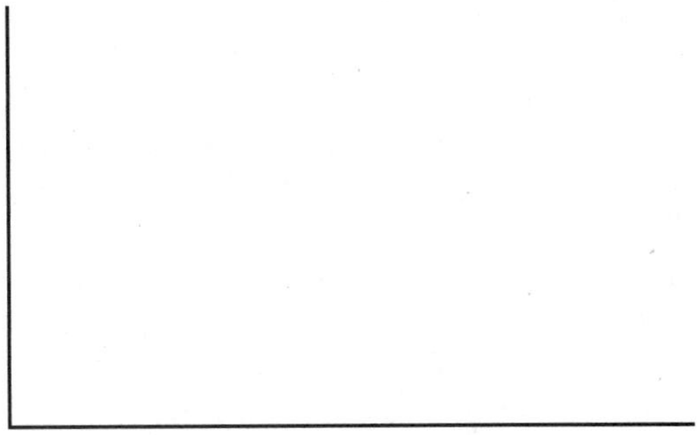

1. In Figure 10.3 draw a productivity curve. Label the axes.
   a. What factor results in a movement along the curve?
   b. What factors shift the curve?
   c. In Figure 10.3, illustrate the effect of a technological change.

Short answer and numeric questions

1. Real GDP is $9 trillion and aggregate hours are 200 billion. What is labor productivity?
2. Aggregate hours are 200 billion and labor productivity is $45 an hour. What is real GDP?
3. What three factors increase labor productivity?

4. Last year, capital per hour of labor grew 6 percent and labor productivity increased 3 percent.

   a. How much did growth in capital per hour of labor contribute to the increase in labor productivity?

   b. How much did human capital growth or technological change contribute to the increase in labor productivity?

CHECKPOINT 10.3

■ **Review the theories of economic growth that explain why growth rates vary over time and across countries.**

Practice Problems 10.3

1. What does classical growth theory say will eventually end economic growth? Does the evidence of history support the prediction of the classical growth theory?

2. What does neoclassical growth theory say about the source of persistent growth in real GDP per person?

3. Why does neoclassical growth theory predict that national levels of real GDP and national growth rates will converge?

4. What is the driving force of growth according to new growth theory?

5. What does new growth theory imply about growth in the global economy?

Solution to Practice Problems 10.3

These questions focus on the three growth theories. You need to know how each theory differs from the others and each theory's conclusion about the persistence of economic growth.

Quick Review

- *Classical growth theory* The clash between an exploding population and limited resources will eventually bring economic growth to an end. Income is driven to the subsistence level.

- *Neoclassical growth theory* Real GDP per person will increase as long as technol-

ogy grows, but no explanation is given for technological growth.

- *New growth theory* Unlimited wants will lead us to ever greater productivity and perpetual economic growth.

1. **What does classical growth theory say will eventually end economic growth? Does the evidence of history support the prediction of the classical growth theory?**

According to classical growth theory, when real GDP per person exceeds the subsistence level, population growth increases and real GDP per person decreases until it returns to the subsistence level. This dismal outcome has not been the case in advanced economies such as the United States because real GDP has remained well above its subsistence level.

2. **What does neoclassical growth theory say about the source of persistent growth in real GDP per person?**

The engine of growth is technological advances. Technological advances lead to increases in the quantity of capital per hour of labor and so increase real GDP per person.

3. **Why does neoclassical growth theory predict that national levels of real GDP and national growth rates will converge?**

According to neoclassical theory, all nations have access to the same technologies, so their productivity curves are the same. Capital is free to roam the globe seeking the highest available profits, so the capital per hour of labor is the same in all nations. As a result, the neoclassical theory predicts that national levels of real GDP per person and real growth rates will converge.

4. **What is the driving force of growth according to new growth theory?**

The driving force for growth in the new growth theory is the incentive to innovate in order to earn profit and an absence of diminishing returns to new knowledge.

5. **What does new growth theory imply about growth in the global economy?**

National growth rates are determined by national incentives to innovate, save, and invest.

Because these incentives depend on factors that are special to each country, national growth rates will not necessarily converge.

Additional Practice Problem 10.3a

How do each of the growth theories reflect the period during which they were developed?

Solution to Additional Practice Problem 10.3a

The classical growth theory was developed during the industrial revolution. Observers such as Thomas Malthus, saw some technological advances and rapid population growth. They combined these two observations into the classical growth theory, which predicts a return to a subsistence level of real GDP.

The neoclassical growth theory was developed in the 1950s, when rapid population growth was no longer a worry and when technological growth and the capital per hour of labor were starting to grow more rapidly. The neoclassical growth theory assigned a key role to these latter two factors and concluded that growth would persist as long as technology advanced.

The new growth theory was developed in the 1980s, when technological growth exploded. The new growth theory assigns importance to technological growth. Based on the observation that technological growth has persisted during the past 200 years, the new growth theory concludes that technology, and so real GDP, will grow forever.

■ Self Test 10.3

Fill in the blanks

The classical growth theory is the same as the ____ (Malthusian; new growth) theory. Classical growth theory says an increase in real GDP per person leads to more rapid growth in ____. Neoclassical growth theory asserts that economic growth continues as long as ____ (the population grows; technology advances). New growth theory predicts that economic growth will persist ____ (temporarily; indefinitely). The ____ growth theory predicts that levels of GDP in different nations will converge; ____ growth

theory predicts that gaps between rich and poor nations can persist.

True or false

1. The classical theory of growth concludes that eventually real GDP per person returns to the subsistence level.

2. According to the neoclassical theory, the rate of technological change does not influence the rate of economic growth.

3. The new growth theory predicts that economic growth can persist indefinitely.

4. Economic growth in the real world suggests that the new growth theory fits the facts more closely than do either the classical growth theory or the neoclassical growth theory.

Multiple choice

1. Classical growth theory predicts that increases in
   a. real GDP per person are permanent and sustainable.
   b. real GDP per person are temporary and not sustainable.
   c. resources permanently increase labor productivity.
   d. resources permanently increase real GDP per person.

2. If real GDP per person is above the subsistence level, then, according to classical growth theory,
   a. the population will increase.
   b. the population will decrease.
   c. the standard of living will continue to improve.
   d. labor productivity will increase.

3. Neoclassical growth theory predicts that economic growth is
   a. only temporary due to overpopulation.
   b. the result of technological advances.
   c. impossible due to extremes in weather.
   d. caused by women entering the workforce.

4. The new growth theory states that
   a. technological advances are the result of random chance.
   b. technological advances are the result of discoveries and choices.
   c. technological advances are the responsibility of the government.
   d. the subsistence income level leads to technological advances.

5. The theory that suggests that our unlimited wants will lead to perpetual economic growth is the
   a. classical growth theory.
   b. sustained growth theory.
   c. neoclassical growth theory.
   d. new growth theory.

6. New growth theory predicts that
   a. national growth rates will not necessarily converge over time.
   b. national growth rates will slowly converge over time.
   c. countries with the highest real GDP per person are likely to be the first to experience a slowing economy.
   d. national growth rates will rise and fall as population rates change.

Short answer and numeric questions

1. What role do technological advances play in each of the three growth theories?
2. What role does population growth play in each of the three growth theories?
3. What role do diminishing returns play in the new growth theory?
4. Which growth theory is most pessimistic about the prospects for persistent economic growth? Which is most optimistic?

CHECKPOINT 10.4

■ **Describe policies that might speed economic growth.**

Practice Problems 10.4

1. What are the preconditions for economic growth?
2. Why does much of Africa experience slow economic growth?
3. Why is economic freedom crucial for achieving economic growth?
4. What role do property rights play in encouraging economic growth?
5. Explain why, other things remaining the same, a country with a well-educated population has a faster economic growth rate than a country that has a poorly educated population?

Solution to Practice Problems 10.4

These questions stress the role that the government can play to encourage economic growth, by providing the necessary preconditions and by conducting the proper policies.

Quick Review

- *Preconditions for economic growth* The three preconditions are economic freedom, property rights, and markets.
- *Policies to achieve growth* Five policies are to create incentive mechanisms, encourage saving, encourage research and development, encourage international trade, and improve the quality of education.

1. What are the preconditions for economic growth?

Economic freedom, property rights, and markets are the preconditions for economic growth. Economic freedom occurs when people are able to make personal choices, their private property is protected, and they are free to buy and sell in markets. Property rights are the social arrangements that govern the protection of private property. Markets enable people to trade and to save and invest.

2. Why does much of Africa experience slow economic growth?

Much of Africa lacks economic freedom. Property rights are not enforced and markets do not function well. These African countries do not have the preconditions for economic growth.

3. Why is economic freedom crucial for achieving economic growth?

Individuals know more about their own skills and preferences than can the government, or anyone else. Economic freedom allows people to make their own choices and gives incentives to pursue growth-producing activities.

4. What role do property rights play in encouraging economic growth?

Property rights and a legal system to enforce them encourage people to work, save, invest, and accumulate human capital. All of these activities lead to economic growth.

5. Explain why, other things remaining the same, a country with a well-educated population has a faster economic growth rate than a country that has a poorly educated population?

A well-educated population has more skills and so a greater labor productivity. A well-educated population is more likely to create and innovate new technology. A well-educated population adapts faster to new innovations and can implement new technology faster.

Additional Practice Problem 10.4a

In 1949 East and West Germany had about the same real GDP per person. By 1989 West Germany had a real GDP per person more than twice the level of East Germany's. Why did East Germany grow so much more slowly than West Germany over those 40 years?

Solution to Additional Practice Problem 10.4a

In 1949, East Germany was formed with state ownership of capital and land, and virtually no economic freedom. West Germany was formed with private ownership of most capital and land, and significant economic freedom.

West Germany had the preconditions for economic growth; East Germany did not. When East Germany collapsed in 1989, West Germany had more human capital, more capital per hour of labor, and better technology. The different incentives had given West German workers the incentive to acquire human capital, West German investors the incentive to acquire physical capital, and West German entrepreneurs the incentive to innovate new and better technology.

■ Self Test 10.4

Fill in the blanks

____, ____, and ____ are preconditions for economic growth. Policies the government can take to encourage faster economic growth are to ____ (create; discourage) incentive mechanisms; ____ (encourage; discourage) saving; ____ (encourage; discourage) research and development; ____ (encourage; discourage) international trade; and improve the quality of ____ (education; pollution control).

True or false

1. To achieve economic growth, economic freedom must be coupled with a democratic political system.
2. Markets slow specialization and hence slow economic growth.
3. Encouraging saving can increase the growth of capital and stimulate economic growth.
4. Limiting international trade will increase economic growth.

Multiple choice

1. Economic freedom means that
   a. firms are regulated by the government.
   b. some goods and services are free.
   c. people are able to make personal choices and their property is protected.
   d. the rule of law does not apply.

2. Property rights protect
   a. only the rights to physical property.
   b. only the rights to financial property.
   c. all rights except rights to intellectual property.
   d. rights to physical property, financial property, and intellectual property.

3. Which of the following statements is FALSE?
   a. Saving helps create economic growth.
   b. Improvements in quality of education are important for economic growth.
   c. Free international trade helps create economic growth.
   d. Faster population growth is the key to growth in real GDP per person.

4. Saving
   a. slows growth because it decreases consumption.
   b. finances investment which brings capital accumulation.
   c. has no impact on economic growth.
   d. is very low in most East Asian nations.

5. The fastest growing nations today are those with
   a. barriers that significantly limit international trade.
   b. the fastest growing exports and imports.
   c. government intervention in markets to ensure high prices.
   d. few funds spent on research and development.

6. Economic growth is encouraged by
   a. free international trade.
   b. limiting international trade so that the domestic economy can prosper.
   c. discouraging saving, because increased saving means less spending.
   d. None of the above.

Short answer and numeric questions

1. Does persistent economic growth necessarily occur when a nation meets all the preconditions for growth?
2. What role do specialization and trade play in determining economic growth?
3. Is it possible for the government to create a large increase in the economic growth rate, say from 3 percent to 10 percent in a year?

SELF TEST ANSWERS

■ CHECKPOINT 10.1

Fill in the blanks

The growth rate of real GDP equals real GDP in the current year minus real GDP in the previous year divided by real GDP in the <u>previous</u> year, all multiplied by 100. The growth rate of real GDP per person equals the growth rate of real GDP <u>minus</u> the growth rate of the population. The number of years it takes for the level of any variable to double is approximately <u>70</u> divided by the annual percentage growth rate of the variable.

True or false

1. True; page 234
2. True; page 234
3. True; page 235
4. False; page 235

Multiple choice

1. a; page 234
2. b; page 234
3. d; page 234
4. a; page 235
5. b; page 235
6. b; page 235

Short answer and numeric questions

1. 10 percent; 10 percent; 10 percent; page 234.

2. a. 1 percent; 2 percent; –1 percent; 0 percent; page 235
   b. 2000 and 2001; page 234

3. 70 ÷ 4 = 17.5 years; 70 ÷ 5 = 14 years; page 235.

■ CHECKPOINT 10.2

Fill in the blanks

All influences on real GDP growth can be divided into those that increase aggregate hours and <u>labor productivity</u>. Education, training, and job experience increase <u>human capital</u>. The <u>productivity curve</u> is the relationship that shows how labor productivity changes when the amount of physical capital per hour of labor changes with a given state of technology. A change in capital per hour of labor creates a <u>movement along</u> the productivity curve and a technological change creates a <u>shift of</u> the productivity curve. The one third rule tells us that a <u>one</u> percent increase in capital per hour of labor brings a <u>one third</u> percent increase in labor productivity.

True or false

1. True; page 238
2. True; page 239
3. False; page 239
4. True; page 241

Multiple choice

1. b; page 238
2. d; page 238
3. c; page 238
4. d; page 239-240
5. b; page 241
6. c; page 243

Complete the graph

■ **FIGURE 10.4**

Real GDP per hour of labor (1996 dollars)

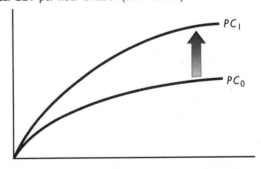

Capital per hour of labor (1996 dollars)

1. The productivity curve is illustrated in Figure 10.4, labeled PC_0.

   a. A change in capital per hour of labor; page 241.

b. A change in human capital or a technological advance; page 241.

c. A technological advance shifts the productivity curve upward from PC_0 to PC_1 in the
figure; page 241.

Short answer and numeric questions

1. Labor productivity is $45 an hour; page 238.
2. Real GDP is $9 trillion; page 238.
3. Saving and investment in physical capital;
expansion of human capital; discovery of
new technologies; page 239-240.
4. a. 1/3 of 6 percent = 2 percent; page 243.
   b. 1 percent; page 243.

■ CHECKPOINT 10.3

Fill in the blanks

The classical growth theory is the same as the
<u>Malthusian</u> theory. Classical growth theory
says an increase in real GDP per person leads to
more rapid growth in <u>population</u>. Neoclassical
growth theory asserts that economic growth
continues as long as <u>technology advances</u>. New
growth theory predicts that economic growth
will persist <u>indefinitely</u>. The <u>neoclassical</u>
growth theory predicts that levels of GDP in
different nations will converge; <u>new</u> growth
theory predicts that gaps between rich and poor
nations can persist.

True or false

1. True; page 245
2. False; page 247
3. True; page 249
4. True; page 252

Multiple choice

1. b; page 245
2. a; page 245
3. b; page 247
4. b; page 249
5. d; page 250-251
6. a; page 252

Short answer and numeric questions

1. In the classical growth theory, advances in
technology start a temporary period of
economic growth; in the neoclassical
growth theory, economic growth continues as long as technology advances; and
in the new growth theory, economic
growth continues indefinitely, in part because technology grows indefinitely;
pages 246, 248, 251.
2. Population growth plays a crucial role
only in the classical growth theory because in that theory population growth
leads the economy back to a subsistence
real income; page 246.
3. The new growth theory assumes that the
economy is not subject to diminishing returns. So as capital accumulates, labor
productivity grows indefinitely; page 250.
4. The most optimistic theory is the new
growth theory, which concludes that economic growth can continue forever. The
most pessimistic theory is the classical
theory, which concludes that the economy
will return to a subsistence level of real income; pages 245, 249.

■ CHECKPOINT 10.4

Fill in the blanks

<u>Economic freedom</u>, <u>property rights</u>, and <u>mar-
kets</u> are preconditions for economic growth.
Policies the government can take to encourage
faster economic growth are to <u>create</u> incentive
mechanisms; <u>encourage</u> saving; <u>encourage</u> research and development; <u>encourage</u> international trade; and improve the quality of <u>educa-
tion</u>.

True or false

1. False; page 255
2. False; page 256
3. True; page 256
4. False; page 257

Multiple choice

1. c; page 255
2. d; page 255
3. d; page 256-257
4. b; page 256
5. b; page 257
6. a; page 257

Short answer and numeric questions

1. No. The preconditions for growth are necessary for growth to occur. But for growth to be persistent, people must face incentives that encourage saving and investment, expansion of human capital, and the discovery and application of new technologies; pages 255-256.

2. Growth begins when people can specialize in the activities in which they have a comparative advantage and trade with each other. As an economy reaps the benefits from specialization and trade, production and consumption grow, real GDP per person increases, and the standard of living rises; page 256.

3. No, the government cannot create a huge increase in the economic growth rate. The government can pursue policies that will nudge the growth rate upward. And, over time, policies that create even small increases in the economic growth rate will have large benefits; page 257.

Money and the Monetary System

Chapter
11

Chapter 11 defines money, describes the U.S. monetary system, and describes the functions of the Federal Reserve System.

■ Define money and describe its functions.

Money is any commodity or token that is generally accepted as a means of payment. Money serves three vital functions. It is a medium of exchange (an object that is generally accepted in return for goods and services), a unit of account (an agreed-upon measure for stating the prices of goods and services), and a store of value (any commodity or token that can be held and exchanged later for goods and services). Money consists of currency (dollar bills and coins) and deposits at banks and other financial institutions. Currency in a bank is not money. Deposits are money but checks are not money. Credit cards, debit cards, and electronic checks are not money. Electronic cash is not sufficiently widely accepted to serve as money today. M1 and M2 are two official measures of money. M1 is currency held outside banks and traveler's checks plus checkable deposits owned by individuals and businesses. M2 is M1 plus savings and time deposits, and money market funds and other deposits. The items in M2 other than M1 are not technically money because they are not a means of payment.

■ Describe the monetary system and explain the functions of banks and other monetary institutions.

The monetary system consists of the Federal Reserve and the banks and other institutions that accept deposits and provide the services that enable people and businesses to make and receive payments. Three types of financial institutions are commercial banks, thrift institutions, and money market funds. A commercial bank makes loans at a higher interest rate than the interest rate it pays on deposits. A bank has four types of assets: cash assets, interbank loans, securities, and loans. A bank's cash assets consist of its reserves and funds that are due from other banks as payments for checks that are being cleared. Monetary institutions create liquidity, lower the costs of lending and borrowing, pool risks, and make payments.

■ Describe the functions of the Federal Reserve System.

The Federal Reserve System is the central bank of the United States. The Fed conducts the nation's monetary policy. The Board of Governors has seven members. There are 12 regional Federal Reserve banks. The Federal Open Market Committee is the Fed's main policy-making committee and consists of the Board of Governors, the president of the Federal Reserve Bank of New York, and four presidents of other regional Federal Reserve banks. The Fed uses three tools to control the quantity of money: required reserve ratios (the minimum percentage of deposits banks must hold as reserves), discount rate (the interest rate at which the Fed stands ready to lend reserves to commercial banks), and open market operations (purchase or sale of government securities by the Fed in the open market). The monetary base is the sum of coins, Federal Reserve notes, and banks' reserves held at the Fed.

EXPANDED CHAPTER CHECKLIST

When you have completed this chapter, you will be able to:

1 Define money and describe its functions.

- Define money and discuss how money serves as a medium of exchange, unit of account, and store of value.
- Categorize currency in a bank, checks, credit cards, debit cards, e-checks, and e-cash as money or not money.
- Define M1 and M2.

2 Describe the monetary system and explain the functions of banks and other monetary institutions.

- Describe the different types of financial institutions.
- Explain how a commercial bank achieves its goal of maximizing its stockholders' long-term wealth.
- Explain the four economic functions of monetary institutions.

3 Describe the functions of the Federal Reserve System.

- Describe the organizational structure of the Fed and the functions of each part of the structure.
- Describe the Fed's policy tools and briefly summarize how each works.
- Define monetary base.

KEY TERMS

- Money (page 264)
- Means of payment (page 264)
- Medium of exchange (page 265)
- Barter (page 265)
- Unit of account (page 265)
- Store of value (page 265)
- Fiat money (page 266)
- Currency (page 266)
- Electronic check (or e-check) (page 268)
- Electronic cash (or e-cash) (page 268)
- M1 (page 269)
- M2 (page 269)
- Monetary system (page 272)
- Commercial bank (page 272)
- Reserves (page 273)
- Required reserve ratio (page 273)
- Excess reserves (page 273)
- Federal funds rate (page 273)
- Savings and loan association (page 274)
- Savings bank (page 274)
- Credit union (page 274)
- Money market fund (page 274)
- Liquid asset (page 276)
- Federal Reserve System (page 279)
- Central bank (page 279)
- Monetary policy (page 279)
- Federal Open Market Committee (page 280)
- Discount rate (page 282)
- Open market operation (page 282)
- Monetary base (page 282)

CHECKPOINT 11.1

■ Define money and describe its functions.

Practice Problems 11.1

1. In the United States today, money includes which of the following items?
    a. Your Visa card
    b. The quarters inside public phones
    c. U.S. dollar bills in your wallet
    d. The check that you have just written to pay for your rent
    e. The loan you took out last August to pay for your school fees

2. In January 2001, currency held by individuals and businesses was $534.9 billion; traveler's checks were $8.1 billion; checkable deposits owned by individuals and businesses were $559.3 billion; savings deposits were $1,889.7 billion; small time deposits were $1,052.6 billion; and money market funds and other deposits were $952 billion.

a. What was M1 in January 2001?

b. What was M2 in January 2001?

Solution to Practice Problems 11.1

These Practice Problems involve definitions of M1 and M2. In the first problem, definitely remember that money is a means of payment.

Quick Review

- *M1* M1 consists of currency held outside banks and traveler's checks plus checkable deposits owned by individuals and businesses. Currency inside banks is not counted.

- *M2* M2 consists of M1 plus savings deposits and small time deposits, money market funds, and other deposits.

1. **In the United States today, money includes which of the following items?**

   a. Your Visa card

   Your Visa card is a credit card and a credit card is not money. It is an ID card that allows for an instant loan.

   b. The quarters inside public phones

   Coins in a pay phone are currency outside the banks, so they are money.

   c. U.S. dollar bills in your wallet

   Dollar bills in your wallet are currency outside the banks, so they are money.

   d. The check that you have just written to pay for your rent

   Checks are not money. The check instructs the banks to transfer money from one person to another, in this case, to transfer money from your account to your landlord's account.

   e. The loan you took out last August to pay for your school fees

   A loan isn't money. When you got the loan you might have received a check, which you turned over to the school. But the check wasn't money. When the school cashed the check it got a transfer of deposit funds from the bank and that was money.

2. **In January 2001, currency held by individuals and businesses was $534.9 billion; traveler's checks were $8.1 billion; checkable deposits owned by individuals and businesses were** $559.3 billion; savings deposits were $1,889.7 billion; small time deposits were $1,052.6 billion; and money market funds and other deposits were $952 billion.

   a. What was M1 in January 2001?

   M1 is the sum of currency, traveler's checks, and checkable deposits owned by individuals and businesses. So, M1 equals $534.9 billion + $8.1 billion + $559.3 billion, which is $1,102.3 billion.

   b. What was M2 in January 2001?

   M2 equals M1 plus savings deposits, small time deposits, and money market funds and other deposits. So M2 equals $1,102.3 billion + $1,889.7 billion + $1,052.6 billion + $952 billion, which is $4,996.6 billion.

Additional Practice Problem 11.1a

You go to the bank and withdraw $200 from your checking account. You keep $100 in cash and deposit the other $100 in your savings account. What is the change in M1? What is the change in M2?

Solution to Additional Practice Problem 11.1a

Your checking account decreased by $200, your currency increased by $100, and your savings account increased by $100. M1, which includes your currency and your checkable deposit, is changed by the decrease in the checking account and the increase in currency. The net effect on M1 is –$200 + $100 = –$100, that is, M1 decreases by $100. M2, which includes your currency, your checkable deposits, and your savings account, does not change. The change in your checkable deposits, –$200, is balanced by the change in your currency, +$100, and the change in your savings account, +100. There was no change in M2.

■ Self Test 11.1

Fill in the blanks

Any commodity or token that is generally accepted as a means of payment is ____. A ____ (unit of account; store of value; medium of exchange) is an object that is generally accepted in return for goods and services. A ____ (unit of account; store of value; medium of exchange) is an agreed-upon measure for stating prices of goods and services. A ____ (unit of account; store of value; medium of exchange) is any commodity or token that can be held and exchanged later for goods and services. Currency inside the banks ____ (is; is not) money and currency outside the banks ____ (is; is not) money. A credit card ____ (is; is not) money. M1 is ____ (more; less) than M2. Checkable deposits ____ (are; are not) part of M1 and savings deposits ____ (are; are not) part of M1.

True or false

1. Using money as a medium of exchange is called barter.

2. Prices in terms of money reflect money's role as a unit of account.

3. Currency is money but checkable deposits at banks are not money.

4. A debit card is not money.

5. M1 and M2 are money.

Multiple choice

1. Which of the following best defines what money is now and what it has been in the past?
   a. currency
   b. currency plus checking deposits
   c. currency plus credit cards
   d. anything accepted as a means of payment

2. For something to be a "means of payment" means that it
   a. is valuable and backed by gold.
   b. is valuable and backed by the government.
   c. can be used to settle a debt.
   d. requires a double coincidence of wants.

3. Which of the following is not a function of money?
   a. unit of account
   b. store of value
   c. unit of debt
   d. medium of exchange

4. Barter is
   a. the exchange of goods and services for money.
   b. the pricing of goods and services with one agreed upon standard.
   c. the exchange of goods and services directly for other goods and services.
   d. a generally accepted means of payment.

5. If someone buries money in a tin can beneath a tree, the money is functioning as a
   a. medium of exchange.
   b. unit of account.
   c. means of payment.
   d. store of value.

6. Credit cards, debit cards, and e-checks are
   a. always counted as money.
   b. not money.
   c. sometimes counted as money, depending on how they are used.
   d. sometimes counted as money, depending on what is purchased.

7. Which of the following counts as part of M1?
   a. $5,000 worth of gold
   b. $5,000 worth of government bonds
   c. $5,000 in a checking account
   d. $5,000 credit line on a credit card

8. M2 equals
   a. M1 and is just another name for currency outside of banks.
   b. M1 plus savings deposits, small time deposits, and money market fund deposits.
   c. M1 minus traveler's checks because they are not really money.
   d. currency plus savings deposits, all time deposits, and money market funds and other deposits.

Short answer and numeric questions

1. Why was it possible at one time to use whale's teeth as money?
2. What are the functions of money?
3. Why is currency money?
4. Why are e-checks not money?
5. Some parts of M2 are not money. Why are these parts included in M2?

CHECKPOINT 11.2

■ **Describe the monetary system and explain the functions of banks and other monetary institutions.**

Practice Problems 11.2

1. What are the institutions that make up the monetary system?
2. What is a bank's "balancing act"?
3. A bank has the following deposits and assets: $320 in checkable deposits, $896 in savings deposits, $840 in small time deposits, $990 in loans to businesses, $400 in outstanding credit card balances, $634 in government securities, $2 in currency, and $30 in its reserve account at the Fed. Calculate the bank's:
    a. Total deposits
    b. Deposits that are part of M1
    c. Deposits that are part of M2
    d. Loans
    e. Securities
    f. Reserves

Solution to Practice Problems 11.2

Banks accept deposits and then use the deposits to make loans and buy securities. Banks maximize stockholders' long-term wealth by collecting a higher interest rate on the loans they make and the securities they buy than the interest rate they pay on deposits. But banks must keep enough funds as reserves to meet depositors' withdrawals. In the United States, banks on the average keep about 7 percent of total deposits in cash assets.

Quick Review

- *Reserves* A bank's reserves consist of the currency in its vault plus the balance on its reserve account at a Federal Reserve Bank.

1. What are the institutions that make up the monetary system?

The monetary system consists of the Federal Reserve and the banks and other institutions that accept deposits and provide the services that enable people and businesses to make and receive payments. Three types of financial institutions that accept deposits that are part of the nation's money are commercial banks, thrift institutions, and money market funds.

2. What is a bank's "balancing act"?

To maximize stockholders' long-term wealth, a bank borrows from depositors at a lower interest rate than it charges the lenders to whom it makes loans. The bank earns no interest on reserves, but it must hold enough reserves to meet depositors' withdrawals. The bank must balance the risks of making loans against the security of holding reserves.

3. A bank has the following deposits and assets: $320 in checkable deposits, $896 in savings deposits, $840 in small time deposits, $990 in loans to businesses, $400 in outstanding credit card balances, $634 in government securities, $2 in currency, and $30 in its reserve account at the Fed. Calculate the bank's:

a. Total deposits

Total deposits are the sum of checkable deposits, $320, savings deposits, $896, and small time deposits, $840, which equals a total of $2,056.

b. Deposits that are part of M1

The only deposits that are part of M1 are checkable deposits, $320.

c. Deposits that are part of M2

All of the bank's deposits are part of M2, so deposits that are part of M2 are $2,056.

d. Loans

Total loans include loans to businesses and credit card balances. Credit card balances are the amount lent to the card holder to pay for purchases. Total loans are $990 + $400, which is $1,390.

e. Securities

Securities are the government securities, $634.

f. Reserves

Reserves are the currency in the bank's vault plus the balance on its reserve account at a Federal Reserve Bank. Reserves are $2 + $30, which equals $32.

Additional Practice Problem 11.2a

The Acme Bank just sold $100 in securities in exchange for a $100 bill. It made a $50 loan, and the borrower left with the cash. It also accepted a $60 cash deposit. How have the bank's reserves changed as a result of all these actions? How have its deposits changed?

Solution to Additional Practice Problem 11.2a

The $100 sale of securities adds $100 to reserves. The $50 loan removes $50 from the bank and out of its reserves, and the $60 deposit adds to reserves. The net result is +$100 − $50 + $60, which is +$110. Acme has $110 more in reserves. The $60 deposit is the only transaction that affects its deposits, so deposits rise by $60.

■ Self Test 11.2

Fill in the blanks

The currency in a bank's vault is part of the bank's ____ (reserves; loans). Banks can borrow or lend reserves in the ____ (reserves; federal funds) market. At commercial banks in the United States, the majority of deposits ____ (are; are not) checkable deposits. An asset that can easily and with certainty be converted into money is called a ____ asset. Banks ____ (lower; raise) the costs of lending and borrowing.

True or false

1. A commercial bank accepts checkable deposits, savings deposits, and time deposits.

2. A commercial bank maximizes its stockholders' long-term wealth by refusing to make any risky loans.

3. When a credit union has excess reserves, it makes loans to its members at an interest rate called the federal funds rate.

4. Thrift institutions provide most of the nation's bank deposits.

5. By lending to a large number of businesses and individuals, a bank lowers the average risk it faces.

Multiple choice

1. A commercial bank's main goal is to
   a. provide loans to its customers.
   b. maximize the long-term wealth of its stockholders.
   c. help the government when it needs money.
   d. lend money to the Federal Reserve banks.

2. A bank divides its assets into four parts:
   a. cash assets, interbank loans, securities, and loans.
   b. reserves, securities, bonds, and loans.
   c. reserves, bonds, cash securities, and interbank loans.
   d. securities, reserves, debts, and interbank cash.

3. A commercial bank's reserves are
   a. bonds issued by the U.S. government that are very safe.
   b. the provision of funds to businesses and individuals.
   c. currency in its vault plus the balance on its reserve account at a Federal Reserve Bank.
   d. savings and time deposits.

4. A bank has $220 in checkable deposits, $796 in savings deposits, $740 in time deposits, $890 in loans to businesses, $300 in outstanding credit card balances, $534 in government securities, $1 in currency in its vault, and $20 in its reserve account at the Fed. The bank's deposits that are part of M1 are equal to
   a. $1,016.
   b. $220.
   c. $796.
   d. $221.

5. All of the following institutions accept deposits from to the general public EXCEPT
   a. money market funds.
   b. thrift institutions.
   c. the Federal Reserve.
   d. commercial banks.

6. Which of the following is a thrift institution?
   a. a savings and loan association
   b. a money fund association
   c. a commercial bank
   d. a loan institution

7. Banks and other monetary institutions perform which of the following functions?
   a. create liquidity
   b. lower costs of borrowing
   c. pool the risks of lending
   d. All of the above answers are correct.

8. We define a liquid asset as
   a. any deposit held at a commercial bank.
   b. bank loans made to low-risk borrowers.
   c. any asset than can be converted into money easily and with certainty.
   d. any deposit held with the Federal Reserve.

Short answer and numeric questions

1. What are a bank's reserves? How does a bank use its account at the Federal Reserve Bank?
2. Which is a larger percentage of M1: commercial bank deposits or thrift institution deposits?
3. What economic functions are performed by the nation's monetary institutions?
4. What does it mean for banks to "pool risk"?

CHECKPOINT 11.3

■ **Describe the functions of the Federal Reserve System.**

Practice Problems 11.3

1. What is the Fed?
2. What is the FOMC?
3. What is the Fed's "power center"?
4. What are the Fed's main policy tools?
5. What is the monetary base?
6. Suppose that at the end of December 2005, the monetary base in the United States is $700 billion, Federal Reserve notes are $650 billion, and banks' reserves at the Fed are $20 billion. Calculate the quantity of coins.

Solution to Practice Problems 11.3

These Practice Problems help you understand the Fed, where its power lies, and its tools. Understanding these points will help you understand a significant part of the ongoing, continuous national debate about macroeconomic policy.

Quick Review

- *Federal Reserve System* The Federal Reserve System is the central bank of the United States. It conducts the nation's monetary policy.

1. What is the Fed?

The Federal Reserve System (Fed) is the central bank of the United States. The Fed conducts the nation's monetary policy, which means that it adjusts the quantity of money in the economy in an effort to influence economic activity. The Fed is organized in 12 Federal Reserve districts, each having a regional Federal Reserve bank. The Fed is overseen by the Board of Governors.

2. What is the FOMC?

The FOMC is the Federal Open Market Committee. It is responsible for determining the nation's monetary policy actions, which are then carried out by the New York Fed. The FOMC consists of the seven members of the Board of Governors, the president of the New York Federal Reserve Bank, and four presidents of the other regional Federal Reserve Banks on a yearly rotating basis.

3. What is the Fed's "power center?"

The Fed's "power center" is the Chairman of the Board of Governors, who, in 2003, is Alan Greenspan. His power comes from control over the internal staff of the Fed and from his public prominence as the person who speaks for the Fed.

4. What are the Fed's main policy tools?

The Fed's main policy tools are required reserve ratios, the discount rate, and open market operations. The required reserve ratio is the minimum percentage of deposits that banks are required to keep as reserves. The discount rate is the interest rate at which the Fed stands ready to lend reserves to commercial banks. Open market operations are the purchase or sale of government securities—U.S. Treasury bills and bonds—by the Federal Reserve in the open market.

5. What is the monetary base?

The monetary base is the sum of the coins, Federal Reserve notes, and banks' reserves at the Fed. It is called the monetary base because it acts like a base upon which the total quantity of the nation's money is constructed.

6. Suppose that at the end of December 2005, the monetary base in the United States is $700 billion, Federal Reserve notes are $650 billion, and banks' reserves at the Fed are $20 billion. Calculate the quantity of coins.

The monetary base is the sum of coins, Federal Reserve notes, and banks' reserves at the Fed. The quantity of coins equals the monetary base minus banks' reserves minus Federal Reserve notes. So the quantity of coins is $700 billion – $650 billion – $20 billion, which is $30 billion.

Additional Practice Problem 11.3a

Banks can borrow reserves from the Federal Reserve. The interest rate they pay on these loans is the discount rate. If the Fed raises the discount rate, what happens to the amount of reserves banks borrow? What is the effect on the monetary base?

Solution to Additional Practice Problem 11.3a

If the Fed raises the discount rate, borrowing reserves becomes more costly. Banks decrease the amount of reserves they borrow from the Fed. The monetary base is the sum of coins, Federal Reserve notes, and banks' reserves at the Fed. Because banks are borrowing fewer reserves, the monetary base decreases.

■ Self Test 11.3

Fill in the blanks

The Fed conducts the nation's ____ policy. There are ____ (2; 6; 12) Federal Reserve Banks. The Fed's main policy-making committee is the ____ (Board of Governors; Federal Open Market Committee). The Fed sets the minimum per-

centage of deposits that must be held as reserves, which is called the ____ (discount rate; required reserve ratio). The interest rate at which the Fed stands ready to lend reserves to commercial banks is the ____ (discount; open market operation) rate. The purchase or sale of government securities by the Federal Reserve is an ____.

True or false

1. The Federal Reserve System is the central bank of the United States.

2. In practice, the power in the Fed resides with the Board of Governors.

3. An open market operation is the purchase or sale of government securities by the Federal Reserve from the U.S. government.

4. If bank deposits fall by $10 million and banks use $1 million of reserves to buy $1 million worth of newly printed bank notes from the Fed, the monetary base does not change.

5. Federal Reserve notes are an asset of the Fed.

Multiple choice

1. Regulating the amount of money in the United States is one of the most important responsibilities of the
   a. State Department.
   b. state governments.
   c. Treasury Department.
   d. Federal Reserve.

2. The Board of Governors of the Federal Reserve System has
   a. 12 members appointed by the president of the United States.
   b. 12 members elected by the public.
   c. seven members appointed by the president of the United States.
   d. seven members elected by the public.

3. The Fed's monetary policy is determined by the
   a. Federal Open Market Committee.
   b. Executive Council to the Governor.
   c. Regional Federal Reserve Banks.
   d. Board of Governors.

4. The most influential position in the Federal Reserve System is the
   a. president of the Federal Reserve Bank of New York.
   b. chairman of the Board of Governors.
   c. chairman of the Federal Reserve Bank presidents.
   d. president of the Federal Reserve Bank of Chicago.

5. The Fed's policy tools include
   a. required reserve ratios, the discount rate, and open market operations.
   b. holding deposits for the U.S. government, reserve requirements, and the discount rate.
   c. setting regulations for lending standards and approving or rejecting loans banks make to large corporations.
   d. supervision of the banking system and buying and selling commercial banks.

6. The minimum percent of deposits that banks must hold is determined by the
   a. interest rate.
   b. discount rate.
   c. required reserve ratio.
   d. federal funds rate.

7. The discount rate is the interest rate that
   a. commercial banks charge their customers.
   b. commercial banks charge each other for the loan of reserves.
   c. the Fed charges the government.
   d. the Fed charges commercial banks for the loan of reserves.

8. The monetary base is the
   a. minimum reserves banks must hold to cover any losses from unpaid loans.
   b. sum of coins, Federal Reserve notes, and banks' reserves at the Fed.
   c. sum of gold and foreign exchange held by the Fed.
   d. sum of government securities and loans held by the Fed.

Short answer and numeric questions

1. How many people are on the Board of Governors of the Federal Reserve System? How are they selected?

2. What is the FOMC and who are its members?

3. Suppose that banks' deposits are $600 billion and that the required reserve ratio is 10 percent.
   a. What is the minimum amount of reserves banks must hold?
   b. Suppose the Federal Reserve lowers the required reserve ratio to 8 percent. Now what is the minimum amount of reserves banks must hold?
   c. Suppose the Federal Reserve raises the required reserve ratio to 12 percent. Now what is the minimum amount of reserves banks must hold?

4. What is the monetary base?

5. Are U.S. government securities an asset or a liability of the Federal Reserve? Are Federal Reserve notes an asset or a liability of the Federal Reserve?

SELF TEST ANSWERS

■ CHECKPOINT 11.1

Fill in the blanks

Any commodity or token that is generally accepted as a means of payment is <u>money</u>. A <u>medium of exchange</u> is an object that is generally accepted in return for goods and services. A <u>unit of account</u> is an agreed-upon measure for stating prices of goods and services. A <u>store of value</u> is any commodity or token that can be held and exchanged later for goods and services. Currency inside the banks <u>is not</u> money and currency outside the banks <u>is</u> money. A credit card <u>is not</u> money. M1 is <u>less</u> than M2. Checkable deposits <u>are</u> part of M1 and savings deposits <u>are not</u> part of M1.

True or false

1. False; page 265
2. True; page 265
3. False; page 266
4. True; page 268
5. False; page 269

Multiple choice

1. d; page 264
2. c; page 264
3. c; pages 264-265
4. c; page 265
5. d; page 265
6. b; pages 267-268
7. c; page 269
8. b; page 269

Short answer and numeric questions

1. It was possible to use whale's teeth as money because whale's teeth were generally accepted as a means of payment. At one time, most people were willing to trade goods and services in exchange for whale's teeth; page 264.
2. Money has three functions. It is a medium of exchange, an object that is generally accepted in return for goods and services. It is a unit of account, an agreed-upon measure for stating the prices of goods and services. And it is a store of value, a commodity or token that can be held and exchanged at a later date for goods and services; page 265.
3. Currency is money because it is generally accepted as a means of payment. It is generally accepted because the government has declared that currency is money, so that currency is fiat money; page 266.
4. E-checks are not money because they are instructions to transfer money from one person's deposit account to another person's deposit account; page 268.
5. Time deposits, money market funds, and some of the savings deposits included in M2 are not money. They are not money because they are not a means of payment. They are included in M2 because they are very easily converted into money; page 269.

■ CHECKPOINT 11.2

Fill in the blanks

The currency in a bank's vault is part of the bank's <u>reserves</u>. Banks can borrow or lend reserves in the <u>federal funds</u> market. At commercial banks in the United States, the majority of deposits <u>are not</u> checkable deposits. An asset that can easily and with certainty be converted into money is called a <u>liquid</u> asset. Banks <u>lower</u> the costs of lending and borrowing.

True or false

1. True; page 272
2. False; page 273
3. False; pages 273-274
4. False; page 274
5. True; page 276

Multiple choice

1. b; page 273
2. a; page 273
3. c; page 273
4. b; page 273
5. c; page 274
6. a; page 274

7. d; page 276

8. c; page 276

Short answer and numeric questions

1. A bank's reserves are the currency in its vault plus the balance on its reserve account at a Federal Reserve bank. A bank uses its account at the Fed to receive and make payments to other banks and to obtain currency; page 273.

2. Commercial bank deposits are a larger percentage of M1 than thrift institution deposits. Commercial bank deposits are about 41 percent of M1, while thrift institution deposits are about 10 percent; page 275.

3. The nation's monetary institutions perform four economic functions: They create liquidity, they lower the cost of lending and borrowing, they pool risks, and they make payments; pages 276-277.

4. "Pooling risk" refers to the point that making loans is risky because the borrower might not repay the loan. If a lender has loaned to only one borrower who does not repay the loan, the lender suffers a large loss. Banks make loans to many different borrowers and "pool" (or gather together) the risk of the loans. Although some loans will not be repaid, the majority will be repaid and so the average risk from failure to be repaid is lower; page 276.

■ CHECKPOINT 11.3

Fill in the blanks

The Fed conducts the nation's <u>monetary</u> policy. There are <u>12</u> Federal Reserve Banks. The Fed's main policy-making committee is the <u>Federal Open Market Committee</u>. The Fed sets the minimum percentage of deposits that must be held as reserves, which is called the <u>required reserve ratio</u>. The interest rate at which the Fed stands ready to lend reserves to commercial banks is the <u>discount</u> rate. The purchase or sale of government securities by the Federal Reserve is an <u>open market operation</u>.

True or false

1. True; page 279

2. False; page 281

3. False; page 282

4. True; page 282

5. False; page 283

Multiple choice

1. d; page 279

2. c; page 280

3. a; page 280

4. b; page 281

5. a; page 281

6. c; page 282

7. d; page 282

8. b; page 282

Short answer and numeric questions

1. There are seven members on the Board of Governors of the Federal Reserve System. They are appointed by the president of the United States and confirmed by the U.S. Senate; page 280.

2. The FOMC is the Federal Open Market Committee and it is the main policy-making committee of the Federal Reserve. The members are the seven members of the Board of Governors, the president of the Federal Reserve Bank of New York, and, on an annual rotating basis, four presidents of the other regional Federal Reserve banks; page 280.

3. a. If the required reserve ratio is 10 percent, banks must keep ($600 billion) × (0.10) = $60 billion as reserves; page 282.

   b. If the required reserve ratio is lowered to 8 percent, banks must keep ($600 billion) × (0.08) = $48 billion as reserves. A decrease in the required reserve ratio decreases the total amount of reserves banks must keep; page 282.

   c. If the required reserve ratio is raised to 12 percent, banks must keep ($600 billion) × (0.12) = $72 billion as reserves. An increase in the required reserve ratio increases the total amount of reserves banks must keep page 282.

4. The monetary base is the sum of coins, Federal Reserve notes, and banks' reserves at the Federal Reserve; page 282.

5. U.S. government securities are the Federal Reserve's largest asset. Federal Reserve notes (currency) are the largest liability of the Fed; pages 282-283.

Money Creation and Control

Chapter 12

CHAPTER IN PERSPECTIVE

Chapter 12 explains how banks create money and how the money supply is controlled by the Fed.

■ Explain how banks create money by making loans.

Banks accept deposits. They hold some deposits as reserves and use the rest to buy government securities and make loans. Deposits are a liability of the bank; reserves, government securities, and loans are assets of the bank. When a check is written, the recipient deposits it in another bank. Deposits and reserves in the first bank decrease and in the second bank increase. The required reserve ratio is the ratio of reserves to deposits that banks are required by regulation to hold. Excess reserves are actual reserves minus required reserves. Banks use excess reserves to buy government securities or make loans. When a bank makes a loan, it deposits the amount loaned in the checkable deposit of the borrower. The bank has now created money. To spend the loan, the borrower writes a check. The bank loses deposits and reserves when the check clears. The bank in which the check is deposited gains the reserves and deposits. This bank now has excess reserves, which it lends. When this loan is spent, a third bank gains reserves and deposits. The process is limited because at each round the change in excess reserves shrinks. The deposit multiplier is the number by which an increase in bank reserves is multiplied to find the resulting increase in bank deposits. The deposit multiplier equals 1 ÷ (required reserve ratio).

■ Explain how the Fed controls the quantity of money.

The Fed changes the quantity of money using three tools: required reserve ratio, discount rate, and open market operations. If the Fed decreases the required reserve ratio, banks hold less reserves. They increase their lending and the quantity of money increases. Changes in the required reserve ratio occur infrequently. If the Fed raises the discount rate, banks borrow less and decrease their lending, thereby decreasing the quantity of money. Changes in the discount rate have a little effect on the quantity of money because banks rarely borrow from the Fed. Open market operations are the Fed's major policy tool. If the Fed buys government securities, banks' reserves increase and excess reserves increase. Banks lend the excess reserves, new deposits are created, and the quantity of money increases. If the Fed sells government securities, banks' reserves decrease and excess reserves decrease. Banks decrease their lending, deposits are destroyed, and the quantity of money decreases. The monetary base changes by the amount of the open market purchase or sale. The money multiplier is the number by which a change in the monetary base is multiplied to find the resulting change in the quantity of money. A currency drain is currency held outside of the banks. The larger the currency drain and the larger the required reserve ratio, the smaller is the money multiplier because banks receive fewer deposits in each round of the multiplier lending and depositing process.

EXPANDED CHAPTER CHECKLIST

When you have completed this chapter, you will be able to:

1 Explain how banks create money by making loans.

- Define the balance sheet and describe the assets and liabilities that appear on a bank's balance sheet.
- Calculate the amount of reserves a bank must hold.
- Calculate a bank's excess reserves.
- Explain how loans made by the banking system create money.
- Define and calculate the deposit multiplier and use it to compute the change in deposits that results from a change in reserves.

2 Explain how the Fed controls the quantity of money.

- Explain how changes in the required reserve ratio and the discount rate affect the quantity of money.
- Describe an open market operation and trace the impact of an open market operation on the quantity of money.
- Explain why there is a multiplier effect from an open market operation and discuss the factors that affect the size of the effect.
- Calculate the money multiplier and use it to determine the effect a change in the monetary base has on the quantity of money.

KEY TERMS

- Balance sheet (page 290)
- Deposit multiplier (page 298)
- Currency drain (page 304)
- Money multiplier (page 306)

CHECKPOINT 12.1

■ Explain how banks create money by making loans.

Practice Problems 12.1

1. How do banks create new deposits by making loans and what factors limit the amount of deposits and loans they can create?
2. The required reserve ratio is 0.1 and banks have no excess reserves. Jamie deposits $100 in his bank. Calculate:
   a. The bank's excess reserves as soon as Jamie makes the deposit.
   b. The maximum amount of loans that the banking system can make.
   c. The maximum amount of new money that the banking system can create.

Solution to Practice Problems 12.1

These Practice Problems concentrate on the role that banks play in creating money. As you work through them, the crucial point to keep in mind is that banks can loan their excess reserves in order to boost their revenue and profit.

Quick Review

- *Excess reserves* Excess reserves equal actual reserves minus required reserves.
- *Deposit multiplier* The number by which an increase in bank reserves is multiplied to find the resulting increase in deposits. In terms of a formula, the deposit multiplier equals $1 \div$ (required reserve ratio). The deposit multiplier is greater than 1.0.

1. How do banks create new deposits by making loans and what factors limit the amount of deposits and loans they can create?

When a bank makes a loan, the bank creates a new deposit for the person who receives the loan. The amount of loans the bank makes and the amount of deposits it creates are limited by the bank's excess reserves because the amount banks can loan equals the amount of their excess reserves. Excess reserves are actual reserves in excess of required reserves. So the factors limiting the amount of deposits and loans a bank can create are the bank's actual reserves and the required reserve ratio, which together determine the amount of the bank's required reserves.

2. The required reserve ratio is 0.1 and banks have no excess reserves. Jamie deposits $100 in his bank. Calculate:

2a. The bank's excess reserves as soon as Jamie makes the deposit.

The new deposit of $100 increases the bank's actual reserves by $100. The bank is required to keep 10 percent of deposits as reserves. So required reserves increase by 10 percent of the deposit, or ($100) × (0.10), which is $10. As a result, excess reserves, which are actual reserves minus required reserves, increase by $100 – $10, which is $90.

2b. The maximum amount of loans that the banking system can make.

To determine the maximum loans that the banking system can create, use the deposit multiplier. The deposit multiplier equals 1 ÷ (required reserve ratio) which in this case is 1 ÷ (0.10) = 10. The increase in deposits is equal to the deposit multiplier times the change in reserves, which is (10) × ($100), or $1,000. Jamie initially deposited $100, so the maximum amount of loans the banking system can create equals the increase in deposits minus Jamie's initial deposit, which is $1,000 – $100 = $900.

2c. The maximum amount of new money that the banking system can create.

The banking system creates money by creating deposits. When a bank in the banking system makes a loan, it does so by creating a deposit. The increase in deposits equals the increase in loans. Because loans increase by $900, the banking system will create $900 of new money.

Additional Practice Problem 12.1a

In Practice Problem 2, how much could Jamie's bank loan? What was the amount of new money created by Jamie's bank?

Solution to Additional Practice Problem 12.1a

Jamie's bank can loan the amount of its excess reserves. When Jamie deposits $100, part (a) of the Practice Problem showed that Jamie's bank has $90 of excess reserves. As a result, Jamie's bank can loan $90. In making this loan, Jamie's bank created a deposit, which is new money. So, Jamie's bank created new money equal to $90.

■ Self Test 12.1

Fill in the blanks

Assets on a bank's balance sheet include ____ (cash; checkable deposits) and ____ (loans; owner's equity). A liability on a bank's balance sheet is ____ (reserves; checkable deposits). Banks ____ (create; do not create) money when they make loans. Any individual bank ____ (can; cannot) create unlimited amounts of money. The deposit multiplier shows that an increase in ____ (money; reserves) can be used to create additional ____ (money; reserves).

True or false

1. The first step in creating a bank is to accept deposits.

2. Checkable deposits are an asset on the bank's balance sheet.

3. A commercial bank's cash and its reserves at a Federal Reserve bank are assets on its balance sheet.

4. Excess reserves increase when the required reserve ratio increases, all other things remaining the same.

5. When banks clear checks, they create money.

6. When a bank increases its loans, it creates money.

7. The deposit multiplier equals the required reserve ratio.

8. Sandy, an immigrant, comes to the United States and deposits $190,000 into a bank. The required reserve ratio is 5 percent. When the entire sequence is completed, deposits increase by $3.8 million.

Multiple choice

1. Which of the following actions is NOT carried out by a bank?
   a. buy government securities
   b. clear checks
   c. make loans
   d. print money

2. A bank's balance sheet is a statement that summarizes
   a. only the bank's loans.
   b. only the bank's reserves.
   c. the bank's assets and liabilities.
   d. the number of banks in a community.

3. Cash in a bank is part of the bank's
   a. owners' equity.
   b. liabilities.
   c. assets.
   d. government securities.

4. Which of the following is a bank liability?
   a. checkable deposits
   b. government securities
   c. equipment
   d. loans

5. If the required reserve ratio is 20 percent, then for every dollar that is deposited in the bank, the bank must
   a. keep 20 cents as reserves.
   b. keep 80 cents as reserves.
   c. loan 80 cents.
   d. loan 20 cents.

6. A bank has checkable deposits of $500,000, loans of $300,000, and government securities of $200,000. If the required reserve ratio is 10 percent, the amount of required reserves is
   a. $20,000.
   b. $30,000.
   c. $50,000.
   d. $500,000.

7. Excess reserves are the
   a. same as the required reserves.
   b. amount of reserves the Fed requires banks to hold.
   c. amount of reserves held above what is required.
   d. amount of reserves a bank holds at the Fed.

8. Keisha writes a $500 check to Larry drawn on Community Bank. Larry deposits the $500 check in his checking account at Neighbors Bank. When the check clears both banks, ____ by $500.
   a. Community Bank's assets decrease
   b. Community Bank's assets increase
   c. Community Bank's liabilities increase
   d. Neighbors Bank's assets decrease

9. Banks can make loans up to an amount equal to their
   a. total deposits.
   b. total reserves.
   c. required reserves.
   d. excess reserves.

10. The banking system can create more money than an initial increase in excess reserves because
    a. banks are sneaky.
    b. the Fed lends money to the commercial banks.
    c. excess reserves are loaned and then deposited in other banks.
    d. banks charge more interest than they pay out.

11. The deposit multiplier equals
    a. 1/(required reserve).
    b. 1/(required reserve ratio).
    c. the required reserve ratio.
    d. 1/(excess reserve ratio).

12. If the required reserve ratio is 15 percent and banks loan all of their excess reserves, a new deposit of $20,000 leads to a total increase in deposits of
    a. $3,000.
    b. $20,000.
    c. $133,333.
    d. $200,000.

Short answer and numeric questions

Assets	Liabilities

1. The First Bank of Townsville has reserves at the Fed of $100, owner's equity of $200, loans of $800, checkable deposits of $1,000, cash of $200, and government securities of $100. Arrange these entries in the balance sheet above.

2. The Bank of Utah has deposits of $500 million and reserves of $60 million. If the required reserve ratio is 10 percent, calculate the bank's excess reserves. How much can the bank loan? If the required reserve ratio is changed to 8 percent, calculate the bank's excess reserves. How much can the bank loan?

3. How does making a loan create a deposit?

Round	Increase in deposits (dollars)	Increase in reserves (dollars)	Increase in excess reserves (dollars)	Loan (dollars)
A				
B				
C				
D				

4. Meg tutors 10 students during finals week and is paid $500 in cash. She deposits the $500 in her bank. The required reserve ratio is 10 percent and banks always loan the maximum possible.
    a. Starting with Meg's $500 deposit, complete the above table.
    b. After the first four rounds, what is the total increase in deposits?
    c. What will be the total increase in deposits?

5. If the required reserve ratio is 10 percent, what is the deposit multiplier? If the required reserve ratio is 5 percent, what is the deposit multiplier? What is the relationship between the required reserve ratio and the deposit multiplier?

CHECKPOINT 12.2

■ **Explain how the Fed controls the quantity of money.**

Practice Problems 12.2
1. Which of the Fed's tools does it use most often?
2. What is the money multiplier? What determines its magnitude?
3. If the Fed makes an open market purchase of $1 million of securities,
    a. Who can sell the securities to the Fed in an open market operation? Does it matter from whom the Fed buys the securities?
    b. What initial changes occur in the economy if the Fed buys from a bank?
    c. What is the process by which the quantity of money changes?
    d. What factors determine how much the quantity of money changes?

Solution to Practice Problems 12.2
These Practice Problems are designed to help you understand how the Fed operates to control the nation's money supply.

Quick Review
- *Open market operation* An open market operation is the purchase or sale of government securities by the Fed in the open market.
- *Money multiplier* The money multiplier is the number by which a change in the monetary base is multiplied to find the resulting change in the quantity of money.

1. **Which of the Fed's tools does it use most often?**
The Fed most frequently uses open market operations.

2. What is the money multiplier? What determines its magnitude?

The money multiplier is the number by which a change in the monetary base is multiplied to find the resulting change in the quantity of money. The factors that determine the magnitude of the money multiplier are the required reserve ratio and the currency drain. If the required reserve ratio or the currency drain increase, the money multiplier will be smaller. Conversely, if the required reserve ratio or the currency drain decrease, the money multiplier will be larger.

3. If the Fed makes an open market purchase of $1 million of securities,

3a. Who can sell the securities to the Fed in an open market operation? Does it matter from whom the Fed buys the securities?

The Fed buys government securities from banks and the public. The Fed does not buy securities from the U.S. government itself. It makes no difference if the Fed buys the securities from the public or banks. If it buys from a bank, the bank's reserves increase by the amount of the purchase as soon as the Fed pays for the securities. If the Fed buys from the public, it pays by check and the bank's reserves increase by the amount of the purchase as soon as the check is deposited. The change in the monetary base is the same in either case.

3b. What initial changes occur in the economy if the Fed buys from a bank?

When the Fed buys securities from a bank, the monetary base increases by $1 million. Ownership of the securities passes from the bank to the Fed and the Fed's assets increase by $1 million. The Fed pays for the securities by increasing the bank's deposits with the Fed by $1 million. So the Fed's liabilities also increase by $1 million. The composition of the bank's assets changes, but the value of the bank's total assets does not change: the bank has $1 million more in reserves and $1 million less in securities.

3c. What is the process by which the quantity of money changes?

After the Fed's open market purchase of government securities, the bank's reserves have in-

creased by $1 million and its deposits have not changed. The bank has $1 million in excess reserves. It will loan these excess reserves and create new deposits which are new money. The borrower writes a check which is deposited in another bank. This bank now has excess reserves that it can loan. This loan creates another new deposit, that is, more new money. The process of depositing, loaning, and creating new deposits continues and the quantity of money increases.

3d. What factors determine how much the quantity of money changes?

Anything that affects the size of the money multiplier affects the change in the quantity of money that will result from this open market operation. The two factors that affect the size of the money multiplier are the required reserve ratio and the currency drain. If the required reserve ratio increases or if the currency drain increases, the money multiplier decreases in magnitude and there is a smaller change in the quantity of money from an open market operation.

Additional Practice Problem 12.2a

If the Fed makes an open market sale of $1 million of government securities to Fleet Bank, what initial changes occur on the Fed's balance sheet and on Fleet Bank's balance sheet? Be sure to tell if each change affects an asset or a liability.

Solution to Additional Practice Problem 12.2a

When the Fed sells $1 million of government securities, the Fed's holding of government securities decreases by $1 million. The Fed decreases Fleet Bank's reserves at the Fed by $1 million. One of the Fed's assets, government securities, and one of its liabilities, reserve deposits, decrease by $1 million. For Fleet Bank, its holdings of government securities increase by $1 million and its reserves at the Fed decrease by $1 million. For Fleet Bank, one of its assets, government securities, increases by $1 million, and another of its assets, reserves at the Fed, decrease by $1 million.

■ Self Test 12.2

Fill in the blanks

An increase in the required reserve ratio ____ (decreases; increases) the quantity of money. An increase in the discount rate ____ (decreases; increases) the quantity of money. When the Fed purchases government securities, it ____ (decreases; increases) the quantity of money. An open market sale of government securities by the Fed ____ (decreases; increases) the monetary base and ____ (decreases; increases) banks' excess reserves. An increase in currency held outside the banks is called ____ (an excess currency removal; a currency drain; a multiplier reserve). If the money multiplier is 2.0, a \$4 million increase in the monetary base will create an increase of ____ (\$2; \$8) million in the quantity of money.

True or false

1. To increase the quantity of money, the Fed can increase the required reserve ratio.

2. When the Fed lowers the discount rate, the quantity of money increases.

3. The Fed's major policy tool is the discount rate.

4. When the Fed sells government securities, it decreases the quantity of banks' reserves.

5. The effect on the money supply when the Fed buys government securities depends on whether the Fed buys the securities from a bank or the general public.

6. When the Fed buys government securities from a bank, the bank has less securities and more reserves.

7. The larger the currency drain, the larger the money multiplier.

8. If the currency drain is 0.25 and the required reserve ratio is 0.1, the money multiplier is 0.675.

Multiple choice

1. The Fed's policy tools are
   a. the excess reserve ratio, required reserve ratios, and the discount rate.
   b. required reserve ratios, the discount rate, and open market operations.
   c. open market operations, excess reserves, and required reserves.
   d. open market operations, closed market operations, and required reserves.

2. When the Fed increases the required reserve ratio, excess reserves ____ and the quantity of money in the economy ____.
   a. increase; increases
   b. increase; decreases
   c. decrease; increases
   d. decrease; decreases

3. The Fed changes the required reserve ratio
   a. never.
   b. more often than it conducts open market operations.
   c. less often than it conducts open market operations.
   d. every time it conducts an open market operation.

4. When the Fed buys or sells securities, it is conducting ____ operation.
   a. a closed door
   b. an open market
   c. a multiplier
   d. a deposit

5. If the Fed buys securities from a commercial bank, the effect on the quantity of money
   a. is larger than when the Fed buys securities from the non-bank public.
   b. is less than when the Fed buys securities from the non-bank public.
   c. is the same as when the Fed buys securities from the non-bank public.
   d. depends on whether the bank was borrowing reserves from another bank.

6. If the Fed buys government securities, then
   a. the quantity of money is not changed, just its composition.
   b. new bank reserves are created.
   c. the quantity of money decreases.
   d. old bank reserves are destroyed.

7. The Citizens First Bank sells $100,000 of government securities to the Fed. This sale
   a. decreases the quantity of money.
   b. decreases the bank's deposits.
   c. increases the bank's required reserves.
   d. increases the quantity of money.

8. The Fed sells $100 million of U.S. government securities to Bank of America. Bank of America's balance sheet shows this transaction as a $100 million ____ in government securities and a $100 million ____ in reserves.
   a. increase; increase
   b. increase; decrease
   c. decrease; increase
   d. decrease; decrease

9. A currency drain is cash
   a. lost in the drain.
   b. draining into the banks.
   c. held outside the banks.
   d. held at the Fed.

10. If the currency drain increases,
    a. the monetary base increases.
    b. banks' reserves decrease.
    c. the quantity of money increases.
    d. banks' reserves increase.

11. The money multiplier is used to determine how much the
    a. monetary base increases when the Fed purchases government securities.
    b. quantity of money increases when the monetary base increases.
    c. monetary base increases when the quantity of money increases.
    d. quantity of money increases when the required reserve ratio increases.

12. The Fed makes an open market operation purchase of $200,000. The currency drain is 0.33 and the required reserve ratio is 0.10. By

how much does the quantity of money increase?
   a. $250,000
   b. $333,333
   c. $2,000,000
   d. $500,000

Short answer and numeric questions

1. What three policy tools does the Federal Reserve possess? Briefly explain how each works to increase the quantity of money.

Round	Increase in currency (dollars)	Increase in deposits (dollars)	Increase in reserves (dollars)	Increase in excess reserves (dollars)
A			1,000	1,000
B	___	___	___	___
C	___	___	___	___
D	___	___	___	___

2. Suppose the Fed buys $1,000 of government securities from Hayward National Bank. The required reserve ratio is 0.10 and the currency drain is 0.20. Suppose that all banks loan all of their excess reserves. Complete the above table. Calculate the total increase in deposits and currency following the first four rounds of the multiplier process.

Round	Increase in currency (dollars)	Increase in deposits (dollars)	Increase in reserves (dollars)	Increase in excess reserves (dollars)
A			1,000	1,000
B	___	___	___	___
C	___	___	___	___
D	___	___	___	___

3. Suppose the Fed buys $1,000 of government securities from Fremont National Bank. The required reserve ratio is 0.10 percent and the currency drain is 0.50. Suppose that all banks loan all of their excess reserves. Complete the above table. Calculate the total increase in deposits and currency following the first four rounds of the multiplier process.

4. In which question, 2 or 3, was the increase in the quantity of money largest after four rounds?

5. Calculate the money multiplier when the required reserve ratio is 0.10 and the currency drain is 0.25 percent. Calculate the money multiplier when the required reserve ratio is 0.10 and the currency drain is 0.60. As the currency drain increases, what happens to the magnitude of the money multiplier?

6. Why does an increase in the required reserve ratio or in the currency drain decrease the magnitude of the money multiplier?

SELF TEST ANSWERS

■ CHECKPOINT 12.1

Fill in the blanks

Assets on a bank's balance sheet include <u>cash</u> and <u>loans</u>. A liability on a bank's balance sheet is <u>checkable deposits</u>. Banks <u>create</u> money when they make loans. Any individual bank <u>cannot</u> create unlimited amounts of money. The deposit multiplier shows that an increase in <u>reserves</u> can be used to create additional <u>money</u>.

True or false

1. False; page 290
2. False; page 292
3. True; page 292
4. False; pages 292-293
5. False; pages 293-294
6. True; pages 295-296
7. False; page 298
8. True; page 298

Multiple choice

1. d; page 290
2. c; page 290
3. c; page 290
4. a; page 292
5. a; page 292
6. c; page 292
7. c; page 293
8. a; page 293
9. d; page 295
10. c; page 296
11. b; page 298
12. c; page 298

Short answer and numeric questions

Assets		Liabilities	
Cash	200	Deposits	1,000
Reserves at the Fed	100		
Loans	800		
Government securities	100	Owner's equity	200

1. The completed balance sheet is above; page 295.

2. The Bank of Utah's required reserves are $(0.10) \times (\$500$ million$) = \$50$ million, so it has excess reserves of $10 million. It can loan the amount of its excess reserves, $10 million. If the required reserve ratio is 8 percent, the bank's required reserves are $40 million and so the bank has $20 million of excess reserves. When the required reserve ratio decreases, the amount the bank can loan increases; page 293.

3. When a bank makes a loan, the bank deposits the loan in the borrower's checkable deposit. For instance, when Emma borrows $30,000 to buy machines for her business, the bank places the $30,000 in Emma's checkable deposit. As a result, when a loan is made, an equal sized deposit is created; page 295.

Round	Increase in deposits (dollars)	Increase in reserves (dollars)	Increase in excess reserves (dollars)	Loan (dollars)
A	500.00	500.00	450.00	450.00
B	450.00	450.00	405.00	405.00
C	405.00	405.00	364.50	364.50
D	364.50	364.50	328.05	328.05

4. a. The completed table is above; page 297.
   b. The total increase in deposits after the first four rounds is $1,719.50.
   c. The total increase in deposits is the deposit multiplier, 10, multiplied by the increase in reserves, $500, or $10.0 \times \$500.00$, which equals $5,000; page 298.

5. The deposit multiplier equals 1/(required reserve ratio). When the required reserve ratio is 10 percent, the deposit multiplier is $1 \div (0.10) = 10$. When the required reserve ratio is 5 percent, the deposit multiplier is $1 \div (0.05) = 20$. When the required reserve ratio is smaller, the deposit multiplier is larger; page 298.

■ CHECKPOINT 12.2

Fill in the blanks

An increase in the required reserve ratio <u>decreases</u> the quantity of money. An increase in the discount rate <u>decreases</u> the quantity of money. When the Fed purchases government securities, it <u>increases</u> the quantity of money. An open market sale of government securities by the Fed <u>decreases</u> the monetary base and <u>decreases</u> banks' excess reserves. An increase in currency held outside the banks is called <u>a currency drain</u>. If the money multiplier is 2.0, a $4 million increase in the monetary base will create an increase of <u>$8</u> million in the quantity of money.

True or false

1. False; page 300
2. True; page 300
3. False; page 300
4. True; page 300
5. False; page 301
6. True; page 301
7. False; page 306
8. False; page 307

Multiple choice

1. b; page 300
2. d; page 300
3. c; page 300
4. b; page 300
5. c; pages 301-303
6. b; page 301
7. d; page 301
8. b; page 303
9. c; page 304
10. b; page 304
11. b; page 306
12. d; pages 306-307

Short answer and numeric questions

1. The Fed's policy tools are required reserve ratios, the discount rate, and open market operations. A decrease in the required reserve ratio increases banks' excess reserves, which allows them to increase their loans. So, when the Fed lowers the required reserve ratio, the quantity of money increases. The required reserve ratio affects the money multiplier. The discount rate has little effect on the quantity of money because banks rarely borrow from the Fed. An open market purchase of government securities increases banks' excess reserves and increases the quantity of money. An open market operation changes the monetary base; page 300.

Round	Increase in currency (dollars)	Increase in deposits (dollars)	Increase in reserves (dollars)	Increase in excess reserves (dollars)
A			1,000.00	1,000.00
B	200.00	800.00	800.00	720.00
C	144.00	576.00	576.00	518.40
D	103.68	414.72	414.72	373.25

2. The completed table is above. After four rounds, currency increases by $447.68, deposits increase by $1,790.72, and the quantity of money increases by the sum of the increase in currency and the increase in deposits, which is $2,238.40; page 305.

Round	Increase in currency (dollars)	Increase in deposits (dollars)	Increase in reserves (dollars)	Increase in excess reserves (dollars)
A			1,000	1,000
B	500.00	500.00	500.00	450.00
C	225.00	225.00	225.00	202.50
D	101.25	101.25	101.25	91.13

3. The completed table is above. After four rounds, currency increases by $826.25, deposits increase by $826.25, and the quantity of money increases by the sum of the increase in currency and the increase in deposits, which is $1,652.50; page 305.

4. The increase in the quantity of money is greater when the currency drain is smaller, in question 2; page 307.

5. To answer this question, use two formulas. First use $L = (1 - C) \times (1 - R)$ where C is the currency drain, and R is the required reserve ratio. (L in this formula is the ratio of the loan in one round of the multiplier process to the

loan in the prior round.) Then calculate the money multiplier, which equals $1 \div (1 - L)$. When $R = 0.10$ and $C = 0.25$, $L = 0.675$, so the money multiplier equals 3.08. When $R = 0.10$ and $C = 0.60$, $L = 0.360$, so the money multiplier equals 1.56. As the currency drain increases, the magnitude of the money multiplier decreases; pages 306-307.

6. The money multiplier exists because of the process of loaning, depositing the proceeds in another bank, and then making another loan. The more each bank loans, the greater the final increase in the quantity of money and the larger the money multiplier. If the required reserve ratio increases in size, banks will be able to loan less of any additional deposit they receive. And if the currency drain increases, less is deposited in a bank and the bank will be able to loan less. Because an increase in the required reserve ratio and an increase in the currency drain decrease the amount that can be loaned, both decrease the size of the money multiplier; page 306.

Chapter

Money, Interest, and Inflation

13

Chapter 13 discusses how the quantity of money determines the nominal interest rate. It studies the relationship between the quantity of money and the price level as well as between money growth and inflation.

■ **Explain what determines the demand for money and how the demand for money and the supply of money determine the *nominal* interest rate.**

The inventory of money that households and firms choose to hold is the quantity of money demanded. The nominal interest rate is the opportunity cost of holding money. The demand for money curve shows the quantity of money demanded at each nominal interest rate. An increase in the price level or real GDP increases the demand for money and the demand for money curve shifts rightward. The supply of money is a fixed quantity on any given day. Equilibrium in the money market determines the nominal interest rate. When the Fed increases the quantity of money, the nominal interest rate falls, and when the Fed decreases the quantity of money, the nominal interest rate rises.

■ **Explain how in the long run, the quantity of money determines the price level and money growth brings inflation.**

A one-time increase in the quantity of money lowers the nominal interest rate in the short run. In the long run, a one-time increase in the quantity of money brings an equal percentage increase in the price level and the nominal interest rate returns to its initial value. The quantity theory of money is the proposition when real GDP equals potential GDP, an increase in the quantity of money brings an equal percentage increase in the price level. The equation of exchange states that the quantity of money multiplied by the velocity of circulation equals nominal GDP. An increase in the quantity of money, with no change in potential GDP or velocity, leads to the same percentage increase in the price level. In rates of change, money growth plus velocity growth equals inflation plus real GDP growth. An increase in the growth of the quantity of money, with no change in the growth of velocity or real GDP, leads to an equal increase in the inflation rate. A hyperinflation is inflation at a rate that exceeds 50 percent a month.

■ **Identify the costs of inflation and the benefits of a stable value of money.**

The four costs of inflation are tax costs, shoe-leather costs, confusion costs, and uncertainty costs. Inflation is a tax. With inflation, households and business lose purchasing power, which is the tax on holding money. Inflation interacts with the income tax to lower saving and investment. Shoe-leather costs are costs that arise from an increase in the amount of running around that people do to try to avoid losses from the falling value of money. Confusion costs are costs of making errors because of rapidly changing prices. Uncertainty costs arise because long-term planning is difficult, so people have a shorter-term focus. Investment falls and the growth rate slows.

EXPANDED CHAPTER CHECKLIST

When you have completed this chapter, you will be able to:

1 **Explain what determines the demand for money and how the demand for money and the supply of money determine the *nominal* interest rate.**

- Discuss the factors that influence the demand for money.
- Explain the relationship between the nominal interest rate, the real interest rate, and the inflation rate.
- Draw a figure to illustrate the money market and indicate the money market equilibrium.
- Explain how the nominal interest rate changes when the Fed changes the quantity of money.

2 **Explain how in the long run, the quantity of money determines the price level and money growth brings inflation.**

- Explain the relationship between a change in the quantity of money and the money market in the long run
- Use the quantity theory of money and the equation of exchange to describe the relationship between a change in the quantity of money and the price level.
- Explain the relationship between a change in the growth rate of the quantity of money and the inflation rate.

3 **Identify the costs of inflation and the benefits of a stable value of money.**

- Explain why inflation is a tax.
- List and discuss the four costs of inflation.
- Explain why high inflation as well as unpredictable inflation impose costs on society.

KEY TERMS

- Quantity of money demanded (page 315)
- Demand for money (page 316)
- Supply of money (page 319)
- Quantity theory of money (page 327)
- Velocity of circulation (page 327)
- Equation of exchange (page 327)
- Hyperinflation (page 331)

CHECKPOINT 13.1

■ **Explain what determines the demand for money and how the demand for money and the supply of money determine the *nominal* interest rate.**

Practice Problems 13.1

1. The figure shows the demand for money curve.

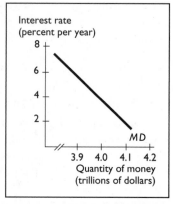

Interest rate (percent per year)

Quantity of money (trillions of dollars)

a. If the quantity of money is $4 trillion, what is the nominal interest rate?

b. If real GDP increases, how will the interest rate change? Explain the process that brings about the change in the interest rate.

c. In part (a), the Fed decreases the quantity of money to $3.9 trillion. Will bond prices rise or fall? Why? What happens to the nominal interest rate?

2. Suppose that banks increase the fee they charge for credit cards, introduce a user fee on every credit card purchase, and increase the interest rate on outstanding credit card balances.

a. How would the demand for money change?

b. How would the nominal interest rate change?

Solution to Practice Problems 13.1

These problems show how the nominal interest rate is determined in the money market. You will use the supply and demand model introduced in Chapter 4.

Quick Review

- *Shifts in the demand for money curve* When real GDP, the price level, or financial technology change, the demand for money curve shifts.

- *Equilibrium nominal interest rate* The equilibrium nominal interest rate occurs where the demand for money curve intersects the supply curve because at this interest rate the quantity of money demanded equals the quantity supplied.

1a. If the quantity of money is $4 trillion, what is the nominal interest rate?

The nominal interest rate is 4 percent a year because the quantity of money demanded equals $4 trillion when the interest rate is 4 percent.

1b. If real GDP increases, how will the interest rate change? Explain the process that brings about the change in the interest rate.

The interest rate rises. When real GDP increases, the demand for money increases. As a result, at the initial interest rate of 4 percent a year, people want to hold more money, so they sell bonds. The price of a bond falls and the interest rate rises.

1c. In part (a), the Fed decreases the quantity of money to $3.9 trillion. Will bond prices rise or fall? Why? What happens to the nominal interest rate?

At an interest rate of 4 percent a year, people want to hold $4 trillion. Only $3.9 trillion is available so they sell bonds. The price of a bond falls and the interest rate rises. The figure shows that when the quantity of money decreases to $3.9 trillion, the nominal interest rate rises to 6 percent a year.

2. Suppose that banks increase the fee they charge for credit cards, introduce a user fee on every credit card purchase, and increase the interest rate on outstanding credit card balances.

2a. How would the demand for money change?

People will use their credit cards less because it is more expensive to use credit cards. The demand for money increases as people use money for more transactions.

2b. How would the nominal interest rate change?

An increase in the demand for money raises the nominal interest rate.

Additional Practice Problems 13.1a

Tomorrow all stores will install retinal scanner identification machines, which allow people to make a purchase without having to carry a credit card. What effect will this technological advance have on the demand for money and on the nominal interest rate?

Solution to Additional Practice Problem 13.1a

This change in technology makes credit purchases more attractive for consumers and merchants. There is an increase in credit purchases and a decrease in the purchases made with money. The demand for money decreases. People want to hold less money than they are actually holding. They buy bonds. The price of a bond rises and the nominal interest rate falls.

■ Self Test 13.1

Fill in the blanks

The nominal interest rate equals the real interest rate ____ (plus; minus; divided by) the inflation rate. The opportunity cost of holding money is the ____ (price level; nominal interest rate). An increase in real GDP ____ (increases; decreases) the demand for money and shifts the demand for money curve ____ (rightward; leftward). An increase in the price level ____ (increases; decreases) the demand for money and shifts the demand for money curve ____ (rightward; leftward). If the nominal interest rate is above the equilibrium level, people ____ (buy; sell) bonds, the price of a bond ____ (rises; falls), and the interest rate ____ (rises; falls). If the Fed decreases the quantity of money, the nominal interest rate ____ (rises; falls).

True or false

1. The real interest rate is the opportunity cost of holding money.

2. An increase in real GDP shifts the demand for money curve leftward.

3. If the price of a government bond rises, the interest rate on the bond rises.

4. When the interest rate is above its equilibrium level, people buy bonds and the interest rate falls.

5. An increase in the quantity of money lowers the interest rate.

Multiple choice

1. The quantity of money demanded
   a. is infinite.
   b. has no opportunity cost.
   c. is the quantity that balances the benefit of holding an additional dollar of money against the opportunity cost of doing so.
   d. is directly controlled by the Fed.

2. Which of the following statements is correct?
   a. Nominal interest rate = Real interest rate − Inflation rate
   b. Nominal interest rate = Real interest rate + Inflation rate
   c. Nominal interest rate = Inflation rate − Real interest rate
   d. Nominal interest rate = Inflation rate + Price index

3. The opportunity cost of holding money is the
   a. real interest rate.
   b. nominal interest rate.
   c. inflation rate.
   d. time it takes to go to the ATM or bank.

4. The demand for money curve shows the relationship between the quantity of money demanded and
   a. the nominal interest rate.
   b. the real interest rate.
   c. the inflation rate.
   d. real GDP.

5. The demand for money ____ when the price level rises.
   a. increases
   b. decreases
   c. remains constant
   d. None of the above answers is correct.

6. Every day, ____ adjusts to make the quantity of money demanded equal the quantity of money supplied.
   a. the inflation rate
   b. the nominal interest rate
   c. the quantity of money
   d. potential GDP

7. If the nominal interest rate is above its equilibrium level, then
   a. people sell financial assets and the interest rate falls.
   b. people buy financial assets and the interest rate falls.
   c. the demand for money curve shifts rightward and the interest rate rises.
   d. the supply of money curve shifts leftward and the interest rate rises.

8. When the Fed increases the quantity of money, the
   a. equilibrium interest rate falls.
   b. equilibrium interest rate rises.
   c. demand for money curve shifts rightward.
   d. supply of money curve shifts leftward.

Complete the graph

Nominal interest rate (percent per year)	Quantity of money, (trillions of 1996 dollars)
5	1.2
6	1.0
7	0.8
8	0.6
9	0.4
10	0.2

1. The table above has data on the nominal interest rate and the quantity of money demanded.
   a. Using the data, label the axes and plot the demand for money curve in Figure 13.1 (on the next page).

■ **FIGURE 13.1**

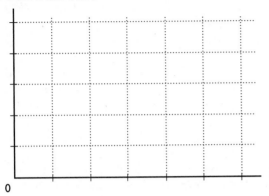

b. Suppose the Fed sets the quantity of money at $0.6 trillion. Plot this quantity in Figure 13.1. What is the equilibrium nominal interest rate?

c. Suppose the Fed wants the nominal interest rate to equal 6 percent a year. What action must the Fed take?

Short answer and numeric questions

1. What are the benefits from holding money?

2. What is the opportunity cost of holding money and why is this the opportunity cost?

3. What effect will an increase in real GDP have on the demand for money curve?

4. Suppose a government bond pays $100 in interest each year. If you buy the bond for $1,000, what is the interest rate? If you buy the bond for $2,000 dollars, what is the interest rate? As the price of the bond increases, what happens to the interest rate?

5. How can the Fed lower the nominal interest rate?

CHECKPOINT 13.2

■ **Explain how in the long run, the quantity of money determines the price level and money growth brings inflation.**

Practice Problems 13.2

1. In 1999, the Canadian economy was at full employment. Real GDP was $886 billion, the nominal interest rate was around 6 percent per year, the inflation rate was 2 percent a year, the price level was 110, and the velocity of circulation was constant at 10.

 a. Calculate the real interest rate.

 b. If the real interest rate remains unchanged when the inflation rate increases to 4 percent a year, explain how the nominal interest rate changes.

 c. What was the quantity of money in Canada?

2. If the quantity of money grows at a rate of 10 percent a year and potential GDP grows at 3 percent a year, what is the inflation rate in the long run?

Solution to Practice Problems 13.2

Remember that in growth rates, money growth plus velocity growth equals inflation plus real GDP growth. Also, potential GDP growth and velocity growth are not influenced by the growth rate of the quantity of money.

Quick Review

- *Inflation rate in the long run* In the long run and other things remaining the same, a given percentage change in the quantity of money brings an equal percentage change in the price level.

- *Quantity theory of money* The proposition that when real GDP equals potential GDP, an increase in the quantity of money brings an equal percentage increase in the price level.

- *Equation of exchange* An equation that states that the quantity of money multiplied by the velocity of circulation equals the price level multiplied by real GDP, that is $M \times V = P \times Y$.

1. In 1999, the Canadian economy was at full employment. Real GDP was $886 billion, the nominal interest rate was around 6 percent per year, the inflation rate was 2 percent a year, the price level was 110, and the velocity of circulation was constant at 10.

 1a. Calculate the real interest rate.

The real interest rate equals the nominal interest rate minus the inflation rate, so the real interest rate is 6 percent a year minus 2 percent a year, which equals 4 percent a year.

> **1b. If the real interest rate remains unchanged when the inflation rate increases to 4 percent a year, explain how the nominal interest rate changes.**

The nominal interest rate equals the real interest rate plus the inflation rate. When the inflation rate is 4 percent a year and the real interest rate equals 4 percent a year, the nominal interest rate is 4 percent a year plus 4 percent a year, which is 8 percent a year.

> **1c. What was the quantity of money in Canada?**

Use the equation of exchange, $M \times V = P \times Y$. Velocity, V, is 10, real GDP, Y, is $886 billion, and the price level P, is 110. Rewriting the equation as $M = (P \times Y) \div V = (\$975 \text{ billion}) \div 10 = \$97.5$ billion. So the quantity of money in Canada is $97.5 billion.

2.If the quantity of money grows at a rate of 10 percent a year and potential GDP grows at 3 percent a year, what is the inflation rate in the long run?

With velocity constant, the inflation rate equals the growth rate of the quantity of money minus the growth rate of potential GDP. The inflation rate equals 10 percent a year minus 3 percent a year, which is 7 percent a year.

Additional Practice Problem 13.2a

The quantity of money is $90 billion, real GDP is $900 billion, and the price level is 110. Find the velocity of circulation.

Solution to Additional Practice Problem 13.2a

The velocity of circulation is the number of times in a year that the average dollar of money gets used to buy final goods and services. The velocity of circulation is calculated using the formula $V = (P \times Y) \div M$. Nominal GDP, which equals $P \times Y$, is $990 billion. So velocity equals ($990 billion) $\div$ $90 billion = 11.

■ Self Test 13.2

Fill in the blanks

Other things remaining the same, a given percentage increase in the quantity of money brings an equal percentage ____ (increase; decrease) in the price level in the long run. An increase in the quantity of money ____ (lowers; raises; does not change) the nominal interest rate in the short run and ____ (lowers; raises; does not change) the nominal interest rate in the long run. The proposition that when real GDP equals potential GDP, an increase in the quantity of money brings an equal percentage increase in the price level is the ____ (quality; inflation; quantity) theory of money. If the velocity of circulation does not change, the inflation rate equals the growth rate of the ____ (quantity of money; nominal interest rate) ____ (minus; divided by) the growth rate of real GDP.

True or false

1. If the inflation rate is 2 percent a year and the real interest rate is 4 percent a year, the nominal interest rate is 6 percent a year.

2. In the long run, an increase in the quantity of money raises the price level and leaves the nominal interest rate unchanged.

3. $M \times P = V \times Y$ is the equation of exchange.

4. According to the quantity theory of money, in the long run with other things remaining the same, a 5 percent increase in the quantity of money brings a 5 percent increase in the price level.

5. According to the quantity theory of money, if the quantity of money grows 2 percent a year faster, the inflation rate falls by 2 percent a year.

Multiple choice

1. In the long run, the price level adjusts
   a. so that the real interest rate equals the nominal interest rate.
   b. so that the inflation rate equals zero.
   c. to achieve money market equilibrium at the long-run equilibrium interest rate.
   d. None of the above answers is correct.

2. If the equilibrium real interest rate is 4 percent a year and the inflation rate is 4 percent

a year, then the nominal interest rate is ____ percent a year.
a. 4
b. 8
c. 0
d. 6

3. Other things remaining the same, if the quantity of money increases by a given percentage, then in the long run the ____ by the same percentage.
a. price level rises
b. price level falls
c. real interest rate rises
d. real interest rate falls

4. In the long run, an increase in the quantity of money ____ the price level and ____ the nominal interest rate.
a. raises; raises
b. raises; does not change
c. raises; lowers
d. does not change; raises

5. Suppose that $P \times Y$ is $5,000 million a year and the quantity of money is $500 million. Then the velocity of circulation is
a. 50.
b. 500.
c. 10.
d. 20.

6. The quantity theory of money is a proposition about the
a. Fed's operating procedures to change the quantity of money.
b. relationship between nominal and real interest rates.
c. relationship between a change in the quantity of money and the price level.
d. relationship between financial assets and currency demanded.

7. If the quantity of money grows at 3 percent a year, velocity does not grow, and real GDP grows at 2 percent a year, then the inflation rate equals ____ percent a year.
a. 6
b. 5
c. 1
d. –1

8. Hyperinflation is
a. inflation caused by negative growth in the quantity of money.
b. inflation at a rate that exceeds 50 percent a month.
c. inflation caused by excessive growth in the demand for money.
d. inflation at a rate that exceeds 5 percent a month.

Short answer and numeric questions
1. In the long run, what is the effect of a 5 percent increase in the quantity of money, other things remaining the same?

2. The table gives data for the nation of Quantoland, a small nation to the south. In 2002, 2003, and 2004, real GDP equals potential GDP.

Year	Quantity of money (billions of dollars)	Velocity of circulation	Price level (1996 = 100)	Real GDP (billions of 1996 dollars)
2002	100	11	____	1,000
2003	110	11	____	1,000
2004	121	11	____	1,000

a. Complete the table.
b. Calculate the percentage change in the quantity of money in 2003 and 2004. Then calculate the percentage change in the price level in 2003 and 2004.
c. What key proposition is illustrated in your answer to part (b)?

3. In the long run, if real GDP grows at 3 percent a year, velocity does not change, and the quantity of money grows at 5 percent a year, what is the inflation rate?

4. What is a hyperinflation? What leads to hyperinflation?

CHECKPOINT 13.3

■ **Identify the costs of inflation and the benefits of a stable value of money.**

Practice Problem 13.3

Suppose that you have $1,000 in your savings account and the bank pays an interest rate of 5 percent a year. The inflation rate is 3 percent a year. The government taxes the interest you earn on your deposit at 20 percent.
  a. Calculate the nominal after-tax interest rate that you earn.
  b. Calculate the real after-tax interest rate you earn.

Solution to Practice Problem 13.3

The interaction of income taxes and inflation is an important real world cost of inflation. As you work the Practice Problem, think about what your after-tax real interest rate will be after you graduate and your income tax rate is higher.

Quick Review

  • *The inflation rate and income tax* Inflation increases the nominal interest rate, and because income taxes are paid on nominal interest income, the true income tax rate rises with inflation.

Suppose that you have $1,000 in your savings account and the bank pays an interest rate of 5 percent a year. The inflation rate is 3 percent a year. The government taxes the interest you earn on your deposit at 20 percent.

  a. Calculate the nominal after-tax interest rate that you earn.

In a year you earn interest income of $50, which is 5 percent of $1,000. You pay the government 20 percent, or $10. The interest income you earn after the tax payment is $40. The after-tax nominal interest rate is ($40 ÷ $1,000) × 100, which is 4.0 percent a year.

  b. Calculate the real after-tax interest rate you earn.

The real after-tax interest rate equals the nominal after-tax interest rate, 4 percent a year, minus the inflation rate, 3 percent a year. So the

real after-tax interest rate is 4 percent a year – 3 percent a year, which equals 1 percent a year.

Additional Practice Problem 13.3a

In the island of Atlantis where you live, the inflation rate has been varying between 3 percent a year and 10 percent a year in recent years. You are willing to lend money if you are guaranteed a real interest rate of at least 2 percent a year. There are potential borrowers, but they will borrow only if they are guaranteed a real interest rate of not more than 5 percent a year.
  a. Can you successfully make a loan if everyone can accurately predict the inflation rate?
  b. Can you successfully make a loan if neither you nor the borrowers can accurately predict the inflation rate?

Solution to Additional Practice Problem 13.3a

  a. Can you successfully make a loan if everyone can accurately predict the inflation rate?

If you and the potential borrowers can accurately predict the inflation rate, it is possible to make a loan. If everyone knows the inflation rate is 10 percent a year, you are willing to lend as long as you receive a nominal interest rate of at least 12 percent a year. Borrowers are willing to pay a real interest rate of no more than 5 percent a year, so borrowers are willing to agree to a loan as long as the nominal rate is no more than 15 percent a year. Because they are willing to pay up to 15 percent a year and you are willing to take as little as 12 percent a year, you can make a loan and charge a nominal interest rate between 12 percent a year and 15 percent a year. Similarly, if everyone knows the inflation rate is 3 percent a year, a loan can be made with a nominal interest rate between 5 percent a year and 8 percent a year.

  b. Can you successfully make a loan if neither you nor the borrowers can accurately predict the inflation rate?

To receive a real interest rate of at least 2 percent a year you must receive a nominal interest rate of at least 12 percent a year in case inflation is 10 percent a year. If borrowers pay a nominal interest rate of 12 percent a year and inflation is 3 percent a year, they are paying a real interest rate of 9 percent a year, well above their maximum real interest rate of 5 percent a year. Because the inflation rate could be as low as 3 percent a year, borrowers are not willing to take a loan at a nominal interest rate of more than 8 percent a year (inflation of 3 percent a year plus a real interest rate of 5 percent a year). Because of the uncertainty about the inflation rate, you don't make the loan.

■ Self Test 13.3

Fill in the blanks

Inflation ____ (is; is not) a tax. The higher the inflation rate, the ____ (lower; higher) the true income tax rate on income from capital. During an inflation, the costs that arise from an increase in the velocity of circulation of money and an increase in the amount of running around to avoid incurring losses from the falling value of money are ____ (shoe-leather; confusion) costs. Increased uncertainty about inflation leads to a ____ (rise; fall) in investment.

True or false

1. Inflation is a tax.

2. The "shoe-leather costs" of inflation are the result of the increase in the velocity of circulation when inflation increases.

3. One of the benefits of inflation is that it makes the value of money change, which benefits both borrowers and lenders.

4. When there is a high inflation rate, the growth rate slows.

5. No country in the world has experienced hyperinflation since the end of the 1950s.

Multiple choice

1. All of the following are costs of inflation EXCEPT
   a. tax costs.
   b. confusion costs.
   c. uncertainty costs.
   d. government spending costs.

2. Becky holds $30,000 as money. After a year during which inflation was 5 percent a year, the inflation tax over that year is
   a. $500.
   b. $1,000.
   c. $1,500.
   d. $3,000.

3. Suppose a country has a real interest rate of 4 percent a year and an inflation rate of 3 percent a year. If the income tax rate is 20 percent, then the real after-tax interest rate is
   a. 2.6 percent a year.
   b. 4.0 percent a year.
   c. 5.6 percent a year.
   d. 7.0 percent a year.

4. Shoe-leather costs arise from inflation because the velocity of circulation of money ____ as the inflation rate ____.
   a. increases; falls
   b. decreases; rises
   c. increases; rises
   d. None of the above answers is correct.

5. A consequence of hyperinflation is that people
   a. who make fixed-payment loans to others receive higher payments as inflation increases.
   b. spend time trying to keep their money holdings near zero.
   c. receive higher nominal raises, which increases their purchasing power for goods and services.
   d. want to lend funds because interest rates are so high.

6. The uncertainty costs of inflation cause people to
   a. increase long-run investment.
   b. increase investment causing growth to decrease.
   c. focus on the short run, which decreases investment and slows growth.
   d. focus on the long run, which increases investment and speeds growth.

7. The costs of inflation ____ when inflation is more rapid and ____ when inflation is more unpredictable.
   a. increase; increase
   b. increase; decrease
   c. decrease; increase
   d. increase; do not change

8. It is estimated that if the inflation rate is lowered from 3 percent a year to 0 percent a year, the growth rate of real GDP will rise by ____ percentage points a year.
   a. 0.06 to 0.09
   b. 1 to 3
   c. 2.3
   d. 3.2

Short answer and numeric questions

1. Jose holds $600 of money. If the inflation rate is 5 percent a year, calculate Joe's inflation tax.

2. The real interest rate is 2 percent a year and the inflation rate is zero percent a year. If the income tax rate is 25 percent, what is the real after-tax interest rate? If the inflation rate rises to 6 percent a year, what is the real after-tax interest rate? If the inflation rate rises to 10 percent a year, what is the real after-tax interest rate?

3. Why does the velocity of circulation increase in a hyperinflation?

4. On what factors does the cost of inflation depend?

SELF TEST ANSWERS

■ CHECKPOINT 13.1

Fill in the blanks

The nominal interest rate equals the real interest rate <u>plus</u> the inflation rate. The opportunity cost of holding money is the <u>nominal interest rate</u>. An increase in real GDP <u>increases</u> the demand for money and shifts the demand for money curve <u>rightward</u>. An increase in the price level <u>increases</u> the demand for money and shifts the demand for money curve <u>rightward</u>. If the nominal interest rate is above the equilibrium level, people <u>buy</u> bonds, the price of a bond <u>rises</u>, and the interest rate <u>falls</u>. If the Fed decreases the quantity of money, the nominal interest rate <u>rises</u>.

True or false

1. False; page 316
2. False; page 318
3. False; page 321
4. True; page 321
5. True; page 321

Multiple choice

1. c; page 315
2. b; page 316
3. b; page 316
4. a; page 316
5. a; page 317
6. b; page 319
7. b; page 321
8. a; page 321

Complete the graph

1. a. Figure 13.2 plots the demand for money curve; page 316.
   b. Figure 13.2 shows the supply of money curve when the Fed sets the quantity of money at $0.6 trillion. The equilibrium nominal interest rate is 8 percent a year at the intersection of the *MD* and *MS* curves; page 319.
   c. If the Fed wants to lower the interest rate to 6 percent a year, it increases the quantity of money to $1.0 trillion; page 321.

■ **FIGURE 13.2**

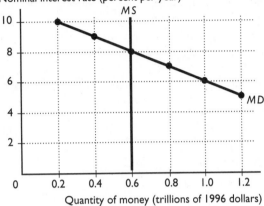

Nominal interest rate (percent per year)

Quantity of money (trillions of 1996 dollars)

Short answer and numeric questions

1. The sources of benefit from holding money are that you can make payments and do transactions; page 315.

2. The opportunity cost of holding money is the nominal interest rate. By holding money rather than a financial asset, the nominal interest rate is forgone. For instance, if Seemi can earn 5 percent a year on a bond, then holding $1,000 in money costs her $50 a year; page 315.

3. An increase in real GDP increases the demand for money and shifts the demand for money curve rightward; page 316.

4. When the price of the bond is $1,000, the interest rate equals ($100 ÷ $1,000) × 100, which is 10 percent. When the price of the bond is $2,000, the interest rate equals ($100 ÷ $2,000) × 100, which is 5 percent. When the price of the bond increases, the interest rate falls; page 320-321.

5. If the Fed wants to lower the interest rate, it increases the quantity of money; page 321.

■ CHECKPOINT 13.2

Fill in the blanks

Other things remaining the same, a given percentage increase in the quantity of money brings an equal percentage <u>increase</u> in the price level in the long run. An increase in the quantity of money <u>lowers</u> the nominal interest rate in the short run and <u>does not change</u> the nominal interest rate in the long run. The proposition that when real GDP equals potential GDP, an increase in the quantity of money brings an equal percentage increase in the price level is the <u>quantity</u> theory of money. If the velocity of circulation does not change, the inflation rate equals the growth rate of the <u>quantity of money minus</u> the growth rate of real GDP.

True or false

1. True; page 324
2. True; pages 325-326
3. False; page 327
4. True; page 329
5. False; page 330

Multiple choice

1. c; page 323
2. b; page 324
3. a; pages 325-326, 329
4. b; pages 325-326
5. c; page 327
6. c; page 327
7. c; page 329
8. b; page 331

Short answer and numeric questions

1. Other things remaining the same, in the long run a 5 percent increase in the quantity of money leads to a 5 percent increase in the price level; page 325-326, 329.
2. The completed table is below.

Year	Quantity of money (billions of dollars)	Velocity of circulation	Price level (1996 = 100)	Real GDP (billions of 1996 dollars)
2002	100	11	<u>110.0</u>	1,000
2003	110	11	<u>121.0</u>	1,000
2004	121	11	<u>133.1</u>	1,000

  a. Use the equation of exchange to solve for the price level; pages 328.
  b. In 2003, the percentage change in the quantity of money is [($110 billion – $100

billion) ÷ $100 billion] × 100, which is 10 percent.
In 2004, the percentage change in the quantity of money is [($121 billion – $110 billion) ÷ $110 billion] × 100, which also is 10 percent.
In 2003, the percentage change in the price level is [(121.0 – 110.0) ÷ 110.0] × 100, which is 10 percent.
In 2004, the percentage change in the price level is [(133.1 – 121.0) ÷ 121.0] × 100, which also is 10 percent.
  c. The answer to part (b) illustrates the quantity theory of money, which is the proposition that, when real GDP equals potential GDP, an increase in the quantity of money brings an equal percentage increase in the price level; page 327.
3. The inflation rate equals money growth plus velocity growth minus real GDP growth. Velocity does not grow, so the inflation rate equals 5 percent a year minus 3 percent a year, which is 2 percent a year; page 329.
4. A hyperinflation is inflation at a rate that exceeds 50 percent a month. A hyperinflation is the result of extraordinarily rapid growth in the quantity of money; page 331.

■ CHECKPOINT 13.3

Fill in the blanks

Inflation <u>is</u> a tax. The higher the inflation rate, the <u>higher</u> the true income tax rate on income from capital. During an inflation, the costs that arise from an increase in the velocity of circulation of money and an increase in the amount of running around to avoid incurring losses from the falling value of money are <u>shoe-leather</u> costs. Increased uncertainty about inflation leads to a <u>fall</u> in investment.

True or false

1. True; page 333
2. True; page 334
3. False; page 334
4. True; page 335
5. False; page 336

Multiple choice

1. d; page 333
2. c; page 333
3. a; page 333-334
4. c; page 334
5. b; page 334
6. c; page 335
7. a; page 336
8. a; page 336

Short answer and numeric questions

1. With an inflation of 5 percent a year, Jose losses ($600 × 0.05) = $30 in purchasing power. His money will buy only $570 worth of goods and services. Jose is paying an inflation tax of $30; page 333.

2. The real after-tax interest rate equals the nominal after-tax interest rate minus the inflation rate. When inflation is zero percent a year, the nominal interest rate equals the real interest, which is 2 percent a year. With a 25 percent income tax, the nominal after-tax interest rate equals 1.5 percent a year, so the real after-tax interest rate is 1.5 percent a year. When the inflation rate is 6 percent a year, the nominal interest rate equals the real interest rate, 2 percent a year, plus the inflation rate, 6 percent, which is 8 percent a year. The nominal after-tax interest rate is 6 percent a year, so the real after-tax interest rate equals 6 percent a year minus the inflation rate, 6 percent a year, which is zero percent a year. When the inflation rate equals 10 percent a year, the nominal interest rate is 12 percent a year so the nominal after-tax interest rate is 9 percent a year. As a result, the real after-tax interest rate is 9 percent a year − 10 percent a year, which is −1 percent a year. In this case, the real after-tax interest rate is negative; page 333.

3. The velocity of circulation increases because people try to spend their money as rapidly as possible to avoid incurring losses from the falling value of money; page 334.

4. The costs of an inflation depend on its rate and its predictability. The higher the rate, the greater is the cost and the more unpredictable the rate, the greater is the cost; page 335.

AS-AD and the Business Cycle

Chapter 14

CHAPTER IN PERSPECTIVE

■ Provide a technical definition of recession and describe the history of the U.S. business cycle.

A business cycle has two phases, expansion and recession, and two turning points, a peak and a trough. A standard definition of recession is a decrease in real GDP that lasts for at least two quarters. The United States has experienced 32 complete business cycles since 1854. The average length of an expansion is 35 months and the average length of a recession is 18 months. Since World War II, the average recession has been 11 months and the average expansion has been 59 months.

■ Explain the influences on aggregate supply.

Moving along the aggregate supply (*AS*) curve, the only influence on production plans that changes is the price level. All other influences on production plans, which include the money wage rate and the money price of other resources, remain constant. Along the potential GDP line, when the price level changes, the money wage rate and the money prices of other resources change by the same percentage as the change in the price level. Aggregate supply changes when potential GDP changes, the money wage rate changes, or the money prices of other resources change. Anything that changes potential GDP changes aggregate supply and shifts the aggregate supply curve.

■ Explain the influences on aggregate demand.

The quantity of real GDP demanded is the total amount of final goods and services produced in the United States that people, businesses, governments, and foreigners plan to buy. A change in the price level changes the quantity of real GDP demanded and brings a movement along the aggregate demand curve. A change in the price level brings changes in the buying power of money, the real interest rate, and the real prices of exports and imports, which influence the quantity of real GDP demanded. The factors that change aggregate demand are expectations about the future, fiscal policy and monetary policy, and the state of the world economy. The aggregate demand multiplier is an effect that magnifies changes in expenditure plans and brings potentially large fluctuations in aggregate demand.

■ Explain how fluctuations in aggregate demand and aggregate supply create the business cycle.

Fluctuations in aggregate demand and aggregate supply lead to changes in real GDP and the price level. The changes in real GDP are the business cycle. If real GDP exceeds potential GDP, an inflationary gap exists, which is eliminated by a decrease in aggregate supply and a rise in the price level. If real GDP is less than potential GDP, a deflationary gap exists, which is eliminated by an increase in aggregate supply and a fall in the price level.

EXPANDED CHAPTER CHECKLIST

When you have completed this chapter, you will be able to:

1 Provide a technical definition of recession and describe the history of the U.S. business cycle.

- State the standard definition of recession.
- Describe a business cycle.
- Discuss the history of the U.S. business cycle, including the average length of an expansion and recession, and how the length has changed since World War II.

2 Explain the influences on aggregate supply.

- Describe the relationship between potential GDP and the quantity of real GDP supplied over the business cycle.
- List the influence on production plans that changes the quantity of real GDP supplied and leads to a movement along the *AS* curve.
- Explain why an increase in the price level increases the quantity of real GDP supplied.
- Discuss the factors that change aggregate supply and shift the *AS* curve.

3 Explain the influences on aggregate demand.

- Discuss the influence of the price level for expenditure plans.
- Draw an *AD* curve and discuss the factors that change aggregate demand and shift the *AD* curve.
- Discuss the *AD* multiplier.

4 Explain how fluctuations in aggregate demand and aggregate supply create the business cycle.

- Describe and illustrate how fluctuations in aggregate demand change real GDP and the price level.

- Describe and illustrate how fluctuations in aggregate supply change real GDP and the price level.
- Define an inflationary gap and explain how real GDP returns to potential GDP.
- Define a deflationary gap and explain how real GDP returns to potential GDP.

KEY TERMS

- Recession (page 342)
- Stagflation (page 360)
- Inflationary gap (page 362)
- Deflationary gap (page 362)

CHECKPOINT 14.1

■ Provide a technical definition of recession and describe the history of the U.S. business cycle.

Practice Problem 14.1

The table shows real GDP in Canada from the first quarter of 1989 to the fourth quarter of 1993.

Billions of 1996 dollars				
	Quarter			
Year	1	2	3	4
1989	700	703	705	706
1990	711	709	705	698
1991	689	691	694	696
1992	696	697	699	702
1993	708	712	716	722

a. In which quarter was Canada at a business-cycle peak?
b. In which quarter was Canada at a business-cycle trough?
c. Did Canada experience a recession during these years?
d. In what periods did Canada experience an expansion?

Solution to Practice Problem 14.1

This Practice Problem will help you to recognize the phases of a business cycle. Remember that an expansion runs from a trough to a peak, and recession runs from a peak to a trough.

Quick Review

- *Business cycle* The business cycle is the fluctuation in economic activity from an expansion to a peak to a recession to a trough and then to another expansion.
- *Recession* The conventional definition of a recession is a decrease in real GDP that lasts for at least six months.

a. In which quarter was Canada at a business-cycle peak?

Canada was at a business cycle peak in the first quarter of 1990. In the quarters prior to the first quarter of 1990, real GDP is increasing. In the quarters following the first quarter of 1990, real GDP is decreasing.

b. In which quarter was Canada at a business-cycle trough?

Canada was at a business cycle trough in the first quarter of 1991. In the quarters prior to the first quarter of 1991, real GDP is decreasing. In the quarters following the first quarter of 1991, real GDP is increasing.

c. Did Canada experience a recession during these years?

Canada experienced a recession between the first quarter of 1990 and the first quarter of 1991. During these four quarters, Canada's real GDP decreased each quarter.

d. In what periods did Canada experience an expansion?

Canada experienced an expansion from the first quarter of 1989 to the first quarter of 1990 and then from the first quarter of 1991 to the fourth quarter of 1993.

Additional Practice Problem 14.1a

A country's real GDP grows at 5 percent a year for six years, slows to 0.5 percent a year for one year, and then increases back to 5 percent a year. Has the country experienced a recession?

Solution to Additional Practice Problem 14.1a

The standard definition of a recession is a decrease in real GDP that lasts for at least two quarters. The country has not experienced a decrease in real GDP so by the standard definition, a recession has not occurred.

■ Self Test 14.1

Fill in the blanks

A business cycle moves from an expansion to a ____ (peak; trough; recession), then to a ____ (peak; trough; recession), and then to a ____ (peak; trough; recession). A decrease in real GDP that lasts for at least two quarters is a ____. In the United States since 1854, the average length of an expansion is ____ (6; 35; 120) months and the average length of a recession is ____ (2; 18; 61) months. During the years since World War II the average expansion has ____ (shortened; lengthened) and the average recession has ____ (shortened; lengthened).

True or false

1. A recession begins at a trough and ends at a peak.
2. An expansion is a period during which real GDP decreases.
3. In the United States since 1854, there have been ten complete business cycles.
4. Potential GDP is not always equal to real GDP.

Multiple choice

1. The business cycle is
   a. a regular up and down movement in production and jobs.
   b. an irregular up and down movement in production and jobs.
   c. a regular movement in price changes.
   d. an irregular movement in price changes.

2. The turning point that reflects the end of an expansion is a
   a. peak.
   b. recession.
   c. trough.
   d. trend.

3. A standard definition of recession is a decrease in real GDP that lasts for at least two
   a. years.
   b. quarters.
   c. months.
   d. weeks.

4. Which organization or agency identifies and dates business-cycle phases and turning points in the United States?
   a. Bureau of Economic Analysis
   b. Department of Commerce
   c. National Bureau of Economic Research
   d. Federal Reserve System

5. Since 1854, the NBER has identified
   a. 82 complete business cycles.
   b. 32 expansions and 25 recessions.
   c. 32 complete business cycles.
   d. 25 expansions and 32 recessions.

6. During the twentieth century, recessions
   a. have shortened and expansions have lengthened.
   b. were as long as expansions.
   c. have lengthened and expansions have shortened.
   d. None of the above answers is correct.

Complete the graph

1. Identify when the economy in Figure 14.1 is experiencing recession.

■ FIGURE 14.1

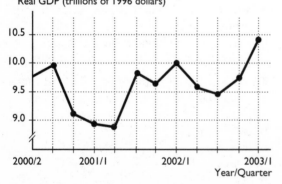

Real GDP (trillions of 1996 dollars)

Short answer and numeric questions

1. What is the standard definition of a recession?

2. Since World War II, how have the length of the average expansion and the average recession changed?

CHECKPOINT 14.2

■ Explain the influences on aggregate supply.

Practice Problem 14.2

In May 2000, armed men took over the Parliament in Fiji and held the Prime Minister and other people as hostages. This action led to many other events. Explain the effect of each of the following events on Fiji's aggregate supply:

   a. Downtown Suva (the capital of Fiji) was heavily looted and businesses were destroyed.
   b. Dock workers in Australia refused to handle cargo to and from Fiji, including raw material going to Fiji's garment industry.
   c. The number of tourists fell and many hotels closed.
   d. As unemployment increased, the workweek was shortened.
   e. The fresh tuna industry boomed with increased sales to Japan and the United States.
   f. With widespread shortages, suppose that the unionized workers demanded higher wages and got them.

Solution to Practice Problems 14.2

To answer this Practice Problem remember that aggregate supply changes when any influence on production plans other than the price level changes. Changes in the price level lead to changes in the aggregate quantity supplied.

Quick Review

* *Factors that change aggregate supply* Aggregate supply decreases and the aggregate supply curve shifts leftward when potential GDP decreases, when the money wage rate rises, or when the money price of other resources rises.

a. **Downtown Suva (the capital of Fiji) was heavily looted and businesses were destroyed.**

As businesses were destroyed, real GDP supplied at each price level decreased. Aggregate supply decreased and the *AS* curve shifted leftward.

b. **Dock workers in Australia refused to handle cargo to and from Fiji, including raw material going to Fiji's garment industry.**

The actions of the dock workers decreased the resources available to Fiji's garment industry. The quantity of real GDP supplied at the current price level decreased. Aggregate supply decreased and the *AS* curve shifted leftward.

c. **The number of tourists fell and many hotels closed.**

As hotels closed, the quantity of tourist services supplied decreased. The quantity of real GDP supplied at the current price level decreased. Aggregate supply decreased and the *AS* curve shifted leftward.

d. **As unemployment increased, the workweek was shortened.**

As the workweek was shortened, the quantity of real GDP supplied at the current price level decreased. Aggregate supply decreased and the *AS* curve shifted leftward.

e. **The fresh tuna industry boomed with increased sales to Japan and the United States.**

As the tuna industry expanded, production increased. Aggregate supply increased and the *AS* curve shifted rightward.

f. **With widespread shortages, suppose that the unionized workers demanded higher wages and got them.**

As the money wage rate rises, for a given price level, the real wage rate rises. Some firms decrease production and others close. The quantity of real GDP supplied at the current price level decreased. Aggregate supply decreased and the *AS* curve shifted leftward.

Additional Practice Problem 14.2a
Describe the effect of advances in computer software during the last decade on aggregate supply and the *AS* curve.

Solution to Additional Practice Problem 14.2a
Advances in computer software mean that the same quantity of output can be produced by fewer workers. Some workers who were formerly employed as typists or data entry clerks now produce other goods and services. Aggregate supply increases and the *AS* curve shifts rightward.

■ Self Test 14.2

Fill in the blanks

Moving along the aggregate supply curve, as the price level rises, the quantity of real GDP supplied ____ (decreases; does not change; increases) because the real wage rate ____ (falls; rises). Moving along the potential GDP line, the money wage rate ____ (changes; does not change) when the price level changes. When potential GDP increases, a ____ (movement along; shift of) the *AS* curve occurs. When the money wage rate changes, a ____ (movement along; shift of) the *AS* curve occurs.

True or false

1. Along the aggregate supply curve, a rise in the price level decreases the quantity of real GDP supplied.

2. A rise in the price level decreases potential GDP.

3. Anything that changes potential GDP shifts the aggregate supply curve.

4. An increase in potential GDP shifts the aggregate supply curve rightward.

Multiple choice

1. Moving along the potential GDP line, the money wage rate changes by the same percentage as the change in the price level so that the real wage rate
   a. increases.
   b. decreases.
   c. stays at the full-employment equilibrium level.
   d. increases or decreases.

2. The aggregate supply curve is
   a. upward sloping.
   b. downward sloping.
   c. a vertical line.
   d. a horizontal line.

3. When the price level falls,
   a. the *AS* curve shifts rightward.
   b. there is a movement up along the *AS* curve.
   c. the *AS* curve shifts leftward.
   d. there is a movement down along the *AS* curve.

4. As the price level rises relative to costs and the real wage rate falls, profits _____ and the number of firms in business _____.
   a. increase; increases
   b. increase; decreases
   c. decrease; increases
   d. decrease; decreases

5. When potential GDP increases,
   a. the *AS* curve shifts rightward.
   b. there is a movement up along the *AS* curve.
   c. the *AS* curve shifts leftward.
   d. there is a movement down along the *AS* curve.

6. If the money wage rate rises,
   a. the *AS* curve shifts rightward.
   b. there is a movement up along the *AS* curve.
   c. the *AS* curve shifts leftward.
   d. there is a movement down along the *AS* curve.

Complete the graph

1. The table gives the aggregate supply schedule and potential GDP schedule for a nation.

Price level (GDP deflator 1996 = 100)	Quantity of real GDP supplied (trillions of 1996 dollars)	Potential GDP (trillions of 1996 dollars)
140	17	13
130	15	13
120	13	13
110	11	13
100	9	13

   a. Label the axes and then plot the *AS* curve and potential GDP line in Figure 14.2.
   b. Suppose the money wage rate falls. Show the effect of this change on aggregate supply and potential GDP in Figure 14.2.

■ **FIGURE 14.2**

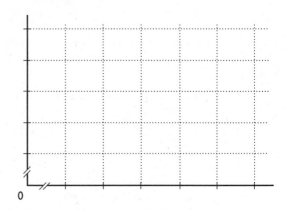

Short answer and numeric questions

1. Why does the *AS* curve slope upward?

2. Why does the aggregate supply curve shift when the money wage rate rises? Why doesn't the potential GDP line also shift?

3. What is the effect on aggregate supply if the money price of oil rises?

CHECKPOINT 14.3

■ **Explain the influences on aggregate demand.**

Practice Problem 14.3

Mexico has signed free trade agreements with many countries, including the United States, Canada, and the European Union. Explain the effect of each of the following events on Mexico's aggregate demand in the short run:

 a. The price level in Mexico increases faster than that in its trading partners.
 b. The government of Mexico cuts taxes.
 c. The United States and Canada experienced strong economic growth.
 d. The European Union goes into a recession.
 e. The Mexican government sets new environmental standards that require factories to upgrade their production facilities.
 f. Mexico adopts an expansionary monetary policy and increases the quantity of money.

Solution to Practice Problem 14.3

To answer this Practice Problem, remember that a change in any factor that influences expenditure plans other than the price level brings a change in aggregate demand and a shift in the *AD* curve.

Quick Review

 • *Factors that change aggregate demand* Aggregate demand changes and the aggregate demand curve shifts if expected future income, inflation, or profit change; if the government or the Federal Reserve take steps that change expenditure plans, such as changes in taxes or in the quantity of money; or the state of the world economy changes.

 a. The price level in Mexico increases faster than that in its trading partners.
A faster rise in Mexico's price level means that Mexican exports become relatively more expensive. Its trading partners want to buy fewer goods from Mexico. The quantity demanded of Mexican real GDP decreases. Because the decrease is the result of the increase in the Mexican price level, this is a movement along the Mexican *AD* curve.

 b. The government of Mexico cuts taxes.
A tax cut increases aggregate demand. The Mexican *AD* curve shifts rightward.

 c. The United States and Canada experienced strong economic growth.
Strong economic growth in the United States and Canada increases the demand for Mexican exports by U.S. and Canadian citizens. Aggregate demand in Mexico increases and the *AD* curve shifts rightward.

 d. The European Union goes into a recession.
If the European Union goes into a recession, the demand for Mexican exports decreases. Aggregate demand in Mexico decreases and the Mexican *AD* curve shifts leftward.

 e. The Mexican government sets new environmental standards that require factories to upgrade their production facilities.
As factories purchase the equipment to upgrade their production facilities, investment increases. Aggregate demand in Mexico increases and the *AD* curve shifts rightward.

 f. Mexico adopts an expansionary monetary policy and increases the quantity of money.
If Mexico increases the quantity of money, aggregate demand increases and the *AD* curve shifts rightward.

Additional Practice Problem 14.3a
Suppose the president of the United States makes a series of speeches proposing that all citizens receive a large tax cut. If people think a tax cut is unlikely to occur, what is the effect on aggregate demand? If many people believe that the tax cuts will occur, what is the effect on aggregate demand?

Solution to Additional Practice Problem 14.3a

If people think a large tax cut is unlikely to occur, there is no change in expected future income. Aggregate demand does not change. If many people believe that the tax cuts will occur, expected future income increases. When expected future income increases, aggregate demand increases.

■ Self Test 14.3

Fill in the blanks

An increase in the price level ____ (decreases; increases) the quantity of real GDP demanded and a ____ (movement along; shift of) the aggregate demand curve occurs. An increase in expected future income shifts the *AD* curve ____ (leftward; rightward). A tax cut shifts the *AD* curve ____ (leftward; rightward). A decrease in foreign income shifts the *AD* curve ____ (leftward; rightward).

True or false

1. As the price level falls, other things remaining the same, the quantity of real GDP demanded increases.
2. An increase in expected future income will not increase aggregate demand until the income actually increases.
3. A decrease in government purchases shifts the aggregate demand curve rightward.
4. An increase in income in Mexico decreases aggregate demand in the United States because Mexicans will buy more Mexican-produced goods.

Multiple choice

1. When the price level rises there is a ____ the aggregate demand curve.
   a. rightward shift of
   b. movement down along
   c. leftward shift of
   d. movement up along

2. A rise in the price level
   a. raises the buying power of money.
   b. decreases the prices of exports.
   c. lowers the buying power of money.
   d. increases aggregate demand.

3. When the price level rises, the real interest rate ____ and the quantity of real GDP demanded ____.
   a. rises; increases
   b. rises; decreases
   c. falls; increases
   d. falls; decreases

4. A change in any of the following factors except ____ shifts the aggregate demand curve.
   a. expectations about the future
   b. the money wage rate
   c. monetary and fiscal policy
   d. the state of the world economy

5. Which of the following produces a leftward shift in the aggregate demand curve?
   a. a decrease in expected future profit
   b. an increase in the price level
   c. a tax cut
   d. an increase in foreign income

6. When investment increases, the increase in aggregate demand is ____ the change in investment.
   a. greater than
   b. smaller than
   c. the same as
   d. unrelated to

Complete the graph

1. Figure 14.3 shows an aggregate demand curve.

■ FIGURE 14.3

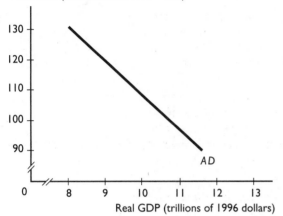

Price level (GDP deflator, 1996 = 100)

a. Suppose that government purchases increase. In Figure 14.3, illustrate the effect of this fiscal policy.

b. Suppose the Federal Reserve decreases the quantity of money. In Figure 14.3, illustrate the effect of this monetary policy.

Short answer and numeric questions

1. Why does an increase in the price level decrease the quantity of real GDP demanded?

2. Expected future profit increases. Explain the effect on aggregate demand.

3. The government increases its taxes. What is the effect on aggregate demand?

4. What is the aggregate demand multiplier?

CHECKPOINT 14.4

■ Explain how fluctuations in aggregate demand and aggregate supply create the business cycle.

Practice Problem 14.4

In the U.S. economy, real GDP equals potential GDP. Then the following events occur one at a time:
• A deep recession hits the world economy.

• The world oil price rises by a large amount.
• U.S. businesses expect future profits to fall.
   a. Explain the effects of each event on aggregate demand and aggregate supply in the United States.
   b. Explain the effect of each event separately on the U.S. real GDP and price level.
   c. Explain the combined effect of all the events together on the U.S. real GDP and price level.
   d. Which event, if any, brings stagflation?

Solution to Practice Problem 14.4

We use the *AS-AD* model to study the economic fluctuations that occur in a business cycle. This Practice Problem studies the effects of changes in aggregate demand and aggregate supply on the price level and real GDP.

Quick Review

• *Effect of decrease in aggregate demand* A decrease in aggregate demand, everything else remaining the same, lowers the price level and decreases real GDP.

• *Effect of decrease in aggregate supply* A decrease in aggregate supply, everything else remaining the same, raises the price level and decreases real GDP.

In the U.S. economy, real GDP equals potential GDP. Then the following events occur one at a time:

• **A deep recession hits the world economy.**

• **The world oil price rises by a large amount.**

• **U.S. businesses expect future profits to fall.**

a. **Explain the effect of each event on aggregate demand and aggregate supply in the United States.**

When a recession in the world economy occurs, income in the rest of the world declines. People in the rest of the world decrease their demand for U.S.-produced goods. U.S. aggregate demand decreases. U.S. aggregate supply does not change.

A large oil price hike is an increase in the money price of a resource. An increase in the money price of a resource decreases aggregate supply but has no effect on aggregate demand.

A decrease in expected future profits decreases investment. Aggregate demand decreases. Aggregate supply does not change.

b. Explain the effect of each event separately on the U.S. real GDP and price level.

The world recession decreases aggregate demand. There is no change in aggregate supply. The *AD* curve shifts leftward in the figure from AD_0 to AD_1, and the *AS* curve does not shift. In the figure, the price level falls and real GDP decreases.

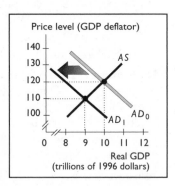

The rise in oil prices decreases aggregate supply. There is no change in aggregate demand. The *AS* curve shifts leftward from AS_0 to AS_1, and the *AD* curve does not shift. The price level rises and real GDP decreases.

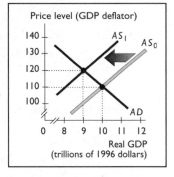

The decrease in expected future profit has the same effect as the world recession because both events decrease aggregate demand with no effect on aggregate supply. The price level falls and real GDP decreases.

c. Explain the combined effect of all the events together on the U.S. real GDP and price level.

All three events decrease real GDP. So real GDP decreases. The effect on the price level is ambiguous: If the oil price hike dominates, the price level rises but if the other two effects dominate, the price level falls.

d. Which event, if any, brings stagflation?

Stagflation is the combination of recession (falling real GDP) and inflation (rising price level). The rise in the price of oil decreases GDP and raises the price level, so it brings stagflation.

Additional Practice Problem 14.4a

In the late 20th century, the French government passed a law limiting the workweek in most industries to 35 hours. At the same time the government also passed laws limiting imports of genetically engineered food. Explain the effects of each event separately on aggregate demand and aggregate supply and on the equilibrium price level and real GDP. Explain the combined effect of the events on real GDP and the price level.

Solution to Additional Practice Problem 14.4a

The decrease in the workweek decreases the supply and so decreases aggregate supply. The *AS* curve shifts leftward. The equilibrium price level rises and equilibrium real GDP decreases.

When food imports are limited, the French people buy more French-produced food. Aggregate demand increases and the *AD* curve shifts rightward. The equilibrium price level rises and equilibrium real GDP increases.

When the effects are combined, the price level rises because separately each event raises the price level. It is not possible to predict the total effect on real GDP because the first event decreases real GDP and the second event increases real GDP.

■ Self Test 14.4

Fill in the blanks

An increase in aggregate demand ____ (decreases; increases) real GDP. An increase in aggregate supply ____ (lowers; raises) the price level. Stagflation is a combination of ____ (expansion; recession) and a ____ (falling; rising) price level. When real GDP exceeds potential GDP, ____ (an inflationary; a deflationary) gap exists. When potential GDP exceeds real GDP, ____ (an inflationary; a deflationary) gap exists.

True or false

1. Starting from full employment, an increase in aggregate demand increases real GDP above potential GDP.

2. Starting from full employment, a decrease in aggregate demand shifts the aggregate demand curve leftward and creates an inflationary gap.

3. Starting from full employment, an increase in aggregate demand shifts the aggregate demand curve rightward and creates an inflationary gap.

4. A deflationary gap brings a rising price level to eliminate the gap.

Multiple choice

1. Which of the following statements is correct?
   a. Changes in the price level shift the aggregate demand curve.
   b. Aggregate supply cannot fluctuate.
   c. The level of real GDP does not depend on fluctuations in aggregate demand or aggregate supply.
   d. Changes in aggregate demand and aggregate supply generate the business cycle.

2. An increase in investment ____ aggregate demand, the aggregate demand curve shifts ____ and the economy is in the ____ phase of the business cycle.
   a. decreases; rightward; expansion
   b. increases; rightward; expansion
   c. decreases; leftward; recession
   d. increases; rightward; recession

3. If the price of oil rises, the
   a. AD curve shifts rightward, real GDP increases, and the price level rises.
   b. AS curve shifts leftward, the price level rises, and real GDP decreases.
   c. AD curve and the AS curve shift leftward, real GDP decreases, and the price level rises.
   d. AD curve and the AS curve shift rightward, the price level rises, and real GDP decreases.

4. Stagflation is a combination of ____ real GDP and a ____ price level.
   a. increasing; rising
   b. increasing; falling
   c. decreasing; rising
   d. decreasing; falling

5. An inflationary gap is created when real GDP is ____ potential GDP.
   a. greater than
   b. equal to
   c. less than
   d. greater than, equal to, or less than

6. An economy is at full employment. If aggregate demand increases,
   a. an inflationary gap is created and the AS curve shifts leftward as the money wage rate rises.
   b. an inflationary gap is created and the AD curve shifts leftward.
   c. an inflationary gap is created and potential GDP increases to close the gap.
   d. a deflationary gap is created and the AS curve shifts leftward as the money wage rate falls.

Complete the graph

1. Figure 14.4 shows an economy. Suppose people expect an increase in future profits.

■ **FIGURE 14.4**

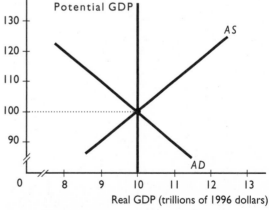

Price level (GDP deflator, 1996 = 100)

a. In Figure 14.4, show the effect of the change in expectations on the price level and real GDP.

b. In Figure 14.4, show how the economy returns to potential GDP.

2. Figure 14.5 shows an economy. Show the effect of a rise in the price of oil on the price level and real GDP.

■ **FIGURE 14.5**

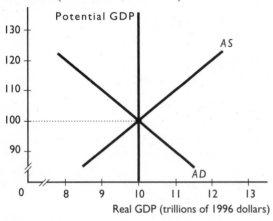

Price level (GDP deflator, 1996 = 100)

Real GDP (trillions of 1996 dollars)

Short answer and numeric questions

1. What is stagflation? What can create stagflation?

2. What is an inflationary gap and how is it eliminated?

SELF TEST ANSWERS

■ CHECKPOINT 14.1

Fill in the blanks

A business cycle moves from an expansion to a peak, then to a recession, and then to a trough. A decrease in real GDP that lasts for at least two quarters is a recession. In the United States since 1854, the average length of an expansion is 35 months and the average length of a recession is 18 months. During the years since World War II the average expansion has lengthened and the average recession has shortened.

True or false

1. False; page 342
2. False; page 342
3. False; page 342
4. True; page 345

Multiple choice

1. b; page 342
2. a; page 342
3. b; page 342
4. c; page 342
5. c; page 342
6. a; page 343

Complete the graph

1. A recession runs from the third quarter of 2000 to the second quarter of 2001 and from the first quarter of 2002 to the third quarter of 2002; page 342.

Short answer and numeric questions

1. The standard definition of a recession is a decrease in real GDP that lasts for at least two quarters (six months); page 342.
2. Since World War II, the average expansion has lengthened and the average recession has shortened; page 343.

■ CHECKPOINT 14.2

Fill in the blanks

Moving along the aggregate supply curve, as the price level rises, the quantity of real GDP supplied increases because the real wage rate falls. Moving along the potential GDP line, the money wage rate does not change when the price level changes. When potential GDP increases, a shift of the AS curve occurs. When the money wage rate changes, a shift of the AS curve occurs.

True or false

1. False; page 346
2. False; page 346
3. True; page 349
4. True; page 349

Multiple choice

1. c; page 346
2. a; page 347
3. d; page 346
4. a; page 348
5. a; page 349
6. c; page 350

Complete the graph

■ FIGURE 14.6

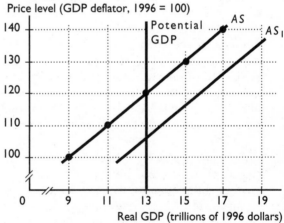

Price level (GDP deflator, 1996 = 100)

Real GDP (trillions of 1996 dollars)

1. a. Figure 14.6 labels the axes. The aggregate supply curve is labeled AS; page 347.

   b. The fall in the money wage rate has no effect on potential GDP, so the potential GDP line does not change. Aggregate supply, however, increases so the AS curve shifts rightward, to an AS curve such as AS_1; page 350.

Short answer and numeric questions

1. The movement along the *AS* curve brings a change in the real wage rate (and changes in the real cost of other resources whose money prices are fixed). If the price level rises, the real wage rate falls.

   A fall in the real wage rate boosts a firm's profit. The number of firms in business increases.

   If the price level rises relative to costs, fewer firms will want to shut down, so more firms operate.

   If the price level rises and the money wage rate does not change, an extra hour of labor that was previously unprofitable becomes profitable. So, the quantity of labor demanded increases and production increases.

   For the economy as a whole, as the price level rises, the quantity of real GDP supplied increases; pages 347-348.

2. An increase in the money wage rate increases firms' costs. The higher are firms' costs, the smaller is the quantity that firms are willing to supply at each price level. Aggregate supply decreases and the *AS* curve shifts leftward. A change in the money wage rate does not change potential GDP. Potential GDP depends only on the economy's real ability to produce and on the full-employment quantity of labor, which occurs at the equilibrium real wage rate. The equilibrium real wage rate can occur at any money wage rate; page 350.

3. If the money price of oil rises, firm's costs increase. The higher are firms' costs, the smaller is the quantity that firms are willing to supply at each price level. Aggregate supply decreases and the aggregate supply curve shifts leftward; page 350.

■ CHECKPOINT 14.3

Fill in the blanks

An increase in the price level <u>decreases</u> the quantity of real GDP demanded and a <u>movement along</u> the aggregate demand curve occurs. An increase in expected future income shifts the *AD* curve <u>rightward</u>. A tax cut shifts the *AD* curve <u>rightward</u>. A decrease in foreign income shifts the *AD* curve <u>leftward</u>.

True or false

1. True; page 352
2. False; page 354
3. False; page 355
4. False; page 356

Multiple choice

1. d; page 353
2. c; page 352
3. b; page 353
4. b; page 354
5. a; pages 354-355
6. a; page 356

Complete the graph

■ FIGURE 14.7

Price level (GDP deflator, 1996 = 100)

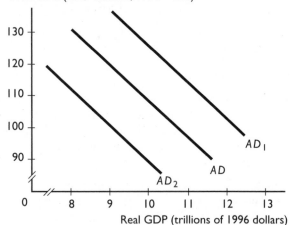

1. a. In Figure 14.7, an increase in government purchases increases aggregate demand and shifts the *AD* curve rightward, from *AD* to *AD*₁; page 355.

   b. In Figure 14.7, a decrease in the quantity of money decreases aggregate demand and shifts the *AD* curve leftward, from *AD* to *AD*₂; page 355.

Short answer and numeric questions

1. An increase in the price level decreases the quantity of real GDP demanded because an increase in the price level lowers the buying power of money, raises the real interest rate, raises the real prices of exports, and lowers the real price of imports; pages 352-354.

2. An increase in expected future profit increases the investment that firms plan to undertake and increases aggregate demand; page 354.

3. The government can influence aggregate demand by changing taxes. When the government increases taxes, aggregate demand decreases; page 355.

4. The aggregate demand multiplier is an effect that magnifies changes in expenditure and increases fluctuations in aggregate demand. For example, an increase in investment increases aggregate demand and increases income. The increase in income induces an increase in consumption expenditure so aggregate demand increases by more than the initial increase in investment; page 356.

■ CHECKPOINT 14.4

Fill in the blanks

An increase in aggregate demand <u>increases</u> real GDP. An increase in aggregate supply <u>lowers</u> the price level. Stagflation is a combination of <u>recession</u> and a <u>rising</u> price level. When real GDP exceeds potential GDP, <u>an inflationary</u> gap exists. When potential GDP exceeds real GDP, <u>a deflationary</u> gap exists.

True or false

1. True; page 358
2. False; page 362
3. True; page 362
4. False; page 362

Multiple choice

1. d; page 358
2. b; pages 358-359
3. b; page 360

4. c; page 360
5. a; page 362
6. a; page 362

Complete the graph

■ FIGURE 14.8

Price level (GDP deflator, 1996 = 100)

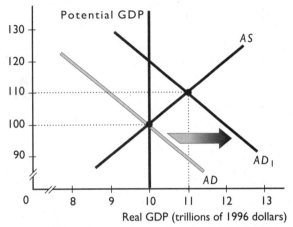

1. a. An increase in expected future profit increases firms' investment which increases aggregate demand. The aggregate demand curve shifts rightward from *AD* to *AD*₁ in Figure 14.8. The equilibrium price level rises to 110 and equilibrium real GDP increases to $11 trillion; page 360.

■ FIGURE 14.9

Price level (GDP deflator, 1996 = 100)

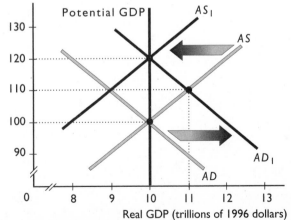

b. An inflationary gap now exists. The money wage rate rises and aggregate supply decreases. In Figure 14.9, the *AS* curve shifts leftward. Eventually the *AS* curve moves to AS_1. Real GDP returns to potential GDP, $10 trillion, and the price level rises to 120; page 362.

■ FIGURE 14.10

Price level (GDP deflator, 1996 = 100)

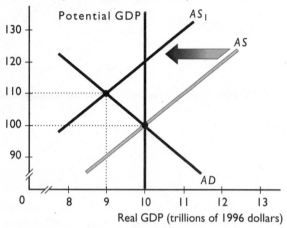

Real GDP (trillions of 1996 dollars)

2. Figure 14.10 shows the effect of a rise in the price of oil. Aggregate supply decreases and the *AS* curve shifts leftward from *AS* to AS_1. Real GDP decreases to $9 trillion and the price level rises to 110; page 360.

Short answer and numeric questions

1. Stagflation is a combination of recession (falling real GDP) and inflation (rising price level). Stagflation can be created by a decrease in aggregate supply; page 360.

2. An inflationary gap is a gap that exists when real GDP exceeds potential GDP. An inflationary gap brings a rising price level. Workers have experienced a fall in the buying power of their wages, and firms' profits have increased. Employment exceeds full employment. Workers demand higher wages. As the money wage rate rises, aggregate supply decreases and the aggregate supply curve shifts leftward. Eventually, real GDP will return to potential GDP and the inflationary gap is eliminated; page 362.

Chapter 15

Aggregate Expenditure

■ **Distinguish between autonomous expenditure and induced expenditure and explain how real GDP influences expenditure plans.**

Aggregate *planned* expenditure is planned consumption expenditure plus planned investment plus planned government purchases plus planned net exports. Aggregate *planned* expenditure does not always equal real GDP. Induced expenditure are the components of aggregate expenditure that change when real GDP changes; autonomous expenditure are the components of aggregate expenditure that do not change when real GDP changes. The consumption function is the relationship between consumption expenditure and disposable income. The marginal propensity to consume, *MPC*, is the fraction of a change in disposable income that is spent on consumption. When real GDP increases, imports increase. The marginal propensity to import is the fraction of an increase in real GDP spent on imports.

■ **Explain how real GDP adjusts to achieve equilibrium expenditure.**

Equilibrium expenditure occurs when aggregate *planned* expenditure equals real GDP. It occurs at the point where the *AE* curve intersects the 45° line. If aggregate planned expenditure is less than real GDP, an unplanned increase in inventories occurs. Firms decrease production and real GDP decreases until real GDP equals aggregate planned expenditure and the economy is at equilibrium expenditure. If aggregate planned expenditure exceeds real GDP, an unplanned decrease in inventories occurs. Firms increase production and real GDP increases. The economy moves to its equilibrium expenditure.

■ **Describe and explain the expenditure multiplier.**

The multiplier is the amount by which a change in any component of autonomous expenditure is multiplied to determine the change that it creates in equilibrium expenditure and real GDP. The multiplier is greater than 1 because an increase in autonomous expenditure induces further changes in aggregate expenditure. If we ignore income taxes and imports, the multiplier equals $1 \div (1 - MPC)$. The multiplier is larger if the *MPC* is larger. Imports and income taxes reduce the size of the multiplier. In general, the multiplier equals $1 \div (1 - \text{slope of } AE \text{ curve})$. An expansion is triggered by an increase in autonomous expenditure that increases aggregate planned expenditure and real GDP.

■ **Derive the *AD* curve from equilibrium expenditure.**

The *AE* curve is the relationship between aggregate planned expenditure and real GDP, when all other influences on expenditure plans remain the same. The *AD* curve is the relationship between the quantity of real GDP demanded and the price level. When the price level rises, aggregate planned expenditure decreases, the *AE* curve shifts downward, and equilibrium expenditure decreases. When the price level rises, aggregate planned expenditure increases, the *AE* curve shifts upward, and equilibrium expenditure increases. Each point of equilibrium expenditure corresponds to a point on the *AD* curve.

EXPANDED CHAPTER CHECKLIST

When you have completed this chapter, you will be able to:

1 **Distinguish between autonomous expenditure and induced expenditure and explain how real GDP influences expenditure plans.**

- Define aggregate planned expenditure and explain why aggregate planned expenditure does not always equal real GDP.
- Compare autonomous expenditure and induced expenditure.
- Describe the consumption function and define the marginal propensity to consume, *MPC*.
- List the influences on consumption and describe their effect on the consumption function.
- Define the marginal propensity to import.

2 **Explain how real GDP adjusts to achieve equilibrium expenditure.**

- Describe the relationship between aggregate planned expenditure and real GDP and illustrate aggregate expenditure with an *AE* curve.
- Discuss how equilibrium expenditure is determined and illustrate equilibrium expenditure using the *AE* curve and a 45° line.
- Describe the convergence to equilibrium when aggregate planned expenditure does not equal real GDP.

3 **Describe and explain the expenditure multiplier.**

- Define the multiplier.
- Explain the relationship between the *MPC* and the multiplier.
- Discuss why income taxes and imports reduce the size of the multiplier and state the general formula for the multiplier, $1 \div (1 -$ slope of *AE* curve).
- Describe what initiates a business cycle expansion or recession and discuss the impact

of the multiplier in creating expansions and recessions.

4 **Derive the *AD* curve from equilibrium expenditure.**

- Discuss the differences between the *AE* curve and the *AD* curve.
- Explain the effect of a change in the price level on aggregate planned expenditure, the *AE* curve, and equilibrium expenditure.
- Derive the *AD* curve.

KEY TERMS

- Aggregate planned expenditure (page 371)
- Autonomous expenditure (page 372)
- Induced expenditure (page 372)
- Consumption function (page 372)
- Marginal propensity to consume *(MPC)* (page 374)
- Marginal propensity to import (page 376)
- Equilibrium expenditure (page 380)
- Multiplier (page 384)
- Marginal tax rate (page 387)

CHECKPOINT 15.1

■ **Distinguish between autonomous expenditure and induced expenditure and explain how real GDP influences expenditure plans.**

Practice Problems 15.1

1. If the marginal propensity to consume is 0.8 and if disposable income increases by $0.5 trillion, by how much will consumption expenditure change?
2. If Americans decrease the fraction of each dollar of disposable income they spend on consumption, how will the U.S. consumption function change?
3. If Americans decide to decrease consumption expenditure by a fixed number of dollars, how will the U.S. consumption function change?
4. Suppose that expected future disposable income increases. Explain how this change in ex-

pectation will influence the consumption function.

5. The figure shows the Canadian consumption function. Calculate the marginal propensity to consume and autonomous consumption in Canada.

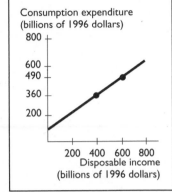

Solution to Practice Problems 15.1

These problems study the consumption function, which is the basic building block of aggregate expenditure. The problems look at the slope of the consumption function, and the influences that create a movement along the consumption function or a shift of the consumption function.

Quick Review

- *Autonomous expenditure* Expenditure that does not change when real GDP changes.
- *Consumption function* The relationship between consumption expenditure and disposable income, other things remaining the same.
- *Marginal propensity to consume, MPC* The fraction of a change in disposable income that is spent on consumption.

1. **If the marginal propensity to consume is 0.8 and if disposable income increases by $0.5 trillion, by how much will consumption expenditure change?**

The change in consumption expenditure equals the change in disposable income multiplied by the marginal propensity to consume, which is ($0.5 trillion) × (0.8) = $0.4 trillion.

2. **If Americans decrease the fraction of each dollar of disposable income they spend on consumption, how will the U.S. consumption function change?**

When the fraction of each dollar of disposable income spent on consumption decreases, the

MPC decreases. The *MPC* is the slope of the consumption function. So the consumption function becomes less steep.

3. **If Americans decide to decrease consumption expenditure by a fixed number of dollars, how will the U.S. consumption function change?**

The decrease in consumption expenditure by a fixed number of dollars is a decrease in autonomous consumption. The consumption function shifts downward.

4. **Suppose that expected future disposable income increases. Explain how this change in expectation will influence the consumption function.**

When expected future disposable income increases, people increase their consumption expenditure today. The consumption function shifts upward.

5. **The figure shows the Canadian consumption function. Calculate the marginal propensity to consume and autonomous consumption in Canada.**

The *MPC* is the slope of the consumption function and equals the change in consumption expenditure divided by the change in disposable income that brought it about. The figure shows that when disposable income increases from $400 billion to $600 billion, consumption expenditure increases from $360 billion to $490 billion. The *MPC* equals ($130 billion) ÷ ($200 billion), which is 0.65. Autonomous consumption is the amount of consumption when income equals zero and equals the y-axis intercept, $100 billion.

Additional Practice Problems 15.1a

If disposable income increases by $1.5 trillion and the marginal propensity to consume (*MPC*) is 0.8, what is the change in consumption expenditure? If the *MPC* equals 0.6, what is the change in consumption expenditure? What is the relationship between the *MPC* and the change in consumption expenditure for a given change in disposable income?

Solution to Additional Practice Problem 15.1a

The change in consumption expenditure equals the *MPC* times the change in disposable income. When the *MPC* is 0.8, the change in consumption expenditure equals ($1.5 trillion) × (0.8), which is $1.2 trillion. When the *MPC* is 0.6, the change in consumption expenditure is ($1.5 trillion) × (0.6), which is $0.9 trillion. The larger the *MPC*, the greater the change in consumption expenditure for a given change in disposable income.

■ Self Test 15.1

Fill in the blanks

Aggregate planned expenditure _____ (does not always equal; always equals) real GDP. The components of aggregate expenditure that change when real GDP changes are _____ (induced; autonomous) expenditure. The components of aggregate expenditure that do not change when real GDP changes are _____ (induced; autonomous) expenditure. The _____ is the relationship between consumption expenditure and disposable income. The marginal propensity to consume equals the change in consumption expenditure _____ (plus; multiplied by; divided by) the change in disposable income that brought it about. The slope of the consumption function equals the _____. A change in disposable income is shown by a _____ (shift in; movement along) the consumption function, and a change in the buying power of money is shown by a _____ (shift in; movement along) the consumption function. Imports _____ (are; are not) a component of induced expenditure.

True or false

1. Induced expenditure increases as real GDP increases.

2. The slope of the consumption function is less than the slope of the 45° line.

3. The marginal propensity to consume equals consumption expenditure divided by disposable income.

4. The consumption function shifts when the buying power of net assets changes.

Multiple choice

1. The four components of aggregate expenditure are
   a. consumption expenditure, interest, gross spending, and net spending.
   b. consumption expenditure, investment, government purchases of goods and services, and net income.
   c. consumption expenditure, interest, government purchases of goods and services, and net exports.
   d. consumption expenditure, investment, government purchases of goods and services, and net exports.

2. Which of the following is true?
   a. Actual aggregate expenditure does not always equal real GDP.
   b. Aggregate planned expenditure always equals real GDP.
   c. Actual aggregate expenditure always equals real GDP.
   d. Aggregate planned expenditure and actual aggregate expenditure always equal real GDP.

3. Autonomous expenditure is the component of
   a. aggregate expenditure that changes when real GDP changes.
   b. induced expenditure that changes when real GDP changes.
   c. aggregate planned expenditure that changes only when government purchases of goods and services change.
   d. aggregate expenditure that does not change when real GDP changes.

4. The components of aggregate expenditure that change when real GDP changes are
   a. unplanned expenditure.
   b. induced expenditure.
   c. planned expenditure.
   d. autonomous expenditure.

5. The consumption function is the relationship between ___, other things remaining the same.
   a. consumption expenditure and saving
   b. real GDP and net taxes
   c. consumption expenditure and disposable income
   d. net taxes and disposable income

6. When disposable income increases from $9 trillion to $10 trillion, consumption expenditure increases from $6 trillion to $6.8 trillion. The *MPC* is
   a. 1.00.
   b. 0.80.
   c. 0.60.
   d. 0.68.

Complete the graph

1. The table has data on consumption expenditure and disposable income.

Disposable income (trillions of 1996 dollars)	Consumption expenditure, (trillions of 1996 dollars)
0.0	0.4
1.0	1.2
2.0	2.0
3.0	2.8
4.0	3.6
5.0	4.4

   a. Using the data, label the axes and plot the consumption function in Figure 15.1.
   b. Indicate the amount of autonomous consumption expenditure in Figure 15.1.
   c. What is the amount of saving if disposable income equals $1.0 trillion? $4.0 trillion?
   d. Calculate the marginal propensity to consume.
   e. Suppose the real interest rate falls and consumers increase their consumption by $0.6 trillion at every level of disposable income. Draw the new consumption function in Figure 15.1. What is the amount of autonomous consumption now?

■ **FIGURE 15.1**

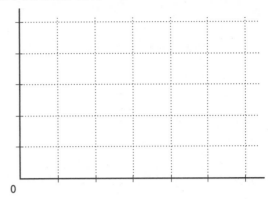

Short answer and numeric questions

1. What is the relationship between actual aggregate expenditure and real GDP? Between aggregate planned expenditure and real GDP?

2. What is the difference between autonomous expenditure and induced expenditure?

3. In a graph with a consumption function, what does the *MPC* equal? What does autonomous consumption equal?

4. The table shows the change in consumption expenditure when a change in disposable income occurs. Complete the table by calculating the marginal propensities to consume.

Change in disposable income (trillions of 1996 dollars)	Change in consumption expenditure (trillions of 1996 dollars)	Marginal propensity to consume, *MPC*
2	1.8	___
1	0.9	___
4	3.0	___

CHECKPOINT 15.2

■ **Explain how real GDP adjusts to achieve equilibrium expenditure.**

Practice Problem 15.2

1. The table gives the components of real GDP in billions of dollars.

	Y	C	I	G	X	M
A	100	110	50	60	60	15
B	200	170	50	60	60	30
C	300	230	50	60	60	45
D	400	290	50	60	60	60
E	500	350	50	60	60	75
F	600	410	50	60	60	90

a. Calculate aggregate planned expenditure when real GDP is $200 billion.

b. Calculate aggregate planned expenditure when real GDP is $600 billion.

c. Calculate equilibrium expenditure.

d. If real GDP is $200 billion, explain the process that moves the economy toward equilibrium expenditure.

e. If real GDP is $600 billion, explain the process that moves the economy toward equilibrium expenditure.

Solution to Practice Problem 15.2

This Practice Problem calculates equilibrium expenditure, and studies the forces that move aggregate expenditure toward equilibrium expenditure. If aggregate planned expenditure exceeds real GDP, firms increase production and real GDP increases. If aggregate planned expenditure is less than real GDP, firms decrease production and real GDP decreases.

Quick Review

- *Equilibrium expenditure* The level of aggregate expenditure that occurs when aggregate planned expenditure equals real GDP.

1. **The table gives the components of real GDP in billions of dollars.**

   a. **Calculate aggregate planned expenditure when real GDP is $200 billion.**

   Aggregate planned expenditure equals $C + I + G + X - M$. When real GDP is $200 billion, ag-gregate planned expenditure is $170 billion + $50 billion + $60 billion + $60 billion − $30 billion, which is $310 billion.

   b. **Calculate aggregate planned expenditure when real GDP is $600 billion.**

   Aggregate planned expenditure equals $C + I + G + X - M$. When real GDP is $600 billion, aggregate planned expenditure is $410 billion + $50 billion + $60 billion + $60 billion − $90 billion, which equals $490 billion.

   c. **Calculate equilibrium expenditure.**

   Equilibrium expenditure occurs when real GDP equals aggregate planned expenditure. When real GDP equals $400 billion, aggregate planned expenditure equals $400 billion. So, equilibrium expenditure occurs when real GDP is $400 billion.

   d. **If real GDP is $200 billion, explain the process that moves the economy toward equilibrium expenditure.**

   When GDP is $200 billion, aggregate planned expenditure exceeds real GDP. An unplanned decrease in investment occurs. Firms increase production to restore their inventories. Real GDP increases. Firms continue to increase production as long as aggregate planned expenditure exceeds real GDP. When real GDP reaches $400 billion, aggregate planned expenditure equals real GDP. The economy is at equilibrium expenditure. The unplanned inventory change is zero and firms have no reason to change production.

   e. **If real GDP is $600 billion, explain the process that moves the economy toward equilibrium expenditure.**

   When real GDP is $600 billion, aggregate planned expenditure of $490 billion is less than real GDP. An unplanned increase in investment occurs. Firms decrease production to restore their inventories. Real GDP decreases. Firms continue to decrease production as long as aggregate planned expenditure is less than real GDP. When real GDP reaches $400 billion, aggregate planned expenditure equals real GDP. The economy is at equilibrium expenditure.

Additional Practice Problem 15.2a

The table gives the components of real GDP in billions of dollars. Draw the aggregate expenditure curve and find the equilibrium expenditure.

Y	C	I	G	X	M
50	50	20	25	25	10
100	85	20	25	25	15
150	120	20	25	25	20
200	155	20	25	25	25
250	190	20	25	25	30
300	225	20	25	25	35

Solution to Additional Practice Problem 15.2a

Aggregate planned expenditure equals $C + I + G + X - M$. To construct the AE curve add the components of aggregate planned expenditure together for each level of real GDP. The AE curve is illustrated in Figure 15.2, along with a 45° line. Equilibrium expenditure occurs at the level of real GDP where the AE curve intersects the 45° line. The equilibrium expenditure is $200 billion.

■ FIGURE 15.2

Aggregate planned expenditure (billions of dollars)

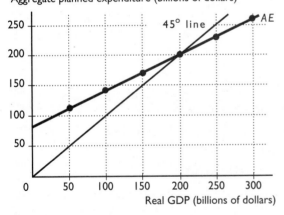

■ Self Test 15.2

Fill in the blanks

Aggregate planned expenditure equals ____ plus ____ plus ____ plus ____ minus ____. As real GDP increases, aggregate planned expenditure ____ (increases; does not change; decreases). Equilibrium expenditure occurs when aggregate planned expenditure is the level of aggregate expenditure that equals ____. When aggregate planned expenditure exceeds real GDP, an unplanned ____ (increase; decrease) in inventories occurs and firms ____ (increase; decrease) production.

True or false

1. Equilibrium expenditure occurs at the intersection of the aggregate expenditure curve and the 45° line.

2. If planned expenditure is less than real GDP, inventories increase.

3. If aggregate planned expenditure exceeds real GDP, inventories decrease and firms decrease production.

4. If unplanned investment occurs, then the aggregate expenditure is not at its equilibrium level.

Multiple choice

1. The AE curve illustrates the relationship between
   a. aggregate planned expenditure and real GDP.
   b. real GDP and actual expenditure.
   c. real GDP and the interest rate.
   d. the interest rate and aggregate planned expenditure.

2. Equilibrium expenditure occurs when
   a. aggregate planned expenditure equals real GDP.
   b. disposable income equals real GDP.
   c. disposable income equals consumption expenditures plus imports.
   d. real GDP plus net taxes equals disposable income.

3. When aggregate planned expenditure exceeds real GDP, there is
   a. a planned decrease in inventories.
   b. a planned increase in inventories.
   c. an unplanned decrease in inventories.
   d. an unplanned increase in inventories.

4. If aggregate planned expenditure is greater than real GDP,
   a. an unplanned decrease in inventories leads to an increase in production.
   b. an unplanned increase in inventories leads to a decrease in production.
   c. a planned decrease in inventories leads to an decrease in production.
   d. a planned increase in inventories leads to an increase in production.

5. If real GDP equals aggregate planned expenditure, then
   a. inventories rise above their target levels.
   b. inventories fall below their target levels.
   c. inventories equal their target levels.
   d. None of the above answers are necessarily correct because there is no relationship between inventories and aggregate planned expenditure.

6. Equilibrium expenditure is the level of expenditure at which
   a. firms' inventories are zero.
   b. firms' inventories are at the desired level.
   c. firms produce more output than they sell.
   d. None of the above answers is correct.

Complete the graph

1. The table gives the components of aggregate planned expenditure in trillions of 1996 dollars.

GDP	C	I	G	X	M	AE
0.0	0.6	0.4	0.2	0.2	0.2	—
1.0	1.2	0.4	0.2	0.2	0.4	—
2.0	1.8	0.4	0.2	0.2	0.6	—
3.0	2.4	0.4	0.2	0.2	0.8	—
4.0	3.0	0.4	0.2	0.2	1.0	—
5.0	3.6	0.4	0.2	0.2	1.2	—

   a. Complete the table.
   b. Label the axes in Figure 15.3 and then plot the AE curve.
   c. In Figure 15.3, show the equilibrium expenditure.
   d. Over what range of GDP is there an unplanned increase in inventories? An unplanned decrease?
   e. What is the amount of planned and actual investment when GDP equals $3.0 trillion?

■ **FIGURE 15.3**

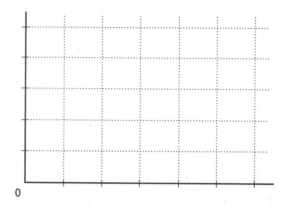

Short answer and numeric questions

1. What is the relationship between aggregate planned expenditure and real GDP? Explain the relationship.

2. In a diagram with an AE curve, what does the 45° line represent? Why is equilibrium expenditure determined by the intersection of the aggregate expenditure curve and the 45° line?

3. If aggregate planned expenditure is less than real GDP, what forces drive the economy to equilibrium expenditure?

CHECKPOINT 15.3

■ **Describe and explain the expenditure multiplier.**

Practice Problems 15.3

1. An economy has no imports or taxes, the MPC is 0.80, and real GDP is $150 billion. If businesses increase investment by $5 billion:
   a. Calculate the multiplier.
   b. Calculate the change in real GDP.
   c. Calculate the new level of real GDP.
   d. Explain why real GDP increases by more than $5 billion.

2. An economy has no imports or taxes. An increase in autonomous expenditure of $2 trillion

increases equilibrium expenditure by $8 trillion:

a. Calculate the multiplier.

b. Calculate the marginal propensity to consume.

c. What happens to the multiplier if an income tax is introduced in this economy?

Solution to Practice Problems 15.3

The multiplier is useful to help understand events you see in the real world, and it also might be featured prominently on exams. The Practice Problems give you valuable practice working with it. To solve the Practice Problems, remember the definition of the multiplier and the formulas to calculate it.

Quick Review

*   *Multiplier* The multiplier is the amount by which a change in any component of autonomous expenditure is magnified or multiplied to determine the change that it generates in equilibrium expenditure and real GDP.
*   *Basic multiplier formula* The defining multiplier formula is:

$$\text{Multiplier} = \frac{\text{Change in equilibrium expenditure}}{\text{Change in autonomous expenditure}}.$$

Multiplier and the MPC With no imports or income taxes, the multiplier is:

$$\text{Multiplier} = \frac{1}{(1 - MPC)}.$$

*   *Multiplier, imports and income taxes* With imports and income taxes, the multiplier is:

$$\text{Multiplier} = \frac{1}{(1 - \text{slope of the } AE \text{ curve})}.$$

1. An economy has no imports or taxes, the *MPC* is 0.80, and real GDP is $150 billion. If businesses increase investment by $5 billion, calculate:

1a. The multiplier.
With no taxes or imports, the multiplier equals $1 \div (1 - MPC)$. The *MPC* is 0.8, so the multiplier equals $1 \div (1 - 0.8)$, which equals 5.0.

1b. The change in real GDP.
The change in real GDP is equal to the multiplier times the change in investment, which is $5 \times \$5$ billion = $25 billion.

1c. The new level of real GDP.
Real GDP increases by $25 billion from $150 billion to $175 billion.

1d. Explain why real GDP increases by more than $5 billion.
The increase in investment increases real GDP, which, in turn, increases income and induces an additional increase in consumption expenditure. So real GDP increases because of the increase in investment *and* the increase in consumption expenditure.

2. An economy has no imports or taxes. An increase in autonomous expenditure of $2 trillion increases equilibrium expenditure by $8 trillion. Calculate:

2a. The multiplier.
The multiplier equals the change in equilibrium expenditure divided by the change in autonomous expenditure. The multiplier equals $8 trillion ÷ $2 trillion, which is 4.

2b. The marginal propensity to consume.
With no taxes and no imports, the multiplier equals $1/(1 - MPC)$. The multiplier is 4, so set $1/(1 - MPC)$ equal to 4 and solve. The *MPC* is 0.75.

2c. What happens to the multiplier if an income tax is introduced in this economy?
When an income tax is introduced, the smaller are the changes in disposable income and real GDP that result from a given change in autonomous expenditure. The slope of the *AE* curve becomes smaller and the multiplier becomes smaller.

Additional Practice Problem 15.3a

Suppose there are no income taxes or imports. How would the following events affect equilibrium expenditure and real GDP?

a. Investment increases by $40 billion and the *MPC* equals 0.6.

b. The president and Congress agree to increase military spending by $100 billion and the *MPC* is 0.8.

Solution to Additional Practice Problem 15.3a

a. **Investment increases by $40 billion and the MPC equals 0.6.**

The increase in investment is an increase in autonomous expenditure. The change in equilibrium expenditure and real GDP equals the multiplier times the change in autonomous expenditure. The multiplier equals $1 \div (1 - MPC)$ $= 1 \div (1 - 0.6) = 2.5$. The change in equilibrium expenditure and real GDP equals $(2.5) \times (\$40$ billion), which is $100 billion. Equilibrium expenditure and real GDP increase by $100 billion.

b. **The president and Congress agree to increase military spending by $100 billion and the MPC is 0.8.**

The increase in military spending is an increase in government purchases and is an increase in autonomous expenditure. The change in equilibrium expenditure and real GDP equals the multiplier times the change in autonomous expenditure. The multiplier equals $1 \div (1 - MPC)$. Because the *MPC* equals 0.8, the multiplier is 5.0. The change in equilibrium expenditure and real GDP equals $(5.0) \times (\$100$ billion), which is $500 billion.

■ Self Test 15.3

Fill in the blanks

The multiplier equals the change in equilibrium expenditure ____ (minus; divided by; multiplied by) the change in autonomous expenditure. The multiplier is ____ (less than; greater than) 1. If there are no taxes or imports, the multiplier equals 1 divided by 1 minus the ____. Imports and income taxes make the multiplier ____ (larger; smaller). A recession is started by ____ (an increase; a decrease) in autonomous expenditure.

True or false

1. The multiplier is greater than 1.

2. If the multiplier equals 4, then a $0.25 trillion increase in investment increases real GDP by $1.0 trillion.

3. The smaller the marginal propensity to consume, the larger is the multiplier.

4. A country that has a high marginal tax rate has a larger multiplier than a country with a low marginal tax rate, other things being the same.

Multiple choice

1. The multiplier is equal to the change in ____ divided by the change in ____.
   a. autonomous expenditure; equilibrium expenditure
   b. dependent expenditure; autonomous expenditure
   c. real GDP; equilibrium expenditure
   d. equilibrium expenditure; autonomous expenditure

2. The multiplier is larger than one because
   a. an increase in autonomous expenditure induces further increases in aggregate expenditure.
   b. additional expenditure induces lower incomes.
   c. an increase in autonomous expenditure brings about a reduction in the real interest rate.
   d. an increase in autonomous expenditure induces further decreases in aggregate expenditure.

3. The multiplier equals 5 and there is a $3 million increase in investment. Equilibrium expenditure
   a. decreases by $15 million.
   b. increases by $3 million.
   c. increases by $5 million.
   d. increases by $15 million.

4. In an economy with no income taxes or imports, the marginal propensity to consume is 0.80. The multiplier is
   a. 0.20.
   b. 0.80.
   c. 1.25.
   d. 5.00.

5. An increase in the marginal tax rate _____ the multiplier.
   a. increases
   b. decreases
   c. has no effect on
   d. can either increase or decrease

6. Which of the following increases the magnitude of the multiplier?
   a. a decrease in the marginal propensity to consume
   b. an increase in autonomous spending
   c. an increase in the marginal income tax rate
   d. a decrease in the marginal propensity to import

7. If the slope of the *AE* curve is 0.5, then the multiplier equals
   a. 5.
   b. 4.
   c. 3.
   d. 2.

8. At the beginning of a recession, the multiplier
   a. offsets the initial cut in autonomous expenditure and slows the recession.
   b. reinforces the initial cut in autonomous expenditure and adds force to the recession.
   c. offsets the initial cut in autonomous expenditure and reverses the recession.
   d. reinforces the initial cut in autonomous expenditure and reverses the recession.

Complete the graph

1. In the "Complete the Graph" problem in Checkpoint 15.2, you plotted an aggregate expenditure curve. Now suppose that government purchases increase by $1.2 trillion to $1.4 trillion at every level of real GDP.
   a. In Figure 15.3, in which you plotted the initial aggregate expenditure curve, plot the new aggregate expenditure curve.
   b. What is the new equilibrium expenditure? By how much did equilibrium expenditure change?

c. What is the slope of the *AE* curve?
d. What is the multiplier? Use the multiplier to find the change in equilibrium expenditure.

Short answer and numeric questions

Marginal propensity to consume, MPC	Multiplier
0.9	___
0.8	___
0.7	___
0.6	___
0.5	___
0.4	___

1. The table gives various values for the marginal propensity to consume. Suppose there are no income taxes or imports. Complete the table by calculating the values of the multiplier. What is the relationship between the *MPC* and the multiplier?

2. Why is the multiplier greater than 1?

3. How does the multiplier affect business cycle turning points?

CHECKPOINT 15.4

■ **Derive the *AD* curve from equilibrium expenditure.**

Practice Problem 15.4

An economy has the following aggregate expenditure schedules:

Real GDP (trillions of 1996 dollars)	Aggregate planned expenditure in trillions of 1996 dollars when the price level is		
	110	100	90
0	1.0	1.5	2.0
1	1.5	2.0	2.5
2	2.0	2.5	3.0
3	2.5	3.0	3.5
4	3.0	3.5	4.0
5	3.5	4.0	4.5
6	4.0	4.5	5.0

a. Make a graph to show three *AE* curves.
b. Find the equilibrium expenditure at each price level.

c. Construct the aggregate demand schedule and plot the aggregate demand curve.

Solution to Practice Problem 15.4

This Practice Problem demonstrates how to derive the *AD* curve. Points on the aggregate demand schedule are the points of equilibrium expenditure.

Quick Review

- *Equilibrium expenditure* The level of aggregate expenditure that occurs when aggregate planned expenditure equals real GDP.

- *Aggregate demand* The real GDP at equilibrium expenditure and the associated price level are the aggregate demand schedule.

a. Make a graph to show three *AE* curves.

The figure shows the three *AE* curves. These curves are graphed using the data in the problem. Each *AE* curve is identified with its price level. The light line in the figure is the 45° line.

b. Find the equilibrium expenditure at each price level.

Equilibrium expenditure is determined where the *AE* curve intersects the 45° line. So in the figure, when the price is 90, equilibrium expenditure is $4 trillion; when the price level is 100, equilibrium expenditure is $3 trillion; and when the price level is 110, equilibrium expenditure is $2 trillion.

c. Construct the aggregate demand schedule and plot the aggregate demand curve.

The table shows the aggregate demand schedule. The aggregate demand schedule is the combination of price level and equilibrium expenditure found in part (b) of the problem. The figure to the right plots this aggregate demand schedule and shows the aggregate demand curve. The aggregate demand curve has been derived from the equilibrium expenditure model.

Price level	Quantity of real GDP demanded (trillions of 1996 dollars)
90	4
100	3
110	2

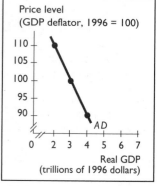

Additional Practice Problem 15.4a

■ FIGURE 15.4

Aggregate planned expenditure (trillions of 1996 dollars)

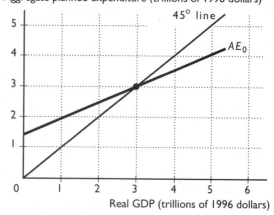

Real GDP (trillions of 1996 dollars)

1. Figure 15.4 shows the *AE* curve, AE_0, when the price level is 100.

   a. In the figure, show what occurs when the price level rises to 110 and aggregate planned expenditure decreases by $1 trillion at every level of real GDP. What is the new equilibrium expenditure?

b. In the figure, show what occurs when the price level falls to 90 and aggregate planned expenditure increases by $1 trillion at every level of real GDP. What is the new equilibrium expenditure?

c. Use the results from parts (a) and (b) to draw an aggregate demand curve in Figure 15.5.

■ **FIGURE 15.5**

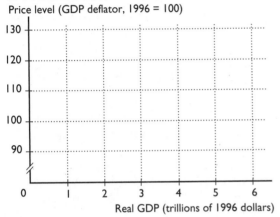

Solution to Additional Practice Problem 15.4a

a. **In the figure, show what occurs when the price level rises to 110 and aggregate planned expenditure decreases by $1 trillion at every level of real GDP. What is the new equilibrium expenditure?**

Figure 15.6 shows the new aggregate expenditure curve, labeled AE_1. The new equilibrium expenditure is $1 trillion, where the AE_1 curve intersects the 45° line.

b. **In the figure, show what occurs when the price level falls to 90 and aggregate planned expenditure increases by $1 trillion at every level of real GDP. What is the new equilibrium expenditure?**

Figure 15.6 shows the new aggregate expenditure curve, labeled AE_2. The new equilibrium expenditure is $5 trillion.

■ **FIGURE 15.6**

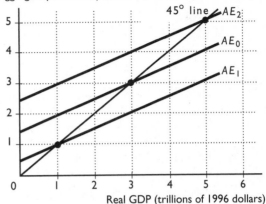

c. **Use the results from parts (a) and (b) to draw an aggregate demand curve in Figure 15.5.**

Each point of equilibrium expenditure corresponds to a point on the AD curve. When the price level is 110, real GDP is $1 trillion. When the price level is 100, real GDP is $3 trillion. And when the price level is 90, real GDP is $5 trillion. These points and the aggregate demand curve are shown Figure 15.7.

■ **FIGURE 15.7**

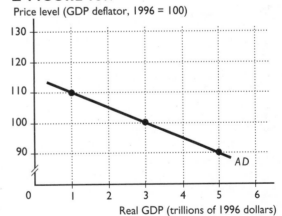

■ Self Test 15.4

Fill in the blanks

The ____ (AE; AD) curve is derived from the ____ (AE; AD) curve. The ____ (AE; AD) curve is the relationship between aggregate planned expenditure and real GDP. The ____ (AE; AD) curve is the relationship between the quantity of real GDP demanded and the price level. The ____ (AE; AD) curve is upward sloping and the ____ (AE; AD) curve is downward sloping. The ____ (AE; AD) curve shifts when the price level changes. There is a movement along the ____ (AE; AD) curve when the price level changes.

True or false

1. There is no relationship between equilibrium expenditure and the *AD* curve.

2. A change in the price level results in a movement along the *AD* curve.

3. A change in the price level results in a movement along the *AE* curve.

4. Each point of equilibrium expenditure on the *AE* curve corresponds to a point on the *AD* curve.

Multiple choice

1. A movement along the *AE* curve arises from a change in ____ and a movement along the AD curve arises from a change in ____.
   a. real GDP; the price level
   b. real GDP; real GDP
   c. the price level; the price level
   d. the price level; real GDP

2. The level of equilibrium expenditure at each price level determines
   a. the points on the *AD* curve.
   b. aggregate planned production.
   c. the price level.
   d. full employment.

3. A change in the price level
   a. shifts the *AE* curve and creates a movement along the *AD* curve.
   b. creates a movement along the *AE* curve and shifts in the *AD* curve.
   c. shifts the *AE* curve and the *AD* curve in the same direction.
   d. shifts the *AE* curve and the *AD* curve in opposite directions.

4. The *AD* curve is the relationship between
   a. aggregate planned expenditure and the price level.
   b. aggregate planned expenditure and the quantity of real GDP demanded.
   c. the quantity of real GDP demanded and the price level.
   d. the quantity of real GDP demanded and the unemployment rate.

Short answer and numeric questions

1. What is the relationship between the *AE* curve and the *AD* curve?

2. What is the effect on the *AE* curve when the price level rises? What is the effect on the *AD* curve when the price level rises?

SELF TEST ANSWERS

■ CHECKPOINT 15.1

Fill in the blanks

Aggregate planned expenditure <u>does not always equal</u> real GDP. The components of aggregate expenditure that change when real GDP changes are <u>induced</u> expenditure. The components of aggregate expenditure that do not change when real GDP changes are <u>autonomous</u> expenditure. The <u>consumption function</u> is the relationship between consumption expenditure and disposable income. The marginal propensity to consume equals the change in consumption expenditure <u>divided by</u> the change in disposable income that brought it about. The slope of the consumption function equals the <u>marginal propensity to consume</u>. A change in disposable income is shown by a <u>movement along</u> the consumption function, and a change in the buying power of money is shown by a <u>shift in</u> the consumption function. Imports <u>are</u> a component of induced expenditure.

True or false

1. True; page 372
2. True; page 373
3. False; page 374
4. True; page 375

Multiple choice

1. d; page 371
2. c; page 371
3. d; page 372
4. b; page 372
5. c; page 372
6. b; page 374

Complete the graph

1. a. Figure 15.8 plots the consumption function, labeled CF_0; page 373.
   b. Autonomous consumption is $0.4 trillion, the y-intercept of curve CF_0 in Figure 15.8; page 373.
   c. If disposable income is $1.0 trillion, consumption expenditure is $1.2 trillion, so saving is –$0.2 trillion. If disposable in-

■ FIGURE 15.8

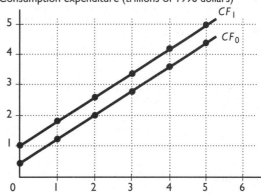

Consumption expenditure (trillions of 1996 dollars)

Disposable income (trillions of 1996 dollars)

come is $4.0 trillion consumption expenditure is $3.6 trillion, so saving is $0.4 trillion; page 373.
   d. The marginal propensity to consume is 0.80; page 374.
   e. The new consumption function is labeled CF_1 in Figure 15.4. Autonomous consumption is $1 trillion; page 373.

Short answer and numeric questions

1. Actual aggregate expenditure always equals real GDP. Aggregate planned expenditure does not necessarily equal real GDP. Actual expenditure equals planed expenditure plus the unplanned change in firms' inventories. If aggregate planned expenditures exceeds real GDP, the change in firms' inventories is smaller than planned, and if aggregate planned expenditure is less than real GDP, the change in firms' inventories is larger than planned; page 371.

2. Autonomous expenditure is the components of aggregate expenditure that do not change when real GDP changes. Induced expenditure is the components of aggregate expenditure that change when real GDP changes; page 372.

3. The MPC equals the slope of the consumption function. Autonomous consumption equals the y-axis intercept; pages 373-374.

4. The completed table is below.

Change in disposable income (trillions of 1996 dollars)	Change in consumption expenditure (trillions of 1996 dollars)	Marginal propensity to consume, MPC
2	1.8	0.90
1	0.9	0.90
4	3.0	0.75

The marginal propensity to consume is the change in consumption expenditure divided by the change in disposable income that brought it about; page 374.

■ CHECKPOINT 15.2

Fill in the blanks

Aggregate planned expenditure equals <u>consumption expenditure</u> plus <u>investment</u> plus <u>government purchases of goods and services</u> plus <u>exports</u> minus <u>imports</u>. As real GDP increases, aggregate planned expenditure <u>increases</u>. Equilibrium expenditure is the level of aggregate expenditure that occurs when aggregate planned expenditure equals <u>real GDP</u>. When aggregate planned expenditure exceeds real GDP, an unplanned <u>decrease</u> in inventories occurs and firms <u>increase</u> production.

True or false

1. True; page 380
2. True; page 381
3. False; page 381
4. True; page 381

Multiple choice

1. a; page 378
2. a; page 380
3. c; page 381
4. a; page 381
5. c; page 381
6. b; page 381

Complete the graph

1. a. Aggregate planned expenditure equals $C + I + G + X - M$. The completed table follows; page 379.

GDP	C	I	G	X	M	AE
0.0	0.6	0.4	0.2	0.2	0.2	<u>1.2</u>
1.0	1.2	0.4	0.2	0.2	0.4	<u>1.6</u>
2.0	1.8	0.4	0.2	0.2	0.6	<u>2.0</u>
3.0	2.4	0.4	0.2	0.2	0.8	<u>2.4</u>
4.0	3.0	0.4	0.2	0.2	1.0	<u>2.8</u>
5.0	3.6	0.4	0.2	0.2	1.2	<u>3.2</u>

b. Figure 15.9 shows the aggregate planned expenditure curve; page 379.

■ FIGURE 15.9

Aggregate planned expenditure (trillions of 1996 dollars)

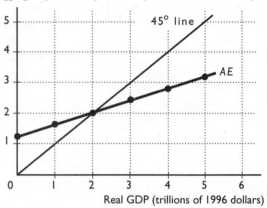

Real GDP (trillions of 1996 dollars)

c. A 45° line has been added to Figure 15.9. Equilibrium expenditure is where the 45° line intersects the aggregate expenditure curve, so equilibrium expenditure is $2 trillion; page 380.

d. An unplanned increase in inventories occurs when real GDP exceeds aggregate planned expenditure. In Figure 15.9, real GDP exceeds planned expenditure when real GDP is greater than $2 trillion; pages 380-381.

An unplanned decrease in inventories occurs when real GDP is less than aggregate planned expenditure. In Figure 15.9, real GDP is less than planned expenditure when real GDP is less than $2 trillion; pages 380-381.

e. When GDP is $3 trillion, planned investment is $0.4 trillion. When GDP is $3 trillion, aggregate planned expenditure is $2.4 trillion, so there is an unplanned increase in inventories of $0.6 trillion. The actual investment is $1 trillion, the sum of planned investment plus the unplanned change in inventories; page 381.

Short answer and numeric questions

1. As real GDP increases, aggregate planned expenditure increases, so there is a positive relationship between real GDP and aggregate planned expenditure. Aggregate planned expenditure increases when real GDP increases because, as real GDP increases, induced expenditure increases; pages 378-379.

2. Along the 45° line real GDP equals aggregate planned expenditure. Equilibrium expenditure occurs when aggregate planned expenditure equals real GDP, which is the point where the *AE* curve intersects the 45° line; page 380.

3. If aggregate planned expenditure is less than real GDP, people are spending less than firms are producing. There is an unplanned increase in inventories. Firms decrease production, and real GDP decreases. Firms continue to decrease production until the unplanned inventory change is zero. When this occurs, real GDP and aggregate expenditure are in equilibrium; page 381.

■ CHECKPOINT 15.3

Fill in the blanks

The multiplier equals the change in equilibrium expenditure <u>divided by</u> the change in autonomous expenditure. The multiplier is <u>greater than</u> 1. If there are no taxes or imports, the multiplier equals 1 divided by 1 minus the <u>marginal propensity to consume</u>. Imports and income taxes make the multiplier <u>smaller</u>. A recession is started by <u>a decrease</u> in autonomous expenditure.

True or false

1. True; pages 384, 386
2. True; page 384
3. False; page 387
4. False; page 387

Multiple choice

1. d; page 385
2. a; page 386
3. d; page 384
4. d; pages 386-387
5. b; page 387
6. d; page 387
7. d; page 387
8. b; page 388

Complete the graph

■ FIGURE 15.10

Aggregate planned expenditure (trillions of 1996 dollars)

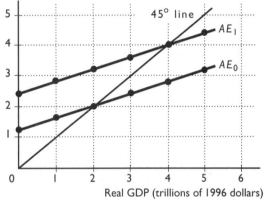

1. a. Figure 15.10 has the new *AE* curve, labeled AE_1 and the initial curve labeled AE_0; page 385.

   b. Equilibrium expenditure increases by $2 trillion to $4 trillion; page 385.

   c. The slope of the *AE* curve equals ($0.4 trillion) ÷ ($1.0 trillion), which is 0.40; page 385.

   d. The multiplier is $\dfrac{1}{(1-\text{slope of the }AE\text{ curve})}$.

   Thus the multiplier is $\dfrac{1}{(1-0.4)}$ = 1.67. The change is equal to the multiplier multiplied by the change in autonomous expenditure, which is (1.67) × ($1.2 trillion). The change in equilibrium expenditure is $2.0 trillion; page 385.

Short answer and numeric questions

1. The multiplier equals $1 \div (1 - MPC)$. The completed table is below. As the MPC increases, the multiplier increases in size; pages 386-387.

Marginal propensity to consume, MPC	Multiplier
0.9	10.0
0.8	5.0
0.7	3.3
0.6	2.5
0.5	2.0
0.4	1.7

2. The multiplier exceeds 1 because an initial change in autonomous expenditure leads to changes in induced expenditure. As a result, the change in aggregate expenditure exceeds the initial change in autonomous expenditure; page 386.

3. The forces that bring business-cycle turning points are the swings in autonomous expenditure such as investment and exports. The multiplier gives momentum to the economy's new direction; page 388.

■ CHECKPOINT 15.4

Fill in the blanks

The _AD_ curve is derived from the _AE_ curve. The _AE_ curve is the relationship between aggregate planned expenditure and real GDP. The _AD_ curve is the relationship between the quantity of real GDP demanded and the price level. The _AE_ curve is upward sloping and the _AD_ curve is downward sloping. The _AE_ curve shifts when the price level changes. There is a movement along the _AD_ curve when the price level changes.

True or false

1. False; pages 390-391
2. True; pages 390-391
3. False; pages 390-391
4. True; pages 390-391

Multiple choice

1. a; page 390
2. a; page 390
3. a; pages 390-391
4. c; page 390

Short answer and numeric questions

1. The _AE_ curve is used to derive the _AD_ curve. Each point of equilibrium expenditure on the _AE_ curve corresponds to a point on the _AD_ curve; page 390.

2. When the price level rises, the _AE_ curve shifts downward and there is a movement up along the _AD_ curve. When the price level falls, the _AE_ curve shifts upward and there is a movement down along the _AD_ curve; pages 390-391.

Fiscal and Monetary Policy Effects

Chapter

16

Chapter 16 provides a description of both fiscal and monetary processes and policies. On the fiscal side, first the federal budget process is outlined. Then fiscal policies are identified and illustrated using the *AD-AS* model. On the monetary side, the basics of how monetary policy affects the economy are discussed, and then the *AD-AS* model is used to illustrate monetary policy. The limits to both fiscal and monetary policy are examined.

■ **Describe the federal budget process and explain the effects of fiscal policy.**

The federal budget is an annual statement of the expenditures, tax receipts, and surplus or deficit of the United States. If tax receipts exceed expenditures, the government has a budget surplus and if expenditures exceed tax receipts, the government has a budget deficit. Fiscal policy can be discretionary, which is policy initiated by an act of Congress, or automatic, which is policy that is triggered by the state of the economy. The government purchases multiplier and the tax multiplier show that aggregate demand changes by more than an initiating change in government purchases or taxes. If real GDP is less than potential GDP, an increase in government purchases or a tax cut can move the economy to potential GDP. If real GDP is greater than potential GDP, a decrease in government purchases or a tax hike can move the economy to potential GDP. A cut in taxes or an increase in government purchases of productive services increases aggregate supply and potential GDP, as well as aggregate demand. The use of discretionary fiscal policy is seriously hampered by law-making time lags, by estimating potential GDP, and by economic forecasting. Automatic stabilizers are features of fiscal policy that stabilize real GDP without explicit action by the government.

■ **Describe the Federal Reserve's monetary policy process and explain the effects of monetary policy.**

Monetary policy is determined by the Federal Open Market Committee (FOMC). The Fed's purchase or sale of government securities affects the nominal interest rate and, in the short run, also the real interest rate. Changes in the interest rate impact decisions regarding investment, consumption, and net exports. When the Fed increases (decreases) the quantity of money, the interest rate falls (rises) and aggregate demand increases (decreases). To fight inflation, the Fed conducts an open market sale. The interest rate rises and expenditure decreases. The multiplier decreases aggregate demand. The *AD* curve shifts leftward and real GDP and the price level both decrease. If the Fed is worried about recession, it conducts an open market purchase, which lowers the interest rate. Aggregate demand increases so that real GDP and the price level increase. Monetary policy has no law-making lag, but estimating potential GDP is hard and economic forecasting is error prone. In addition, monetary policy has the drawback that it depends on how private decision makers respond to a change in the interest rate.

EXPANDED CHAPTER CHECKLIST

When you have completed this chapter, you will be able to:

1 Describe the federal budget process and explain the effects of fiscal policy.

- Define budget surplus, balanced budget, and budget deficit.
- Describe the federal budget time line.
- Define discretionary fiscal policy and automatic fiscal policy.
- Describe the government purchases multiplier and the tax multiplier, and explain why both exist.
- Define the balanced budget multiplier.
- Explain and illustrate how fiscal policy can eliminate a deflationary gap and an inflationary gap.
- State why fiscal policy has supply-side effects.
- Discuss the limitations to discretionary fiscal policy.
- Explain the operation of the automatic stabilizers and define induced taxes and needs-tested spending.

2 Describe the Federal Reserve's monetary policy process and explain the effects of monetary policy.

- Describe the Fed's monetary policy process.
- Explain how the Fed influences the interest rate in the short run and long run.
- Illustrate the effects when the Fed raises and when it lowers the interest rate.
- Discuss the ripple effect of the Fed's actions and explain the role played by the multiplier.
- Explain and illustrate in an *AD-AS* figure how the Fed fights inflation and recession.
- Describe the limitations to monetary policy.

KEY TERMS

- Federal budget (page 398)
- Budget surplus (page 398)
- Budget deficit (page 398)
- Balanced budget (page 398)
- Discretionary fiscal policy (page 400)
- Automatic fiscal policy (page 400)
- Government purchases multiplier (page 401)
- Tax multiplier (page 401)
- Balanced budget multiplier (page 401)
- Automatic stabilizers (page 408)
- Induced taxes (page 408)
- Needs-tested spending (page 408)
- Beige Book (page 410)

CHECKPOINT 16.1

■ Describe the federal budget process and explain the effects of fiscal policy.

Practice Problems 16.1

1. Classify each of the following as discretionary fiscal policy or automatic fiscal policy or neither:
   a. A decrease in tax receipts in a recession
   b. Additional expenditure to upgrade highways
   c. An increase in the public education budget
   d. A purchase of $1 billion of medicines to treat AIDS sufferers in Africa
   e. A cut in funding for NASA during an expansion
2. Explain the change in aggregate demand when:
   a. Government purchases increase by $100 billion, which the government spends on national defense.
   b. Taxes are increased by $100 billion.
   c. Both (a) and (b) occur simultaneously.

Solution to Practice Problems 16.1

The difference between a discretionary fiscal policy and an automatic policy is whether the policy is initiated by an act of Congress or whether the policy is already in place and is triggered automatically by the state of the economy. Discretionary fiscal policies are hampered by law-making time lags, estimating potential GDP, and economic forecasting.

Quick Review

- *Discretionary fiscal policy* Fiscal policy action that is initiated by an act of Congress.
- *Automatic fiscal policy* Fiscal policy that is triggered by the state of the economy.
- *Government purchases multiplier* The magnification effect of a change in government purchases on aggregate demand.
- *Tax multiplier* The magnification effect of a change in taxes on aggregate demand.

1. Classify each of the following as discretionary fiscal policy or automatic fiscal policy or neither:

1a. A decrease in tax receipts in a recession

During a recession, tax receipts automatically fall as workers are laid off and their incomes decrease. So the decrease in tax receipts is an example of induced taxes and is an automatic fiscal policy.

1b. Additional expenditure to upgrade highways

To further upgrade highways, Congress must approve the increase in the budget. Because Congress must pass a law to increase spending, it is a discretionary fiscal policy.

1c. An increase in the public education budget

Similar to part (b), an act of Congress is required to increase the public education budget, so the policy is a discretionary fiscal policy.

1d. A purchase of $1 billion of medicines to treat AIDS sufferers in Africa

The purchase of medicines for AIDS sufferers must be approved by an act of Congress, so the policy is a discretionary fiscal policy.

1e. A cut in funding for NASA during an expansion

A cut in NASA's funding cannot be made without passing an act of Congress. Because the cut requires Congressional action, it is a discretionary fiscal policy.

2. Explain the change in aggregate demand when:

2a. Government purchases increase by $100 billion, which the government spends on national defense.

The $100 billion increase in government purchases leads to an increase in aggregate demand that is greater than $100 billion because of the government purchases multiplier. The initial government purchases of $100 billion induces an increase in consumer expenditure, which brings a further increase in aggregate demand. A multiplier process ensues so that aggregate demand increases by more than $100 billion.

2b. Taxes are increased by $100 billion.

The tax hike decreases aggregate demand by more than $100 billion because of the tax multiplier. The tax hike decreases disposable income. The decrease in disposable income decreases consumption expenditure. With decreased consumption expenditure, employment and incomes fall, and consumption expenditure falls further. A multiplier process ensues.

2c. Both (a) and (b) occur simultaneously.

Aggregate demand increases. The increase in aggregate demand from the increase in government purchases is larger than the decrease in aggregate demand from the tax hike. The balanced budget multiplier is positive—a simultaneous and equal increase in government purchases and taxes results in an increase in aggregate demand.

Additional Practice Problem 16.1a

What is the balanced budget multiplier and why is it greater than zero?

Solution to Additional Practice Problem 16.1a

The balanced budget multiplier is the magnification effect on aggregate demand of *simultaneous* changes in government purchases and taxes that leave the budget balance unchanged. The balanced budget multiplier is not zero—it is positive—because the size of the government purchases multiplier is larger than the size of the tax multiplier. That is, a $1 increase in government purchases increases aggregate demand by more than a $1 increase in taxes decreases aggregate demand. So when both government purchases and taxes increase by $1, aggregate demand still increases.

■ Self Test 16.1

Fill in the blanks

The national debt is ____ (tax receipts minus expenditures; the amount of debt outstanding that arises from past budget deficits). ____ (Automatic; Discretionary) fiscal policy is a fiscal policy action that is initiated by an act of Congress; ____ (automatic; discretionary) fiscal policy is a fiscal policy action triggered by the state of the economy. The government purchases multiplier is the magnification of a change in government purchases on aggregate ____ (demand; supply). A tax cut ____ (increases; decreases) aggregate supply and shifts the *AS* curve ____ (rightward; leftward). One limitation of discretionary fiscal policy is the ____ (needs-tested lag; law-making time lag).

True or false

1. Other things the same, a tax cut decreases the national debt.

2. The Bush tax cut package approved by Congress in 2002 is an example of discretionary fiscal policy.

3. The government purchases multiplier is the magnification effect of a change in aggregate demand on government purchases of goods and services.

4. The magnitude of the tax multiplier is smaller than the government purchases multiplier.

5. If government purchases and taxes increase by the same amount, aggregate demand does not change.

6. To eliminate an inflationary gap, the government could decrease its purchases of goods and services.

7. A tax cut increases aggregate supply but does not increase aggregate demand, so it increases real GDP and lowers the price level.

8. Automatic stabilizers are features of fiscal policy that work to stabilize real GDP without explicit action by the government.

Multiple choice

1. The annual statement of the expenditures, tax receipts, and surplus or deficit of the government of the United States is the federal
   a. surplus record.
   b. deficit record.
   c. budget.
   d. spending.

2. When government expenditures are less than tax receipts, the government has a budget
   a. with a positive balance.
   b. deficit.
   c. surplus.
   d. with a negative debt.

3. National debt decreases in a given year when a country has a
   a. budget deficit.
   b. balanced budget.
   c. budget supplement.
   d. budget surplus.

4. The Employment Act of 1946 states that it is
   a. the duty of the federal government to give jobs to all citizens.
   b. the policy and the responsibility of the federal government to promote maximum employment.
   c. the responsibility of the federal government to hire all who are unemployed.
   d. wise and compassionate to force business to hire the unemployed.

5. An example of automatic fiscal policy is
   a. an interest rate cut, initiated by an act of Congress.
   b. an increase in the quantity of money.
   c. a tax cut, initiated by an act of Congress.
   d. a decrease in tax receipts, triggered by the state of the economy.

6. The government purchases multiplier is the magnification effect of a change in government purchases on
   a. aggregate demand.
   b. the budget deficit.
   c. tax receipts.
   d. None of the above answers is correct.

7. The magnitude of the tax multiplier is ____ the magnitude of the government purchases multiplier.
   a. equal to
   b. greater than
   c. smaller than
   d. the inverse of

8. Discretionary fiscal policy works to close a deflationary gap by shifting the
   a. *AD* curve leftward.
   b. *AS* curve leftward.
   c. *AD* curve leftward and the *AS* curve leftward.
   d. *AD* curve rightward.

9. If the economy is at an above full-employment equilibrium, ____ gap exists and discretionary fiscal policy that ____ aggregate demand will return real GDP to potential GDP.
   a. an inflationary; increases
   b. an inflationary; decreases
   c. a deflationary; increases
   d. a deflationary; decreases

10. The supply-side effects of a tax cut ____ potential GDP and ____ aggregate supply.
    a. increase; increase
    b. increase; decrease
    c. decrease; increase
    d. decrease; decrease

11. If a tax cut increases aggregate demand more than aggregate supply, real GDP ____ and the price level ____.
    a. increases; rises
    b. increases; falls
    c. decreases; rises
    d. decreases; falls

12. Discretionary fiscal policy is handicapped by
    a. law-making time lags, induced taxes, and automatic stabilizers.
    b. law-making time lags, estimating potential GDP, and economic forecasting.
    c. economic forecasting, law-making time lags, and induced taxes.
    d. automatic stabilizers, law-making time lags, and estimating potential GDP.

Complete the graph

■ **FIGURE 16.1**

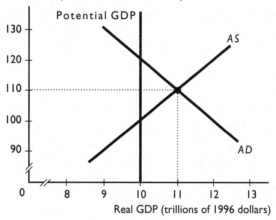

1. Figure 16.1 illustrates the economy.
   a. Is there an inflationary gap or a deflationary gap present?
   b. What type of fiscal policy might be used to restore the economy to full employment?
   c. In Figure 16.1, illustrate the effect of the policy you suggested in your answer to part (b).

Short answer and numeric questions

1. What happens to the national debt if the government has a $100 billion budget deficit?

2. How can the government use fiscal policy to eliminate a deflationary gap?

3. What are the demand-side effects of a tax cut? What are the supply-side effects? Why does a tax cut have supply-side effects?

4. It is not easy to determine potential GDP. Why does this fact hamper the use of discretionary fiscal policy?

5. What are automatic stabilizers? Can they eliminate a recession?

CHECKPOINT 16.2

■ Describe the Federal Reserve's monetary policy process and explain the effects of monetary policy.

Practice Problems 16.2

1. If the Fed cuts the quantity of money, explain how each of the following items changes:
   a. Businesses' purchases of new capital equipment
   b. Households' purchases of new cars and houses
   c. Foreigners' purchases of U.S.-made goods and services
   d. Americans' purchases of Canadian-made goods and services

2. What is the multiplier effect of monetary policy? How does it work? How does the size of the expenditure multiplier influence the size of the multiplier effect of monetary policy?

Solution to Practice Problems 16.2

The first Practice Problem studies the ripple effects of the Fed's actions. The second Practice Problem studies the multiplier effects of the Fed's actions. These effects exist not only in theory but also in practice, so the Practice Problems give you some excellent insights into the many ways the Fed influences economic activity.

Quick Review

- *Ripple effects from monetary policy* When the Fed increases the interest rate, three main events follow: investment and consumption expenditure decrease; the price of the dollar rises on the foreign exchange market and net exports decrease; a multiplier effect induces a further decrease in consumption expenditure and aggregate demand.

1. If the Fed cuts the quantity of money, explain how each of the following items changes:

   1a. Businesses' purchases of new capital equipment

A reduction in the quantity of money raises the interest rate. The interest rate is the opportunity cost of the funds used to finance investment. When the opportunity cost of investment increases, businesses decrease their purchases of new capital equipment.

   1b. Households' purchases of new cars and houses

A reduction in the quantity of money raises the interest rate. The interest rate is the opportunity cost of the funds used to finance the purchase of big-ticket consumer items. When the opportunity cost rises, households delay their purchases of new cars and houses.

   1c. Foreigners' purchases of U.S.-made goods and services

When the interest rate in the United States rises relative to the interest rate in other countries, people buy dollars and sell other currencies. With more dollars demanded, the price of the dollar rises on the foreign exchange market. The rise in the price of the dollar means that foreigners must now pay more for U.S.-made goods and services. U.S. exports decrease.

   1d. Americans' purchases of Canadian-made goods and services

When the interest rate in the United States rises relative to the interest rate in other countries, people buy dollars and sell other currencies. With more dollars demanded, the price of the dollar rises on the foreign exchange market. The rise in the price of the dollar means U.S. residents now pay less for Canadian-made goods and services. U.S. imports from Canada increase.

2. What is the multiplier effect of monetary policy? How does it work? How does the size of the expenditure multiplier influence the size of the multiplier effect of monetary policy?

When the Fed increases the quantity of money, the interest rate falls, and the foreign exchange value of the dollar falls. As the interest rate falls, investment and consumption expenditure increase. With the fall in the foreign exchange value of the dollar, U.S. exports increase and U.S. imports decrease. Aggregate expenditure increases because investment, consumption expenditure, and net exports, which are part of autonomous expenditure, increase. As autonomous expenditure increases, the expenditure multiplier determines the increase in aggregate demand. The larger the expenditure multiplier, the larger the increase in aggregate demand and the larger is the multiplier effect of monetary policy.

Additional Practice Problem 16.2a

What is an advantage that monetary policy has over fiscal policy?

Solution to Additional Practice Problem 16.2a

Monetary policy has an advantage over fiscal policy because it cuts out the law-making time lags. The FOMC meets eight times a year and can conduct telephone meetings between its scheduled meetings. And the actual actions that change the quantity of money are daily actions taken by the New York Fed operating under the guidelines decided by the FOMC. So monetary policy is a continuous policy process and is not subject to a long decision lag.

■ Self Test 16.2

Fill in the blanks

The Beige Book is a ____ (book that outlines the Fed's current monetary policy; report summarizing economic conditions). In the ____ (long; short) run, the Fed has no control over the real interest rate. To raise the interest rate, the FOMC instructs the New York Fed to ____ (purchase; sell) securities in the open market. When the interest rate rises, investment and consumption expenditure ____ (increase; decrease) and net exports ____ (increase; decrease). When the Fed eases to fight recession, the aggregate ____ (demand; supply) curve shifts ____ (leftward; rightward).

True or false

1. The FOMC meets once a year in January to determine the nation's monetary policy.

2. In the short run, when the Fed changes the nominal interest rate, the real interest rate also changes.

3. If the Fed fears a recession, it lowers the interest rate.

4. A change in the interest rate changes net exports.

5. The Fed's monetary policy works by changing aggregate supply.

6. If the Fed's monetary policy raises the interest rate, aggregate demand decreases.

7. To combat a recession, the Fed lowers taxes, which increases aggregate demand and shifts the aggregate demand curve rightward.

8. Monetary policy is a perfect stabilization tool because it does not have law-making time lags.

Multiple choice

1. The FOMC is the
   a. report the Fed gives to Congress twice a year.
   b. group within the Fed that makes the monetary policy decisions.
   c. report that summarizes the economy across Fed districts.
   d. name of the meeting the Fed has with Congress twice a year.

2. The Fed affects aggregate demand through monetary policy by changing
   a. the quantity of money and influencing the interest rate.
   b. tax rates and influencing disposable income.
   c. the quantity of money and determining government purchases.
   d. government purchases and influencing the budget balance.

3. If the Fed sells securities, in the short run the interest rate
   a. rises.
   b. is not affected.
   c. falls.
   d. might either rise or fall.

4. When the Fed increases the nominal interest rate, the real interest rate
   a. temporarily rises.
   b. permanently rises.
   c. temporarily falls.
   d. permanently falls.

5. In the long run, the Fed's policies can influence
   a. the real interest rate.
   b. the inflation rate.
   c. induced taxes.
   d. income taxes.

6. If the Fed decreases the interest rate, which of the following occurs?
   a. Investment increases.
   b. Consumption expenditure decreases.
   c. The price of the dollar on the foreign exchange market increases.
   d. Net exports decreases.

7. If the Fed increases the interest rate, which of the following occur?
   a. The price of the dollar on the foreign exchange market increases.
   b. Investment increases.
   c. Aggregate demand increases.
   d. Net exports increases.

8. The Fed increases the interest rate when it
   a. fears recession.
   b. wants to increase the quantity of money.
   c. fears inflation.
   d. wants to encourage bank lending.

9. Decreasing the quantity of money shifts the aggregate demand curve _____, so that real GDP _____ and the price level _____.
   a. rightward; increases; rises
   b. leftward; decreases; rises
   c. rightward; increases; falls
   d. leftward; decreases; falls

10. To fight a recession, the Fed can
    a. lower the interest rate by buying securities.
    b. lower the interest rate by selling securities.
    c. raise the interest rate by buying securities.
    d. raise the interest rate by selling securities.

11. When the economy is in a recession, the Fed can _____ the interest rate, which _____ aggregate demand and _____ real GDP.
    a. lower; increases; decreases
    b. raise; decreases; increases
    c. lower; increases; increases
    d. raise; increases; decreases

12. An advantage monetary policy has over fiscal policy is that monetary policy
    a. can be quickly changed and implemented.
    b. is coordinated with fiscal policy.
    c. is approved by the president of the United States.
    d. affects consumption expenditure and investment without impacting international trade.

Complete the graph

■ **FIGURE 16.2**

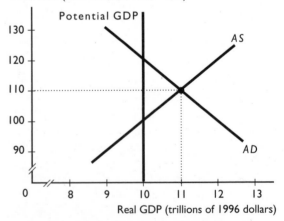

Price level (GDP deflator, 1996 = 100)

1. Figure 16.2 illustrates the economy.
   a. What type of monetary policy is used to restore the economy to full employment?
   b. In Figure 16.2, illustrate the effect of the policy you suggested in your answer to part (a).

c. In Figure 16.1, you answered a similar question about fiscal policy. Compared to using fiscal policy, what is an advantage of using monetary policy to restore the economy to potential GDP? Compared to monetary policy, what is an advantage of using fiscal policy?

Short answer and numeric questions

1. How does the Fed keep the public informed about the state of the economy and its monetary policy decisions?

2. In the short run, how does the Fed affect the real interest rate? In the long run, how does the Fed affect the real interest rate?

3. Suppose the Fed increases the quantity of money. In the short run, what is the effect on the interest rate? On investment? On aggregate demand?

4. How does monetary policy affect the price of the dollar on the foreign exchange market? In your answer, explain the case in which the Fed raises the interest rate.

5. Suppose the Fed is concerned that the economy is entering a recession. What policy can the Fed pursue and what is the effect of the policy on real GDP and the price level?

■ SELF TEST ANSWERS

■ CHECKPOINT 16.1

Fill in the blanks

The national debt is <u>the total amount of debt outstanding that arises from past budget deficits</u>. <u>Discretionary</u> fiscal policy is a fiscal policy action that is initiated by an act of Congress; <u>automatic</u> fiscal policy is a fiscal policy action triggered by the state of the economy. The government purchases multiplier is the magnification of a change in government purchases on aggregate <u>demand</u>. A tax cut <u>increases</u> aggregate supply and shifts the *AS* curve <u>rightward</u>. One limitation of discretionary fiscal policy is the <u>law-making time lag</u>.

True or false

1. False; page 398
2. True; page 400
3. False; page 401
4. True; page 401
5. False; page 401
6. True; page 403
7. False; pages 401, 405
8. True; page 407

Multiple choice

1. c; page 398
2. c; page 398
3. d; page 398
4. b; page 400
5. d; page 400
6. a; page 401
7. c; page 401
8. d; page 402
9. b; page 403
10. a; page 404
11. a; page 406
12. b; page 407

Complete the graph

1. a. There is an inflationary gap because real GDP exceeds potential GDP; page 403.
   b. The economy will return to full employment with a tax hike or a decrease in government purchases; page 403.

■ FIGURE 16.3

Price level (GDP deflator, 1996 = 100)

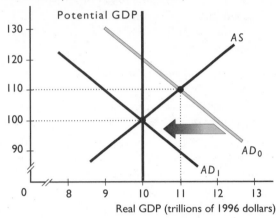

Real GDP (trillions of 1996 dollars)

c. Figure 16.3 shows the results of the suggested policy. Aggregate demand decreases and the *AD* curve shifts leftward from AD_0 to AD_1. Real GDP decreases from $11 trillion to $10 trillion and the price level falls from 110 to 100; page 403.

Short answer and numeric questions

1. If the government has a $100 billion budget deficit, the national debt increases by $100 billion; page 398.

2. A deflationary gap exists when real GDP is less than potential GDP. The government can eliminate the deflationary gap by increasing aggregate demand. The government can increase aggregate demand by increasing its purchases of goods and services or by cutting taxes; page 402.

3. A tax cut increases disposable income, which increases consumption expenditure and aggregate demand. A tax cut creates an incentive to work and save. So a tax cut increases the supply of labor and the supply of saving. An increase in the supply of labor increases the equilibrium quantity of labor employed. An increase in the supply of saving increases the equilibrium quantity of investment and capital. With larger quantities of labor and capital, potential GDP increases and so does

aggregate supply. So a decrease in taxes increases aggregate supply; page 404.

4. It is not easy to tell whether real GDP is below, above, or at potential GDP. So a discretionary fiscal action can move real GDP *away* from potential GDP instead of toward it; page 407.

5. Automatic stabilizers are features of fiscal policy that stabilize real GDP without explicit action by the government. Automatic stabilizers include induced taxes and needs-tested spending. Induced taxes and needs-tested spending decrease the multiplier effect of a change in autonomous expenditure. So they moderate both expansions and recessions and make real GDP more stable. But they cannot eliminate a recession; page 407.

■ CHECKPOINT 16.2

Fill in the blanks

The Beige Book is a <u>report summarizing economic conditions</u>. In the <u>long</u> run, the Fed has no control over the real interest rate. To raise the interest rate, the FOMC instructs the New York Fed to <u>sell</u> securities in the open market. When the interest rate rises, investment and consumption expenditure <u>decrease</u> and net exports <u>decrease</u>. When the Fed eases to fight recession, the aggregate <u>demand</u> curve shifts <u>rightward</u>.

True or false

1. False; page 410
2. True; page 411
3. True; page 412
4. True; page 413
5. False; page 415
6. True; page 415
7. False; page 416
8. False; page 417

Multiple choice

1. b; page 410
2. a; page 411
3. a; page 411
4. a; page 411
5. b; page 411
6. a; page 413
7. a; page 413
8. c; page 415
9. d; page 415
10. a; page 416
11. c; page 416
12. a; page 417

Complete the graph

■ **FIGURE 16.4**

Price level (GDP deflator, 1996 = 100)

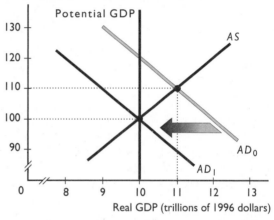

1. a. The economy will return to full employment with a decrease in the quantity of money; page 415.

   b. Figure 16.4 shows the results of the decrease in the quantity of money. Aggregate demand decreases and the *AD* curve shifts leftward from AD_0 to AD_1. Real GDP decreases from $11 trillion to potential GDP of $10 trillion and the price level falls from 110 to 100; page 415.

   c. The advantage of using monetary policy is that there is no law-making lag. The actions that change the quantity of money are taken each day. The advantage of using fiscal policy is that the impact on aggregate demand is direct. The effects of monetary policy are indirect and depend on how private decisions respond to a change in the interest rate. These responses are hard to forecast and vary from one situation to another in unpredictable ways; page 417.

Short answer and numeric questions

1. To keep the public informed about the state of the economy, the Fed makes available the Beige Book, which is a report that summarizes the current economic conditions in each Federal Reserve district and each sector of the economy. After each FOMC meeting the FOMC announces its decisions and describes its view of the likelihood that its goals of price stability and sustainable economic growth will be achieved. The minutes of the FOMC meeting are released only after the next meeting. The Fed is required to report twice a year to the House of Representatives Committee on Financial Services, at which time the Fed chairman testifies before the committee; page 410.

2. In the short run, the Fed can determine the nominal interest rate by changing the quantity of money in circulation. In the short run, the expected inflation rate is determined by recent monetary policy and inflation experience. So when the Fed changes the nominal interest rate, the real interest rate also changes, temporarily.

   In the long run, saving supply and investment demand determine the real interest rate in global financial markets. So in the long run, the Fed influences the nominal interest rate by the effects of its policies on the inflation rate. But it does not directly control the nominal interest rate, and it has no control over the real interest rate; page 411.

3. If the Fed increases the quantity of money, the interest rate falls, investment increases and aggregate demand increases; page 412.

4. Suppose the interest rate rises relative to the interest rate in other countries. Some people will want to move funds into the United States from other countries to take advantage of the higher interest rate they can now earn on U.S. bank deposits and bonds. When money is moved into the United States, people buy dollars and sell other currencies. With more dollars demanded, the price of the dollar rises on the foreign exchange market; page 413.

5. When the Fed is concerned that the economy is entering a recession, it makes an open market purchase. The interest rate falls. The quantity of investment and other interest-sensitive expenditure increases. Net exports also increases. With an increase in aggregate expenditure, the multiplier increases aggregate demand. Real GDP increases and the price level rises; page 416.

Chapter

17

The Short-Run Policy Tradeoff

Chapter 17 discusses the relationship between inflation and unemployment in the short run and the relationship between the long-run Phillips curve and the short-run Phillips curve. It also discusses how the Fed can influence the expected inflation rate.

■ **Describe the short-run tradeoff between inflation and unemployment.**

The short-run Phillips curve shows the relationship between the inflation rate and the unemployment rate when the natural unemployment rate and expected inflation rate remain constant. The downward-sloping short-run Phillips curve indicates a tradeoff between inflation and unemployment. The short-run Phillips curve is another way of looking at the upward-sloping aggregate supply curve, because a change in real GDP also changes the unemployment rate and a change in the price level also changes the inflation rate. The relationship between output and unemployment is called Okun's Law. Okun's Law states that for each percentage point that the unemployment rate is above the natural unemployment rate, there is a 2 percent gap between real GDP and potential GDP.

■ **Distinguish between the short-run and the long-run Phillips curves and describe the shifting tradeoff between inflation and unemployment.**

The long-run Phillips curve is a vertical line that shows the relationship between inflation and unemployment when the economy is at full employment. At full employment, the unemployment rate is the natural unemployment rate, but the inflation rate can take on any value. So along the long-run Phillips curve, there is no long-run tradeoff between inflation and unemployment. When the expected inflation rate changes, the short-run Phillips curve shifts to intersect the long-run Phillips curve at the new expected inflation rate. The natural rate hypothesis is the proposition that when the money growth rate changes, the unemployment rate changes temporarily and eventually returns to the natural unemployment rate. If the natural unemployment rate changes, both the long-run Phillips curve and the short-run Phillips curve shift.

■ **Explain how the Fed can influence the expected inflation rate and how expected inflation influences the short-run tradeoff.**

The expected inflation rate helps set the money wage rate and other money prices. To forecast inflation, people use data about past inflation and other relevant variables, as well as economic science. The presence of long-term labor contracts means that the short-run tradeoff between inflation and unemployment responds gradually to a change in the expected inflation rate. If the Fed pursues a surprise inflation reduction, inflation slows but at the cost of recession. If the Fed pursues a credible announced inflation reduction, the expected inflation rate falls along with the inflation rate and there is no accompanying loss of output or increase in unemployment.

EXPANDED CHAPTER CHECKLIST

When you have completed this chapter, you will be able to:

1 Describe the short-run tradeoff between inflation and unemployment.

- Define, describe, and illustrate the short-run Phillips curve.
- Explain why the short-run Phillips curve is another way of looking at the upward sloping aggregate supply curve.
- Explain and use Okun's Law.
- Explain why aggregate demand fluctuations that bring movements along the aggregate supply curve also bring movements along the short-run Phillips curve.

2 Distinguish between the short-run and the long-run Phillips curves and describe the shifting tradeoff between inflation and unemployment.

- Describe and illustrate the long-run Phillips curve and explain how it differs from the short-run Phillips curve.
- Illustrate the effect of a change in the expected inflation rate on the long-run Phillips curve and the short-run Phillips curve.
- Explain the natural rate hypothesis.
- Illustrate the effect of a change in the natural unemployment rate on the long-run Phillips curve and the short-run Phillips curve.

3 Explain how the Fed can influence the expected inflation rate and how expected inflation influences the short-run tradeoff.

- Define rational expectation.
- Describe the economy following a surprise inflation reduction by the Fed.
- Describe the economy following a credible announced inflation reduction by the Fed.

KEY TERMS

- Short-run Phillips curve (page 424)
- Okun's Law (page 425)
- Long-run Phillips curve (page 430)
- Expected inflation rate (page 432)
- Natural rate hypothesis (page 433)
- Rational expectation (page 439)

CHECKPOINT 17.1

■ **Describe the short-run tradeoff between inflation and unemployment.**

Practice Problem 17.1

1. The table describes five possible situations that might arise in 2003, depending on the level of aggregate demand in that year. Potential GDP is $7 trillion, and the natural unemployment rate is 5 percent.

	Price level (2002 = 100)	Unemployment rate (percentage)
A	102.5	9
B	105.0	6
C	106.0	5
D	107.5	4
E	110.0	3

   a. Calculate the inflation rate for each possible outcome.
   b. Use Okun's Law to find the real GDP associated with each unemployment rate in the table.
   c. What is the expected inflation rate in 2003?
   d. What is the expected price level in 2003?
   e. Plot the short-run Phillips curve for 2003.
   f. Plot the aggregate supply curve for 2003.
   g. Mark the points *A, B, C, D,* and *E* on each curve that correspond to the data provided in the table and the data that you have calculated.

Solution to Practice Problem 17.1

This problem focuses on the connections between the short-run Phillips curve and the aggregate supply curve.

Quick Review

- *Short-run Phillips curve* A curve that shows the relationship between the inflation rate and the unemployment rate when the natural unemployment rate and the expected inflation rate remain constant.

- *Okun's Law* For each percentage point that the unemployment rate is above the natural unemployment rate, there is a 2 percent gap between real GDP and potential GDP.

a. Calculate the inflation rate for each possible outcome.

The inflation rate equals the change in the price level divided by the initial price level, all multiplied by 100. So, for row *A*, the inflation rate equals $\frac{102.5 - 100.0}{100.0} \times 100$, or 2.5 percent. The rest of the inflation rates are calculated similarly.

	Inflation rate (percent per year)
A	2.5
B	5.0
C	6.0
D	7.5
E	10.0

b. Use Okun's Law to find the real GDP associated with each unemployment rate in the table.

Okun's Law states that for each percentage point that the unemployment rate is above the natural unemployment rate, there is a 2 percent gap between real GDP and potential GDP. In row *A* the unemployment rate is 9 percent. The natural unemployment rate is 5 percent, so the unemployment rate is 4 percentage points above the natural unemployment rate. So real GDP is (2) × (4 percent) = 8 percent below potential GDP. Potential GDP is $7 trillion, so real GDP is (8 percent) × ($7 trillion) = $0.56 trillion dollars below potential GDP. Real GDP equals $7 trillion minus $0.56 trillion, which is $6.44 trillion. The rest of the real GDP calculations are similar.

	Real GDP (trillions of 2002 dollars)
A	6.44
B	6.86
C	7.00
D	7.14
E	7.28

c. What is the expected inflation rate in 2003?

People expect that the economy will be at potential GDP so the unemployment rate equals the natural unemployment rate. At the natural unemployment rate of 5 percent, the table shows that the price level is 106. The inflation rate is 6 percent a year and so the expected inflation rate is 6 percent a year.

d. What is the expected price level in 2003?

With an expected inflation rate of 6 percent, the expected price level is 106.

e. Plot the short-run Phillips curve for 2003.

The short-run Phillips curve for 2003 shows the relationship between the inflation rate and the unemployment rate when the natural unemployment rate is 5 percent and the expected inflation rate is 6 percent a year.

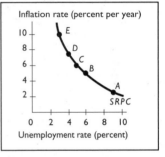

f. Plot the aggregate supply curve for 2003.

The aggregate supply curve is plotted in the figure. The price levels are given in the problem and the corresponding real GDPs are calculated from Okun's Law in part (b).

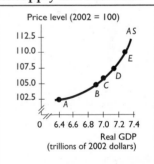

g. Mark the points *A*, *B*, *C*, *D*, and *E* on each curve that correspond to the data provided in the table and the data that you have calculated.

The figures in part (e) and part (f) have the points labeled.

Additional Practice Problem 17.1a

In the Practice Problem, what is the role of the aggregate demand curve?

Solution to Additional Practice Problem 17.1a

When aggregate demand increases, everything else remaining the same, there is a movement up along the aggregate supply curve. Real GDP increases and the price level rises. At the same time, the unemployment rate decreases and the inflation rate rises. There is a movement up along the short-run Phillips curve.

When aggregate demand decreases, everything else remaining the same, there is a movement down along the aggregate supply curve. Real GDP decreases and the price level falls. At the same time, the unemployment rate increases and the inflation rate falls. There is a movement down along the short-run Phillips curve.

■ Self Test 17.1

Fill in the blanks

The short-run Phillips curve is the curve that shows the relationship between the _____ (price level; inflation rate; nominal interest rate) and the _____ (quantity of real GDP supplied; unemployment rate; real interest rate) when the natural unemployment rate and expected inflation rate remain constant. The short-run Phillips curve is _____ (downward; upward) sloping. Okun's Law states that for each percentage point that the unemployment rate is above the natural unemployment rate, there is a _____ (2; 6) percent gap between real GDP and potential GDP. A change in aggregate demand that leads to a movement along the aggregate supply curve also leads to a _____ (shift in; movement along) the short-run Phillips curve.

True or false

1. The short-run Phillips curve shows the tradeoff between the natural unemployment rate and the expected inflation rate.

2. Moving along a short-run Phillips curve, the price of a lower unemployment rate is a higher inflation rate.

3. Okun's Law states that for each percentage point that real GDP is less than potential GDP, there is a 2 percent gap between the unemployment rate and the natural unemployment rate.

4. Points on the short-run Phillips curve correspond to points on the aggregate supply curve.

5. Aggregate demand fluctuations bring movements along the aggregate supply curve and along the short-run Phillips curve.

Multiple choice

1. The short-run Phillips curve shows the relationship between
   a. the inflation rate and the interest rate.
   b. real GDP and the inflation rate.
   c. the unemployment rate and the interest rate.
   d. the inflation rate and the unemployment rate.

2. The short-run Phillips curve is
   a. vertical at the natural unemployment rate.
   b. upward sloping.
   c. downward sloping.
   d. horizontal at the expected inflation rate.

3. Moving along the short-run Phillips curve, as the unemployment rate increases the inflation rate
   a. decreases.
   b. increases.
   c. remains unchanged.
   d. might increase, not change, or decrease.

4. If real GDP exceeds potential GDP, then employment is _____ full employment and the unemployment rate is _____ the natural unemployment rate.
   a. below; above
   b. equal to; below
   c. above; below
   d. above; above

5. Okun's Law states that for every percentage point that the unemployment rate is above the natural rate, there is a _____ percent gap between real GDP and potential GDP.
   a. 1
   b. 1.5
   c. 2
   d. 2.5

6. When a movement up along the aggregate supply curve occurs, there is also a
   a. movement down along the short-run Phillips curve.
   b. movement up along the short-run Phillips curve.
   c. rightward shift of the short-run Phillips curve.
   d. leftward shift of the short-run Phillips curve.

7. When aggregate demand increases, there is a movement ____ along the *AS* curve and ____ along the short-run Phillips curve.
   a. up; up
   b. up; down
   c. down; up
   d. down; down

8. By looking at the data on inflation and unemployment for the United Kingdom and the United States, we see
   a. a neat, tight tradeoff between the variables in both countries.
   b. a positive relationship between the variables in both countries.
   c. no neat, tight tradeoff between the variables in both countries.
   d. that the relationship in the United States is positive and in the United Kingdom the relationship is negative.

Complete the graph

1. The table has data on the inflation rate and the unemployment rate.

Inflation rate (percent per year)	Unemployment rate (percentage)
2	12
3	8
4	5
5	3
6	2

   a. Using the data, label the axes and plot the short-run Phillips curve in Figure 17.1. Label the curve *SRPC*.

■ **FIGURE 17.1**

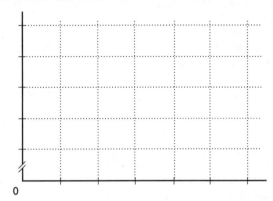

   b. What is the effect of a decrease in the unemployment rate from 8 percent to 5 percent? Show the effect in Figure 17.1.
   c. How does your answer to question (b) indicate the presence of a tradeoff?

Short answer and numeric questions

1. What does the slope of the short-run Phillips curve indicate about the tradeoff between inflation and unemployment?

2. The table gives data for an economy. Suppose that for this economy the natural unemployment rate is 5 percent and potential GDP is $8 trillion.

Unemployment rate (percentage)	Real GDP (trillions of 1996 dollars)
4	____
5	____
6	____
7	____

   a. What is Okun's Law?
   b. Using Okun's Law, complete the table by calculating real GDP for each unemployment rate.

3. What is the effect on the aggregate supply curve and on the short-run Phillips curve of an increase in aggregate demand?

CHECKPOINT 17.2

■ **Distinguish between the short-run and the long-run Phillips curves and describe the shifting tradeoff between inflation and unemployment.**

Practice Problems 17.2

1. The figure shows a short-run Phillips curve and a long-run Phillips curve.

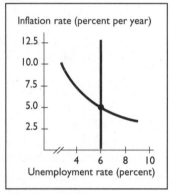

a. Label the two curves to identify which is the long-run curve and which is the short-run curve.

b. What is the expected inflation rate?

c. What is the natural unemployment rate?

d. If the expected inflation rate increases to 7.5 percent a year, show the new short-run and long-run Phillips curves.

e. If the natural unemployment rate increases to 8 percent, show the new short-run and long-run Phillips curves.

2. In the economy illustrated in the figure above, aggregate demand starts to grow more rapidly, and eventually, the inflation rate rises to 10 percent a year. Explain the course of unemployment and inflation in this economy.

Solution to Practice Problems 17.2

This Practice Problem emphasizes the relationship between the short-run Phillips curve and the long-run Phillips curve. There are several key points: The long-run Phillips curve is vertical at the natural unemployment rate. The short-run Phillips curve intersects the long-run Phillips curve at the expected inflation rate. Changes in the expected inflation rate shift only the short-run Phillips curve, and changes in the natural unemployment rate shift both the short-run and long-run Phillips curves.

Quick Review

- *Long-run Phillips curve* The long-run Phillips curve is the vertical line that shows the relationship between inflation and unemployment when the economy is at full employment.

- *Factor that shifts the long-run Phillips curve* An increase (decrease) in the natural unemployment rate shifts the long-run (and short-run) Phillips curve rightward (leftward).

1a. Label the two curves to identify which is the long-run curve and which is the short-run curve.

The curves are labeled in the figure to the right. The long-run Phillips curve is the vertical line labeled *LRPC* and the short-run Phillips curve is the downward-sloping curve labeled *SRPC*.

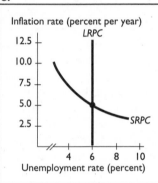

1b. What is the expected inflation rate?
The expected inflation rate is the inflation rate where the short-run Phillips curve and the long-run Phillips curve intersect. The expected inflation rate is 5 percent a year.

1c. What is the natural unemployment rate?
The long-run Phillips curve is vertical at the natural unemployment rate. The natural unemployment rate is 6 percent.

1d. If the expected inflation rate increases to 7.5 percent a year, show the new short-run and long-run Phillips curves.

When the expected inflation rate increases to 7.5 percent a year, the short-run Phillips curve shifts upward but the long-run Phillips curve does not shift. The new short-run Phillips curve intersects

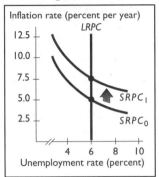

the long-run Phillips curve at the new expected inflation rate. The figure shows that the short-run Phillips curve shifts upward from $SRPC_0$ to $SRPC_1$.

1e. If the natural unemployment rate increases to 8 percent, show the new short-run and long-run Phillips curves.

An increase in the natural unemployment rate shifts *both* the short-run Phillips curve and the long-run Phillips curve rightward. In the figure the long-run Phillips curve shifts rightward from

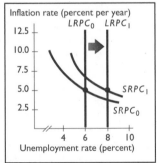

$LRPC_0$ to $LRPC_1$ and the short-run Phillips curve shifts rightward from $SRPC_0$ to $SRPC_1$. The new short-run Phillips curve intersects the new long-run Phillips curve at the expected inflation rate.

2. In the economy illustrated in the figure, aggregate demand starts to grow more rapidly, and eventually, the inflation rate rises to 10 percent a year. Explain the course of unemployment and inflation in this economy.

As the inflation rate comes to be expected, the short-run Phillips curve shifts upward, from $SRPC_0$ to $SRPC_1$ in the figure. Eventually the short-run Phillips curve intersects the long-run

Phillips curve at the expected inflation rate of 10 percent a year. As the inflation rate rises, the unemployment rate initially falls below the natural unemployment rate, shown by the arrows along

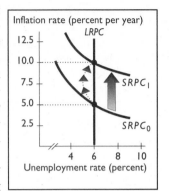

the dotted line. Gradually the unemployment rate returns to the natural unemployment rate.

Additional Practice Problem 17.2a

Explain how the inflation rate and unemployment rate might simultaneously increase.

Solution to Additional Practice Problem 17.2a

If the natural unemployment rate increases and simultaneously the inflation rate rises, the long-run and short-run Phillips curves shift rightward. It is possible for the economy to move from a point on its old short-run Phillips curve to a point on its new short-run Phillips curve such that both the inflation rate and the unemployment rate increase.

■ Self Test 17.2

Fill in the blanks

The long-run Phillips curve is a _____ (vertical; horizontal) line that shows the relationship between inflation and unemployment when the economy is at full employment. The long-run Phillips curve tells us that _____ (any; only one) inflation rate is possible at the natural unemployment rate. A change in the expected inflation rate _____ (shifts; does not shift) the long-run Phillips curve and _____ (shifts; does not shift) the short-run Phillips curve. The _____ (natural rate hypothesis; constant natural unemployment rate theory) is the proposition that when the growth rate of the quantity of money changes, the unemployment rate _____ (permanently; temporarily) changes. A change in the natural unemployment rate _____ (shifts; does not shift) the long-run Phillips curve and _____ (shifts; does not shift) the short-run Phillips curve.

True or false
1. The long-run Phillips curve is horizontal because it shows that at the expected inflation rate, any unemployment rate might occur.
2. An increase in the expected inflation rate shifts the long-run Phillips curve.
3. An increase in the expected inflation rate shifts the short-run Phillips curve.
4. The natural rate hypothesis states that an increase in the growth rate of the quantity of money temporarily decreases the unemployment rate.
5. A change in the natural unemployment rate shifts both the short-run and long-run Phillips curves.

Multiple choice
1. The long-run Phillips curve is the relationship between
   a. unemployment and the price level at full employment.
   b. unemployment and the rate of inflation at the expected price level.
   c. inflation and real GDP at full employment.
   d. inflation and unemployment when the economy is at full employment.

2. The long-run Phillips curve is
   a. upward sloping.
   b. downward sloping.
   c. horizontal.
   d. vertical.

3. The inflation rate that is used to set the money wage rate and other money prices is the
   a. natural inflation rate.
   b. actual inflation rate.
   c. expected inflation rate.
   d. cost of living inflation rate.

4. Burger King is paying $8 an hour to its servers. If the expected inflation rate is 10 percent a year, then to keep the real wage rate constant in a year the money wage rate must
   a. rise to $8.80 an hour.
   b. fall to $7.20 an hour.
   c. stay at $8.00 an hour.
   d. rise to $8.10 an hour.

5. When the expected inflation rate ____, the short-run Phillips curve shifts ____.
   a. falls; upward
   b. rises; upward
   c. rises; downward
   d. None of the above because a change in the expected inflation rate only shifts the long-run Phillips curve.

6. The natural rate hypothesis states that
   a. only natural economic policies can bring a permanent reduction in the unemployment rate.
   b. changes in the growth rate of the quantity of money temporarily change the unemployment rate.
   c. it is natural for the unemployment rate to exceed the inflation rate.
   d. it is natural for the unemployment rate to be less than the natural unemployment rate.

7. If the natural unemployment rate decreases, then the short-run Phillips curve ____ and the long-run Phillips curve ____.
   a. does not shift; shifts leftward
   b. shifts leftward; shifts leftward
   c. shifts rightward; shifts leftward
   d. shifts rightward; shifts rightward

8. The natural unemployment rate
   a. changes because of changes in frictional and structural unemployment.
   b. never changes.
   c. always increases.
   d. decreases when the inflation rate increases.

Complete the graph
1. The table has data on a nation's short-run

Phillips curve. In this nation, the natural unemployment rate equals 5 percent.

Inflation rate (percent per year)	Unemployment rate (percentage)
2	12
3	8
4	5
5	3
6	2

■ **FIGURE 17.2**

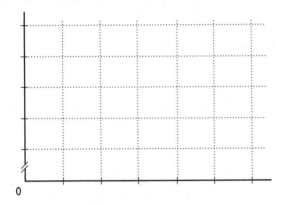

a. Draw both the short-run Phillips curve and long-run Phillips curve in Figure 17.2.
b. What is the expected inflation rate?
c. Suppose the expected inflation rate falls by 1 percentage point. Show the effect of this change on the short-run Phillips curve and long-run Phillips curve in Figure 17.2.

■ **FIGURE 17.3**

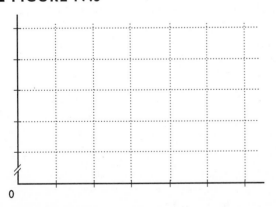

2. In Figure 17.3, redraw your initial short-run and long-run Phillips curves from Figure 17.2. Suppose that the natural unemploy-

ment rate falls to 3 percent and the expected inflation rate does not change. In Figure 17.3, show the effect of this change.

Short answer and numeric questions

1. In the *AS-AD* model, does the aggregate demand curve, the aggregate supply curve, or the potential GDP line best correspond to the long-run Phillips curve?

2. How does an increase in the expected inflation rate change the short-run and long-run Phillips curves?

3. What is the natural rate hypothesis?

4. How does an increase in the natural unemployment rate change the short-run and long-run Phillips curves?

CHECKPOINT 17.3

■ **Explain how the Fed can influence the expected inflation rate and how expected inflation influences the short-run tradeoff.**

Practice Problem 17.3

The figure shows the short-run and long-run Phillips curves. The current inflation rate is 5 percent a year.
a. Inflation is expected to remain at 5 percent next year. If the

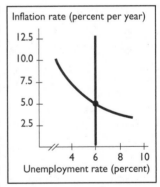

Fed slows the money growth rate, explain the effect of the Fed's action on inflation and unemployment next year.

b. If the Fed announces that it will slow the money growth rate such that inflation will fall to 2.5 percent a year and everyone believes the Fed, explain the effect of the Fed's action on inflation and unemployment next year.

c. Inflation is expected to remain at 5 percent next year. If the Fed slows the money growth rate such that inflation will fall to 2.5 percent a year and keeps it there for many years, explain the effect of the Fed's action on inflation and unemployment.

Solution to Practice Problem 17.3

This Practice Problem studies the effect on the economy of a credible announced inflation reduction and a surprise inflation reduction. You will see why the Fed wants a reputation as a credible inflation fighter.

Quick Review

- *Surprise inflation reduction* A surprise inflation reduction slows inflation but at the cost of recession.
- *Credible announced inflation reduction* A credible announced inflation reduction lowers the inflation rate but with no accompanying loss of output or increase in unemployment.

a. **Inflation is expected to remain at 5 percent next year. If the Fed slows the money growth rate, explain the effect of the Fed's action on inflation and unemployment next year.**

Because no one expected the Fed's action, the expected inflation rate does not change and the short-run Phillips curve does not shift. The economy moves along the short-run Phillips curve. As the inflation rate falls below 5 percent, the unemployment rate rises above 6 percent.

b. **If the Fed announces that it will slow the money growth rate such that inflation will fall to 2.5 percent a year and everyone believes the Fed, explain the effect of the Fed's action on inflation and unemployment next year.**

If the Fed's announcement is credible, the expected inflation rate falls. The short-run Phillips curve shifts downward. The inflation rate falls to 2.5 percent a year and the unemployment rate remains at 6 percent.

c. **Inflation is expected to remain at 5 percent next year. If the Fed slows the money growth rate such that inflation will fall to 2.5 percent a year and keeps it there for many years, explain the effect of the Fed's action on inflation and unemployment.**

The inflation rate falls below 5 percent a year and the unemployment rate rises above 6 percent. As time passes and people see that the inflation rate remains low, they start to expect the lower inflation rate. As the expected inflation rate falls, the short-run Phillips curve shifts downward. The unemployment rate decreases. Eventually the expected inflation rate equals the actual inflation rate of 2.5 percent a year and the unemployment rate returns to 6 percent.

Additional Practice Problem 17.3a

Suppose in part (b) of the Practice Problem, the Fed announces that it will slow the money growth rate such that inflation will fall to 2.5 percent a year but no one believes the Fed. The Fed actually carries out its policy. Explain the effect of the Fed's action on inflation and unemployment. Based on your answer to this question, should the Fed be concerned about its credibility?

Solution to Additional Practice Problem 17.3a

Because no one believes the Fed, the actual slowdown in the money growth rate and the reduction in inflation take people by surprise. The economy moves along its short-run Phillips curve. The inflation rate falls and the unemployment rate rises. Eventually people come to believe the Fed and the expected inflation rate falls. The short-run Phillips curve shifts downward and the unemployment rate decreases.

The Fed should be concerned about its credibility. *Only* if the Fed has credibility can it make an announcement about reducing inflation that reduces the inflation rate without an increase in the unemployment rate.

■ Self Test 17.3

Fill in the blanks

When all the relevant data and economic science are used to forecast inflation, the forecast is called _____ (an accurate prediction; a rational expectation; an accurate expectation). A change in the expected inflation rate changes the short-run Phillips curve _____ (rapidly; gradually). A surprise inflation reduction will result in a temporarily _____ (higher; lower) unemployment rate than a credible announced inflation reduction.

True or false

1. The expected inflation rate never changes.

2. A change in the expected inflation rate shifts the short-run Phillips curve gradually.

3. A surprise inflation reduction does not increase the unemployment rate.

4. A credible announced inflation reduction leads to a large increase in the unemployment rate.

5. When the Fed slowed inflation in 1981, the consequence was recession.

Multiple choice

1. A rational expectation of the inflation rate is
   a. a forecast based, in part, on the forecasted monetary policy of the Fed.
   b. an expected inflation rate between 1 percent a year and 5 percent a year.
   c. a forecast based on the historical evolution of the inflation rate over the last 100 years.
   d. an expected inflation rate between 5 percent a year and 10 percent a year.

2. A major ingredient in a forecast of inflation is a forecast of the actions of the
   a. Office of the Treasury.
   b. president.
   c. Congress.
   d. Fed.

3. A change in the expected inflation rate shifts the
   a. long-run Phillips curve slowly.
   b. short-run and long-run Phillips curves slowly.
   c. short-run and long-run Phillips curves quickly.
   d. short-run Phillips curve slowly.

4. The existence of long-term labor contracts means that the short-run tradeoff responds
   a. more than proportionally to a change in the expected inflation rate.
   b. gradually to a change in the expected inflation rate.
   c. immediately to a change in the expected inflation rate.
   d. None of the above because the existence of long-term labor contracts eliminates the influence of the expected inflation rate on the short-run tradeoff.

5. A surprise inflation reduction comes at the cost of
   a. a higher expected inflation rate.
   b. an increase in real GDP.
   c. recession.
   d. a decrease in the natural unemployment rate.

6. A credible announced inflation reduction policy is one that
   a. has monetary policy slowly increasing the quantity of money.
   b. the public is told about *after* the policy change has occurred.
   c. the public is told about before policy changes have occurred and that is believed by the public.
   d. depends only on fiscal policy changes that have been publicly debated and implemented.

7. If the Fed makes a credible announcement that its policy aims to reduce inflation, the
   a. long-run Phillips curve shifts downward.
   b. short-run Phillips curve shifts downward.
   c. long-run Phillips curve shifts upward.
   d. short-run Phillips curve shifts upward.

8. In 1981, the Fed
   a. implemented a surprise inflation reduction policy and created an expansion.
   b. implemented a surprise inflation reduction policy and created a recession.
   c. credibly announced an inflation reduction policy and created a recession.
   d. credibly announced an inflation reduction policy and created an expansion.

Short answer and numeric questions

1. What short-run effects does a surprise inflation reduction have on the short-run and long-run Phillips curves and the unemployment rate? What long-run effects does it have?

2. What short-run effects does a credible announced inflation reduction have on the short-run and long-run Phillips curves and the unemployment rate? What long-run effects does it have?

3. How do the long-run effects of a surprise inflation reduction compare to the effects of a credible announced inflation reduction?

SELF TEST ANSWERS

■ CHECKPOINT 17.1

Fill in the blanks

The short-run Phillips curve is the curve that shows the relationship between the <u>inflation rate</u> and the <u>unemployment rate</u> when the natural unemployment rate and expected inflation rate remain constant. The short-run Phillips curve is <u>downward</u> sloping. Okun's Law states that for each percentage point that the unemployment rate is above the natural unemployment rate, there is a <u>2</u> percent gap between real GDP and potential GDP. A change in aggregate demand that leads to a movement along the aggregate supply curve also leads to a <u>movement along</u> the short-run Phillips curve.

True or false

1. False; page 424
2. True; page 424
3. False; page 425
4. True; page 426
5. True; page 427

Multiple choice

1. d; page 424
2. c; page 424
3. a; page 424
4. c; page 425
5. c; page 425
6. b; page 426
7. a; page 427
8. c; page 428

Complete the graph

1. a. Figure 17.4 plots the short-run Phillips curve, labeled *SRPC*; page 424.
   b. The decrease in the unemployment rate brings a rise in the inflation rate. There is a movement along the short-run Phillips curve, as indicated by the movement from point *A* to point *B*; page 424.
   c. The movement indicates a tradeoff because a decrease in the unemployment rate has a rise in the inflation rate as the price; page 424.

■ FIGURE 17.4

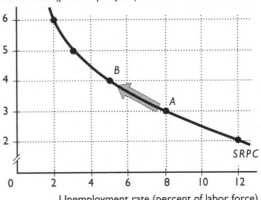

Inflation rate (percent per year)

Short answer and numeric questions

1. The slope of the short-run Phillips curve is negative, which indicates that as the unemployment rate decreases, the inflation rate increases. So the price of a lower unemployment rate is a higher inflation rate; page 424.

2. a. Okun's Law states that for each percentage point that the unemployment rate is above the natural unemployment rate, there is a 2 percent gap between real GDP and potential GDP; page 425.

Unemployment rate (percentage)	Real GDP (trillions of 1996 dollars)
4	<u>8.16</u>
5	<u>8.00</u>
6	<u>7.84</u>
7	<u>7.68</u>

   b. The completed table is above. When the unemployment rate is 7 percent, it is 2 percentage points above the natural unemployment rate. According to Okun's Law, real GDP is (2) × (2 percent) or 4 percent below potential GDP. So real GDP is (4 percent) × ($8 trillion) or $0.32 trillion below potential GDP. Real GDP is $8 trillion minus $0.32 trillion, which is $7.68 trillion; page 425.

3. When aggregate demand increases, the aggregate demand curve shifts rightward and

there is a movement up along the aggregate supply curve. The price level rises and real GDP increases. As the price level rises the inflation rate rises and as real GDP increases the unemployment rate decreases. There is a movement up along the short-run Phillips curve; page 427.

■ CHECKPOINT 17.2

Fill in the blanks

The long-run Phillips curve is a <u>vertical</u> line that shows the relationship between inflation and unemployment when the economy is at full employment. The long-run Phillips curve tells us that <u>any</u> inflation rate is possible at the natural unemployment rate. A change in the expected inflation rate <u>does not shift</u> the long-run Phillips curve and <u>shifts</u> the short-run Phillips curve. The <u>natural rate hypothesis</u> is the proposition that when the growth rate of the quantity of money changes, the unemployment rate <u>temporarily</u> changes. A change in the natural rate of unemployment <u>shifts</u> the long-run Phillips curve and <u>shifts</u> the short-run Phillips curve.

True or false

1. False; page 430
2. False; page 432
3. True; page 432
4. True; page 433
5. True; page 434

Multiple choice

1. d; page 430
2. d; page 430
3. c; page 432
4. a; page 432
5. b; page 432
6. b; page 433
7. b; page 434
8. a; page 435

Complete the graph

■ **FIGURE 17.5**

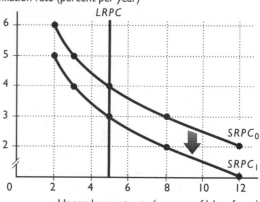

1. a. Figure 17.5 plots the short-run Phillips curve, labeled $SRPC_0$ and the long-run Phillips curve, labeled $LRPC$; page 430.

   b. The expected inflation rate is 4 percent a year because that is the inflation rate at which the short-run Phillips curve intersects the long-run Phillips curve; page 432.

   c. The new short-run Phillips curve is illustrated as $SRPC_1$; page 432.

■ **FIGURE 17.6**

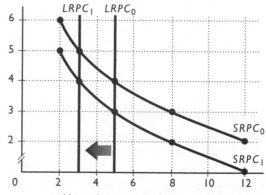

2. The initial short-run Phillips curve is labeled $SRPC_0$ and the initial long-run Phillips curve is labeled $LRPC_0$ in Figure 17.6. The decrease in the natural unemployment rate by 2 per-

centage points shifts both the long-run Phillips curve leftward from $LRPC_0$ to $LRPC_1$ and the short-run Phillips curve leftward from $SRPC_0$ to $SRPC_1$. The new short-run Phillips curve and the new long-run Phillips curve intersect at the expected inflation rate; page 435.

Short answer and numeric questions

1. The potential GDP line best corresponds to the long-run Phillips curve. The potential GDP line shows that a change in the price level does not change potential GDP and has no effect on the natural unemployment rate. The long-run Phillips curve shows that a change in the inflation rate does not change the natural unemployment rate; page 431.

2. An increase in the expected inflation rate shifts the short-run Phillips curve upward but does not change the long-run Phillips curve; page 432.

3. The natural rate hypothesis is the proposition that when the money supply growth rate changes (so that the growth rate of aggregate demand changes), the unemployment rate changes temporarily and eventually returns to the natural unemployment rate. An increase in the money supply growth rate increases the inflation rate and temporarily lowers the unemployment rate but eventually the unemployment rate returns to the natural unemployment rate. The fall in the unemployment rate was only temporary; page 433

4. An increase in the natural unemployment rate shifts *both* the long-run and short-run Phillips curves rightward; page 434.

■ CHECKPOINT 17.3

Fill in the blanks

When all the relevant data and economic science are used to forecast inflation, the forecast is called <u>a rational expectation</u>. A change in the expected inflation rate changes the short-run Phillips curve <u>gradually</u>. A surprise inflation reduction will result in a temporarily <u>higher</u>

unemployment rate than a credible announced inflation reduction.

True or false

1. False; page 439
2. True; page 440
3. False; page 440
4. False; page 441
5. True; page 441

Multiple choice

1. a; page 439
2. d; page 439
3. d; page 440
4. b; page 440
5. c; page 440
6. c; page 441
7. b; page 441
8. b; page 441

Short answer and numeric questions

1. In the short run, a surprise inflation reduction does not change the short-run or long-run Phillips curve. The economy moves down along the short-run Phillips curve. The inflation rate falls and the unemployment rate rises. In the long run, the inflation reduction is no longer a surprise. The short-run Phillips curve shifts downward. The long-run Phillips curve does not change. The inflation rate falls and the unemployment rate returns to the natural unemployment rate; page 440.

2. In the short run, a credible announced inflation reduction shifts the short-run Phillips curve downward. It has no effect on the long-run Phillips curve. Because the announcement is credible, the inflation rate falls and the unemployment rate does not change. The long-run effects are identical to the short-run effects; page 441.

3. The long-run effects of a surprise inflation reduction are the same as the short-run effects of a credible announced inflation reduction. In both cases the short-run Phillips curve shifts downward and the inflation rate

falls with no change in the unemployment rate. The reason for the similarity is that in both instances people revise the expected inflation rate downward. In the case of the surprise inflation reduction, the expected inflation rate is revised downward because of the actual experience with lower inflation. In the case of the credible announcement, the expected inflation rate is revised downward because people are aware in advance of the Fed's policy; pages 440-441.

Fiscal and Monetary Policy Debates

Chapter

18

Chapter 18 discusses the relative strength of fiscal policy and monetary policy, whether they should be used to help stabilize the economy, and if they are used, what they should target.

■ **Discuss whether fiscal policy or monetary policy is the better stabilization tool.**

A change in the quantity of money changes the interest rate, which influences interest-sensitive components of aggregate expenditure. If a change in the quantity of money brings a large change in the interest rate because the demand for money is relatively insensitive to the interest rate and aggregate expenditure is highly sensitive to the interest rate, monetary policy is powerful. The more predictable the demand for money and investment demand, the more predictable is the effect of monetary policy. An increase in government purchases or a tax cut increases aggregate demand and real GDP, which increases the demand for money and raises the interest rate. The higher interest rate decreases investment, which counteracts the effects of the initial increase in aggregate expenditure. If the interest rate rise is small and a given change in the interest rate has a small effect on aggregate expenditure, the crowding-out effect is small and fiscal policy is powerful. Discretionary fiscal policy actions create policy goal conflicts because it is not clear which of the many spending programs or tax laws should be changed. Monetary policy has fewer policy goal conflicts than fiscal policy and is more flexible.

■ **Explain the rules-versus-discretion debate and compare Keynesian and monetarist policy rules.**

Three broad approaches to the Fed's monetary policy are discretionary policy, which is policy based on the judgments of policymakers, fixed-rule policy, which is policy that is pursued independently of the state of the economy, and feedback-rule policy, which is policy that responds to changes in the economy. For an aggregate demand shock under a fixed-rule policy, in which the quantity of money remains constant, the economy returns to potential GDP when aggregate supply changes. A feedback rule offsets the initial change in aggregate demand. Feedback-rule policies are difficult to use if potential GDP is uncertain, if there are policy lags that exceed forecast horizons, or if the policy creates uncertainty. Aggregate supply shocks result in larger changes in the price level with a feedback rule.

■ **Assess whether policy should target the price level rather than real GDP.**

Two possible targets for monetary policy are real GDP and the price level. In the face of shocks to aggregate supply, stabilizing real GDP means destabilizing the price level and stabilizing the price level means destabilizing real GDP. Monetary policy also can weight fluctuations in real GDP and the price level to keep variations in both within an acceptable range. Stabilizing the price level also stabilizes the expected inflation rate and the money wage rate, which means it decreases fluctuations in aggregate supply. Arguments in favor of a positive inflation rate rather than a zero inflation are flawed.

EXPANDED CHAPTER CHECKLIST

When you have completed this chapter, you will be able to:

1 Discuss whether fiscal policy or monetary policy is the better stabilization tool.

- Discuss and illustrate the transmission of monetary policy and explain the conditions under which monetary policy is powerful.
- Discuss the transmission of fiscal policy and explain the conditions under which fiscal policy is powerful.
- Describe fiscal policy goal conflicts and monetary policy goal conflicts.
- Discuss why monetary policy is the preferred stabilization tool in normal times.

2 Explain the rules-versus-discretion debate and compare Keynesian and monetarist policy rules.

- Define discretionary monetary policy, fixed-rule policy, and feedback-rule policy.
- Describe the policies pursued by a monetarist and by a Keynesian activist.
- Describe and illustrate how a fixed-rule and a flexible-rule policy respond to changes in aggregate demand.
- Explain why some economists believe fixed rules are better than feedback rules.
- Describe and illustrate how a fixed-rule policy and a flexible-rule policy respond to a change in aggregate supply.

3 Assess whether policy should target the price level rather than real GDP.

- Explain the effects on the economy of real GDP targeting and price level targeting.
- Describe how monetary policy can target something less extreme than either real GDP or the price level.

- Discuss how targeting the price level can help stabilize aggregate supply.
- Present and evaluate arguments for positive inflation.

KEY TERMS

- Liquidity trap (page 451)
- Discretionary monetary policy (page 454)
- Fixed-rule policy (page 454)
- Feedback-rule policy (page 454)
- Monetarist (page 456)
- Keynesian activist (page 457)

CHECKPOINT 18.1

■ Discuss whether fiscal policy or monetary policy is the better stabilization tool.

Practice Problems 18.1

1. The Fed decreases the quantity of money.
   a. Use a graph like Figure 18.1 of the text to work out the effects of the Fed's policy on the interest rate, the quantity of money demanded, and investment.
   b. Explain the effects of the Fed's policy on aggregate expenditure and aggregate demand.
   c. Explain the conditions that make the Fed's policy more effective.
2. If a change in the quantity of money leads to a large change in the interest rate and investment is very sensitive to the interest rate, would a decrease in government purchases be an effective fiscal policy? Explain why or why not.

Solution to Practice Problems 18.1

The Practice Problems study the effects of fiscal policy and monetary policy. Both policy tools affect aggregate demand, but the size of the change in aggregate demand depends on the demand for money and investment demand. Fiscal policy is powerful when monetary policy is weak and monetary policy is powerful when fiscal policy is weak.

Quick Review

- *Strength of monetary policy* The more insensitive the quantity of money demanded to a change in the interest rate, and the more sensitive investment demand and other components of aggregate expenditure are to a change in the interest rate, the more powerful is monetary policy.

- *Strength of fiscal policy* The power of fiscal policy depends on the strength of the crowding-out effects that counteract it.

1. The Fed decreases the quantity of money.

1a. **Use a graph like Figure 18.1 to work out the effects of the Fed's policy on the interest rate, the quantity of money demanded, and investment.**

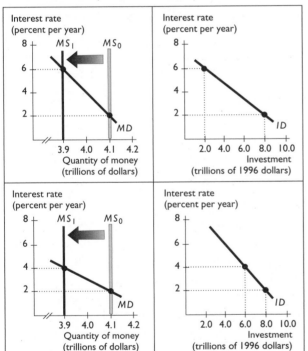

In the top left figure when the quantity of money decreases from $4.1 trillion to $3.9 trillion, the interest rate rises from 2 percent a year to 6 percent a year. In the top right figure, when the interest rate rises from 2 percent a year to 6 percent a year, there is a movement along the investment demand curve and investment demand de-

mand decreases from $8 trillion to $2 trillion, a decrease of $6 trillion.

In the bottom left figure when the quantity of money decreases from $4.1 trillion to $3.9 trillion, the interest rate rises from 2 percent a year to 4 percent a year. In the bottom right figure, when the interest rate rises from 2 percent a year to 4 percent a year, there is a movement along the investment demand curve and investment demand decreases from $8 trillion to $6 trillion, a decrease of $2 trillion.

1b. **Explain the effects of the Fed's policy on aggregate expenditure and aggregate demand.**

The decrease in investment decreases aggregate expenditure. Aggregate demand decreases.

1c. **Explain the conditions that make the Fed's policy more effective.**

The Fed's policy is more powerful the larger the resulting change in aggregate demand. The reduction in aggregate demand will be larger the bigger the reduction in investment resulting from a given increase in the interest rate. And the increase in the interest rate will be larger the less sensitive is the demand for money to the interest rate.

In the figure, the Fed's policy is more powerful in the top left figure and the top right figure. In the top left figure, the demand for money is less sensitive to the interest rate than in the bottom left figure. And in the top right figure, investment demand is more sensitive to a change in the interest rate than in the bottom right figure.

2. If a change in the supply of money leads to a large change in the interest rate and investment is very sensitive to the interest rate, would a decrease in government purchases be an effective fiscal policy? Explain why or why not.

When government expenditure decreases, aggregate demand decreases, which decreases real GDP. The decrease in real GDP decreases the demand for money. The interest rate falls.

Investment is very sensitive to the interest rate, so investment increases by a large amount. The increase in investment counteracts the decrease in government expenditure, which limits the effect of the fiscal policy action. So a decrease in government expenditure is not a powerful fiscal policy.

Additional Practice Problem 18.1a

In the figures that answered Practice Problem 1, when is fiscal policy powerful? Why?

Solution to Additional Practice Problem 18.1a

Fiscal policy is powerful when the demand for money is sensitive to the interest rate and investment demand is insensitive to the interest rate. In this case the crowding-out effect is smaller.

So fiscal policy is powerful in the left bottom figure, where the demand for money is sensitive to the interest rate and in the right bottom figure, where investment demand is insensitive to the interest rate.

■ Self Test 18.1

Fill in the blanks

If the demand for money is not sensitive to the interest rate, monetary policy is ____ (less; more) powerful. If investment demand is not sensitive to the interest rate, fiscal policy is ____ (less; more) powerful. In a liquidity trap, monetary policy ____ (is very powerful; has no effect) and fiscal policy ____ (is very powerful; has no effect). Discretionary fiscal policy ____ (is; is not) subject to goal conflicts. Monetary policy has ____ (more; fewer) goal conflicts than discretionary fiscal policy. (Fiscal policy; Monetary policy; Neither fiscal policy nor monetary policy) is clearly the best stabilization policy.

True or false

1. Monetary policy is more powerful the more sensitive investment demand is to the interest rate.

2. Fiscal policy is more powerful the less sensitive investment demand is to the interest rate.

3. In a liquidity trap, monetary policy is extremely powerful.

4. A major reason fiscal policy suffers from goal conflicts is because there are only a few spending programs and tax laws that can be changed.

5. Monetary policy can be undertaken more rapidly than fiscal policy.

Multiple choice

1. When the Fed implements monetary policy, it changes
   a. the supply of money, which changes the interest rate, which changes investment.
   b. the supply of money, which changes investment, which changes the interest rate.
   c. the interest rate, which changes investment, which changes the supply of money.
   d. investment, which changes the supply of money, which changes the interest rate.

2. One of the factors that determines the power of monetary policy is the responsiveness of
   a. the supply of money to the interest rate.
   b. the demand for money to the interest rate.
   c. investment to the level of potential GDP.
   d. the unemployment rate to the natural unemployment rate.

3. In which case is fiscal policy the strongest?
   a. There is a large crowding-out effect.
   b. The multiplier is large.
   c. Aggregate expenditure is very sensitive to a change in the interest rate.
   d. A change in real GDP results in a large change in the demand for money.

4. If the demand for money is not sensitive to the interest rate and investment is sensitive to the interest rate, fiscal policy is ____ and monetary policy is ____.
   a. powerful; powerful
   b. powerful; weak
   c. weak; powerful
   d. weak; weak

5. The term "goal conflicts" refers to the situation in which
   a. fiscal and monetary policy conflict in their goals.
   b. stabilization policy can have side effects that conflict with other goals.
   c. the announcement of policy goals is in conflict with the reality of their actions.
   d. goals are not made clear by either monetary or fiscal policy authorities.

6. The three main goals of monetary policy are
   a. price level stability, real GDP stability, and income redistribution.
   b. price level stability, real GDP stability, and financial market stability.
   c. real GDP stability, financial market stability, and income redistribution.
   d. provision of goods and services, financial market stability, and price level stability.

7. Discretionary fiscal policy is
   a. volatile, because it responds to rapidly changing political agendas.
   b. flexible, because discretionary fiscal policy is passed quickly through Congress.
   c. coherent, because the Fed dictates it according to its monetary policy.
   d. inflexible, because fiscal policy is political in nature.

8. To deal with normal fluctuations in the economy,
   a. there is no clear winner between monetary policy and fiscal policy.
   b. monetary policy is more flexible and therefore preferred.
   c. fiscal policy is superior with its use of automatic stabilizers and discretionary action.
   d. neither fiscal policy nor monetary policy can do anything to dampen these common occurrences.

Complete the graph

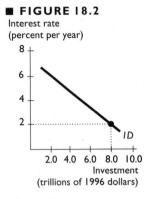

■ **FIGURE 18.1**
Interest rate (percent per year)

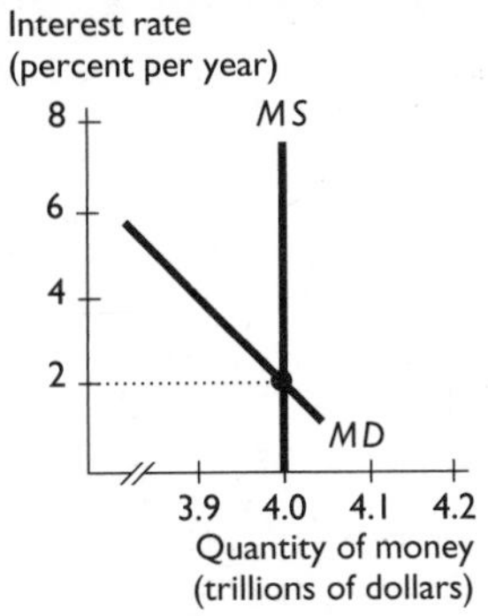

■ **FIGURE 18.2**
Interest rate (percent per year)

1. Figures 18.1 and 18.2 show the money market and the investment demand curve.
   a. The government increases government purchases. What is the effect on real GDP and the price level?
   b. What happens to the demand for money when government purchases increase? Use Figure 18.1 to illustrate the effect.
   c. What is the effect of this fiscal policy on investment? Use Figure 18.2 to illustrate the effect.
   d. Relate your answer to part (c) to the crowding-out effect.
   e. How does the size of the crowding-out effect relate to the strength of the fiscal policy?

Short answer and numeric questions

1. Explain why monetary policy is more powerful if the quantity of money demanded is insensitive to the interest rate.
2. What is a liquidity trap? What is the relationship between a liquidity trap and monetary policy?
3. What are the three main fiscal policy goals? How might stabilization lead to a goal conflict?
4. Why is monetary policy considered more flexible than fiscal policy?
5. Is fiscal policy or monetary policy best for handling the normal fluctuations in economic activity? Why?

CHECKPOINT 18.2

■ **Explain the rules-versus-discretion debate and compare Keynesian and monetarist policy rules.**

Practice Problem 18.2

The economy shown in the figure is initially on aggregate demand curve AD_0 and aggregate supply curve AS. Then aggregate demand decreases, and the aggregate demand curve shifts leftward to AD_1.

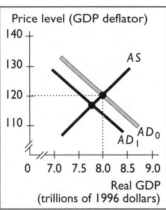

a. What are the initial equilibrium real GDP and price level?

b. If the decrease in aggregate demand is temporary and the Fed adopts a fixed-rule policy, what happens to real GDP and the price level?

c. If the decrease in aggregate demand is temporary and the Fed adopts a feedback-rule policy, what happens to real GDP and the price level?

d. If the decrease in aggregate demand is permanent and the Fed adopts a fixed-rule policy, what happens to real GDP and the price level?

e. If the decrease in aggregate demand is permanent and the Fed adopts a feedback-rule policy, what happens to real GDP and the price level?

Solution to Practice Problem 18.2

This Practice Problem helps you see the differences the Fed's policy can make. To solve this problem, remember that a fixed-rule policy leaves real GDP and the price level to fluctuate and a feedback-rule policy tries to restore full employment as quickly as possible.

Quick Review

- *Fixed-rule policy* A fixed-rule policy is a policy that is pursued independently of the state of the economy. A fixed-rule monetary policy is to keep the quantity of money constant.

- *Flexible-rule policy* A flexible-rule policy is a policy that specifies how policy actions respond to changes in the state of the economy. A flexible-rule monetary policy is to increase the quantity of money when aggregate demand decreases and decrease the quantity of money when aggregate demand increases.

a. What are the initial equilibrium real GDP and price level?

The initial equilibrium is where the aggregate demand curve intersects the aggregate supply curve. Equilibrium real GDP is $8 trillion and the equilibrium price level is 120.

b. If the decrease in aggregate demand is temporary and the Fed adopts a fixed-rule policy, what happens to real GDP and the price level?

In the short run, real GDP and the price level move to the intersection of AD_1 and AS, so the price level falls to 118 and real GDP decreases to $7.8 trillion. If the Fed is using a fixed-rule policy, the changes in the price level and real GDP do not bring any change in policy. Because the change in aggregate demand is temporary, in the long run the AD curve shifts back to AD_0 and the price level and real GDP return to their original values of 120 and $8 trillion.

c. If the decrease in aggregate demand is temporary and the Fed adopts a feedback-rule policy, what happens to real GDP and the price level?

The Fed increases the quantity of money to keep the AD curve at AD_0. The price level stays at 120 and real GDP stays at $8 trillion. When the shock ends, the Fed decreases the supply of money to keep the AD curve at AD_0.

d. If the decrease in aggregate demand is permanent and the Fed adopts a fixed-rule policy, what happens to real GDP and the price level?

Real GDP decreases to $7.8 trillion and the price level falls to 118. Unemployment is above the natural unemployment rate, so the money wage rate decreases. Aggregate supply increases and the aggregate supply curve shifts rightward. Eventually, real GDP returns to potential GDP of $8 trillion. The price level falls to 110.

e. If the decrease in aggregate demand is permanent and the Fed adopts a feedback-rule policy, what happens to real GDP and the price level?

Real GDP remains at $8 trillion and the price level remains at 120. The Fed increases the quantity of money so that the AD curve remains at AD_0.

Additional Practice Problem 18.2a

Can monetary policy offset fluctuations in aggregate supply so that neither the price level nor real GDP changes? Explain your answer.

Solution to Additional Practice Problem 18.2a

It is not possible for monetary policy to offset fluctuations in aggregate supply so that neither the price level nor real GDP changes. A negative aggregate supply shock raises the price level and decreases real GDP.

Monetary policy changes aggregate demand. If monetary policy aims to restore real GDP to potential GDP, it increases aggregate demand. Real GDP increases, as desired, but the price level rises more than otherwise. Similarly, if monetary policy aims to offset the initial increase in the price level, it decreases aggregate demand. The price level falls, as desired, but real GDP decreases more than otherwise.

■ Self Test 18.2

Fill in the blanks

A policy that is pursued independently of the state of the economy is a ____ (fixed-rule; feedback-rule) policy and a policy that specifies how policy actions respond to changes in the state of the economy is a ____ (fixed-rule; feedback-rule) policy. A monetarist favors ____ (fixed-rule; feedback-rule) policies and a Keynesian activist favors ____ (fixed-rule; feedback-rule) policies. When faced with a deflationary gap, a fixed-rule policy ____ (increases; decreases; does not change) the quantity of money while a feedback-rule policy ____ (increases; decreases; does not change) the quantity of money. The fact that there is uncertainty about potential GDP favors ____ (fixed-rule; feedback-rule) policies. After being hit by a negative aggregate supply shock, in the long run the price level is higher when using a ____ (fixed-rule; feedback-rule) policy.

True or false

1. An example of a feedback-rule policy is to keep the quantity of money growing at a constant rate to make the average inflation rate equal to zero.

2. Advocates of fixed rules propose that the Fed increase the quantity of money when aggregate demand decreases.

3. A feedback-rule policy attempts to pull the economy out of a deflationary gap by using a policy action.

4. Because it is difficult to forecast future economic conditions, feedback-rule policies are better than fixed-rule policies.

5. Feedback-rule policies react only to aggregate demand shocks and not to aggregate supply shocks.

Multiple choice

1. Monetary policy that is based on the judgments of the policymakers about current needs of the economy is called ____ monetary policy.
   a. fixed-rule
   b. sure-thing
   c. feedback-rule
   d. discretionary

2. A fixed-rule policy is policy
   a. determined by policymakers who use their own judgment to decide what is needed.
   b. that is determined by a preset list of rules.
   c. that is followed regardless of the state of the economy.
   d. determined by the unemployment rate.

3. Economists who believe fluctuations in the quantity of money are the main source of economic fluctuations are
   a. Keynesians.
   b. monetarists.
   c. feedback advocates.
   d. fiscalists.

4. To eliminate a deflationary gap with a fixed-rule monetary policy, the Fed will
   a. increase the supply of money.
   b. decrease the supply of money.
   c. not change the supply of money.
   d. None of the above answers is correct.

5. A Keynesian activist is likely to prefer a ____ policy.
   a. rigid-rule
   b. fixed-rule
   c. feedback-rule
   d. directed-rule

6. Reasons given to support a fixed-rule monetary policy include all of the following EX-CEPT
   a. potential GDP is not known.
   b. the price level is not known.
   c. policy lags are longer than the forecast horizon.
   d. feedback-rule policies are less predictable than fixed-rule policies.

7. When an economy experiences a negative aggregate supply shock, the policy rule that waits for real wage rates to change and move the economy back to potential GDP is the ____ policy.
   a. fixed-rule
   b. discretionary
   c. feedback-rule
   d. directed-rule

8. To eliminate a deflationary gap that is the result of a supply shock, a feedback-rule monetary policy that targets real GDP will ____ the quantity of money.
   a. decrease
   b. increase
   c. not change
   d. None of the above answers is correct.

Complete the graph

1. Figure 18.3 shows the economy in its initial equilibrium with real GDP equal to potential GDP of $10 trillion and the price level equal to 100.

■ **FIGURE 18.3**

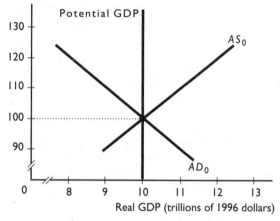

Price level (GDP deflator, 1996 = 100)

   a. Suppose a negative aggregate supply shock hits so that in the short run, the new equilibrium price level is 110. In Figure 18.3, illustrate the effect of this aggregate supply shock. What is equilibrium real GDP?
   b. Suppose that monetary policy follows a feedback-rule policy that moves real GDP back to potential GDP. In Figure 18.3, illustrate the effect of the monetary policy. What is the equilibrium price level?

Short answer and numeric questions

1. What are the three general approaches to monetary policy that the Fed can follow?

2. If the Fed is following a fixed-rule policy, how does it respond to a decrease in aggre-

gate demand? To a decrease in aggregate supply?

3. If the Fed is following a feedback-rule policy, how does it respond to a decrease in aggregate demand?

4. Suppose it takes two years for monetary policy to have an effect and recessions last for only one year. What implication does this have for monetary policy?

CHECKPOINT 18.3

■ **Assess whether policy should target the price level rather than real GDP.**

Practice Problems 18.3

1. Suppose that the economy experiences a positive aggregate supply shock and the Fed reacts to this shock by adjusting its monetary policy. Explain the effect of the Fed's action on real GDP and the price level if the Fed places:
   a. No weight on real GDP fluctuations.
   b. No weight on inflation.
   c. Equal weight on inflation and real GDP fluctuations.

2. Suppose that in 2005, the inflation rate is 3 percent a year and potential GDP is $12 trillion. Faced with a decrease in aggregate supply, the Fed decides that it wants to keep the inflation rate between 1 percent and 5 percent a year and to keep real GDP within the range $11.9 trillion to $12.1 trillion.
   a. Is the Fed placing more weight on inflation or on real GDP?
   b. What actions will the Fed take?

Solution to Practice Problem 18.3

The Practice Problems help you understand how the effects on the economy differ according to the focus of the Fed's target. If the Fed stabilizes real GDP, it destabilizes the price level. If the Fed stabilizes the price level, it destabilizes real GDP.

Quick Review

- *Real GDP target* If monetary policy targets real GDP, an increase in aggregate supply is met with a decrease in aggregate demand and the price level falls; and a decrease in aggregate supply is met with an increase in aggregate demand and the price level rises.

- *Price level target* If monetary policy targets the price level, an increase in aggregate supply is met with an in increase in aggregate demand and the real GDP increases; and a decrease in aggregate supply is met with a decrease in aggregate demand and real GDP decreases.

1. Suppose that the economy experiences a positive aggregate supply shock and the Fed reacts to this shock by adjusting its monetary policy. Explain the effect of the Fed's action on real GDP and the price level if the Fed places:

   1a. No weight on real GDP fluctuations.
   If the Fed places no weight on real GDP fluctuations, the Fed is targeting the price level. The Fed increases the supply of money to avoid the falling price level associated with a positive aggregate supply shock. Real GDP increases but the price level remains the same.

   1b. No weight on inflation.
   If the Fed places no weight on inflation, the Fed is targeting real GDP. The Fed decreases the supply of money to avoid the increasing real GDP associated with a positive aggregate supply shock. The price level falls but real GDP remains the same.

   1c. Equal weight on inflation and real GDP fluctuations.
   If the Fed puts equal weight on inflation and real GDP fluctuations, the Fed might decrease the supply of money, or it might increase the supply of money, or it might even do nothing. The outcome will be between the outcomes of the previous two answers, so real GDP will increase and the price level will fall.

2. Suppose that in 2005, the inflation rate is 3 percent a year and potential GDP is $12 trillion. Faced with a decrease in aggregate supply, the Fed decides that it wants to keep the inflation rate between 1 percent and 5 percent

a year and to keep real GDP within the range $11.9 trillion to $12.1 trillion.

2a. Is the Fed placing more weight on inflation or on real GDP?

The Fed is placing more weight on real GDP. The Fed will accept a decrease in real GDP of $0.1 trillion from potential GDP, which is less than 1 percent. The Fed is willing to accept a 2 percentage point deviation from the midpoint of 3 percent a year, which is a deviation of 66.7 percent.

2b. What actions will the Fed take?

The decrease in aggregate supply raises the price level and decreases real GDP. The Fed is more concerned with the decrease in real GDP, so it increases the supply of money. Aggregate demand increases. The price level rises and real GDP moves to its target range.

Additional Practice Problem 18.3a

Suppose in Practice Problem 2, the Fed now wants to keep the inflation rate between 2.9 percent a year and 3.1 percent a year and is willing to allow real GDP to range between $11 trillion to $13 trillion. How will this change in targets affect the Fed's monetary policy?

Solution to Additional Practice Problem 18.3a

The Fed is now placing more weight on the inflation rate and less weight on real GDP. Now when confronted with a decrease in aggregate supply, the Fed will *decrease* the quantity of money to decrease aggregate demand and keep the inflation rate within its acceptable range. The change in the Fed's targets changes its monetary policy.

■ Self Test 18.3

Fill in the blanks

Targeting _____ (real GDP; the price level) is equivalent to targeting the unemployment rate. If policy targets real GDP, aggregate supply shocks result in the policy destabilizing _____ (real GDP; the price level). If monetary policy targets the price level, an increase in aggregate supply is met with _____ (an increase; a decrease) in the quantity of money. If monetary

policy targets _____ (real GDP; the price level), it also helps stabilize aggregate supply.

True or false

1. The only possible target for stabilization policy is real GDP.

2. If monetary policy targets real GDP, it attempts to offset aggregate supply shocks.

3. If monetary policy targets real GDP, it destabilizes the price level.

4. It is possible for stabilization policy to put weight on fluctuations in both real GDP and the price level.

5. By stabilizing the price level, monetary policy also helps make aggregate supply more stable.

Multiple choice

1. Targeting real GDP is equivalent to targeting
   a. inflation.
   b. unemployment.
   c. labor supply.
   d. the tax rate.

2. Two possible targets for monetary policy are
   a. real GDP and the price level.
   b. real GDP and potential GDP.
   c. low taxes and low inflation.
   d. low taxes and zero inflation.

3. If monetary policy targets real GDP, an increase in aggregate supply is met by _____ in the quantity of money and _____ in aggregate demand.
   a. an increase; an increase
   b. an increase; a decrease
   c. a decrease; an increase
   d. a decrease; a decrease

4. If the Fed targets real GDP and the economy experiences an aggregate supply shock, then
   a. monetary policy will not move the economy toward potential GDP.
   b. the price level will fluctuate.
   c. the price level will be effectively stabilized.
   d. both real GDP and the price level will be stabilized.

5. If the Fed targets the price level, an increase in aggregate supply means that the Fed takes actions to
   a. increase aggregate demand.
   b. decrease aggregate demand.
   c. increase aggregate supply.
   d. decrease aggregate supply.

6. Targeting the price level brings the "free lunch" of a more stable aggregate supply because
   a. productivity is more stable.
   b. government purchases are more stable.
   c. the expected price level is more stable.
   d. real GDP is less stable.

7. Arguments in favor of positive inflation rather than zero inflation include all of the following EXCEPT
   a. the inflation rate must exceed the nominal interest rate.
   b. inflation lubricates the labor market.
   c. the nominal interest rate cannot fall below zero.
   d. ALL of the above are arguments in favor of positive inflation.

8. The "zero lower bound" argument suggests that a low inflation rate
   a. increases the length of recessions because the nominal interest rate cannot be less than zero.
   b. increases the unemployment rate because the real wage rate is sticky.
   c. reduces real GDP fluctuations if a feedback-rule policy is followed.
   d. reduces aggregate demand and aggregate supply fluctuations and leads to price stability.

Short answer and numeric questions

1. Does it matter whether the Fed targets real GDP or the price level when faced with a decrease in aggregate demand? Does it matter which the Fed targets if it is faced with a decrease in aggregate supply?

2. Must the Fed target *only* real GDP or *only* the price level?

3. What is the "free lunch" associated with targeting the price level?

4. What are the arguments for positive rather than zero inflation? What are the flaws in each argument?

SELF TEST ANSWERS

■ CHECKPOINT 18.1

Fill in the blanks

If the demand for money is not sensitive to the interest rate, monetary policy is <u>more</u> powerful. If investment demand is not sensitive to the interest rate, fiscal policy is <u>more</u> powerful. In a liquidity trap, monetary policy <u>has no effect</u> and fiscal policy <u>is very powerful</u>. Discretionary fiscal policy <u>is</u> subject to goal conflicts. Monetary policy has <u>fewer</u> goal conflicts than discretionary fiscal policy. <u>Neither fiscal policy nor monetary policy</u> is clearly the best stabilization policy.

True or false

1. True; page 448
2. True; page 450
3. False; page 451
4. False; page 451
5. True; page 452

Multiple choice

1. a; page 448
2. b; page 448
3. b; page 450
4. c; page 450
5. b; page 451
6. b; page 452
7. d; page 452
8. b; page 452

Complete the graph

1. a. The increase in government purchases increases real GDP and raises the price level; page 450.
   b. The increase in real GDP increases the demand for money and the demand for money curve shifts rightward. Figure 18.4 illustrates a rightward shift in the demand for money curve. The interest rate rises; page 450.
   c. The rise in the interest rate decreases investment. In Figure 18.5 there is a movement up along the investment demand curve; page 450.

■ FIGURE 18.4

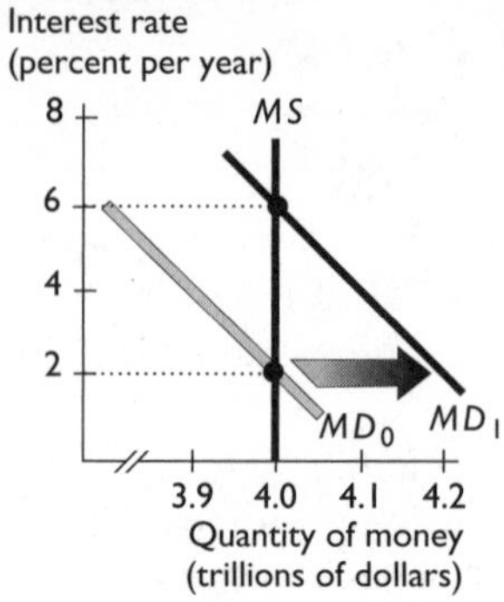

Interest rate (percent per year)

Quantity of money (trillions of dollars)

■ FIGURE 18.5

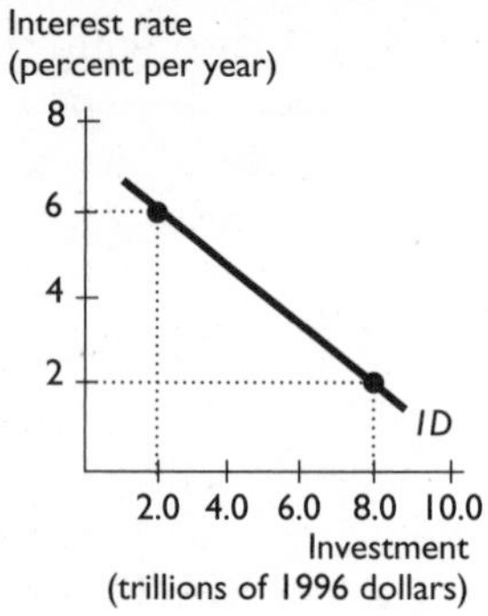

Interest rate (percent per year)

Investment (trillions of 1996 dollars)

d. The increase in government purchases decreases investment. The decrease in investment is the crowding-out effect; page 450.

e. The larger the crowding-out effect, that is, the greater the decrease in investment, the weaker the effect of the fiscal policy. So the more the interest rate rises and the more sensitive investment is to the rise in the interest rate, the weaker is fiscal policy; page 450.

Short answer and numeric questions

1. When the quantity of money demanded is relatively insensitive to the interest rate, a change in the interest rate brings a small change in the quantity of money demanded. Then, when the quantity of money increases by a given amount, the decrease in the interest rate is large. The larger the decrease in the interest rate, the larger is the change in investment and aggregate expenditure, and the more powerful the monetary policy; page 448.

2. A liquidity trap is an interest rate at which people are willing to hold any quantity of money. In a liquidity trap, a change in the quantity of money has no effect on the interest rate. So a change in the quantity of money has no effect on aggregate expenditure. Monetary policy has no effect; page 451.

3. The three fiscal policy goals are to provide public goods and services, to redistribute income, and to stabilize aggregate demand.

The main source of conflict that arises from stabilization is the very large number of spending programs and tax laws in place and the difficulty of changing all of them to balance the costs and benefits of one against the costs and benefits of others; page 451.

4. Monetary policy is more flexible than fiscal policy. The Fed and its policy committee, the FOMC, can quickly take policy actions. Every day, the Fed monitors the financial markets and watches for signs that its policy needs to be tweaked to keep the economy on course; page 452.

5. Monetary policy is best for handling the normal fluctuations in economic activity because it can be changed quickly; page 452.

■ CHECKPOINT 18.2

Fill in the blanks

A policy that is pursued independently of the state of the economy is a <u>fixed-rule</u> policy and a policy that specifies how policy actions respond to changes in the state of the economy is a <u>feedback-rule</u> policy. A monetarist favors <u>fixed-rule</u> policies and a Keynesian activist favors <u>feedback-rule</u> policies. When faced with a deflationary gap, a fixed-rule policy <u>does not change</u> the quantity of money while a feedback-rule policy <u>increases</u> the quantity of money. The fact that there is uncertainty about potential GDP favors <u>fixed-rule</u> policies. After being hit by a negative aggregate supply shock, in the long run the price level is higher when using a <u>feedback-rule</u> policy.

True or false

1. False; page 454
2. False; page 456
3. True; page 457
4. False; pages 457-458
5. False; page 460

Multiple choice

1. d; page 454
2. c; page 454
3. b; page 456

4. c; page 456
5. c; page 457
6. b; page 457-458
7. a; page 460
8. b; page 460

Complete the graph

■ FIGURE 18.6

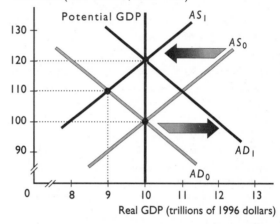

1. a. The negative aggregate supply shock decreases aggregate supply and shifts the aggregate supply curve leftward from AS_0 to AS_1. Figure 18.6 shows that the price level rises to 110 and real GDP decreases to $9 trillion; page 459.

   b. If the Fed follows a feedback-rule policy that restores real GDP back to potential GDP, it increases the quantity of money, which increases aggregate demand. In Figure 18.6, the aggregate demand curve shifts rightward, from AD_0 to AD_1. Real GDP equals potential GDP of $10 trillion and the price level rises to 120; page 460.

Short answer and numeric questions

1. The Fed can follow discretionary monetary policy (in which the policy is based on the judgments of policy makers about the current needs of the economy), a fixed-rule policy (in which the policy is pursued independently of the state of the economy), or a feedback-rule policy (in which the policy ac-

tions respond to changes in the economy); page 454.

2. If the Fed is following a fixed-rule policy, in the face of a decrease in aggregate demand it does nothing. And it does nothing in the face of a decrease in aggregate supply. A fixed-rule policy does *not* respond to the current state of the economy; pages 456, 460.

3. If the Fed is following a feedback-rule policy, in the face of a decrease in aggregate demand the Fed increases the quantity of money and lowers the interest rate, which increases aggregate demand; page 457.

4. If it takes two years for monetary policy to have an effect and recessions last for only one year, a feedback-rule policy will be difficult. If the Fed's feedback-rule policy increases the quantity of money when the economy is in a recession then in two years when aggregate demand responds by increasing, the economy will be out of the recession and in an expansion. So monetary policy based on feedback rules might increase aggregate demand when aggregate demand is increasing strongly already. Monetary policy runs the risk of boosting the inflation rate rather than fighting the recession; page 458.

■ CHECKPOINT 18.3

Fill in the blanks

Targeting <u>real GDP</u> is equivalent to targeting the unemployment rate. If policy targets real GDP, aggregate supply shocks result in the policy destabilizing <u>the price level</u>. If monetary policy targets the price level, an increase in aggregate supply is met with <u>an increase</u> in the quantity of money. If monetary policy targets <u>the price level,</u> it also helps stabilize aggregate supply.

True or false

1. False; page 462
2. True; page 462
3. True; page 462
4. True; page 464
5. True; page 465

Multiple choice

1. b; page 462
2. a; page 462
3. d; page 462
4. b; page 462
5. a; page 463
6. c; page 465
7. a; page 466
8. a; page 467

Short answer and numeric questions

1. A decrease in aggregate demand lowers the price level and decreases real GDP. Regardless of the Fed's target, the appropriate monetary policy is to increase the quantity of money, which increases aggregate demand. An increase in aggregate demand can return real GDP and the price level back to their original levels.

   If the Fed is faced with a decrease in aggregate supply the choice of target is important. If the Fed is targeting real GDP, the appropriate monetary policy is to increase the quantity of money, which can return real GDP to its original level but with a rise in the price level. Or if the Fed is targeting the price level, the appropriate monetary policy is to decrease the quantity of money, which can return the price level to its original level but with a decrease in real GDP; pages 462-463.

2. The Fed does not need to limit itself to targeting either real GDP or the price level because the Fed can target weighted combinations of real GDP and the price level; page 464.

3. Monetary policy influences the money wage rate and the money prices of other resources through the expected price level. A change in the expected price level changes the money wage rate and the money prices of other resources and so changes aggregate supply. Stabilizing the price level stabilizes the expected price level (and expected inflation rate) and also makes aggregate supply more stable. Directly targeting the price level brings the "free lunch" of a more stable ag-

gregate supply and more stable real GDP. Targeting the price level gives a "free lunch"; page 465.

4. The first argument in favor of positive inflation is that inflation lubricates the labor market and that a long-run tradeoff between inflation and unemployment exists. It is alleged that unemployment increases at a lower inflation rate because the real wage gets stuck at too high a level. While there is plenty of evidence that money wage rates are sticky, there is no evidence that they are stickier downward than upward. The natural rate hypothesis appears to be correct, so this argument for positive inflation is incorrect.

The second argument is that the nominal interest rate cannot fall below zero. The claim is that expansionary monetary policy cannot be used to get the economy out of recession if the nominal interest rate is zero, so in such a situation recession will last longer. Because the nominal interest rate will be zero more frequently the lower is the inflation rate, the economy will spend longer in recession, on the average, the lower is the inflation rate. But even if the nominal interest rate does not fall, when money is injected into the economy, more money brings more spending by way of an exchange rate effect and a buying power of money effect, which can move the economy out of recession; page 466.

International Trade

Chapter

19

In Chapter 19 we see that all countries can benefit from free trade but, despite this fact, countries nevertheless restrict trade.

■ **Describe the patterns and trends in international trade.**

The goods and services that we buy from people in other countries are called imports. The goods and services that we sell to people in other countries are called exports. Goods comprise 72 percent of U.S. exports and 84 percent of U.S. imports. The rest of U.S. international trade is in services. Trade has grown over time. Between 1960 and 2002 exports grew from 5 percent of total output to 10 percent, and imports grew from 4 percent to 14 percent. The biggest U.S. trading partner is Canada, followed by Mexico, Japan, and China. The balance of trade is the value of exports minus the value of imports. In 2002, the United States had a trade deficit.

■ **Explain why nations engage in international trade and why trade benefits all nations.**

Comparative advantage enables countries to gain from trade. A nation has a comparative advantage in producing a good if it can produce that good at a lower opportunity cost than another country. To achieve the gains from trade, a nation specializes in the production of the goods and services in which it has a comparative advantage and then trades with other nations. By specializing and trading, a nation can consume at a point beyond its production possibilities frontier. Repeatedly performing the same task and becoming more productive at producing a particular good or service is called learning-by-doing. Learning-by-doing can lead to dynamic comparative advantage.

■ **Explain how trade barriers reduce international trade.**

A tariff is a tax on a good that is imposed by the importing country when an imported good crosses its international boundary. A tariff on a good reduces imports of that good, increases domestic production of the good, and reduces the gains from trade. A quota is a specified maximum amount of a good that may be imported in a given period of time.

■ **Explain the arguments used to justify trade barriers and show why they are incorrect but also why some barriers are hard to remove.**

The three main arguments for protection and restriction of trade are the national security argument, the infant-industry argument, and the dumping argument. Each of these arguments is flawed. Fatally flawed arguments for protection are that protection saves jobs, allows us to compete with cheap foreign labor, brings diversity and stability, penalizes lax environmental standards, protects national culture, and prevents rich countries from exploiting developing countries. Tariffs are imposed in some nations to gain revenue for the government. Trade is restricted is because of rent seeking.

EXPANDED CHAPTER CHECKLIST

When you have completed this chapter, you will be able to:

1 Describe the patterns and trends in international trade.

- Discuss U.S. international trade in goods and services and describe the trends in the volume of trade.
- Discuss the United States' major trading partners and the trading blocs in which the United States is a member.
- Define balance of trade.

2 Explain why nations engage in international trade and why trade benefits all nations.

- Discuss the relationship between comparative advantage and opportunity cost.
- Explain how the production possibilities frontier can be used to determine the opportunity cost of producing a good.
- Use the production possibilities frontier to demonstrate the gains from trade.

3 Explain how trade barriers reduce international trade.

- Define tariff and quota.
- Explain the effects of a tariff and a quota on domestic consumers, domestic producers, and the domestic government.

4 Explain the arguments used to justify trade barriers and show why they are incorrect but also why some barriers are hard to remove.

- Discuss the three main arguments for protection and explain why each argument is invalid.
- Discuss the six fatally flawed arguments (saving jobs, competing with cheap foreign labor, bringing diversity and stability, penalizing lax environmental standards, pro-

tecting national culture, and preventing exploitation) for protection.
- Explain why governments and rent seekers are in favor of protection.

KEY TERMS

- Balance of trade (page 477)
- Learning-by-doing (page 484)
- Dynamic comparative advantage (page 484)
- Tariff (page 486)
- Nontariff barrier (page 486)
- Quota (page 488)
- Infant-industry argument (page 491)
- Dumping (page 492)
- Rent seeking (page 496)

CHECKPOINT 19.1

■ Describe the patterns and trends in international trade.

Practice Problem 19.1

Use the link on your Foundations Web site to answer the following questions:
  a. In 1990, what percentage of Canadian production was exported to the United States and what percentage of total goods and services bought by Canadians was imported from the United States?
  b. In 2000, what percentage of Canadian production was exported to the United States and what percentage of total goods and services bought by Canadians was imported from the United States?

Solution to Practice Problem 19.1

Although trade is not a major part of the U.S. economy, this Practice Problem illustrates how important trade with just the United States is to Canada.

Quick Review

- *Imports* The goods and services that we buy from people in other countries are called imports.

- *Exports* The goods and services that we sell to people in other countries are called exports.

a. In 1990, what percentage of Canadian production was exported to the United States and what percentage of total goods and services bought by Canadians was imported from the United States?

In 1990, Canadian exports to the United States were 16.5 percent of Canadian production. Canadian imports from the United States were 14.4 percent of the total goods and services bought by Canadians.

b. In 2000, what percentage of Canadian production was exported to the United States and what percentage of total goods and services bought by Canadians was imported from the United States?

In 2000, Canadian exports to the United States were 34.6 percent of Canadian production. Canadian imports from the United States were 27 percent of the total goods and services bought by Canadians.

Additional Practice Problem 19.1a

Citibank, an American firm, provides financial services to firms in France. Describe how the United States and France categorize these financial services.

Solution to Additional Practice Problem 19.1a

For the United States, the services rendered by Citibank are exports to France. For France, the services rendered by Citibank are imports from the United States.

■ Self Test 19.1

Fill in the blanks

Manufactured goods account for ____ (8; 28; 58) percent of U.S. imports. ____ (Canada; Mexico; The United Kingdom; Japan) is the United States' biggest trading partner. The United States ____ (is; is not) a member of NAFTA, the North American Free Trade Agreement. In the United States between 1960 and 2002, trade ____ (decreased; increased) as a fraction of total output.

True or false

1. The United States exports more services than goods.

2. In 2002, 1 percent of total U.S. output was exported.

3. Canada, Mexico, and Japan are the biggest U.S. trading partners.

4. In 2002, the United States imported a larger value of goods and services than it exported.

Multiple choice

1. Goods and services that we buy from people in other countries are called
   a. imports.
   b. exports.
   c. inputs.
   d. raw materials.

2. The largest fraction of U.S. imports is ____ and the largest fraction of U.S. exports ____.
   a. industrial materials; industrial materials
   b. industrial materials; manufactured goods
   c. manufactured goods; industrial materials
   d. manufactured goods; manufactured goods

3. Goods account for about ____ percent of U.S. exports and services account for about ____ percent of U.S. exports.
   a. 51; 49
   b. 72; 28
   c. 28; 72
   d. 100; 0

4. If a college student from North Carolina State University travels to Germany, the money spent on hotels and sight seeing in Germany is counted as services
   a. exported to America.
   b. imported to Germany.
   c. exported to Germany.
   d. exported from America.

5. The largest U.S. trading partner is
   a. Canada.
   b. Mexico.
   c. Japan.
   d. the European Union.

6. The balance of trade equals
   a. the value of imports minus the value of exports.
   b. the value of exports minus the value of imports.
   c. the value of imports.
   d. the value of exports.

Short answer and numeric questions

1. French cheese is flown to the United States abroad a United Airlines plane. Classify these transactions from the vantage point of the United States and from the vantage point of France.

2. How has the amount of international trade changed in the United States between 1960 and 2002?

3. What is NAFTA and what is its goal?

CHECKPOINT 19.2

■ **Explain why nations engage in international trade and why trade benefits all nations.**

Practice Problem 19.2

During most of the Cold War, the United States and Russia did not trade with each other. The United States produced manufactured goods and farm produce. Russia produced manufactured goods and farm produce. Suppose that in the last year of the Cold War, the United States could produce 100 million units of manufactured goods or 50 million units of farm produce and Russia could produce 30 million units of manufactured goods or 10 million units of farm produce.
   a. What was the opportunity cost of 1 unit of farm produce in the United States?
   b. What was the opportunity cost of 1 unit of farm produce in Russia?

c. Which country had a comparative advantage in producing farm produce?

d. With the end of the Cold War and the opening up of trade between Russia and the United States, which good did the United States import from Russia?

e. Did the United States gain from this trade? Explain why or why not.

f. Did Russia gain from this trade? Explain why or why not.

Solution to Practice Problem 19.2

This Practice Problem shows that when opportunity costs between countries diverge, comparative advantage enables countries to gain from international trade.

Quick Review

- *Comparative advantage* A nation has a comparative advantage in a good when its opportunity cost of producing the good is lower than another nation's opportunity cost of producing the good.

a. What was the opportunity cost of 1 unit of farm produce in the United States?

In the United States, to produce 50 million units of farm produce, 100 million units of manufactured goods are forgone. So the opportunity cost of 1 unit of farm produce is (100 million units of manufactured goods) ÷ (50 million units of farm produce), which is 2 units of manufactured goods.

b. What was the opportunity cost of 1 unit of farm produce in Russia?

In Russia, to produce 10 million units of farm produce, 30 million units of manufactured goods are forgone. The opportunity cost of 1 unit of farm produce is (30 million units of manufactured goods) ÷ (10 million units of farm produce), which is 3 units of manufactured goods.

c. Which country had a comparative advantage in producing farm produce?

The opportunity cost of producing farm produce was less in the United States than in Russia, so the United States had the comparative advantage in farm produce.

d. With the end of the Cold War and the opening up of trade between Russia and the United States, which good did the United States import from Russia?

Russia had the comparative advantage in producing manufactured goods. The opportunity cost of producing 1 unit of a manufactured good in Russia was 1/3 of a unit of farm produce. The opportunity cost of producing 1 unit of manufactured good in the United States was 1/2 of a unit of farm produce. So the United States imported manufactured goods from Russia.

e. Did the United States gain from this trade? Explain why or why not.

The United States gained from this trade because it ended up with more of both goods.

f. Did Russia gain from this trade? Explain why or why not.

Russia also gained from this trade for the same reason that the United States gained: Russia ended up with more of both goods. When countries specialize in the good in which they have a comparative advantage and then trade, both countries gain.

Additional Practice Problem 19.2a

In Practice Problem 19.2, suppose that new technology becomes available so that the production of manufactured goods doubles in the United States and Russia. Now which good does the United States import from Russia?

Solution to Additional Practice Problem 19.2a

In the United States when 200 million units of manufactured goods are produced, 50 million units of farm produce are forgone. The opportunity cost of 1 unit of manufactured goods is (50 million units of farm produce) ÷ (200 million units of manufactured goods), which is 1/4 unit of farm produce.

In Russia when 60 million units of manufactured goods are produced, 10 million units of farm produce are forgone. The opportunity cost of 1 unit of manufactured goods is (10 million units of farm produce) ÷ (60 million units of manufactured goods), which is 1/6 unit of farm produce.

Russia still has the comparative advantage in manufactured goods. So the United States continues to import manufactured goods from Russia.

■ Self Test 19.2

Fill in the blanks

A country has a comparative advantage in producing a good if it can produce the good at ____ (higher; lower) opportunity cost than another country. If the world price of clothing is less than the price in the United States with no international trade and the United States imports clothing from Asia, U.S. buyers of clothing ____ (gain; lose) and Asian producers of clothing ____ (gain; lose). Trade ____ (allows; does not allow) a nation to produce at a point beyond its production possibilities frontier. Trade ____ (allows; does not allow) a nation to consume at a point beyond its production possibilities frontier.

True or false

1. Only the exporting country gains from free international trade because it has a comparative advantage.

2. The United States has a comparative advantage in the production of a good if the opportunity cost of producing that good is higher in the United States than in most other countries.

3. A country cannot reap any gains from international trade if it has an absolute advantage in producing all goods and services.

4. In World War II, U.S. shipbuilders became more productive by repeatedly producing the same type of boat, a phenomenon called learning-by-doing.

Multiple choice

1. The fundamental force that drives trade between nations is
   a. the government.
   b. NAFTA.
   c. absolute advantage.
   d. comparative advantage.

2. A nation will import a good if its
   a. no-trade, domestic price is equal to the world price.
   b. no-trade, domestic price is less than the world price.
   c. no-trade, domestic price is greater than the world price.
   d. All of the above answers are correct.

3. When Italy buys Boeing jets, the price Italy pays is ____ than if they produced their own jets and the price Boeing receives is ____ than it could receive from an additional U.S. buyer.
   a. lower; lower
   b. higher; higher
   c. lower; higher
   d. higher; lower

4. When a good is imported, the domestic production ____ and the domestic consumption ____.
   a. increases; increases
   b. increases; decreases
   c. decreases; increases
   d. decreases; decreases

5. You can tell that specialization and trade make a country better off because then the country can consume at a point
   a. outside its production possibilities frontier.
   b. inside its production possibilities frontier.
   c. on its production possibilities frontier.
   d. on the trading partner's production possibilities frontier.

6. People can become more productive just by repeatedly producing a particular good or service. This is called
   a. learning-by-doing.
   b. learning-by-boredom.
   c. absolute advantage.
   d. dynamic absolute advantage.

Complete the graph

1. Figure 19.1 shows the U.S. demand and supply curves for wheat.

■ **FIGURE 19.1**

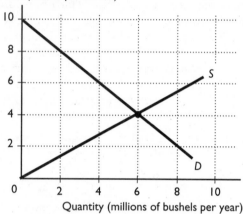

Price (dollars per bushel)

a. In the absence of international trade, what is the price of a bushel of wheat in the United States?
b. If the world price of a bushel of wheat is $6 a bushel, will the United States import or export wheat? Above what world price for wheat will the United States export wheat? Below what world price for wheat will the United States import wheat?

2. Figure 19.2 has the U.S. and French *PPFs*.

■ **FIGURE 19.2**

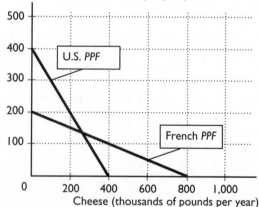

Computer chips (thousands per year)

a. What is the opportunity cost of a computer chip in the United States? In France?

Who has the comparative advantage in producing computer chips?

b. What is the opportunity cost of a pound of cheese in the United States? In France? Who has the comparative advantage in producing cheese?

c. When the United States and France trade, who exports chips and who exports cheese?

d. The United States produced 200,000 computer chips and 200,000 pounds of cheese before trade. France produced 100,000 computer chips and 400,000 pounds of cheese. Label as point *A* the point that shows the total chip and cheese production before trade.

e. The United States and France both specialize according to comparative advantage after trade. Label as point *B* the point that shows the total chip and cheese production after trade. How does point *B* compare to point *A*?

Short answer and numeric questions

1. The table has the U.S. demand and supply schedules for potatoes.

Price (dollars per ton)	Quantity supplied (tons per year)	Quantity demanded (tons per year)
400	38	58
500	42	52
600	46	46
700	50	40
800	54	34
900	58	28

a. If there is no international trade, what is the equilibrium price and quantity?

b. If the world price of potatoes is $800 a ton, what is the quantity supplied and the quantity demanded in the United States? Does the United States import or export potatoes? What quantity?

c. If the world price of potatoes rises to $900 a ton, what is the quantity supplied and the quantity demanded in the United States? Does the United States import or export potatoes? What quantity?

d. Would the United States ever import potatoes?

2. Suppose the United States and France produce only ice cream and cheese. The United States can produce 50 tons of ice cream or 100 tons of cheese and France can produce 20 tons of ice cream or 120 tons of cheese.

a. What is the opportunity cost of a ton of ice cream in France? In the United States? Which nation has the comparative advantage in producing ice cream?

b. What is the opportunity cost of a ton of cheese in France? In the United States? Which nation has the comparative advantage in producing cheese?

c. If France and the United States trade, what does the United States import? What does it export?

d. Before trade the United States produced 25 tons of ice cream and 50 tons of cheese and France produced 10 tons of ice cream and 60 tons of cheese. What is the total production of ice cream? Of cheese?

e. After trade, France and the United States specialize according to comparative advantage. What is the total amount of ice cream produced? Of cheese?

f. Compare your answers to (d) and (e).

3. What are the gains from trade? How do countries obtain the gains from trade?

4. What is dynamic comparative advantage?

CHECKPOINT 19.3

■ **Explain how trade barriers reduce international trade.**

Practice Problems 19.3

1. Before 1995, the United States imposed tariffs on goods imported from Mexico and Mexico imposed tariffs on goods imported from the United States. In 1995, Mexico joined NAFTA. U.S. tariffs on imports from Mexico and Mexican tariffs on imports from the United States

are gradually being removed. Explain how the removal of tariffs will change:

a. The price that U.S. consumers pay for goods imported from Mexico.
b. The quantity of U.S. imports from Mexico.
c. The quantity of U.S. exports to Mexico.
d. The U.S. government's tariff revenue from trade with Mexico.

2. In 2000, the U.S. government placed a ban on potato imports from Canada. Explain how the ban influences:

a. The price that U.S. consumers pay for potatoes.
b. The quantity of potatoes consumed in the United States.
c. The price received by Canadian potato growers.
d. The U.S. and Canadian gains from trade.

Solution to Practice Problems 19.3

Think in terms of the supply and demand model. Imposing a tariff or a quota raises the domestic price, which changes the quantity demanded and the quantity supplied.

Quick Review

- *Tariff* A tariff is a tax on a good that is imposed by the importing country when an imported good crosses its international boundary.
- *Quota* A quota is a specified maximum amount of a good that may be imported in a given period of time.

1a. The price that U.S. consumers pay for goods imported from Mexico.

When the tariff is removed U.S. consumers pay less for goods imported from Mexico.

1b. The quantity of U.S. imports from Mexico.

As the price falls, the quantity of Mexican goods demanded by U.S. consumers increases, so the quantity of U.S. imports from Mexico increases.

1c. The quantity of U.S. exports to Mexico.

When the tariff is removed Mexican consumers pay less for goods exported from the United

States. So the quantity of U.S. goods demanded by Mexican consumers increases and the quantity of U.S. exports to Mexico increases.

1d. The U.S. government's tariff revenue from trade with Mexico.

When the tariff reaches zero, so that trade is totally free of tariffs, the U.S. government's tariff revenue is zero.

2. In 2000, the U.S. government placed a ban on potato imports from Canada. Explain how the ban influences:

2a. The price that U.S. consumers pay for potatoes.

The ban decreases the supply of imported potatoes and raises the price paid by U.S. consumers.

2b. The quantity of potatoes consumed in the United States.

As the price of potatoes rises, the quantity of potatoes consumed in the United States falls.

2c. The price received by Canadian potato growers.

Because Canadian producers cannot export their potatoes to the United States, the supply of potatoes in Canada increases and the price of potatoes falls.

2d. The U.S. and Canadian gains from trade.

The U.S. and Canadian gains from trade are decreased. Anything that limits international trade decreases the gains from trade.

Additional Practice Problem 19.3a

For many years Japan conducted extremely slow, detailed, and costly safety inspections of *all* U.S. cars imported into Japan. In terms of trade, what was the effect of this inspection? How did the inspection affect the price and quantity of cars in Japan?

Solution to Additional Practice Problem 19.3a

Japan's safety inspection (which has since been eliminated) was an example of a nontariff barrier to trade. It served a role similar to tariffs and quotas. The safety inspection added to the cost of selling cars in Japan. It raised the price of U.S. produced cars in Japan and decreased the quantity of U.S. cars sold. The Japanese government, however, received no tariff revenue.

■ Self Test 19.3

Fill in the blanks

A tax on a good that is imposed by the importing country when an imported good crosses its international boundary is a ____ (quota; tariff) and a specified maximum amount of a good that may be imported in a given period of time is a ____ (quota; tariff). A tariff ____ (raises; lowers) the price paid by domestic consumers and ____ (increases; decreases) the quantity produced by domestic producers. A quota ____ (raises; lowers) the price paid by domestic consumers and ____ (increases; decreases) the quantity produced by domestic producers.

True or false

1. If the United States imposes a tariff, the price paid by U.S. consumers does not change.

2. If a country imposes a tariff on rice imports, domestic production of rice will increase and domestic consumption of rice will decrease.

3. A tariff increases the gains from trade for the exporting country.

4. A quota on imports of a particular good specifies the minimum quantity of that good that can be imported in a given period.

Multiple choice

1. A tax on a good that is imposed by the importing country when an imported good crosses its international boundary is a
   a. quota.
   b. nontariff barrier.
   c. tariff.
   d. sanction.

2. The average U.S. tariff was highest in the
   a. 1930s.
   b. 1940s.
   c. 1970s.
   d. 1980s.

3. Suppose the world price of a shirt is $10. If the United States imposes a tariff of $5 a shirt, then the price of a shirt in the
   a. United States falls to $5.
   b. United States rises to $15.
   c. world falls to $5.
   d. world rises to $5.

4. When a tariff is imposed on a good, the ____ increases.
   a. domestic quantity purchased
   b. domestic quantity produced
   c. quantity imported
   d. quantity exported

5. When a tariff is imposed on a good, domestic consumers ____ and domestic producers ____.
   a. win; lose
   b. lose; win
   c. win; win
   d. lose; lose

6. Which of the following parties benefits from a quota but not from a tariff?
   a. the government
   b. domestic producers
   c. domestic consumers
   d. the person with the right to import the good

Complete the graph

1. Figure 19.3 shows the supply of and demand for sugar in the United States.

   ### ■ FIGURE 19.3

   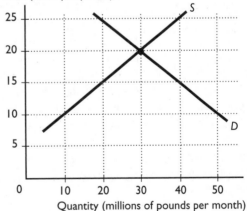

   a. If the world price of sugar is 10¢ a pound, draw the world price line in the figure. What is the quantity consumed in the United States, the quantity produced in the United States, and the quantity imported?

b. Suppose the government imposes a 5¢ a pound tariff on sugar. Show the effect of the tariff in Figure 19.3 After the tariff, what is the quantity consumed in the United States, the quantity produced in the United States, and the quantity imported?

Short answer and numeric questions

1. Suppose the U.S. government imposes a tariff on steel. How does the tariff affect the price of steel? How does it affect U.S. steel consumers? U.S. steel producers?

2. Suppose the U.S. government imposes a quota on steel. How does the quota affect the price of steel? How does it affect U.S. steel consumers? U.S. steel producers?

3. Why do consumers lose from a tariff?

CHECKPOINT 19.4

■ **Explain the arguments used to justify trade barriers and show why they are incorrect but also why some barriers are hard to remove.**

Practice Problems 19.4

1. Japan sets quotas on imports of rice. California rice growers would like to export more rice to Japan. What are Japan's arguments for restricting imports of Californian rice? Are these arguments correct? Who loses from this restriction of trade?

2. The United States has, from time to time, limited imports of steel from Europe. What is the argument that the United States has used to justify this quota? Who wins from this restriction? Who loses?

3. The United States maintains a quota on imports of textiles. What is the argument for this quota? Is this argument flawed? If so, explain why.

Solution to Practice Problem 19.4

Free trade promotes prosperity for all countries. Protection reduces the potential gains from trade. These Practice Problems discuss the arguments

for protection and show the range of issues in the free trade versus protection debate.

Quick Review

- *Rent seeking* Lobbying and other political activity that seeks to capture the gains from trade.

1. **Japan sets quotas on imports of rice. California rice growers would like to export more rice to Japan. What are Japan's arguments for restricting imports of Californian rice? Are these arguments correct? Who loses from this restriction of trade?**

Japan has used a number of arguments, but they are all incorrect. Japan has argued that Japanese rice is of a higher quality than U.S. rice, but if Japanese consumers detect a quality difference, they can purchase Japanese rice rather than U.S. rice. Japan has argued that rice is part of Japanese national heritage, but if Japanese consumers want to protect this part of their heritage, they can buy exclusively Japanese rice rather than U.S. rice. The major losers from the Japanese quota are Japanese consumers who must pay a higher price for rice.

2. **The United States has, from time to time, limited imports of steel from Europe. What is the argument that the United States has used to justify this quota? Who wins from this restriction? Who loses?**

In past decades, the United States asserted that the steel industry was needed because it played a major role in national defense. With the use of more exotic materials in defense armaments, the national defense argument has passed into history. More recently, the United States has, at times, argued that Europeans were dumping steel in the United States. Both of these arguments are likely not the true reason for the quotas. The quotas are the result of political lobbying by steel producers and steel workers. They are the result of rent seeking by steel producers and steel workers. The winners from the quotas are the steel producers and steel workers. The losers are all U.S. steel consumers.

3. **The United States maintains a quota on imports of textiles. What is the argument for**

this quota? Is this argument flawed? If so, explain why.

U.S. textile producers and textile workers assert that the U.S. textile industry needs protection because of cheap foreign labor. This argument is flawed. The United States does not have a comparative advantage in textiles because textiles can be produced by low-productivity, low-wage workers. U.S. workers have a higher productivity and command a higher wage. Other nations have a comparative advantage in producing textiles.

Additional Practice Problem 19.4a

In each of the three Practice Problems, identify who is rent seeking.

Solution to Additional Practice Problem 19.4a

Rent seeking is lobbying and other political activity that seeks to capture the gains from trade. In Practice Problem 1, the Japanese rice farmers are rent seeking. In Practice Problem 2, the U.S. steel producers and U.S. steel workers are rent seeking. And in Practice Problem 3, U.S. textile producers and U.S. textile workers are rent seeking.

■ Self Test 19.4

Fill in the blanks

The assertion that it is necessary to protect a new industry to enable it to grow into a mature industry that can compete in world markets is the ____ (infant-industry; maturing-industry) argument. Dumping occurs when ____ (U.S. jobs are lost to cheap foreign labor; a foreign firm sells its exports at a lower price than its cost of production). Protection ____ (is; is not) necessary to bring diversity and stability to our economy. Protection ____ (is; is not) necessary to prevent rich countries from exploiting developing countries. The major reason why international trade is restricted is because ____ (foreign countries protect their industries; of rent seeking).

True or false

1. The national security argument is the only valid argument for protection.

2. Dumping by a foreign producer is easy to detect.

3. Protection saves U.S. jobs at no cost.

4. International trade is an attractive base for tax collection in developing countries

Multiple choice

1. The national security argument is used by those who assert they want to
   a. increase imports as a way of strengthening their country.
   b. increase exports as a way of earning money to strengthen their country.
   c. limit imports that compete with domestic producers important for national defense.
   d. limit exports to control the flow of technology to third world nations.

2. The argument that it is necessary to protect a new industry to enable it to grow into a mature industry that can compete in world markets is the
   a. national security argument.
   b. diversity argument.
   c. infant-industry argument.
   d. environmental protection argument.

3. ____ occurs when a foreign firm sells its exports at a lower price than its cost of production.
   a. Dumping
   b. The trickle-down effect
   c. Rent seeking
   d. Tariff avoidance

4. The United States
   a. needs tariffs to allow us to compete with cheap foreign labor.
   b. does not need tariffs to allow us to compete with cheap foreign labor.
   d. should not trade with countries that have cheap labor.
   d. will not benefit from trade with countries that have cheap labor.

5. Why do governments in less-developed nations impose tariffs on imported goods and services?
   a. The government gains revenue from the tariff.
   b. The government's low-paid workers are protected from high-paid foreign workers.
   c. The nation's total income is increased.
   d. The country's national security is improved.

6. What is the major reason international trade is restricted?
   a. rent seeking
   b. to allow competition with cheap foreign labor
   c. to save jobs
   d. to prevent dumping

Short answer and numeric questions

1. What is the dumping argument for protection? What is its flaw?

2. How do you respond to a speaker who says that we need to limit auto imports from Japan in order to save U.S. jobs?

3. Why is it incorrect to assert that trade with developing countries exploits the workers in these countries?

SELF TEST ANSWERS

■ CHECKPOINT 19.1

Fill in the blanks

Manufactured goods account for <u>58</u> percent of U.S. imports. <u>Canada</u> is the United States' biggest trading partner. The United States <u>is</u> a member of NAFTA, the North American Free Trade Agreement. In the United States between 1960 and 2002, trade <u>increased</u> as a fraction of total output.

True or false

1. False; page 474
2. False; page 474
3. True; page 475
4. True; page 477

Multiple choice

1. a; page 474
2. d; page 474
3. b; page 474
4. a; page 474
5. a; page 475
6. b; page 477

Short answer and numeric questions

1. From the U.S. vantage, the cheese is an imported good and the air transportation is an exported service. From the French vantage, the cheese is an exported good and the air transportation is an imported service; page 474.

2. Between 1960 and 2002, international trade in the United States expanded. In 1960, U.S. exports were 5 percent of total output and in 2002, exports were 10 percent of total output. In 1960, U.S. imports were 4 percent of the goods and services purchased and in 2002, imports were 14 percent of the goods and services purchased; page 474.

3. NAFTA is the North American Free Trade Agreement. It is an agreement among Canada, the United States, and Mexico to make trade among the three nations easier and freer; page 475.

■ CHECKPOINT 19.2

Fill in the blanks

A country has a comparative advantage in producing a good if it can produce the good at <u>lower</u> opportunity cost than another country. If the world price of clothing is less than the price in the United States with no international trade and the United States imports clothing from Asia, U.S. buyers of clothing <u>gain</u> and Asian producers of clothing <u>gain</u>. Trade <u>does not allow</u> a nation to produce at a point beyond its production possibilities frontier. Trade <u>allows</u> a nation to consume at a point beyond its production possibilities frontier.

True or false

1. False; page 484
2. False; pages 478-479
3. False; page 484
4. True; page 484

Multiple choice

1. d; page 478
2. c; page 479-480
3. c; page 478
4. c; page 481
5. a; page 484
6. a; page 484

Complete the graph

1. a. In the absence of international trade, the equilibrium price of a bushel of wheat in the United States is $4; pages 478-479.

   b. If the world price of a bushel of wheat is $6 a bushel, the United States will export wheat because the world price exceeds the no-trade price. If the price of wheat exceeds $4 a bushel, the United States will export wheat. If the price of wheat is less than $4 a bushel, the United States will import wheat; pages 479-481.

2. a. The opportunity cost of a computer chip in the United States is 1 pound of cheese. In France, the opportunity cost of a computer chip is 4 pounds of cheese. The

United States has the comparative advantage in chips; page 481.

b. The opportunity cost of a pound of cheese in the United States is 1 computer chip. In France, the opportunity cost is of a pound of cheese 1/4 of a computer chip. France has the comparative advantage in cheese; page 481.

c. The United States has the comparative advantage in chips, so it will specialize in producing chips and export chips to France. France will specialize in cheese and export cheese to the United States; page 483.

d. The point is labeled in Figure 19.4; page 483-484.

■ **FIGURE 19.4**

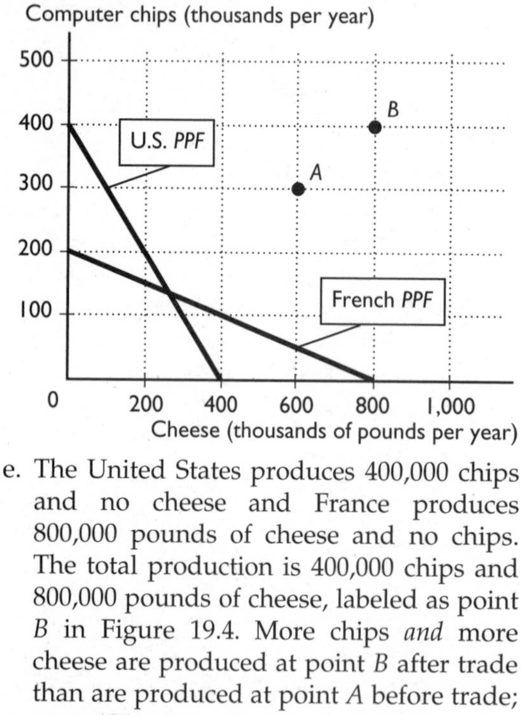

Computer chips (thousands per year)

e. The United States produces 400,000 chips and no cheese and France produces 800,000 pounds of cheese and no chips. The total production is 400,000 chips and 800,000 pounds of cheese, labeled as point B in Figure 19.4. More chips *and* more cheese are produced at point B after trade than are produced at point A before trade; page 484.

Short answer and numeric questions

1. a. In the absence of international trade, the equilibrium price is $600 a ton and the equilibrium quantity is 46 tons; page 478.

b. In the United States, the quantity supplied is 54 tons and the quantity demanded is 34

tons. The United States exports 20 tons of potatoes; page 478.

c. In the United States, the quantity supplied is 58 tons and the quantity demanded is 28 tons. The United States exports 30 tons of potatoes; page 478.

d. The United States would import potatoes if the world price is less than $600 a ton; page 480.

2. a. In France, the opportunity cost of a ton of ice cream is 6 tons of cheese; in the United States, the opportunity cost of a ton of ice cream is 2 tons of cheese. The United States has the comparative advantage in producing ice cream; page 483.

b. In France, the opportunity cost of a ton of cheese is 1/6 of a ton of ice cream; in the United States, the opportunity cost of a ton of cheese is 1/2 of a ton of ice cream. France has the comparative advantage in producing cheese; page 483.

c. The United States imports cheese and exports ice cream; page 483.

d. 35 tons of ice cream are produced and 110 tons of cheese are produced; page 483.

e. 50 tons of ice cream are produced in the United States and 120 tons of cheese are produced in France; page 483.

f. The world production of ice cream *and* cheese increased, which demonstrates the gains from trade; page 483.

3. The gains from trade occur because after specialization and trade, a country can increase its consumption so that it can consume at a point beyond its production possibilities frontier. To obtain the gains from trade a country must specialize and trade; pages 483-484.

4. Dynamic comparative advantage is comparative advantage from specializing in an activity so that productivity increases because of learning-by-doing; page 484.

■ CHECKPOINT 19.3

Fill in the blanks

A tax on a good that is imposed by the importing country when an imported good enters its boundary is called a <u>tariff</u> and a specified maximum amount of a good that may be imported is called a <u>quota</u>. A tariff <u>raises</u> the price paid by domestic consumers and <u>increases</u> the quantity produced by domestic producers. A quota <u>raises</u> the price paid by domestic consumers and <u>increases</u> the quantity produced by domestic producers.

True or false

1. False; pages 487-488
2. True; pages 487-488
3. False; pages 487-488
4. False; page 488

Multiple choice

1. c; page 486
2. a; page 486
3. b; page 487
4. b; pages 487-488
5. b; pages 487-488
6. d; pages 488-489

Complete the graph

■ FIGURE 19.5

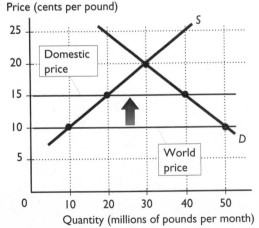

1. a. The world price line is shown in Figure 19.5. 50 million pounds of sugar are consumed in the United States, 10 million pounds are produced in the United States, and 40 million pounds are imported into the United States; pages 486-487.

   b. The tariff increases the domestic price, as shown in the figure. The quantity consumed in the United States decreases to 40 million pounds, the quantity produced in the United States increases to 20 million pounds, and the amount imported decreases to 20 million pounds; pages 486-487.

Short answer and numeric questions

1. The tariff raises the price of steel. U.S. steel consumers decrease the quantity they purchase and U.S. steel producers increase the quantity they produce; pages 486-487.

2. The quota has the same effects as the tariff in the previous question. The quota raises the price of steel. U.S. steel consumers decrease the quantity purchased and U.S. steel producers increase the quantity produced; pages 488-489.

3. Consumers lose from a tariff because the tariff raises the price they pay and the quantity bought decreases. The tariff makes people pay more than the opportunity cost of the good; page 488.

■ CHECKPOINT 19.4

Fill in the blanks

The assertion that it is necessary to protect a new industry to enable it to grow into a mature industry that can compete in world markets is the <u>infant-industry</u> argument. Dumping occurs when <u>a foreign firm sells its exports at a lower price than its cost of production</u>. Protection <u>is not</u> necessary to bring diversity and stability to our economy. Protection <u>is not</u> necessary to prevent rich countries from exploiting developing countries. The major reason why international trade is restricted is because <u>of rent seeking</u>.

True or false

1. False; page 491
2. False; page 492
3. False; page 493
4. True; page 496

Multiple choice

1. c; page 491
2. c; page 491
3. a; page 492
4. b; page 493
5. a; page 496
6. a; page 496

Short answer and numeric questions

1. Dumping occurs when a foreign firm sells its exports at a lower price than its cost of production. The dumping argument is flawed for the following reasons. First, it is virtually impossible to detect dumping because it is hard to determine a firm's costs and the fair market price. Second, it is hard to think of a good that is produced by a global natural monopoly. Third, if a firm truly was a global natural monopoly, the best way to deal with it would be by regulation; page 493.

2. Saving jobs is one of the oldest arguments in favor of protection. It is also incorrect. Protecting a particular industry will likely save jobs in that industry but will cost many other jobs in other industries. The cost to consumers of saving a job is many times the wage rate of the job saved; page 493.

3. The assertion that trade with developing countries exploits the workers in these countries is incorrect. Wage rates in some developing countries are very low. But by trading with developing countries, we increase the demand for the goods that these countries produce, and we increase the demand for their labor. When the demand for labor in developing countries increases, the wage rate also increases. So instead of exploiting people in developing countries, trade improves their opportunities and increases their income; page 495.

International Finance

Chapter 20

Chapter 20 examines international finance. It studies how nations keep their international accounts, what determines the balance of payments, and how the value of the dollar is determined in the foreign exchange market.

■ **Describe a country's balance of payments accounts and explain what determines the amount of international borrowing and lending.**

There are three balance of payments accounts, which are the current account, the capital account, and the official settlements account. The current account balance equals exports minus imports, plus net interest and transfers received from abroad. The capital account is a record of foreign investment in the United States minus U.S. investment abroad. The official settlements account is a record of the change in U.S. official reserves. The sum of the balances on the three accounts always equals zero. We pay for imports that exceed the value of our exports by borrowing from the rest of the world. A net borrower is a country that is borrowing more from the rest of the world than it is lending to the rest of the world, and a net lender is a country that is lending more to the rest of the world than it is borrowing from the rest of the world. A debtor nation is a country that during its entire history has borrowed more from the rest of the world than it has lent to it, and a creditor nation is a country that during its entire history has invested more in the rest of the world than other countries have invested in it. Net exports equals the sum of the private sector balance and the government sector balance.

■ **Explain how the exchange rate is determined and why it fluctuates.**

Foreign currency is needed to buy goods or invest in another country. The foreign exchange rate is the price at which one currency exchanges for another and is determined by demand and supply in the foreign exchange market. The quantity of dollars demanded increases when the exchange rate falls. The demand for dollars changes and the demand curve for dollars shifts if the U.S. interest rate differential or the expected future exchange rate changes. A rise in either increases the demand for dollars. The quantity of dollars supplied increases when the exchange rate rises. The supply of dollars changes and the supply curve of dollars shifts if the U.S. interest rate differential or the expected future exchange rate changes. A rise in either decreases the supply of dollars. At the equilibrium exchange rate, the quantity of dollars demanded equals the quantity of dollars supplied. The exchange rate is volatile because factors that change the demand also change the supply. Exchange rate expectations are influenced by purchasing power parity, a situation in which money buys the same amount of goods and services in different currencies, and interest rate parity, a situation in which the interest rate in one currency equals the interest rate in another currency once exchange rate changes are taken into account. The Fed can intervene directly in the foreign exchange market.

EXPANDED CHAPTER CHECKLIST

When you have completed this chapter, you will be able to:

1 Describe a country's balance of payments accounts and explain what determines the amount of international borrowing and lending.

- Define the balance of payment accounts, the current account, the capital account, and the official settlements account.
- Define net borrower, net lender, creditor nation, and debtor nation.
- State the relationship between net exports, the private sector balance, and the government sector balance.
- Discuss whether the United States is borrowing for consumption or investment.

2 Explain how the exchange rate is determined and why it fluctuates.

- Explain the role of the foreign exchange market.
- Define currency appreciation and currency depreciation.
- Discuss the relationship between the exchange rate and the quantity of dollars demanded.
- Explain how a change in the U.S. interest rate differential or in the expected future exchange rate changes the demand for dollars.
- Discuss the relationship between the exchange rate and the quantity of dollars supplied.
- Explain how a change in the U.S. interest rate differential or in the expected future exchange rate changes the supply of dollars.
- Illustrate equilibrium in the foreign exchange market and show how a change in the demand for dollars or supply of dollars changes the exchange rate.
- State how the Fed intervenes in the foreign exchange market.

KEY TERMS

- Balance of payments accounts (page 504)
- Current account (page 504)
- Capital account (page 504)
- Official settlements account (page 504)
- U.S. official reserves (page 504)
- Net borrower (page 506)
- Net lender (page 506)
- Debtor nation (page 506)
- Creditor nation (page 506)
- Private sector balance (page 508)
- Government sector balance (page 508)
- Foreign exchange market (page 511)
- Foreign exchange rate (page 511)
- Currency depreciation (page 511)
- Currency appreciation (page 512)
- U.S. interest rate differential (page 514)
- Purchasing power parity (page 520)
- Interest rate parity (page 522)

CHECKPOINT 20.1

■ Describe a country's balance of payments accounts and explain what determines the amount of international borrowing and lending.

Practice Problem 20.1

It is 2004 and the U.S. economy records the following transactions:

Imports of goods and services, $2,000 billion; interest paid to the rest of the world, $500 billion; interest received from the rest of the world, $400 billion; decrease in U.S. official reserves, $10 billion; government sector balance, $200 billion; saving $1,800 billion; investment $2,000 billion; net transfers, zero.

a. Calculate the current account balance, the capital account balance, the official settlements account balance, and exports of goods and services.

b. Is the United States a debtor or a creditor nation in 2004?

c. If government purchases increase by $100 billion, what happens to the current account balance?

Solution to Practice Problem 20.1

Keep in mind the components of the current account and the capital account and remember that the sum of the current account, capital account, and official settlements account is zero.

Quick Review

- *Current account balance* The current account balance equals net exports plus net interest plus net transfers received from abroad.

It is 2004 and the U.S. economy records the following transactions:

Imports of goods and services, $2,000 billion; interest paid to the rest of the world, $500 billion; interest received from the rest of the world, $400 billion; decrease in U.S. official reserves, $10 billion; government sector balance, $200 billion; saving $1,800 billion; investment $2,000 billion; net transfers, zero.

a. Calculate the current account balance, the capital account balance, the official settlements account balance, and exports of goods and services.

The current account balance equals net exports plus net interest, which is –$100 billion, plus net transfers, which is zero. Net exports equals the private sector balance plus the government sector balance. The private sector balance equals saving minus investment, or $1,800 billion minus $2,000 billion, which is –$200 billion. The government sector balance is $200 billion. The sum of the private sector balance plus the government sector balance is –$200 billion + $200 billion, which equals zero. So net exports are zero and the current account balance is –$100 billion. Net exports equals zero, so exports equal imports, which is $2,000 billion.

Next calculate the official settlements account balance, which is the negative of the change in U.S. official reserves. When reserves decrease by –$10 billion, the official settlements account balance is $10 billion.

The sum of the current account balance, the capital account balance, and the official settlements account balance is zero. The current account balance is –$100 billion and the official settlements balance is $10 billion, so the capital account balance is $90 billion.

b. **Is the United States a debtor or a creditor nation in 2004?**

Interest payments reflect the value of outstanding debts. The United States is a debtor nation because the value of interest payments received from the rest of the world is less than the value of interest payments made to the rest of the world.

c. **If government purchases increase by $100 billion, what happens to the current account balance?**

Net exports equals the sum of the private sector balance and the government sector balance. The current account balance equals net exports plus net interest and transfers received from abroad. When government purchases increase by $100 billion, the government sector balance decreases by $100 billion, which reduces net exports by $100 billion. The current account balance decreases by $100 billion and so the current account deficit increases by $100 billion.

Additional Practice Problem 20.1a

Suppose the official settlements account equals zero. In this case, what is the relationship between the current account and the capital account? Why does this relationship exist?

Solution to Additional Practice Problem 20.1a

If the official settlements account equals zero, then the deficit in the current account equals the surplus in the capital account. Or, if the official settlements account equals zero, then the surplus in the current account equals the deficit in the capital account. This relationship exists because the sum of the current account, capital account, and the official settlements account equals zero. If the official settlements account equals zero, the current account balance must equal the negative of the capital account balance.

■ Self Test 20.1

Fill in the blanks

The ____ (current; capital; official settlements) account records payments for the imports of goods and services. The ____ (current; capital; official settlements) account records foreign investment in the United States minus U.S. investment abroad. The sum of the balances on current account, capital account, and the official settlements account always equals ____ (zero; 100 percent). The United States is a ____ (debtor; creditor) nation. The United States is borrowing for ____ (consumption; investment).

True or false

1. If foreign investment in the United States increases, and U.S. investment in the rest of the world decreases, the current account shows an increase in exports and a decrease in imports.

2. The official settlements account balance is negative if U.S. official reserves increase.

3. In the year 2002, the United States had a current account deficit.

4. If the United States has a surplus in its capital account and a deficit in its current account, the balance in its official settlements account is zero.

5. In 2002, the United States was a net lender and a debtor nation.

6. If the United States started to run a current account surplus that continued indefinitely, it would immediately become a net lender and would eventually become a creditor nation.

7. Net exports equals the private sector balance minus the government sector balance.

8. In 2002, U.S. borrowing from abroad financed investment.

Multiple choice

1. A country's balance of payments accounts records its
   a. tax receipts and expenditures.
   b. tariffs and nontariff revenue and government purchases.
   c. international trading, borrowing, and lending.
   d. international exports and imports and nothing else.

2. All the following are balance of payments accounts EXCEPT the
   a. capital account.
   b. labor account.
   c. official settlements account.
   d. current account.

3. Which balance of payments account records payments for imports and receipts from exports?
   a. current account
   b. capital account
   c. official settlements account
   d. reserves account

4. The current account balance is equal to
   a. imports − exports + net interest + net transfers.
   b. imports − exports + net interest − net transfers.
   c. exports − imports − net interest + net transfers.
   d. exports − imports + net interest + net transfers.

5. If an investment of $100 million from the United Kingdom is made in the United States, the $100 million is listed as a ____ entry in the ____ account.
   a. positive; current
   b. negative; capital
   c. positive; capital
   d. negative; current

6. If the United States receives $200 billion of foreign investment and at the same time invests a total of $160 billion abroad, then the U.S.
   a. capital account balance increases by $40 billion.
   b. current account must be in surplus.
   c. balance of payments must be negative.
   d. capital account balance decreases by $40 billion.

7. In the balance of payments accounts, changes in U.S. official reserves are recorded in the
   a. current account.
   b. capital account.
   c. official settlements account.
   d. international currency account.

8. If a country has a current account balance of $100 billion and the official settlements account balance is zero, then the country's capital account balance must be
   a. equal to $100 billion.
   b. positive but not necessarily equal to $100 billion.
   c. equal to –$100 billion.
   d. negative but not necessarily equal to –$100 billion.

9. A country that is borrowing more from the rest of the world than it is lending is called a
   a. net lender.
   b. net borrower.
   c. net debtor.
   d. net creditor.

10. A debtor nation is a country that
    a. borrows more from the rest of the world than it lends to it.
    b. lends more to the rest of the world than it borrows from it.
    c. during its entire history has invested more in the rest of the world than other countries have invested in it.
    d. during its entire history has borrowed more from the rest of the world than it has lent to it.

11. Comparing the U.S. balance of payments in 2002 to the rest of the world, we see that the
    a. United States has the largest current account surplus.
    b. U.S. current account is similar in size to most developed nations.
    c. United States has the largest capital account deficit.
    d. United States has the largest current account deficit.

12. According to the U.S. balance of payments accounts in 2002, U.S. international borrowing is used for
    a. private and public investment.
    b. private consumption.
    c. government expenditure.
    d. private and public saving.

Short answer and numeric questions

1. What is recorded in the U.S. current account? In its capital account? In its official settlements account?

2. If its official settlements account equals zero, what will a country's capital account equal if it has a $350 billion current account deficit?

3. The table has balance of payment data for the United States.

Item	(billions of dollars)
U.S. investment abroad	400
Exports of goods and services	1,000
Net transfers	0
Change in official reserves	10
Net interest	0
Foreign investment in the United States	800

   a. What is the capital account balance?
   b. What is the official settlements balance?
   c. What is the current account balance?
   d. What is the value of imports of goods and services?

4. What is a net borrower? A debtor nation? Is it possible for a nation to be net borrower and yet not be a debtor nation?

5. The table has data for the United States.

Item	(billions of dollars)
Saving	1,600
Investment	1,900
Government purchases	1,300
Net taxes	1,400

   a. What is the private sector balance?
   b. What is the government sector balance?
   c. What is net exports?

CHECKPOINT 20.2

■ Explain how the exchange rate is determined and why it fluctuates.

Practice Problem 20.2

Suppose that yesterday, the U.S. dollar was trading on the foreign exchange market at 100 yen per dollar. Today, the U.S. dollar is trading at 105 yen per dollar.

   a. Which of the two currencies (the dollar or the yen) has appreciated and which has depreciated today?
   b. List the events that could have caused to-day's change in the value of the U.S. dollar on the foreign exchange market.
   c. Did the events that you have listed in part (b) change the demand for U.S. dollars, the supply of U.S. dollars, or both the demand for and supply of U.S. dollars?
   d. If the Fed had tried to stabilize the value of the U.S. dollar at 100 yen per dollar, what action would it have taken?
   e. In part (d), what effect would the Fed's actions have had on U.S. official reserves?

Solution to Practice Problem 20.2

To solve this Practice Problem, remember that the demand and supply of dollars changes when the U.S. interest rate differential changes and when the expected future exchange rate changes.

Quick Review

*   *U.S. interest rate differential* On the foreign exchange market, an increase in the U.S. interest rate differential increases the demand for dollars and decreases the supply of dollars.

*   *Expected future exchange rate* On the foreign exchange market, a rise in the expected future exchange rate increases the demand for dollars and decreases the supply of dollars.

Suppose that yesterday, the U.S. dollar was trading on the foreign exchange market at 100 yen per dollar. Today, the U.S. dollar is trading at 105 yen per dollar.

   a. Which of the two currencies (the dollar or the yen) has appreciated and which has depreciated today?

Today, the dollar buys more yen so the dollar has more value. The dollar has appreciated. Yesterday, 1 yen bought 1 cent. Today, 1 yen cannot buy 1 cent, so the yen has depreciated.

   b. List the events that could have caused today's change in the value of the U.S. dollar on the foreign exchange market.

The factors that change the demand for and supply of dollars are the U.S. interest rate differential and the expected future exchange rate. Because the dollar rose in value, an increase in the U.S. interest rate differential—either a rise in the U.S. interest rate and/or a fall in the Japanese interest rate—or a rise in the expected future exchange rate both raise the value of the dollar.

   c. Did the events that you have listed in part (b) change the demand for U.S. dollars, the supply of U.S. dollars, or both the demand for and supply of U.S. dollars?

The events changed *both* the demand for dollars and the supply of dollars. Both events increased the demand for dollars and decreased the supply of dollars.

   d. If the Fed had tried to stabilize the value of the U.S. dollar at 100 yen per dollar, what action would it have taken?

The dollar increased in value. To prevent the dollar from rising in value, the Fed would have sold dollars in the foreign exchange market to increase the supply of dollars and keep the value at 100 yen per dollar.

e. **In part (d), what effect would the Fed's actions have had on U.S. official reserves?**

In part (d), when the Fed sells dollars it buys foreign currency. U.S. official reserves would have increased.

Additional Practice Problem 20.2a

How and why does an increase in the expected future exchange rate change the demand for U.S. dollars and the demand curve for dollars? How and why does an increase in the expected future exchange rate change the supply of U.S. dollars and the supply curve of dollars? What is the effect on the equilibrium exchange rate?

Solution to Additional Practice Problem 20.2a

An increase in the expected future exchange rate increases the demand for U.S. dollars and shifts the demand curve rightward. The demand for U.S. dollars increases because at the current exchange rate people want to buy U.S. dollars now and sell them in the future at the higher expected exchange rate. An increase in the expected future exchange rate decreases the supply of U.S. dollars and shifts the supply curve leftward. The supply of U.S. dollars decreases because people would rather keep the dollars until they can sell them in the future at the higher expected exchange rate. Because the demand for dollars increases and the supply of dollars decreases, the current equilibrium exchange rate rises.

■ Self Test 20.2

Fill in the blanks

The price at which one currency exchanges for another is called a foreign _____ (exchange rate; interest rate). If the dollar falls in value against the Mexican peso, the dollar has _____ (appreciated; depreciated). A rise in exchange rate _____ (decreases; increases) the quantity of U.S. dollars demanded. An increase in the demand for dollars shifts the demand curve for dollars _____ (leftward; rightward) and an increase in the supply of dollars shifts the supply curve of dollars _____ (leftward; rightward). The exchange rate is volatile because an influence that changes the demand for dollars often _____ (changes; does not change) the supply of dollars. An increase in the expected future exchange rate _____ (raises; lowers) the equilibrium exchange rate. Purchasing power parity is equal value of _____ (interest rates; money). If the Fed buys dollars on the foreign exchange market, the exchange rate _____ (rises; falls).

True or false

1. The U.S. foreign exchange rate changes infrequently.

2. If the exchange rate increases from 90 yen per dollar to 110 yen per dollar, the dollar has appreciated.

3. The larger the value of U.S. exports, the larger is the quantity of U.S. dollars demanded.

4. An increase in the U.S. exchange rate increases the supply of U.S. dollars and shifts the supply curve of dollars rightward.

5. A rise in the expected future exchange rate increases the demand for dollars and also the supply of dollars and might raise or lower the exchange rate.

6. The equilibrium U.S. exchange rate is the exchange rate that sets the quantity of dollars demanded equal to the quantity of dollars supplied.

7. An increase in the U.S. interest rate differential raises the U.S. exchange rate.

8. To prevent the price of the euro from falling, the European Central Bank might sell euros on the foreign exchange market.

Multiple choice

1. The foreign exchange market is the market in which
   a. all international transactions occur.
   b. currencies are exchanged solely by governments.
   c. goods and services are exchanged between governments.
   d. the currency of one country is exchanged for the currency of another.

2. When Del Monte, an American company, purchases Mexican tomatoes, Del Monte pays for the tomatoes with
   a. Canadian dollars.
   b. Mexican pesos.
   c. gold.
   d. Mexican goods and services.

3. If today the exchange rate is 100 yen per dollar and tomorrow the exchange rate is 98 yen per dollar, then the dollar ____ and the yen ____.
   a. appreciated; appreciated
   b. appreciated; depreciated
   c. depreciated; appreciated
   d. depreciated; depreciated

4. In the foreign exchange market, as the U.S. exchange rate rises, other things remaining the same, the
   a. quantity of dollars demanded increases.
   b. demand curve for dollars shifts rightward.
   c. demand curve for dollars shifts leftward.
   d. quantity of dollars demanded decreases.

5. In the foreign exchange market, the demand for dollars increases and the demand curve for dollars shifts rightward if the
   a. U.S. interest rate differential increases.
   b. expected future exchange rate falls.
   c. foreign interest rate rises.
   d. U.S. interest rate falls.

6. As the exchange rate ____, the quantity supplied of U.S. dollars ____.
   a. rises; increases
   b. falls; increases
   c. falls; remains the same
   d. rises; decreases

7. In the foreign exchange market, the supply curve of dollars is
   a. upward sloping.
   b. downward sloping.
   c. vertical.
   d. horizontal.

8. Everything else remaining the same, in the foreign exchange market which of the following will increase the supply of U.S. dollars?
   a. The Japanese interest rate rises.
   b. The expected future exchange rate rises.
   c. The U.S. interest rate rises.
   d. The U.S. interest rate differential increases.

9. When there is a shortage of dollars in the foreign exchange market, the
   a. demand curve for dollars shifts leftward to restore the equilibrium.
   b. U.S. exchange rate will appreciate.
   c. U.S. exchange rate will depreciate.
   d. supply curve of dollars shifts leftward to restore the equilibrium.

10. In the foreign exchange market, when the U.S. interest rate rises, the supply of dollars ____ and the foreign exchange rate ____.
    a. increases; rises
    b. increases; falls
    c. decreases; rises
    d. decreases; falls

11. A situation in which money buys the same amount of goods and services in different currencies is called
    a. exchange rate equilibrium.
    b. purchasing power parity.
    c. exchange rate surplus.
    d. exchange rate balance.

12. Interest rate parity occurs when
    a. the interest rate in one currency equals the interest rate in another currency when exchange rate changes are taken into account.
    b. interest rate differentials are always maintained across nations.
    c. interest rates are equal across nations.
    d. prices are equal across nations when exchange rates are taken into account.

Complete the graph

1. Figure 20.1 shows the foreign exchange market for U.S. dollars.

■ **FIGURE 20.1**

Exchange rate (yen per dollar)

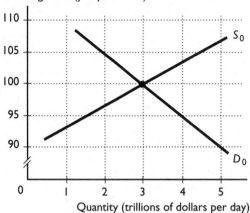

a. What is the equilibrium exchange rate?
b. The U.S. interest rate differential rises. In Figure 20.1, illustrate the effect of this change. What happens to the exchange rate?

2. Figure 20.2 shows the foreign exchange market for U.S. dollars. Suppose people expect that the future exchange rate will be lower. In Figure 20.2, illustrate the effect of this change. What happens to the exchange rate? Has the exchange rate appreciated or depreciated?

■ **FIGURE 20.2**

Exchange rate (yen per dollar)

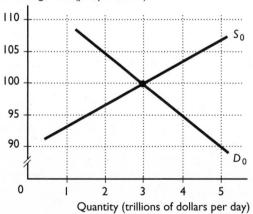

Short answer and numeric questions

1. If the exchange rate rises from 90 yen per dollar to 100 yen per dollar, has the dollar appreciated or depreciated? Has the yen appreciated or depreciated?

2. What is the relationship between the value of U.S. exports and the quantity of U.S. dollars demanded? Why does this relationship exist?

3. What is the relationship between the value of U.S. imports and the quantity of U.S. dollars supplied? Why does this relationship exist?

4. Everything else remaining the same, how will a rise in the Japanese interest rate affect the demand for dollars, the supply of dollars, and the U.S. exchange rate?

5. If the Fed believes the exchange rate is too low and wants to raise it, what action does the Fed undertake in the foreign exchange market? What limits the extent to which the Fed can undertake this action?

SELF TEST ANSWERS

■ CHECKPOINT 20.1

Fill in the blanks

The <u>current</u> account records payments for the imports of goods and services. The <u>capital</u> account records foreign investment in the United States minus U.S. investment abroad. The sum of the balances on current account, capital account, and the official settlements account always equals <u>zero</u>. The United States is a <u>debtor</u> nation. The United States is borrowing for <u>investment</u>.

True or false

1. False; page 504
2. False; page 504
3. True; page 504
4. False; page 504
5. False; page 506
6. True; page 507
7. False; page 508
8. True; page 509

Multiple choice

1. c; page 504
2. b; page 504
3. a; page 504
4. d; page 504
5. c; page 504
6. a; page 504
7. c; page 504
8. c; page 504
9. b; page 506
10. d; page 506
11. d; page 509
12. a; page 509

Short answer and numeric questions

1. The current account records payments for imports, receipts from exports, net interest and net transfers received from abroad. The capital account records foreign investment in the United States minus U.S. investments abroad. The official settlements account records changes in U.S. official reserves, the government's holding of foreign currency; page 504.

2. The current account balance plus the capital account balance plus official settlements account balance sums to zero. So if the official settlements account equals zero, a $350 billion current account deficit means there is a $350 billion capital account surplus; page 504.

3. a. The capital account balance equals foreign investment in the United States minus U.S. investment abroad, which is $400 billion; page 504.

   b. The official settlements balance is the negative of the change in official reserves, or –$10 billion; page 504.

   c. The sum of the current account balance, the capital account balance, and the official settlements account balance is zero. The capital account balance is $400 billion and the official settlements account balance is –$10 billion, so the current account balance is –$390 billion; page 504.

   d. The current account balance equals exports minus imports plus net interest plus net transfers received from abroad. Net interest and net transfers are given as zero. The current account balance is –$390 billion and exports are $1,000 billion, so imports equal $1,390 billion; page 504.

4. A net borrower is a country that is borrowing more from the rest of the world than it is lending to the rest of the world. A debtor nation is a country that during its entire history has borrowed more from the rest of the world than it has lent to it. It is possible for a nation to be a net borrower but not be a debtor nation. A country can be a creditor nation and a net borrower. This situation occurs if a creditor nation is, during a particular year, borrowing more from the rest of the world than it is lending to the rest of the world; page 506.

5. a. The private sector balance equals saving minus investment, so the private sector balance is –$300 billion; page 508.
   b. The government sector balance equals net taxes minus government purchases of goods and services, so the government sector balance is $100 billion; page 508.
   c. The sum of the private sector balance plus the government sector balance equals net exports, so net exports equals –$200 billion; page 508.

■ CHECKPOINT 20.2

Fill in the blanks

The price at which one currency exchanges for another is called a foreign <u>exchange rate</u>. If the dollar falls in value against the Mexican peso, the dollar has <u>depreciated</u>. A rise in the exchange rate <u>decreases</u> the quantity of U.S. dollars demanded. An increase in the demand for dollars shifts the demand curve for dollars <u>rightward</u> and an increase in the supply of dollars shifts the supply curve of dollars <u>rightward</u>. The exchange rate is volatile because an influence that changes the demand for dollars often <u>changes</u> the supply of dollars. An increase in the expected future exchange rate <u>raises</u> the equilibrium exchange rate. Purchasing power parity is equal value of <u>money</u>. If the Fed buys dollars on the foreign exchange market, the exchange rate <u>rises</u>.

True or false

1. False; page 511
2. True; page 512
3. True; page 512
4. False; page 515
5. False; pages 514, 517
6. True; page 518
7. True; page 519
8. False; page 522

Multiple choice

1. d; page 511
2. b; page 511
3. c; pages 511-512

4. d; page 512
5. a; page 514
6. a; page 515
7. a; page 516
8. a; page 517
9. b; page 518
10. c; pages 517, 519
11. b; page 520
12. a; page 522

Complete the graph

■ FIGURE 20.3

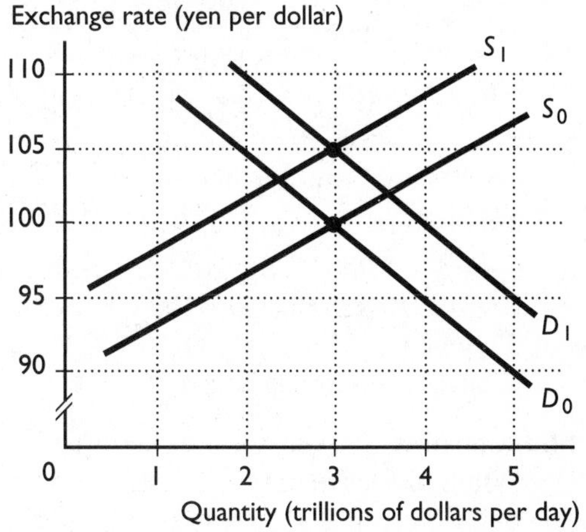

1. a. The equilibrium exchange rate is 100 yen per dollar; page 518.
   b. The increase in the U.S. interest rate differential increases the demand for dollars and shifts the demand curve from D_0 to D_1 in Figure 20.3. The increase in the U.S. interest rate differential also decreases the supply of dollars and shifts the supply curve from S_0 to S_1. The exchange rate rises. In the figure, the exchange rate rises to 105 yen per dollar; page 519.

■ **FIGURE 20.4**

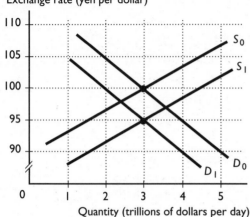

2. The fall in the expected future exchange rate decreases the demand for dollars and increases the supply of dollars. The demand curve shifts leftward from D_0 to D_1 and the supply curve shifts rightward from S_0 to S_1. The exchange falls from 100 yen per dollar to 95 yen per dollar in Figure 20.4. The exchange rate depreciates; page 519.

Short answer and numeric questions

1. When the exchange rate rises from 90 yen per dollar to 100 yen per dollar, the dollar appreciates because the dollar buys more yen. The yen depreciates because it now takes 100 yen to buy a dollar instead of 90 yen to buy a dollar; pages 511-512.

2. The larger the value of U.S. exports, the larger is the quantity of U.S. dollars demanded. This relationship exists because U.S. firms want to be paid for their goods and services in dollars; page 512.

3. The larger the value of U.S. imports, the larger the quantity of U.S. dollars supplied. This relationship exists because U.S. consumers must pay for their imports in foreign currency. To obtain foreign currency, U.S. consumers supply dollars; page 515.

4. An increase in the Japanese interest rate decreases the U.S. interest rate differential. The smaller the U.S. interest rate differential, the smaller is the demand for U.S. assets and the smaller the demand for dollars. And the smaller the U.S. interest rate differential, the greater is the demand for foreign assets and the greater is the supply of dollars. So when the Japanese interest rate rises, the demand for dollars decreases, the supply of dollars increases, and the equilibrium exchange rate falls; page 520.

5. If the Fed wants to raise the exchange rate, it will buy dollars. The Fed would have to sell U.S. official reserves to buy dollars. The Fed is limited by its quantity of official reserves. If the Fed persisted in this action, eventually it would run out of reserves and would be forced to stop buying dollars; page 522.